Cardinal de La Rochefoucauld

CARDINAL DE LA ROCHEFOUCAULD

Leadership and Reform in the French Church

Joseph Bergin

1987
Yale University Press
New Haven and London

Typeset in Linotron Garamond by
Best-set Typesetter Ltd, Hong Kong
Printed and bound by The Bath Press, Avon

Library of Congress Cataloging-in-Publication Data

Bergin, Joseph, 1948–
   Cardinal François de La Rochefoucauld, 1558–1645.

   Bibliography: p.
   Includes index.
   1. La Rochefoucauld, François de, 1558–1645.
2. Cardinals – France – Biography.   3. Counter-Reformation
– France.   4. Catholic Church – France – History – 16th
century.   5. Catholic Church – France – History – 17th
century.   6. France – Church History – 16th century.
7. France – Church History – 17th century.   I. Title.
BX4705.L16B47   1987   282′.092′4   87–14255
ISBN 0–300–04104–7

Contents

Abbreviations

A.D.	Archives départementales
A.A.E.	Archives des Affaires Etrangères
A.N.	Archives Nationales
A.R.S.I.	Archivium Romanum Societatis Jesu
A.S.V.	Archivio Segreto Vaticano
B.V.A.	Biblioteca Apostolica Vaticana
B. Institut	Bibliothèque de l'Institut de France
B.L., Addit Ms.	British Library, Additional Manuscripts
B.N.	Bibliothèque Nationale
B.S.G.	Bibliothèque Ste Geneviève
MS. Fr.	Manuscrit français
N.a.f	Nouvelles acquisitions françaises
Nunz. Fr.	Nunziatura di Francia

Preface

IT IS probably fair to say that it is less difficult to identify historical problems that are worth investigating, or to detect gaps in existing treatments of a period or a topic, than it is to locate the kinds of sources that would enable one to examine them satisfactorily. The present study grew out of a vague desire to work on the French Counter-Reformation church, but it only began to seem feasible when, after much uncertainty and many false leads, I realized that a considerable mass of documentation lay relatively unnoticed and certainly unworked in a Paris library.

The end product has also been a long time in the making, and was even abandoned for a time to enable an entirely different kind of study of Richelieu to be researched and written. Others will judge whether this has been a good or bad thing, and the reaction of one reader of the book on Richelieu to a description of the present study was – 'ah, l'antithèse!'. Other readers may be tempted to think the same, but I can assure them that, for all the obvious differences between the two works, no such intention lies behind the pages that follow.

The time that it has taken to bring this study to completion means that I have accumulated debts of gratitude to many individuals and institutions for their help and advice. I am more than happy to agree with Chateaubriand's remark, 'rien n'est doux comme de publier les services qu'on a reçus'. In doing so, it is only just that my first acknowledgements should go to the librarians of the Bibliothèque Sainte Geneviève in Paris, in whose lovely 'Salle de Réserve' much of the research for this book was done; they were invariably co-operative, understanding and good-humoured however demanding I might happen to be, and my gratitude to them is unqualified. I am equally indebted to Professor Nicola Sutherland, whose astringent reading of successive drafts of my chapters helped to keep me on my toes and to clarify what I wanted to say. At a later stage, the sympathetic criticisms and comments of Dermot Fenlon, John Bossy and Brian Pullan were both encouraging and stimulating. I also received valuable advice and assistance from Bernard Barbiche and Alfred Soman in Paris. Not for the first time, it is a pleasure to thank Nigel Griffin and Mark Greengrass, who have read several chapters in penultimate draft, and done a great deal to improve their argument and style. I was also fortunate to have their assistance, as well as that of Anthony Birley, Gordon Kinder and Jeremy Lawraence at the proofs stage. More generally, I would like to thank my colleagues in the History Department at Manchester, whose company I have enjoyed for nearly a decade now. It may be somewhat invidious to do so, but I would particularly like to mention Ian Kershaw who, although working in a very different field from mine, has been characteristically warm and generous in his encouragement during that time.

Parts of this book have already appeared in print elsewhere. Chapter six was published in a slightly different form under the title 'The Crown, the Papacy and the Reform of the Old Orders in Early Seventeenth-Century France' in the *Journal of Ecclesiastical History*, 33 (1982), pp. 234–55, while some material in the final section of chapter five is based on an article published in the *Historical Journal* 34 (1982), pp. 781–803 as 'The Decline and Fall of the House of Guise as an Ecclesiastical Dynasty'. I wish to acknowledge permission from Cambridge University Press to reproduce both of them here.

Finally, I want to thank John Nicoll and Mary Carruthers at Yale University Press, London. Their praises have already been sung by others, but their efficiency, skill and good humour deserve nothing less than the warmest acknowledgement; it has been a great pleasure to work with them.

Manchester, June 1987.

Introduction

FOR SOME considerable time now, there has been no real dispute among historians that the Counter-Reformation was considerably more than a defensive reaction against the Protestant Reformation, or that it embraced a genuinely Catholic Reform which, like Protestantism itself, grew out of late medieval movements for reform. This more favourable view has been the result of several shifts in the focus of historians' attention. Firstly, in both research and works of synthesis, the emphasis has been displaced from the political to the religious sphere itself. Whereas historians once readily identified the Counter-Reformation with the policies of a Philip II or a Ferdinand II, they have recently been paying increasing attention to the new spiritual forces that were emerging within sixteenth- and seventeenth-century Catholicism – the new religious orders and the enormous spiritual vitality associated with them; the prolonged and considerable labours of the Council of Trent, now chronicled in magisterial fashion; the changing character of the papacy itself – from being a target of reformers everywhere to becoming the engine of a Catholic reformation; and the determined and systematic use of schools, missions and pastoral visitations in an attempt to produce a disciplined clergy, as well as a laity instructed in the basic elements of their religion. These historiographical developments have in turn led to a second shift – away from bishops and ecclesiastical high-politics and towards a sociology of 'religious culture', a term which in itself reflects a growing detachment from, or indifference to, earlier confessional concerns.[1] These two shifts have produced a third, which is no less

1. See Natalie Zemon Davis, 'From Popular Religion to Religious Culture', in Steven Ozment, ed., *Reformation Europe, A Guide to Research* (St Louis, Missouri, 1982), pp. 321–41; and the comments of Philip T. Hoffman, *Church and Community in the diocese of Lyon, 1500–1789* (New Haven, 1984), pp. 1–4.

significant – the explosion of the traditional chronology of the Counter-Reformation, both for France and for Europe as a whole. Instead of occupying the half-century or so after the Council of Trent (Europe) or after the Wars of Religion (France), the Counter-Reformation is increasingly seen as a protracted affair which, although it took time to acquire momentum, nevertheless managed to sustain that momentum throughout the seventeenth and at least part of the eighteenth century. Indeed, some historians have provocatively argued that the high-water mark of the Counter-Reformation, especially in France, coincided with the age of Voltaire and the alleged skepticism, deism and religious disaffection of the Enlightenment.[2]

So much work of this kind has now been done that, despite the occasional warning to the contrary, it is tempting to view the Counter-Reformation as an uncontrollable welling-up of spiritual energy that could not but sweep all before it.[3] Although there would have been nothing like a reform without this energy, a moment's reflection should suffice to realise that such a view of the Counter-Reformation would be excessively one-sided and optimistic. Not only did new divisions and differences of a pastoral or doctrinal kind emerge within the Counter-Reformation church, but most of the age-old problems of church reform had still to be faced; indeed, some of the major new developments of the sixteenth and seventeenth centuries avoided rather than solved them. The rise of new orders did not guarantee the reform of the old ones; the formidable obstacles to the reform of the episcopate and secular clergy remained as intractable as ever; the post-Tridentine papacy's political and secular interests, as Paolo Prodi and others have shown, often had the effect of relegating reform to an inferior position on its list of priorities.[4] Genuine reform 'in head and members' of a church dominated at almost every level by vested interests embedded in an archaic benefice-system would have had to have been revolutionary to be wholly successful, and there was nothing revolutionary about the Counter-Reformation church.[5]

The present study differs in several obvious ways from much recent

2. Among the first to do so was Jean Delumeau, *Le Catholicisme entre Luther et Voltaire* (Paris, 1971). Translated as *Catholicism between Luther and Voltaire* (London, 1977). See Hoffman, *Church and Community*, ch. 5; Jean Quéniart, *Les Hommes, l'église et dieu dans la France du xviiie siècle* (Paris, 1978), part i, for subsequent comments.

3. See, for instance, the strictures of Robert Sauzet, *Contre-réforme et réforme catholique en Bas-Languedoc. Le diocèse de Nîmes au xviie siècle* (Louvain-Paris, 1979).

4. Paolo Prodi, *Il Cardinale Gabriele Paleotti* 2 vols. (Rome, 1959–66), especially vol.ii; *idem.*, *Il Sovrano pontefice. Un corpo e due anime: la monarchia papale nella prima età moderna* (Bologna, 1982); Wolfgang Reinhard, 'Reformpapsttum zwischen Renaissance und Barock', in *Reformatio Ecclesiae. Beiträge zu kirchlichen Reformbemühungen von der Alten Kirche bis zur Neuzeit*, ed. Remigius Bäumer (Paderborn, 1980), pp. 779–96.

5. For a study of the effects of the benefice-system on church policy at the highest level, one that would be repeated throughout the church, see Barbara McClung Hallman, *Italian Cardinals, Reform and the Church as Property 1492–1563* (Los Angeles, 1985).

work in the field of French religious history, though this derives more from its subject-matter and the constraints inherent in it than from disagreements on basic questions of substance. It is not the product of a rejection of contemporary historiography, nor of a desire to put the clock back by reinstating older modes or objects of historical analysis. Having expanded so considerably in the manner described above, Counter-Reformation studies should now be regarded as a broad church, within which different approaches to problems are legitimate and welcome. However, the following pages owe their existence to dissatisfaction with existing treatments of the early phase of the French Counter-Reformation, and of its general significance for the seventeenth-century church.

The term 'Counter-Reformation' has enjoyed much less favour in France than elsewhere in Europe. Because the Catholic revival there took place much later than the Protestant Reformation, French historians have instinctively tended to see it as a self-contained phenomenon, and preferred to speak of a 'renaissance religieuse' flowering spontaneously at the end of the Wars of Religion. The tendency to regard it as an indigenous growth is reinforced by its close connection to powerful new schools of mysticism and spirituality. But such an attitude can be challenged in the way that Lucien Febvre once did for conventional views of the origins of French Protestantism – as a form of historiographical nationalism. The problems of the French church at the end of the religious wars might have been more acute, but they were not fundamentally different to those confronted by reformers and church leaders in other parts of Catholic Europe. Because of the time-lag created by the wars, the ensuing religious revival could draw on ideas and experiences from abroad, and did not generate wholly new solutions to unique problems. The originality of the French Counter-Reformation would not be manifest until the middle decades of the seventeenth century, and was the fruit of a long apprenticeship. For that reason, it seemed worth re-examining more closely the early phase of the Counter-Reformation, and in particular to draw attention to its fitful nature, its tentative search for solutions to familiar problems of reform, and its uneven development.

Another strong, although less clearly articulated assumption in much of the historiography, both old and new, of the French Counter-Reformation is that its true architects and greatest champions were members, not of the upper, but of the middling and lower clergy – celebrated 'saints prêtres' like Bourdoise, Vincent de Paul, Olier, Jean Eudes and others. It is they who are commonly held to have provided the ideas and inspiration which eventually dragged both clergy and their parishioners out of their squalor and ignorance through extensive preaching, missions, charitable work and, especially, seminaries. Not holding major ecclesiastical posts, only they, it would appear, could genuinely understand and set about solving the problems facing the church. Having been held up as models for generations of French clergy since then, they have in many cases become mythological rather than historical figures, and one important result of contemporary research has been to resurrect the far less glamorous context of men, ideas and institutions which made them possible. By contrast, the higher clergy, dominated by the aristocracy and tied to the workings of royal patronage, are held to have been largely incapable of decisive action as reformers: owing everything to the existing system, they were themselves symptoms of the church's malaise, which they could not be expected to cure.

Now it is certainly true that the 'generation of saints' of the mid-seventeenth century deserve a prominent place in any account of the French Counter-Reformation. But excessive attention to them easily produces a distorted vision of both the church they were trying to reform, and of their own contributions to that reform. Outsiders have rarely transformed a system without initiatives and support from within. This is especially true of the French church in the seventeenth century. The traditional picture of the upper clergy, and of the bishops in particular, is largely responsible for this one-sided view of the French Counter-Reformation. But it is one that relies more on anecdote and endlessly repeated cases of neglect, absenteeism or other derelictions of duty by individual bishops, than on an adequate historical investigation of the calibre and activities of the episcopate. Until that has been arrived at, a more balanced interpretation of the strengths and weaknesses of French Catholicism in this period, as well as of success and failure in efforts at reform, will remain impossible.

It would be idle to pretend that the analysis of a single member of the upper clergy could rectify the existing historiographical im-balance. But, as a recent study of the famous Henri Arnauld, Bishop of Angers, demonstrates, such an analysis can help to uncover some at least of the general characteristics of the upper clergy, as well as the range of activities and objectives of reforming prelates.[6] François de La Rochefoucauld (1558–1645) was, in his own time, a much more widely-known and influential figure than Arnauld, even to the point where some contemporaries and historians referred to him as the Charles Borromeo of the French church. Despite the problems posed by such a sobriquet, it ought perhaps to have drawn more attention to him than has been the case, all the more so as he was a fairly typical product of the French church under the later Valois monarchs. He owed his elevation to the episcopate at the age of twenty-six primarily to his aristocratic ancestry. His very longevity, which serves to bridge

6. Isabelle Bonnot, *Hérétique ou saint? Henry Arnauld évêque janséniste d'Angers au xviie siècle* (Paris, 1984).

the gap between the successive generations of the early French Counter-Reformation, should not be allowed to obscure the fact that he was a leading member of the generation of reformers who matured during the last stages of the Wars of Religion, and whose adherence to the Catholic League left an enduring mark on him thereafter. His subsequent, albeit delayed, rise to the dignity of cardinal and a prominent position in the French church, as well as to the presidency of the king's council, also helps us to understand the fortunes of men of his generation after the Wars of Religion. Despite this upward progress, he was never in any sense a political churchman, and the causes that he espoused, beginning with that of the League itself, were of the kind which would normally impede rather than advance individuals with political ambitions.

Forty years ago, Jean Orcibal called attention to 'le rôle capital des individus dans la réforme catholique'. Despite important changes in the way historians approach historical subjects, I would not dissent from that view. But it is not one that determined either the inception or the shape of this study. There are, in any case, a variety of ways in which Orcibal's statement can be applied in practice. What follows, therefore, is not a biography of La Rochefoucauld in the conventional sense of the term. The central theme is indicated by the subtitle – the multifarious connections between leadership and reform that are to be encountered in the French Counter-Reformation church during the half-century or so between La Rochefoucauld's appointment to the see of Clermont in 1585 and his death in 1645. However, it would be misguided to assume that his career and activities are familiar to more than a minority of historians of the period. For that reason, it seemed both reasonable and necessary to present the essential outline of his career in the early chapters. If their framework is broadly biographical, it is not so that as many known facts about him as possible may be packed into them: on the contrary, many facts have been omitted which would probably have found a place in a purely biographical approach. These 'biographical' chapters with which the book opens have another, no less important purpose – to begin a general exploration of the themes of leadership and reform. The leadership which La Rochefoucauld exerted over his fellow clergy was predominantly of a moral kind, based far more on his reputation as a reformer than on his political skill or attainments. The latter were, as we shall see, relatively insignificant, and in any case only materialised well into the later part of his career. The position of eminence that he enjoyed in the French church pre-dated them; indeed, they had the uncommon effect of drawing him into new areas of reform, culminating in the most monumental of all his activities – that of special papal commissioner for the reform of the old orders in France.

By conceiving the biographical chapters along these lines, it is possible to pursue in greater depth some of the main themes of reform as they manifest themselves throughout La Rochefoucauld's career as a whole. It then seemed especially important to present, to the extent that the surviving evidence allows, the broad contours of his reforming activities and ideas as a bishop in his two dioceses of Clermont and Senlis, both because of their importance as the foundations of his reputation as a reformer, and as an insight into the priorities of the first generation of church leaders of the French Counter-Reformation. Likewise, the record of his tenure of the office of grand almoner of France is one in which the two themes of leadership and reform are intimately connected at the highest levels of both church and state.

If a study of La Rochefoucauld's grand almonership takes us into an unfamiliar corner of church affairs, so, in a rather different way, does a study of the reform of the old orders. It is a subject which occupies a curiously exiguous, even non-existent place in most accounts of the French Counter-Reformation. The failure to achieve extensive reforms among them seems to have had the effect of virtually removing the problem altogether from historical attention, almost as if it had never been on the agenda of the Counter-Reformation in the first place. It is a central contention of this book that this was an important field of concern and endeavour for reformers, so important, indeed, that a special commission, supported by the papacy and the crown, was established to deal with the leading old orders. The space devoted to this question may seem disproportionately large, but it is as important to know why individual reforms failed as why they succeeded if we are to grasp the kinds of problem with which the Counter-Reformation church was faced.

It has to be said that the internal politics of religious orders rarely make exciting or cheerful reading, even when reform is at stake, yet they are unavoidable if the attitudes of the orders towards reform, especially where it was being introduced from the outside, are to be understood. Even the infighting which is a characteristic feature of their history in the Counter-Reformation period must be taken account of, if the options open to reformers like La Rochefoucauld, as well as the tactics available to his opponents, are to emerge as an indispensable feature of the success or failure of the different reforms. The final chapters of this study are devoted to his attempts to reform four of the old orders – the canons-regular, Cluny, Cîteaux, and the Mathurins. Even so, there is no place for the Benedictines, whom La Rochefoucauld was also commissioned to reform, largely because he mounted no major initiative among them, but contented himself with supporting and protecting what was perhaps the most famous product of seventeenth-century French monastic reform – the Maurists. With the exception of Cluny and Cîteaux, these orders and their reform present sufficient contrasts to merit attention in separate chapters, while having enough in common to make constant repetition of certain points unnecessary. It will be abundantly obvious by the end that La Rochefoucauld achieved very mixed results as commissioner for the orders, and that a substantial measure of success among the canons-regular was offset by outright failure in Cluny, Cîteaux and the Mathurin order, failure which can in part be attributed to bad judgement and miscalculation on his part.

Despite the length of his career and the range of his activities, there has never been an adequate study of La Rochefoucauld's role in the French Counter-Reformation church. Since his death, he has been suspended somewhere between the pious veneration of a few and the neglect of the many. In the late nineteenth century, Pierre Féret devoted some attention to his career as a reformer, but his work was cursory, and based on limited research.[7] Later, Gabriel de La Rochefoucauld produced a full-scale study which is not without merit, and which attempted to embrace his career as a whole.[8] Since then, only investigations of the history of the religious orders with which La Rochefoucauld was involved have managed to shed new light on particular aspects of his action.[9]

This neglect is all the more surprising in that La Rochefoucauld probably left more personal papers — Richelieu and a few others excepted — than virtually any leading churchman of his day. If historians have not taken advantage of this fact, it may be because the papers are not a faithful reflection of his career as a whole. Only when he becomes a cardinal in 1607 do they become reasonably plentiful, and only when he begins to reform the orders truly bulky. Thus, certain aspects of his career have to be documented, not always satisfactorily it should be said, from other sources. This disparity is inevitably reflected in the structure of the book, in the choice of issues for study, and in the thoroughness with which those issues could be investigated. What is being offered, therefore, is a series of closely connected studies which amount to much less than a biography, but which, it is hoped, will convey something of the range of interests and the extent of the challenges facing anyone involved in the affairs of the French Counter-Reformation church.

7. Pierre Féret, 'Le Cardinal de La Rochefoucauld réformateur', *Revue des questions historiques* 23 (1878), pp. 115–75; *idem.*, *L'Abbaye de Ste Geneviève et la congrégation de France*, 2 vols. (Paris, 1883).
8. Gabriel de La Rochefoucauld, *Un Homme d'église et d'état au commencement du xviie siècle: le cardinal de La Rochefoucauld* (Paris, 1926).
9. See especially the works of Paul Denis, Louis Lekai and Polycarp Zakar cited in the bibliography.

1

The Making of a
Cardinal 1558–1607

I

IT WOULD BE less than truthful to claim that François de La Rochefoucauld is a household name among the galaxy of prelates, mystics and *saints prêtres* who dominate the long history of the French Counter-Reformation. Neither his longevity nor the impressive range of his career has secured for him anything like the reputation of a Bérulle or a Vincent de Paul, let alone of a François de Sales or a Du Perron. Never a real political figure, he espoused causes that were unpopular in many quarters (he was ultramontane and very pro-Jesuit), and fought battles on frontiers that were less than attractive (notably the reform of the court, the episcopate and the monastic orders). He has survived in the historical memory as a name that is fleetingly encountered in a surprisingly high number of religious and ecclesiastical contexts between the mid-1580s and the mid-1640s. But I hope to show that this comparative anonymity, reflects not a lack of importance in his career and activities but rather a vision of the French Counter-Reformation church that is too narrowly and too partially focussed.

La Rochefoucauld's relative obscurity can certainly not be attributed to his social origins. The La Rochefoucaulds were among the oldest and most distinguished of all French aristocratic families, and in the sixteenth century they were beginning to spawn those numerous junior branches that were to be a feature of the family's subsequent history. The future cardinal's father, Charles, Baron of Randan, founded the cadet branch of that name, while the senior branch, which was to produce the famous *Frondeur* and moralist of the mid-seventeenth century, descended through Charles's elder brother, François III, Count of La Rochefoucauld.[1] But family unity remained strong, as is clearly demonstrated by the marriages of the two brothers

1. For a brief genealogy of the La Rochefoucauld family, see Appendices. Older works include André Duchesne, *Généalogie de l'ancienne et illustre maison de La Rochefoucauld* (Paris, 1622). There is also the more up-to-date study by Georges Martin, *Histoire et généalogie de la maison de La Rochefoucauld* (n.p., 1975).

to the two daughters of an Italian count, Galeotti Pico della Mirandola, one of the many exiles, the *fuorusciti*, who, having staunchly supported the French in the long Italian wars against the Habsburgs, were
forced into exile, and flocked to the court of Henri II, where they
clustered around the Queen, Catherine de Medici, or the young
Duchess of Guise, Anne d'Este.[2] The future cardinal's ancestry was
thus doubly illustrious since, as their family name indicates, the sisters
were related to the celebrated humanist of the later fifteenth century,
Giovanni Pico della Mirandola. They arrived in France in 1548, where
Catherine de Medici quickly took them under her wing. Silvia, the
elder of the two, married the Count of La Rochefoucauld only to die in
childbirth in 1554, leaving just the one son.[3] Fulvia, on the other
hand, who was only fifteen when she married Charles de Randan in
June 1555, lived on until 1607, almost long enough to see her only
surviving son made a cardinal.[4] During her short, seven-year marriage
to Charles, she gave birth to five children. François, the second of her
four sons, was born on 8 December 1558, and was baptised shortly
afterwards in the Parisian parish church of St André-des-Arts.

Although the family seat of Randan was situated in the Auvergne, a
fact which was to prove decisive in the career of François and his
brothers, there is little evidence that their parents lived anywhere
except in Paris and at court, to which both were closely attached.
Fulvia left Catherine de Medici's household on her marriage, but
would return to it after her husband's early death. Charles de Randan,
for his part, seems to have owed his advancement to the patronage of
the Duke of Guise, in whose service he fought at Metz against Charles
V in 1552. Such close ties of family and fealty were all the more
unavoidable for the ambitious of the time, especially as factions were
allowed to blossom more than was wise during Henri II's reign. If
anything, the Guise connection was further strengthened by Randan's
marriage, given his young wife's close friendship with Mme de Guise.
With their support, Randan obtained the important post of colonel-
general of the French infantry, and even went on a diplomatic mission
to England and Scotland in 1560, when Guise power was at its
height.[5]

2. For a memorable portrait of these groups and their importance in the political, financial
   and ecclesiastical life of France at this time, see Lucien Romier, *Les Origines politiques des
   guerres de religion*, 2 vols. (Paris, 1913), especially vol. i, ch. 4. On Pico della Mirandola's
   support for France: *ibid.*, i, pp. 249–50; ii, p. 213. See also Frederic J. Baumgartner,
   'Henry II's Italian Bishops: A Study in the Use and Abuse of the Concordat of Bologna',
   Sixteenth Century Journal, 11 (1980), pp. 49–58.
3. Romier, *Les Origines politiques*, i, p. 72, n. 9.
4. For the text of her will and later codicils, B.S.G., MS. 3238, fos. 192–8. The final
   version of her will is dated 15 July 1607, and shows Fulvia Pica to have been just as
   devoted to the Jesuits as her son.
5. *Négociations, lettres et pièces diverses relatives au règne de François II*, ed. Louis Paris (Paris,
   1841), pp. 378, 386–91, 423–4, 445, 478, 538, for his correspondence during that
   mission.

The Wars of Religion were, by then, beginning to loom on the horizon, and would cause serious problems for the La Rochefoucauld clan. The Counts of La Rochefoucauld and Randan soon found themselves on opposite sides of the confessional divide. François III became a Huguenot and moved close to the Prince of Condé, the acknowledged leader of the new church. During the 1560s, he became one of its most prominent figures, and emerged as a major military leader in the decade before his death in the notorious bloodbath of Huguenots in Paris in August 1572, the St Bartholomew's Day Massacre.[6] Charles, on the other hand, remained a firm, even a determined Catholic, in the image of his patrons of the house of Guise. He, too, took part in the religious wars but did not survive the sieges of the first war of 1562. Wounded at Bourges in August 1562, he died during the siege and recapture of Rouen the following November.[7] His death did not break the family's connection with the Guises, as later events would demonstrate.

Randan's death left his widow with the considerable task of rearing five children, a situation which increasing numbers of women would have to face as the religious wars took their toll on heads of families. Fulvia Pica never remarried, either through personal choice or, though we know nothing of the family's economic position at this point, possibly because she was not an eligible match. She soon returned to Catherine de Medici's household, and was only to leave it in 1589 on the queen's death and the outbreak of the final, most violent phase of the wars.[8] She was fortunate to have married into such a well-connected family. Apart from the Guises, she was able to call on the assistance of the Gonzaga Dukes of Nevers (a family to which, incidentally, she was related in her own right) and successive dukes were to become influential patrons of the Randan family.[9] This and her return to court no doubt helped her to prevent the Randans, now divided from the senior branch of the La Rochefoucauld family by religion, from slipping into the obscurity and genteel poverty that might easily have become their lot — as was later to happen to the Richelieu family in analogous circumstances.[10] Instead of having to

---

6. See Emile-G. Léonard, *A History of Protestantism* (London, 1967), ii, pp. 133, 143.
7. On the military and political events of 1562, see J.H.M. Salmon, *Society in Crisis. France in the Sixteenth Century* (London, 1975), pp. 146ff. The Latin and French texts of Randan's epitaph in Rouen cathedral are in *Lettres du cardinal d'Ossat*, ed. Amelot de la Houssaye (Amsterdam, 1714), iii, p. 625, n. 3.
8. Gabriel de La Rochefoucauld, *Homme d'église*, p. 5.
9. On the Gonzaga-Nevers, see Robert R. Harding, *Anatomy of a Power Elite. The Provincial Governors of Early Modern France* (New Haven, Conn. 1978), pp. 145ff; Denis Crouzet, 'Recherches sur la crise de l'aristocratie en France au xvie siècle: les dettes de la maison de Nevers', *Histoire, économie et société* 1 (1982), pp. 7–50.
10. Elizabeth Wirth Marvick, *The Young Richelieu. A Psychoanalytical Study of Leadership* (Chicago, 1983); Joseph Bergin, *Cardinal Richelieu: Power and the Pursuit of Wealth* (London-New Haven, 1985), ch. 1.

retire to the family seat of Randan, they were able to continue living in Paris.

In educating her offspring, Fulvia was especially fortunate in being able to put her connections to excellent use. Given her circumstances, it comes as no surprise that François and his younger brother Alexandre, were destined for ecclesiastical careers from a very early date, though the civil wars were to make such choices problematic for many families. One of their uncles, Jean de La Rochefoucauld, was then abbot of the great monastery of Marmoutier, master of the king's music in the royal chapel, and a close friend of the Guise Cardinals. Accordingly, he took the two boys into his care at the Parisian College of Marmoutier in order to supervise their education. More positively, he found for them, around 1567, a tutor of unusual erudition and seriousness, Jean Courtier, known humanistically as Curterius.[11] It was he who initiated them into the study of the classics and, above all, of the Church Fathers. Indeed, the earliest document we possess about the young François is the preface to one of his translations which Courtier addressed to Abbot Jean a few years later in 1571. In it, he outlined his pedagogical aims: a well-grounded *pietas literata*, which shunned everything in classical learning that was repugnant to Christian values, as well as an aptitude for study without constant supervision.[12] While the over-blown rhetoric of the Renaissance dedicatory epistle needs to be read with caution, there is little doubt that Courtier was eminently successful with the future cardinal; all his life he was to be a lover of books and manuscripts but, equally, he disliked dilettantes and paganisers, particularly among the clergy. His own published works followed the path mapped out by his first tutor, his learning being overwhelmingly theological in character, and his knowledge of the Fathers of the Church extensive.

The education begun under Courtier was continued at the Jesuit College of Clermont in Paris during the 1570s; indeed, Courtier remained in charge of the two brothers throughout their time at the college. The disappearance of the college's records makes it impossible to say when François began there, how long he stayed, or which precise courses of study he took. He obviously completed the arts course, which could take from four to six years depending on individual ability, and almost certainly went on to study philosophy and theology. In 1585, he was described in Rome as 'diu et egregie

---

11. This was stated by Courtier himself in the preface to one of his many translations: *Procopii sophistae christianae variorum in Esaiam prophetam commentariorum epitome, Ioanne Curterio interprete* (Paris, 1580), a work dedicated to his young protégé, La Rochefoucauld.

12. Courtier, *Historiae Ecclesiasticae Scriptores Graeci* (Paris, 1571). A French version of this preface was printed in Michel-Martin de la Morinière, *Les Vertus du vray prélat représentées en la vie de Monseigneur l'Eminentissime Cardinal de la Rochefoucauld* (Paris, 1646), pp. 43–4, and in La Rochefoucauld, *Homme d'église*, pp. 10–11.

versatus' in humane, philosophical and sacred learning.[13] In these disciplines, he would have been taught philosophy by Jacques Commolet, who later achieved notoriety as an impassioned preacher and adherent of the Catholic League; and theology by Richard Flaminius and the Scotsman James Tyrie, who later participated in preparing the *Ratio Studiorum*, the famous charter of Jesuit educational methods.[14] Founded in 1563, the College of Clermont was well attended, and its educational standards high; but it was debarred from giving degrees, owing to the unremitting hostility of the nearby Sorbonne, nor could its students go on to take degrees at the Sorbonne.[15] François probably left the college after six or seven years in 1578 or 1579, his formal education at an end. It is worth noting that he did not make any move, either then or later, to take a degree in law, in Paris or elsewhere, as did many prospective bishops at the time.[16]

In view of La Rochefoucauld's life-long association with the Jesuits, it is appropriate to dwell briefly here on the influence exercised on him by the College of Clermont. In the theological sphere, the Jesuits abandoned entirely the older Augustinian thesis of human corruption and sinfulness in favour of a more audaciously modern emphasis on free will and the capacity of man to contribute positively towards his salvation. While such views were solidly Thomistic in character, they did incorporate some of the best Renaissance humanist thinking and were still being developed and refined during La Rochefoucauld's lifetime. While such theological optimism was later to be attacked, notably by the Jansenists, as a dilution of Christian tradition, in the sixteenth century at least, it underpinned an energetic pastoral activism, the object of which was the defence and reform of Catholicism; it was probably one reason why the Jesuits were able to attract so many able individuals to their ranks, as well as to obtain the broad support of influential groups among both clergy and laity.[17]

In the ecclesiastical and political sphere, Jesuit teaching was no less controversial. Briefly, they taught a modernised version of the Ultra-

---

13. A.S.V., *fondo* Consistoriale, Acta Miscellanea 95, fo. 489.
14. On Commolet, see Philip Benedict, 'The Catholic Response to Protestantism: Church Activity and Popular Piety in Rouen 1560–1600', in *Religion and the People 800–1700*, ed. James Obelkevich (Chapel Hill, N.C., 1979), p. 179; C. Sommervogel, *Bibliographie des auteurs de la Compagnie de Jésus*, 12 vols. (Brussels-Paris 1890–1932) ii, col. 1351 and on Tyrie, vii, pp. 299–300.
15. George Huppert, *The Public Schools of Renaissance France* (Chicago, 1984); R. Chartier, M.M. Compère, D. Julia, *L'Education en France du xviᵉ au xviiiᵉ siècle* (Paris, 1976); Gustave Dupont-Ferrier, *Du collège de Clermont au lycée Louis-le-Grand*, 3 vols. (Paris, 1921–5).
16. See Michel Péronnet, *Les Evêques de l'ancienne France*, 2 vols. (Lille, 1976), i, pp. 482ff.
17. François de Dainville, *Les Jésuites et l'éducation de la société moderne* (Paris, 1940); *idem.*, *L'Education des Jésuites* (Paris, 1978); Antoine Adam, *Du mysticisme à la révolte: Les jansénistes du xviiᵉ siècle* (Paris, 1968), ch. 2.

montanism that the older mendicant orders had always espoused. Because the peculiar position of the orders within the church, especially the large measure of autonomy they enjoyed in relation to the bishops and parish clergy, was based on papal concessions, the orders strongly affirmed the monarchical nature of the church and the absolute superiority of papal authority, even against a general council of the church. For this reason, conciliarism of any kind was anathema to them, as was the so-called *vieille doctrine* of the Sorbonne which defended the 'liberties of the Gallican church' against papal supremacy, the rights of the French crown to full independence in 'temporal' matters, and the authority of bishops in their dioceses, particularly where the activities of religious orders were concerned. In due course, the Jesuits came to be the most outspoken defenders of the orders and papal authority in France, which explains why they were at the centre of most controversies on these questions, and why it was they who were so often singled out for attack in times of tension.[18] Pro-Jesuit and Ultramontane views thus frequently went together, and in no one more completely than in François de La Rochefoucauld. During the 1570s, when he was studying at the College of Clermont, the Jesuits even allowed their pupils to defend theses on papal power, especially that of deposing secular rulers. In a time of endemic civil war, such behaviour could not be purely academic in inspiration and intent, and it inevitably added to the widespread suspicion of both the order and the college. La Rochefoucauld's highly sheltered, religious upbringing seems to have made him more than usually receptive to Jesuit teaching, and he remained faithful to it, as well as to the order, throughout his long career. Their influence would, among other things, virtually ensure that he would later be sympathetic towards, and then a committed supporter of the *bons catholiques* during the final phase of the religious wars. He was only one of the many Jesuit *alumni* who would join the Catholic League.

In the five or six years between leaving the college and his nomination to the see of Clermont, La Rochefoucauld seems to have led a quiet, withdrawn and studious existence. In 1579–80 Courtier, still attached to the family, took him and Alexandre on an extended and leisurely tour of Italy, much of which was spent in Bologna.[19] They

18. The bibliography of the subject is immense. A brief reassessment of gallican ideas is to be found in J.K. Powis, 'The Nature of Gallicanism in late Sixteenth-Century France', *Historical Journal* 26 (1983), pp. 515–30. See also the older works of Victor Martin, *Le Gallicanisme et la réforme catholique. Essai historique sur l'introduction des decrets du concile de Trente en France* (Paris, 1919); idem., *Le Gallicanisme politique et le clergé de France* (Paris, 1929); Charles de Chesneau, *Le Père Yves de Paris et son temps*, 2 vols. (Meaux, 1946–8). Further references will be given when La Rochefoucauld's own role in these controversies is discussed in later chapters.
19. Morinière, *Le Vray prélat*, pp. 97–8; Pierre Rouvier, *De Vita et rebus gestis cardinalis de la Rochefoucauld libri tres* (Paris, 1645), p. 12.

spent large sums on books and manuscripts and, true to Courtier's methods, studied and worked on translations with him.[20] Rome and family relatives around Mantua were also visited, but particularly in Milan, where the great Carlo Borromeo was at the height of a career that would make him the model bishop for Catholic Europe for many generations.[21] It is hardly surprising that many of La Rochefoucauld's biographers should have sought to dramatise this 'historic' encounter between a Counter-Reformation that was already in full swing, and one that was still on the drawing board, but which would in due course also become a model for the rest of Europe. In particular, they argue that it was this meeting which spurred the young scholar to develop a genuine religious vocation, as distinct from the conventional willingness of the younger son to embrace the ecclesiastical state.[22] While Borromeo was later to influence La Rochefoucauld's generation, it has to be said that there is not a fragment of real evidence to support this edifying tale, and one might just as effectively, though equally speculatively, argue that La Rochefoucauld's long stay at Bologna exposed him to the influence of another great figure of the Italian Counter-Reformation, Gabriele Paleotti, Archbishop of Bologna, who was critical of much of Borromeo's rigorist approach to reform.[23] Assuming that La Rochefoucauld was already interested in ecclesiastical questions, we can at least say that his Italian journey exposed him to large-scale, systematic efforts at church reform. We should not forget, however, that he was to remain a simple, tonsured cleric for several years after his Milanese and Italian experiences.

20. B.S.G., MS. 2602, text of Courtier's translations of St Athanasius's preface to the Psalms, done from the 'vieil exemplaire grec de Monsieur Françoys de la Rochefoucault', and dated 'Bologne-la-Grasse, la 10 avril 1580'. Courtier's translation of Procopius (see above, n. 11), which contains a dedication to La Rochefoucauld, is also dated 'Bologna 15 octobris 1579'. These two dates do not prove conclusively that they spent all the intervening time in Bologna, but the nature of their occupations suggests they probably did so. Courtier explicitly refers to the purchase of books and manuscripts in the preface to one of his later translations, *Hieroclis philosophi commentarius in aurea Pythagorearum carmina* (Paris, 1583), p. xi, 'ingens ille Graecorum voluminum thesaurus. . . magnisque sumptibus a vobis comparatis'.
21. La Rochefoucauld, *Homme d'église*, ch. 2, most of which is devoted to this meeting and its significance, and relying almost entirely on the cardinal's seventeenth-century biographers.
22. On Borromeo as the model bishop, see Giuseppe Alberigo, 'Carlo Borromeo come modello di vescovo nella chiesa post-tridentina', *Rivista Storica Italiana* 79 (1967), pp. 1031–52; *idem.*, 'Carlo del mito, Carlo della storia', in *Il grande Borromeo tra storia e fede* (Milan, 1984), pp. 127–219; Bruno Maria Bosatra, 'Ancora sul "vescovo ideale" della riforma cattolica: I lineamenti del pastore tridentino-borromaico', *Scuola Cattolica* 112 (1984), pp. 517–79 (with extensive bibliographical references). The same volume contains a survey by Raymond Darricau of Borromeo's influence in the French church, 'La posterità spirituale di san Carlo Borromeo in Francia nei secoli xvii–xix', at pp. 733–64. La Rochefoucauld figures very prominently in this account, but it differs in scarcely any detail from earlier views.
23. See Paolo Prodi, *Il Cardinale Gabriele Paleotti*, one of the best studies of the Italian Counter-Reformation.

No less significant is the fact that his ecclesiastical career was being closely attended to during these years, especially by his mother and uncle who, in time-honoured fashion, used their connections to good effect. Abbot Jean's close relations with the Guises were especailly valuable, given their prodigious ability to secure benefices for themselves and their clients. In was in this way that, in 1569, the eleven year-old François found himself succeeding his uncle as vicar-general to Cardinal Guise in his Burgundian Abbey of Tournus, and, in 1575, Guise resigned it outright to the young collegian, its revenues, though diminished by the effects of a Huguenot ransack, no doubt enabling him to pursue his studies in the comfort to which those of his rank felt entitled.[24] He became strongly attached to Tournus, and was to remain abbot until his death. Despite his later efforts to reform the old orders, he was to benefit throughout his career, albeit on a relatively modest scale for a cardinal, from the French crown's practice of granting abbeys *in commendam*, itself a major source of decay among the orders.[25]

Even before obtaining his first benefice, La Rochefoucauld had taken an initial step towards entering the ecclesiastical state. On 23 September 1570, while still less than twelve years old, he received the tonsure, the first of the minor orders, from the Bishop of Paris.[26] In itself, the step had no great significance, as it was taken by many young boys, often younger than himself, who subsequently did not seek full priestly orders. More valuable for future advancement, however, was the fact that, sometime in the late 1570s, his uncle obtained for him the reversion (*survivance*) of his office of master in the king's chapel.[27] Once again, earlier biographers allude to his pious and edifying performance of his duties, but he probably did not formally enter the king's ecclesiastical household until Abbot Jean's death in 1583.[28] Until then, the office proved no more of a burden or distraction to him than did his being Abbot of Tournus. Its great value was that, when his turn came to assume his functions, it would put him in an enviable position close to the king, from which he might be plucked should a favourable opportunity for further preferment arise. Indeed, the best proof of this is the very rapidity with

---

24. P. Juenin, *Nouvelle histoire de l'abbaie royale et collégiale de St Philibert et de la ville de Tournus* (Dijon, 1733), pp. 294–5, using original documents, gives the dates as 7 August 1569 and 11 July 1575 respectively.
25. This involved giving a 'regular' benefice (an abbey or priory) to a secular ecclesiastic or even layman who was by the terms of canon law, not qualified to hold it.
26. A.N., Z¹ O 239, unfoliated register of ordinations, 1558–79.
27. Pierre de St Julien de Baleurre, *Recueil de l'antiquité et choses mémorables de l'abbaie et de la ville de Tournus* (Paris, 1581), preface. Dated 1578, this preface is dedicated to La Rochefoucauld, and describes him as holding the office at the time.
28. Abbé Oroux, *Histoire ecclésiastique de la cour de France* (Paris, 1777), ii, pp. 179–80, who refers to him as exercising the office 'en survivance' in 1583.

which he became a bishop – barely a year after his presentation at court.

The Bishop of Clermont, Antoine de Senneterre, died on 14 September 1584, and within less than two weeks, Henri III had nominated François to succeed him.[29] There were several reasons for this choice, and not the least noteworthy aspect of it is that the king did not in this case delegate the right to nominate to a third party, as he frequently did for other dioceses.[30] At a time when royal authority was weakening noticeably in the provinces, an episcopal nomination was an important political act, which could serve to reverse the slide, while at the same time conciliating local feeling. The Randan family seat was, after all, in the Auvergne, and one consequence of the monarchy's weakness was greater pressure to nominate bishops whose family base was in the vacant diocese.[31] Moreover, François's elder brother, Jean-Louis, Count of Randan, had been active in the Auvergne since the late 1570s, being made royal *lieutenant général* there in 1579, and appointed full governor shortly after François was chosen as bishop.[32] The governorship of a province was a major prize in sixteenth-century France, and the see of Clermont would powerfully complement that of Auvergne. From this point of view alone, the two appointments were a major royal recognition for the Randan family. There were other reasons, too, for the king's choice. The powerful cathedral chapter of Clermont still resented having lost the right to elect its own bishop and, consequently, needed to be treated carefully.[33] Also, by the terms of her jointure, Catherine de Medici held title to the county of Clermont, a claim opposed by successive bishops of Clermont.[34] François's nomination may have owed something to her, and she doubtless felt that the son of Fulvia Pica, whom she had recently made head of Henri III's wife's household, would not challenge her rights there. With a number of reasons for acting circumspectly, the king could reasonably see in La Rochefoucauld a bishop who would be at one and the same time welcome in the Auvergne, while remaining closely attached to the crown's interests.

Thus far, La Rochefoucauld's elevation to the episcopal bench followed the classic pattern of the sixteenth century, with the

29. *Négociations diplomatiques de la France avec la Toscane*, ed. Abel Desjardins (Paris, 1859–86), iv, p. 534, Giulio Busini to Belisario Vinta, 2 October 1584; Abel Poitrineau, ed., *Le Diocèse de Clermont* (Paris, 1979), pp. 121–2.
30. Frederic J. Baumgartner, *Change and Continuity in the French Episcopate: The Bishops and the Wars of Religion 1547–1610* (Chapel Hill, N.C., 1986), pp. 41–2.
31. *Ibid.*; Péronnet, *Les Evêques de l'ancienne France*, i, p. 498.
32. *Inventaire des archives communales de Clermont-Ferrand. Fonds Montferrand* (Clermont-Ferrand, 1902), i, pp. 144–5; B.N., MS. Dupuy 937, fo.229, Henri III to marquis de Canillac, informing him that Randan was to succeed the absent marquis de St Hérem.
33. Louis Welter, 'Le Chapitre cathédral de Clermont', *Revue d'histoire de l'église de France* 41 (1955), pp. 41ff.
34. Poitrineau, ed., *Le Diocèse de Clermont*, p. 105.

territorial power and the court connections of the aristocracy playing a far greater part than the personality or the achievements of the candidate. There was no formal process by which candidates for mitres might be selected, nor any recognised career pattern which might establish who deserved them. In La Rochefoucauld's case, there were certainly no achievements to report in 1584, nor any guarantee whatever that he would fulfil the 'promise' to which French kings so commonly referred in proposing their nominees to the pope for confirmation. It is, of course, possible that through his place in the royal chapel, he had made some impression on Henri III but that, even if true, would not in itself suffice to explain his nomination. Besides, despite being a member of one of Henri's own confraternities, there is little reason to think that the cautious, moderate La Rochefoucauld found the king's idiosyncratic religious practices to his taste.[35] He was not the only French bishop of his generation to develop reservations about the system to which he owed his advancement, even if he was to prove one of the few to make a positive effort to alter or improve it.

Although without a degree, not in orders, and under the minimum age for a bishop as required by the Concordat of Bologna, La Rochefoucauld seems to have had little difficulty obtaining papal confirmation in consistory on 29 July 1585. Indeed, at a time when the papacy tended to worry more about the orthodoxy of incoming French bishops than their qualifications, everything it ascertained from the traditional inquiry conducted by the bishop of Paris's officials into his *vita et mores* was to his advantage. The résumé prepared for the consistory in Rome stated boldly that both his parents were Catholic, and that his father had died, arms in hand, for the defence of Catholicism. As for not possessing a degree, it was claimed that sons of the great French nobility were not in the habit of taking them, however extensive their studies.[36] Thus, there was no dissent when his confirmation as bishop was proposed in Rome; as an added favour, he received his bulls *gratis*, and was allowed to retain Tournus for life.[37]

News of the papal confirmation provided the first genuine test of La Rochefoucauld's intentions. There was at this time very little pressure to have oneself consecrated quickly, or at all; many incoming bishops were reluctant ever to assume their obligations in a time of growing insecurity. La Rochefoucauld, however, lost no time in taking major orders, including the priesthood, in late September 1585.[38] A week

---

35. Paris, Bibliothèque de l'Arsénal, MS. 2028, fo.35. For a more positive view of Henri III's religious behaviour, see Mark Greengrass, *France in the Age of Henry IV. The Search for Stability* (London, 1984), pp. 24–5; Jacqueline Boucher, *La Cour de Henri III* (Rennes, 1986), ch. 7.

36. A.S.V., *fondo* Consistoriale, Acta Miscellanea 95, fo. 489.

37. *Ibid.*, Acta Miscellanea 36, fo. 374.

38. A.N., Z¹ O 240, unfoliated register of ordinations 1580–99. The dates on which La Rochefoucauld took orders were 18, 20, 27 and 29 September respectively.

later, on 6 October, he was consecrated bishop by the papal nuncio; the next day, he took possession of his see by proxy.[39] Of course, the question of residence in his new diocese was an even more crucial test than that of consecration. But here the available evidence does not make it clear when he actually began residing in Clermont, and it has been argued that he did not do so for several years, following the example of his mentor in the king's household, the famous Jacques Amyot, Bishop of Auxerre, who did not leave court until after the murder of Henri III in August 1589.[40] Yet it seems highly unlikely that La Rochefoucauld lingered at court for so long. The speed with which he had himself consecrated was unusual for his time, and would have made little sense unless he was intent on residing in his diocese. When he did arrive in Clermont in early 1586, he refused to make the traditional episcopal promise to respect his chapter's privileges, an unlikely gesture for someone on a short, purely formal visit.[41] Two years later, he was elected to represent the ecclesiastical province of Bourges at the Estates General of Blois and, given the rising pro-League feeling in the Auvergne, it seems most unlikely that an unknown courtier-bishop – who would have been instinctively regarded as a king's man – would have been elected. Though individually none of these pieces of evidence is decisive, together they amount to a strong presumption that he became a resident bishop shortly after his consecration, and that he embarked there and then on his public career.

II

With his arrival in Auvergne begins the least satisfactorily document-ed period of La Rochefoucauld's career, though it is clear that he was intensely active there both politically and pastorally. The disappear-ance of his papers, as well as the bulk of the Clermont diocesan archives for the years in question, is particularly regrettable, since it was his long episcopate at Clermont which shaped his commitment and approach to church reform, as will be amply shown in a later chapter. Only a full study of the Catholic League in Auvergne could hope to reveal the detail of his activities during the first decade of his episcopate.[42] But the problem is much less acute than for several other

39. B.S.G., MS. 366, fo. 35, 6 October 1585, certificate of consecration signed by Pierre de Gondi, Bishop of Paris; La Rochefoucauld, *Homme d'église*, p. 40.
40. Oroux, *Histoire ecclésiastique de la cour*, ii, pp. 219–20, gives 1589 as the date.
41. Louise Welter, *La Réforme ecclésiastique au diocèse de Clermont au xvii\ siècle* (Paris, 1956), pp. 24–5.
42. Both A. Imberdis, *Histoire des guerres religieuses en Auvergne*, 2 vols. (Moulins, 1840) and Marc de Vissac, *Chronique de la ligue en Basse-Auvergne* (Riom, 1888) are highly anecdotal and of little value. By contrast, the two short accounts written by Francine Leclercq, published in A.G. Manry, ed., *Histoire de l'Auvergne* (Toulouse, 1974) and Abel Poitrineau, ed., *Le Diocèse de Clermont* (Paris, 1979) respectively, are both valuable.

bishops and dioceses during the final phase of the religious wars, when even the identity of the incumbent of many a diocese remains unclear to this day.

With its 800 or so parishes, Clermont, which was one of the largest dioceses in France, offered unlimited challenge to any energetic young bishop. Not only was it large, but much of it was virtually inaccessible, and late sixteenth-century observers were struck by the penury obtaining in most of the region. It boasted numerous abbeys, priories and other smaller chapters and hospices; some of its abbeys, such as Chaise Dieu, were among the most powerful and wealthy in France, but others belonged to independent congregations like Cluny or Chezal-Benoît. The Clermont cathedral chapter also possessed rights and pretensions which likewise placed limits on his authority. Moreover, the bishop could appoint the parish priests of about only one parish in ten, one of the most unfavourable ratios to be found in the entire French church. The consequences of this for a bishop intent on reform can easily be imagined, as can the slowness with which the calibre of the Clermont clergy improved.[43] Lay patrons or religious establishments controlled the greater number of parishes, and strongly defended their exemption from episcopal control. And, as the special assizes known as *grands jours*, which were held in Clermont in 1583 and 1666, showed, the Auvergne suffered heavily from war damage, and was prey to a lawless nobility that verged on brigandage into the age of Louis XIV.[44]

The bishop's financial position was not much healthier. If national economic trends apply to Clermont, then it is virtually certain that La Rochefoucauld enjoyed much less for most of his years there than the modest 15,000 *livres* which his immediate successors possessed.[45] A 'good' abbey was worth more than that, and La Rochefoucauld probably relied heavily on Tournus to supplement his episcopal revenues. As he confessed repeatedly, his clergy were in a deplorable state, and quite useless for the task of reforming the laity; indeed, they were probably as urgently in need of reform as their flocks. Civil and military disruption made the whole task infinitely more painful, and La Rochefoucauld would later complain of how little he had managed to achieve.

If La Rochefoucauld's priorities in 1586 were the good government and reform of his diocese, he could not, however, ignore the growing politico-religious crisis which had opened two years earlier with the

43. Welter, *La Réforme ecclésiastique*, ch. 1; Poitrineau, *Le Diocèse de Clermont*, pp. 139ff.
44. For those of 1582, and their criticism of ecclesiastical abuses: B.N., MS. Fr. 16508, fos. 577sqq; for the position in 1666, see Arlette Lebigre, *Les Grands Jours d'Auvergne: désordres et répressions au xviie siècle* (Paris, 1976); Albert N. Hamscher, 'Les Réformes judiciaires des grands jours d'Auvergne, 1665–1666', *Cahiers d'Histoire* 21 (1976), pp. 425–42.
45. A.D., Puy-de-Dôme 1G 153, no. 4.

death of the Duke of Anjou, the last Valois heir to the throne (his brother Henri III had no children), and the emergence of the Huguenot leader Henri de Navarre as heir apparent.[46] No doubt, Pope Sixtus V's excommunication and exclusion of Navarre from the succession in 1585 was enough to satisfy an Ultramontane like La Rochefoucauld, but it might not of itself have thrown him headlong into the Catholic League that was then gathering strength.[47]

Apart from these general pressures, the new bishop found, on arriving in Auvergne, that his brothers Jean-Louis and Alexandre – the latter now prior of St Martin-de-Randan – were active and influential there, and favourable to the League. The political and religious position in the province is not easy to summarise. Huguenots were not numerous, and were concentrated in Upper Auvergne; the main Protestant threat came from neighbouring Gévaudan, Velay and the Vivarais. Passions were less inflamed than elsewhere – significantly, Auvergne had not had its *Saint Barthélemy*.[48] Old rivalries between the towns, especially Clermont and Riom, continued in a different guise, and were to determine attitudes to the League and Henri de Navarre. All the towns seem to have disliked paying for the garrisons raised by the Count of Randan, while military operations were usually confined to attempts to control strategic towns.[49] A suspicious Henri III went as far as placing Randan under close surveillance in 1586, and one of the latter's few extant letters, dated December 1586, shows him attempting to refute rumours circulating at court that he was in contact with Navarre.[50] In fact, at this point, Randan made no move to join the Guise-dominated League, but seems to have followed the policy of the family patron, Nevers, which was one of opposition to government by royal favourites such as Epernon or Joyeuse, rather than outright support for the Guises. Randan survived Joyeuse's expedition to Auvergne in 1586, and the following year still resisted Guise pressure to embrace the League after Navarre's important victory at Coutras. Mercurial and probably without great firmness of purpose, he was typical of the local aristocracy which used the wars to establish their power against all-comers.[51]

By contrast, Randan's episcopal brother was entirely without political experience, and was probably in no hurry to acquire it; as his

46. See Salmon, *Society in Crisis*, pp. 234ff; Greengrass, *France in the Age of Henry IV*, pp. 26ff.
47. The papal bull is printed in R. Mousnier, *The Assassination of Henry IV* (London, 1973), Appendix 2, pp. 293ff.
48. Leclercq, 'Le temps des troubles', in *Le Diocèse de Clermont*, pp. 113–14.
49. Leclercq, 'Le temps des troubles', in *Histoire de l'Auvergne*, pp. 266–7.
50. B.N. MS. Fr. 3612, fo. 124, 26 Dec. 1586, letter to Nevers, denouncing the rumour as an attempt to discredit him, and asking Nevers to intercede with Henri III and Catherine de Medici on his behalf.
51. Pierre Richard, *Pierre d'Epinac: la papauté et la ligue française* (Paris, 1902), pp. 246ff.

later career would show, he had little ambition, taste or even talent for politics. If he sympathised with the League before 1588, it was probably on intellectual grounds alone. But in that year, he was plunged into politics through being elected, along with his brother Alexandre, to represent the province of Bourges at the ill-fated Estates General of Blois. Randan had finally joined the League in the previous year, bringing a large section of the Auvergnat nobility with him.[52] The bishop's election confirmed a growing drift towards the League in the province. The invariably laconic records of meetings of the French clergy tell us little about his role at Blois, but as a junior member of the episcopate, he could not rival the grandees of the church and the League, led by Cardinals de Guise and Bourbon, and by Pierre d'Epinac, Archbishop of Lyon, to whom leadership had clearly belonged for several years.[53] A letter written to his patron, Nevers, certainly does not convey an impression of him as a Leaguer fanatic.[54] But then he did not need to be, as the Estates General was overwhelmingly pro-League and determined to force their anti-Huguenot views on Henri III. Here lay the roots of the conflict which would lead to the assassination of the Guise brothers on Henri's orders, an act which almost certainly led many men like La Rochefoucauld to sacrifice their remaining scruples and to declare openly for the League.[55] This was the real importance of the Estates General for the bishop for, as his later career would often reveal, once he had made up his mind, he showed remarkable tenacity, even stubbornness, in following his chosen path.

La Rochefoucauld returned to Auvergne in March 1589, and resided there with few interruptions for nearly twenty years. His brother, whom the Duke of Mayenne (now *lieutenant général* of the kingdom for the League which no longer recognised Henri III) retained as governor of the province, was already campaigning against the Huguenot towns of Upper Auvergne.[56] Henri III did not yet dismiss him, but sent the Marquis d'Effiat to keep an eye on him.[57] Henceforth, the bishop and the governor would lead the League in Auvergne, with François showing the greater determination of the two. He and Alexandre were

52. *La Prise et réduction de plusieurs villes et chasteaux du pay d'Auvergne par Monsieur le comte de Randan* (Paris, 1589), p. 6; Pierre-Victor Palma Cayet, *Chronologie novenaire*, ed. J.A. Buchon (Paris, 1836), p. 117, who claims Randan had been a Leaguer since 1585.
53. Almost inevitably, the Blois assembly was overshadowed by the Guise murders, and existing studies of it are unsatisfactory: Lucien Serbat, *Les Assemblées du clergé de France: origines, organisation, développement 1561–1615* (Paris, 1906), scarcely mentions it; Manfred Orlea, *La Noblesse aux états généraux de 1576 et de 1588* (Paris, 1980), is not definitive; see his brief comments at pp. 160–1.
54. B.N., MS. Fr. 3633, fo. 124, letter of 12 December 1588.
55. Richard, *Pierre d'Epinac*, pp. 325ff; Salmon, *Society in Crisis*, pp. 243ff.
56. *La Prise et réduction de plusieurs villes*, pp. 10–11; *Inventaire sommaire des archives communales de Riom* (Riom, 1892), p. 177.
57. Leclercq, in *Histoire de l'Auvergne*, p. 270.

active in negotiations to win the adherence of the towns. Riom was won over through Alexandre, while François ensured his seigneurial town of Billom would follow suit.[58] But there was a heavy price to pay for this: Clermont, largely out of hostility to Riom, refused to come over and, even after Henri III's death, remained firmly royalist.[59] La Rochefoucauld, along with his servants and those of the clergy loyal to him, was excluded from the town for the next six years. This decision considerably weakened his ability to control and govern his diocese.[60] It was an experience that he shared with many other bishops during the critical last years of the wars.

La Rochefoucauld soon showed his determined support of the League, for it was he and Alexandre who did most to make possible the first meeting of its Estates in Auvergne at Billom in April 1589, for as bishop he was temporal lord of the town.[61] He opened the assembly, presided over its sessions, and welcomed a delegation from Languedoc. According to an eye-witness account, he vigorously defended the action of the *bons catholiques* in defence of the church. The sorry state of France derived from its having forgotten human obligations towards God – in this case the defence of Catholicism – with the unacceptable result that heresy was only prosecuted insofar as it threatened the state. La Rochefoucauld was having no truck with such versions of *raison d'état*, insisting instead on the universal duty to transcend the perfidious 'sagesse humaine et police mondaine' which, he claimed, was often contrary to the laws of God. He alleged that there were those in Clermont who were in contact with Navarre, and that an envoy from Randan had been sent away with the polite assurance, 'nous avons un roi'.[62] This speech had the desired effect, and the deputies enthusiastically followed his lead, accepting the articles of union and taking the oath of loyalty to the League from the bishop's own hands. Clermont and Montferrand were declared rebels and disturbers of the peace, and it was decided to redistribute their offices among League towns; towns still sitting on the fence would be given time to join, and war would be waged on rebels with taxes raised under special commission from Randan. The *taille* would be used to alleviate distress, while Mayenne would be approached for permission to use church *décimes* for military operations in the Auvergne.[63]

58. *Inventaire des archives de Riom*, pp. 177–8; Riom seems to have resisted Randan's attempts to push it into joining the League: Harding, *Anatomy of a Power Elite*, p. 94.

59. *Mémoires de Jehan de Vernyes conseiller du roy et président de la cour des aides de Montferrand 1589–1593* (Paris-Riom, 1874), pp. 39–40. It should be pointed out that these are not 'Memoirs' in the usual sense, but two memoranda dating from 1589 and 1593 respectively, addressed by Vernyes to Henri IV.

60. F. Leclercq, 'Les Etats provinciaux de la ligue en Basse-Auvergne de 1589 à 1594', *Bulletin philologique et historique* (1963), pp. 916–18.

61. *Inventaire des archives de Riom*, p. 179.

62. *La Résolution des trois estats du bas pais d'Auvergne, avec la prise de la ville d'Issoire* (Paris, 1589), pp. 5–14.

63. *Ibid.*, pp. 17–27; Palma Cayet, *Chronologie novenaire*, p. 117.

The bishop and his brothers had finally burned their boats and left no doubt as to where their loyalties now lay. Informed of events in the Auvergne, Henri III dismissed Randan as governor on 20 April 1589, and appointed in his place Charles de Valois, Count of Auvergne.[64] François could not be removed as bishop, but he felt the king's displeasure when he was deprived of his office in the royal chapel.[65] In July, Henri quashed the resolutions of the Estates, and only a few weeks before he was himself assassinated, declared Randan guilty of treason.[66] The League's enemy was now the altogether more formidable Henri de Navarre; for La Rochefoucauld, this meant the issues were even clearer than before, and the duty of resistance all the more binding.

Despite the energetic resolutions of the Estates, Randan failed to prosecute a vigorous military campaign.[67] Charles de Valois began building an effective opposition to him, while the royalist towns refused to answer his call to join the League after Henri III's assassination.[68] Military operations were accompanied by incessant negotiations to limit material destruction. But hopes of a lasting peace or ceasefire foundered because of the mutual suspicion separating the sides. When Randan proposed peace in January 1590 on condition that a Catholic succeed to the throne and that Navarre be excluded, the royalists refused to be drawn or to abandon him, insisting that they would have to seek his approval for a ceasefire, 'pour y obéir comme fidelles subiects'.[69]

These negotiations gave La Rochefoucauld the opportunity to restate his interpretation of the League's principles, with the aim of persuading the royalists that their defence of Navarre's rights was ill-founded. He alleged that they had failed to make any kind of reasoned reply to the League on the Catholic character of the French crown, on the need to prevent it from falling to a heretic, and on the church's judgement of Navarre as delivered by Sixtus V in 1585. How could they claim to remain in the church while rejecting its decisions? 'For what is your answer concerning the authority of the church? Who could be so blind and divorced from reason to argue that one could remain in the church but refuse to recognize it and its authority?' Such themes were to be a constant refrain in his career, and it was no accident that his first significant work should be entitled *De l'Authorité de l'Eglise en ce qui concerne la foy et la religion*. As far as he was

64. Leclercq, 'Les Etats provinciaux', p. 918.
65. Oroux, *Histoire ecclésiastique de la cour*, ii, p. 227.
66. Leclercq, 'Les Etats provinciaux', p. 920.
67. He did, however, capture a number of strategic towns, notably Issoire: *La Prise et reduction de plusieurs villes*, pp. 11ff; Palma Cayet, *Chronologie novenaire*, p. 215.
68. *La Résolution des trois estats*, pp. 38–9, for Randan's summons of 13 August 1589.
69. *Articles proposez à la noblesse du pais d'Auvergne de la part de Monsieur le comte de Randan, avec un discours sur la réplique de la dite noblesse du contraire party par Monsieur l'Evesque de Clermont* (Paris, 1590), pp. 10–14.

concerned, the pope and the Estates General had both spoken, and the latter's judgement could not be impugned without attacking the fundamental laws of the kingdom – the chief of which was the king's obligation to defend the church and the true faith. Religion being the foundation of the kingdom, the king himself owed obedience to the church, and La Rochefoucauld had no doubt that Navarre was incapable of fulfilling such a role; peace with *him* would be but a prelude to further attacks on the church, while even a temporary truce would benefit heresy.[70] There was little room for compromise on fundamentals here, and it is not surprising that La Rochefoucauld believed it essential to carry on the struggle against Navarre by every available means. Such views were an essential part of the arsenal of arguments used by the League, and La Rochefoucauld's exposition of them was not particularly original. If we have dwelt on these two declarations of 1589 and 1590, it is because they are the only surviving sources that offer us a direct insight into his convictions as a Leaguer. Moreover, he expressed them with the forcefulness of someone who had entered the political arena slowly and unwillingly, and primarily out of religious conviction. If, in retrospect, some of his arguments seem to lack political realism, and to stem from a low esteem for politics and the 'sagesse humaine et police mondaine' upon which it was based, it should be remembered that it was precisely Leaguers of this hue that Navarre found it most difficult to deal with effectively in later years.

In fact, a greater burden of leadership was shortly to be thrust on to La Rochefoucauld's shoulders. In March 1590, on the same day as Navarre defeated Mayenne at Ivry, Randan was defeated and killed at the battle of Cros-Rolland, near the important strategic fortress of Issoire.[71] Neither victory was decisive in the short-term, but Randan's defeat proved a military turning-point in Auvergne. He had failed to rally the neutrals, the royalists were now on the offensive, and the League's fortunes dwindled steadily.[72] Randan had benefited from François's solid support, which led one soured observer, Jehan de Vernyes, to attribute the governor's policies 'à l'ambition de son frère. . .qui a plus espéré d'avancement au parti de la rebellion qu'en celui du feu roi'.[73]

If Vernyes really believed his own words, he was singularly mistaken. After a defeat as irreversible as that of March 1590, an ambitious bishop would have begun to tone down his Leaguer

---

70. *Ibid.*, pp. 17–27. This is not the actual text of his speech, but notes taken by someone who was present.
71. See the long account in Palma Cayet, *Chronologie novénaire*, pp. 238ff; *Les Oeconomies royales de Sully*, ed. Bernard Barbiche and David Buisseret, (Paris, 1970), i, p. 253.
72. Leclercq, in *Histoire de l'Auvergne*, p. 272; La Rochefoucauld, *Homme d'église*, pp. 62–4.
73. *Mémoires de Jehan de Vernyes*, p. 41.

opinions and to shift his ground. Yet La Rochefoucauld remained faithful to the League for five more years. By then, the more politically motivated amongst the clergy, especially the bishops, had long since made their peace with Henri IV; a large number, led by La Rochefoucauld's own metropolitan, Renaud de Beaune, Archbishop of Bourges, did so by 1593, when Henri converted to Catholicism, and others followed soon afterwards.[74] In Auvergne, meanwhile, it was only due to the leadership of La Rochefoucauld and the marquis de Canillac that the League did not rapidly fade away, though it took occasional sorties from the nearby Lyonnais by the duc de Nemours and the marquis de Saint-Sorlin to prevent its total military collapse. Frequent truces were arranged, only to be quickly broken. The towns were increasingly war-weary. The League's principal bases were Riom and Billom, where both Capuchin and Jesuit preachers were active. La Rochefoucauld and Canillac continued to convene the Leaguer Estates and to raise money for their cause.[75] The bishop also tried to raise *décimes* from his clergy for the same purpose; as late as March 1594, we find him renewing the collector's commission 'suivant le mandement de monseigneur le duc de Mayenne'.[76]

La Rochefoucauld's stand for the League was well known outside his diocese. It was evidently appreciated by Mayenne, who seems to have made repeated efforts to tempt him into taking on a more prominent role in its affairs. But not even the offer of a place on his 'council of state', which Mayenne made him in early 1591, could persuade him to leave Clermont to assume such a role, and fill the vacuum left by the deaths of Cardinals Guise and Bourbon and by the gradual defection of other leading prelates.[77] Even more convincing evidence of his standing is provided by Mayenne's response, a few months later, to Gregory XIV's reported willingness to show his support for the League by offering to make cardinals of its leading ecclesiastical figures. Apart from the ubiquitous Pierre d'Epinac, Mayenne's only candidate, in May 1591, was La Rochefoucauld, 'prélat très capable et zélé'.[78] Nothing came of this, as Gregory XIV died in October, and neither of his more cautious successors was willing to implement or renew such a commitment. It would be exactly ten years before La Rochefoucauld would next become a candidate for the rank of cardinal.

Yet this should not be taken to mean that Rome was indifferent to him, the decision to appoint him cardinal being fraught with

74. Frederic J. Baumgartner, 'Crisis in the French Episcopacy: the Bishops and the Succession of Henri IV' *Archiv für Reformationsgeschichte* 70 (1979), pp. 276–301.
75. Leclercq, 'Les Etats provinciaux', pp. 923–7.
76. A.N., G 8* 1282, unfoliated *liasse*.
77. *Correspondance de Mayenne*, ed. E. Henry and C. Loriquet (Reims, 1860–2), ii, pp. 282–4, Mayenne to la Rochefoucauld, 16 January 1591.
78. *Ibid* ii, pp. 252–3, Mayenne to Jacques de Diou, League agent in Rome, 22 May 1591.

difficulties which might lead to its being regretted by all concerned. In fact, Rome continued to regard La Rochefoucauld as a faithful ally against Navarre. In May 1592, the newly-elected Clement VIII sent a brief to eleven bishops, of whom La Rochefoucauld was one, demanding an uncompromising stand on the succession issue and on the need for a speedy convocation of an Estates General to elect a Catholic king.[79] A letter from him to Clement in April 1593 shows how firm he remained, although the circumstances in which the letter was written remain obscure. He had evidently failed in his attempts to forbid his clergy to administer the sacraments to Navarre's Catholic followers, and now feared that his failure might lead ordinary people to believe they could be simultaneously good, practising Catholics and supporters of a heretic pretender. He pointed the finger quite clearly at Clermont and several other towns, whose inhabitants he did not hesitate to call enemies of religion.[80] Such a statement may have well been designed to impress the pope, but it was, as we have already seen, characteristic of him.

In these circumstances, it is significant that in an extensive memorandum submitted to Henri IV in 1593 by Jean de Vernyes, president in the Montferrand *cour des aides*, the author, in advising the king on how to recover Auvergne, should have devoted much thought to François and Alexandre de La Rochefoucauld. Vernyes felt the best approach would be through Nevers, to whom François was closely attached.[81] Evidently well informed, but misjudging his man, Vernyes continued:

> Besides, he is of an ambitious disposition, aspiring to higher things, who stands to gain a cardinal's hat from the League. One could keep such hopes alive if the king comes to terms with the pope. . .and in the meantime, offer him a seat in council, for which he would be well equipped.[82]

Vernyes was, in effect, advising Henri to take a leaf out of Mayenne's book, but the king, with so many other problems to resolve and perhaps judging the bishop's obduracy better than Vernyes, never seems to have made any such approach to him. Nor did La Rochefoucauld give him any grounds for doing so. When Riom recognised

---

79. A.S.V., Miscellanea Armarium XLIV, vol. 37, no. 88, brief of 7 May 1592.

80. A.S.V., Nunz. Fr. 42, fos. 24–5, letter of 5 April 1593. He concluded the letter with the hope that ecclesiastical discipline, now 'pene collapsam', would be restored to its 'pristinam dignitatem et pietatem'.

81. *Mémoires*, pp. 68–9: 'parce que ledict évesque a cet honneur d'appartenir au duc de Nevers, et sont fort liés d'amitié'.

82. 'C'est au reste un esprit ambitieux, aspirant aux choses hautes, et qui a à attendre de son parti le chapeau de cardinal. On peut l'entretenir des mesmes esperances si Sa Majesté s'accorde avec le Pape. . .et presentement d'une retenue du conseil d'estat, dont il est très capable.' *Ibid.*, p. 85.

Henri in April 1594, La Rochefoucauld withdrew to his town of Billom, where he held out until Clement VIII formally absolved Henri in August 1595.[83] La Rochefoucauld's submission to Henri the following month was minimal, that of a hard-line Ultramontane — he recognised him only because he now had papal authorisation do do so. The League might be dead but, as Henri would discover, the attitudes that gave rise to it were not.

Even before his recognition of Henri IV, La Rochefoucauld gave further evidence of his political intractability in the affair of the expulsion of the Jesuits from France in the wake of Jean Châtel's abortive attempt to assassinate the king in December 1594. The *parlement* of Paris gave the Jesuits two weeks in which to leave the realm, though some other *parlements* such as Toulouse refused to follow suit.[84] Curiously, within the jurisdiction of the Paris *parlement*, only the Jesuit college at Billom refused to obey the decree. There followed a further decree directed specifically against it, but it proved impossible to enforce. On 30 June 1595, the *parlement* was informed by its procurator-general that only Billom was still resisting, adding that its resistance was covertly supported by 'ceulx qui ont autorité en ladite ville', i.e. La Rochefoucauld and the consuls. A third decree followed, threatening heavy penalties and deprivation of office should officials obstruct its implementation.[85]

When the *parlement's* commissioners arrived in Billom on 8 August, the consuls prudently opted for obedience.[86] But La Rochefoucauld was not prepared to do so. Two days earlier, he drafted a formal protest against the impending expulsion, with the demand that the commissioners insert it into their formal record and that the parties be sent before the *parlement*. The first request was granted, but not the second. The Jesuits, who had been prepared to submit, were now fortified by the bishop's stand, and demanded that at least the *lieutenant général* of the local *bailliage* court be asked to judge the case. Though this petition was granted, the official refused to deal with such a dangerous issue, and ordered the eviction to go ahead. But, for some reason, nothing happened, and months later, on 25 October, we find the *parlement* asking for an examination of, and report on La Rochefoucauld's protest. Whether a further decree confirming the expulsion then followed is not known, but there is no doubt that the Jesuits withdrew from Billom, first to the bishop's château at Mozun, where they were under his personal protection and, later, when this proved insufficient, to Le Puy, which lay just beyond the *parlement's*

83. *Inventaire des archives de Riom*, pp. 21–2.
84. Mousnier, *Assassination of Henry IV*, pp. 217ff.
85. B.N., Dupuy 438, fos. 41–2, 44, for the decrees of April and June 1595.
86. Most of what follows is based on the *procès-verbal* of the expulsion in A.D., Ardèche, *fonds* of *lycée* of Tournon, uncatalogued.

jurisdiction.[87] The court proved inflexible and, not for the last time, La Rochefoucauld demonstrated his determination to support the Jesuits. Within two years, he was again petitioning the crown for a return of the Jesuits to his diocese.

In his protest, La Rochefoucauld assumed full personal responsibility for obstructing the *parlement*, insisting that he did so not as *seigneur* of Billom but as Bishop of Clermont.[88] He did not query the court's motives, which were doubtless sincere, but felt his own were superior. Firstly, he objected that an order recognised by the pope and a general council, that is, the Council of Trent, could not be banished from a Catholic kingdom 'sans grande iniure et preiudice de l'Eglise': to do so would be to institute schism. Secondly, he had a pressing and more personal motive – the disastrous state of his diocese, full of ignorant and incapable clergy. He could not, therefore, hope to discharge his episcopal obligations of reform if deprived of the services of an order of priests universally recognised as the best preachers and teachers of their age. Implicitly, there was much more at stake than the fate of an order of which he happened to be a protector; he saw Gallican and schismatic tendencies at work in the expulsion, and his pastoral and Ultramontane convictions urged him to oppose them.

La Rochefoucauld's defence of the Jesuits ended as it had begun – with a declaration of the duties of his office and the state of his diocese. These sentiments may seem conventional enough, and no one was in a position to gainsay them. But the expulsion was an issue on which the *parlement* was inflexible, and on which it was unwise to provoke it without strong motivation. Once again, La Rochefoucauld's Ultramontane convictions were opposed to the subjection of religion to politics, views doubtless instilled in him by the Jesuits of the College of Clermont. Yet again, the affair demonstrates his disregard for the prevailing political winds. If this seems a peculiar judgement of a man who was Richelieu's predecessor as president of the king's council, we need but note the opinions of him voiced by Ubaldini and Bentivoglio, two of the shrewdest papal nuncios of the early seventeenth century: both found him *too* remote from politics for their liking; in 1617, Bentivoglio even lamented his 'stoicism', by which he meant his detachment from politics rather than a philosophical stance, in what he saw as a time of political drift and 'corruption'.[89]

If La Rochefoucauld had shunned a chance of leadership in the

87. P. Delattre, *Les Establissements des Jésuites en France depuis quatre siècles* (Enghien, Belgium, 1949), i, col. 704.
88. Apart from the copy of the protest in the *procès-verbal* (see n. 85), there is a further copy in the Jesuit archives in Rome, Archivum Romanum Societatis Iesu (A.R.S.I.), Gallia 61, fos. 22–3.
89. B.N., MS. Italien 1264, fos. 373v–4r, for Ubaldini's estimate; Luigi di Steffani, *La Nunziatura di Francia di Guido de Bentivoglio*, 4 vols. (Florence, 1863–70), ii. pp. 21–2, 71.

League under Mayenne – which would have severely compromised him for a long time – he was even less likely to enter the limelight under Henri IV. Leadership within the French church now lay firmly with those who had rallied early on to the king, such as Beaune of Bourges, Gondi of Paris, Cardinal Joyeuse and Du Perron; there was little if any room in such company for Leaguer irreducibles. Henri, in any case, was suspicious of clerical politicians, and kept them at arm's length where seats in council and the formulation of policy were concerned.[90]

III

In any event, La Rochefoucauld was only too happy to return to his pastoral duties once the wars had ended. He resumed residence in the royalist town of Clermont, from which he had been exiled since 1589, but it does not seem that the hostilities of recent years affected the remaining years of his episcopate. This was by no means a foregone conclusion: there were many bishops, both royalist and Leaguer, who were either unable to return to their dioceses at all or who, if they did, found themselves beset with obstruction and opposition of different kinds.[91] Of course, the wars had greatly increased La Rochefoucauld's burden as bishop. He had lost control of part of his clergy and this would be difficult to restore, while secular control of benefices also grew, as did the practice of simony in their acquisition. It is, unfortunately, very difficult to form a satisfactory picture of how he dealt with these problems. But, taking stock of his first ten years as bishop in 1597, he was candid enough to admit that he had achieved little; indeed, his frustration was so great that writing seemed, at least briefly, to be the only way left to him to further the objectives which had proved unattainable in practice.[92] The immediate result of this conclusion was the appearance of his two most substantial works, both published in 1597, the *Authorité de l'Eglise* and the *De la perfection de l'estat ecclésiastique*. Both were intended as contributions to the defence and reform of the church, with the second forming a commentary on

---

90. There is no adequate modern study of the French church under Henri IV. See Jean-Pierre Babelon, *Henri IV* (Paris 1982), pp. 677ff, and the older study of François-Tommy Perrens, *L'Eglise et l'état en France sous Henri IV*, 2 vols. (Paris, 1872).

91. For example, the Bishop of St Flour lost his see in 1593 and, if the Leaguer consuls had had their way, his place would have been taken by Alexandre de La Rochefoucauld: A.S.V., Nunz. Fr. 42, fo. 515, petition to Clement VIII, 1 January 1595.

92. *De l'Estat ecclésiastique* (Lyon, 1597), p. 65: 'A quoy (*reform*) ayant proposé dès mon entrée en ce diocèse d'emploier le peu de moien qui me restait d'une si grande désolation...i'en ay esté tellement empesché par les fléaux que Dieu nous a fait sentir de sa iuste indignation contre nos peschés...i'ay pensé ne devoir servir de celuy seul de l'écriture pour faire déclaration de ce que ie n'ay peu faire'.

some of the peculiar problems that he encountered in Clermont.

But despite the evident temptation to do so, he was not about to retire to his study and continue the work of reform by the pen alone; however admirable and necessary, it was not an option which could ever replace the thankless task of visiting, preaching and administering a large diocese.[93] He seems to have left Clermont rarely before 1608. He conducted visitations, held synods, and founded new religious houses. At the 1599 synod, he published a new set of diocesan statutes, designed to fit pressing, immediate needs and in no way corresponding to any Borromean stereotype.[94] However much the reformer of Milan may have influenced him as a bishop, La Rochefoucauld did not feel the need to publish encyclopaedic legislation, as Borromeo had done. His numerous Clermont synods, both before and after 1599, were much more than legislative exercises: they provided him with opportunities to assemble his clergy and impress on them the imperatives of reform. Legislation could not replace the actual work of reform, any more than could the writing of books.

Moreover, though Henri IV was now a Catholic, former Leaguers continued to be suspicious of him and his religion. The Huguenot threat seemed to them to increase rather than recede, and their fears were further aroused by the Edict of Nantes of 1598.[95] La Rochefoucauld's *Authorité de l'Eglise* of the previous year was a contribution to the controversy which has been described as 'the continuation of the wars of religion by other means'.[96] Directed to and against the Protestant church, it clearly betrayed the unease of an erstwhile Leaguer still far from certain of his own church's future. It was also an Ultramontane tract, for, in his preface, he frankly admitted his indebtedness to the Jesuit theologian, Bellarmine, whose *Controversies*, despite some initial opposition to his views on papal power, were to become the staple of Ultramontane ecclesiology for a long time to come.[97] Against the Protestants, La Rochefoucauld defended the necessity of an authentic tradition which alone enabled the church to define revelation and repudiate error or interpolation. Furthermore, he asserted that only the church could validly and correctly interpret Scripture, which brought him to his primary concern – the question of authority. There was no equivocation here: authority in the church was 'entièrement entre les mains du chef et souverain pasteur d'icelle, et en

93. See ch. 4.
94. *Statuts renouvelez par le Révérend Père François de La Rochefoucauld evesque de Clairmont* (Clermont, 1599). They will be analysed in ch. 4.
95. Frederic J. Baumgartner, 'The Catholic Opposition to the Edict of Nantes 1598–99', *Bibliothèque d'humanisme et renaissance* 40 (1978), pp. 525–37.
96. Jacques Solé, *Le Débat entre protestants et catholiques français de 1598 à 1685*, 4 vols. (Lille-Paris, 1985), part i.
97. See Quentin Skinner, *The Foundations of Modern Political Thought*, 2 vols. (Cambridge, 1978), ii, pp. 179–80.

l'assemblée générale des autres pasteurs authorisée et confirmée par le saint siège apostolique'.[98] There was no concession to conciliarism in this juxtaposition, for the pope enjoyed authority over all bishops in his capacity as bishop of the universal church.[99] All assemblies and councils required his consent. As for secular princes, they had no right whatever to interfere in church affairs; their role was merely to assist the pope once decisions had been taken.[100]

Beliefs like this won La Rochefoucauld the reputation of being one of the most uncompromising Ultramontanes in the seventeenth-century French church. He was to have many occasions to display such a stance, and like defenders of embattled positions everywhere, he was quick to raise the alarm as soon as he detected anti-papal tendencies in France. If he was highly regarded in Rome for such devotion, it is not difficult to see why it would separate him from a large section of the French clergy.

More evidence of La Rochefoucauld's *engagement* and independence was forthcoming in subsequent years. The *Traité de l'Eucharistie* of the 'Huguenot Pope', Duplessis-Mornay, began circulating in 1598, giving rise to a controversy which led to the famous debate between him and Du Perron at Fontainebleau in 1600. According to the diarist Pierre de l'Estoile, the Bishop of Clermont was one of those who attacked Mornay's book, but, unfortunately, he fails to say what form his attack took.[101] However, we do have independent proof that La Rochefoucauld attempted to write, and may have even completed, a book refuting Mornay, but that perhaps only one chapter of it was ever printed. There is no ready explanation for this, except that he may have withdrawn from the fray in order to make way for Du Perron. And, unfortunately, no copy of his treatise, manuscript or printed, has ever come to light.[102]

Altogether more extraordinary was the Marthe Brossier affair, a celebrated case of demonic possession that occurred in 1599 and which was to have worrying political repercussions for Henri IV. The details of the case need not detain us here, but Brossier first caused a storm in Paris with her 'prophesyings' of a Huguenot bloodbath.[103] The Parisian *dévots*, many of them former Leaguers, openly fanned the

98. *De l'authorité de l'église*, pp. 128–9.
99. *Ibid.*, p. 178.
100. *Ibid.*, pp. 183–4.
101. *Journal pour le règne de Henri IV*, ed. L.-R. Lefèvre, vol. i 1589–1600 (Paris, 1948), p. 354.
102. B.S.G., MS. 3238, fo. 527, La Rochefoucauld to his secretary, Jean Desbois, asking him to send him the first, printed chapter of the book. The Jesuits of the college of Clermont later claimed to have a copy of the work: Morinière, *Vray prélat*, p. 348, Rouvier, *Vita*, p. 181.
103. The best account is in Robert Mandrou, *Magistrats et sorciers au xviiᵉ siècle* (Paris, 1968), pp 163ff.

ensuing agitation, which became an indirect attack on the recent and unpopular Edict of Nantes, and the king and the *parlement* had to act energetically to curb the incipient political opposition. La Rochefoucauld only became involved when his brother Alexandre brought Brossier with him to the Auvergne in defiance of a decree of the *parlement* ordering her to be kept under close surveillance at home near Romorantin. The *parlement* reacted quickly to such provocation, and ordered her arrest.[104] But the royal intendants then on mission in Auvergne were unable to carry out this order, since the La Rochefoucaulds kept her well hidden. The intendant Miron wrote that they were too powerful there to be perturbed by a decree or by royal officials, and that the bishop's replies to his remonstrances were unsatisfactory.[105] The *parlement* riposted with a further decree giving the brothers a month to surrender Brossier or have their property seized.[106] This induced them to yield, but in an extraordinary manner which nearly created a serious diplomatic incident: Alexandre took Brossier to Rome, no doubt with his brother's approval, in order to obtain the pope's own judgement on the genuineness of her possession.[107] It took all of Cardinal d'Ossat's formidable skills to prevent this from happening, as well as to persuade Alexandre to abandon his mission and to seek royal forgiveness.[108] Henri IV was extremely angry, and in no mood to forgive either him or the Bishop of Clermont, insisting that the decrees against them should be enforced to the full.[109] We may doubt that they were, since Alexandre disappeared from view, dying in exile in Italy in 1602, while the disturbed state of Auvergne may have reduced Henri's determination to see the full rigours of the law applied to his brother in Clermont.

In contrast to his earlier defence of the Jesuits, La Rochefoucauld does not seem to have written down his reasons for harbouring Brossier and then encouraging the journey to Rome. The intendant Miron merely related that the two brothers 'donnent d'estranges opinions à

---

104. The *parlement* decreed her arrest on 30 December 1599: B.N., Dupuy 379, fos. 147 and 150. A binding error has separated the pages of the decree in this manuscript.
105. B.N., MS. Fr. 18453, fo. 106, Robert Miron to Sully, 24 January 1600.
106. B.N., Dupuy 379, fos. 148–9, decree of 21 March 1600. An earlier decree of 19 February 1600 had threatened similar penalties: A.N., X¹a 1767, fos. 103v–4r.
107. *Correspondance de Pierre de Bérulle*, ed. Jean Dagens, 3 vols. (Paris, 1937–9), i, p. 3, Jacques Leprevost to Bérulle, from Avignon, 15 April 1600. Bérulle was one of the many *dévots* who believed the possession to be genuine.
108. For d'Ossat's activities, see *Correspondance du cardinal d'Ossat*, ed. Amelot de La Houssaye (Amsterdam, 1714), iii, pp. 591, 621; iv, p. 202. See also the letters of ambassador Sillery to the king in A.A.E., Correspondance politique, Rome 18, fo. 229–30, 27 April 1600; fo. 247, 27 May; fo. 262, 29 June; fo. 271, 8 July; fo. 291, 5 August. The size of the correspondence is indicative of how seriously the king and his agents treated the affair.
109. *Lettres inédites du roi Henri IV à Monsieur de Sillery ambassadeur à Rome du 1 avril au 27 juin 1600*, ed. E. Halphen (Paris, 1866), pp. 58–9, letter of 12 May 1600; A.A.E., Rome 18, fo. 259, Henri IV to Sillery, 14 July 1600.

tout le monde', without specifying what they were.[110] In all probability, however, La Rochefoucauld agreed with the *dévots* in refusing to accept that a case of possession be judged by a civil court on the basis of evidence from lawyers and medical doctors – this was an area of ecclesiastical competence and religious belief.[111]

La Rochefoucauld was not the principal actor in the Brossier case, but it came at a significant point in his career. When viewed alongside his writing and activity since the expulsion of the Jesuits, it belongs to a coherent pattern of behaviour which shows that he remained an unreconciled Leaguer, albeit an essentially unpolitical one, in at least one specific sense: his allegiance to the crown was conditional upon its support for the church, and Henri IV was not the ideal *fidei defensor*. By the same token, agitation such as that of the Brossier case, showed the king how far he still had to go in appeasing many ex-Leaguers, and here, too, it was the unpolitical among them who proved the most recalcitrant. Only royal policy initiatives could signal a more conciliatory attitude to them. One of these would have been the formal acceptance of the decrees of the Council of Trent by the French crown, but Henri did not feel strong enough to brave the opposition to such a move.[112] On the other hand, after much petitioning from La Rochefoucauld among many others, the king did allow the Jesuits to return to France in 1603.[113] This and a number of other concessions to the church seriously reduced distrust of Henri, while his personal efforts to win the confidence of individual ex-Leaguers were no less patient.[114] All set the tone for the religious and ecclesiastical *détente* that characterised the last years of his reign.

In the circumstances, there was every possibility that La Rochefoucauld, who continued to remain in his diocese, would become a *persona grata*. One sign of this, for example, was the king's prompt reply to his petition of 1603 that the Jesuits be allowed to return to their former houses in his diocese.[115] In fact, his return to favour began

---

110. B.N., MS. Fr. 18453, fo. 106, Miron to Sully, 24 January 1600.

111. Still the best study of the *milieux des dévots* which formed in the aftermath of the Wars of Religion and which were to be so important in the religious life of the following century, is Jean Dagens, *Bérulle et les origines de la restauration catholique* (Paris, 1952). I wish to thank Dr Alfred Soman for his help on the Brossier affair.

112. He did come close to doing so, and only backed down at the last minute: see Victor Martin, *Gallicanisme et réforme catholique*, pp. 303ff.; *idem.*, *Les négociations du nonce Silingardi évêque de Modène relatives à la publication du concile de Trente en France 1599–1601* (Paris, 1919).

113. H. Fouqueray, *Histoire de la Compagnie de Jésus en France des origines à la suppression*, 5 vols. (Paris, 1910–25), ii; A. Drouin, 'L'Expulsion des Jésuites sous Henri IV et leur rappel', *Revue d'histoire moderne* 3 (1901–2), pp. 5–28, 593–609; Paul Calendini, 'Henri IV et les Jésuites de 1602 à 1604', *Annales Fléchoises*, 12 (1911), pp. 69–92.

114. Mark Greengrass, *France in the Age of Henry IV*, pp. 160–1.

115. A.R.S.I., Toulouse 20, no. 73, copy of royal *brevet* permitting Jesuits to return to Mauriac.

much earlier than this, though the circumstances behind it remain mysterious. For, only eighteen months after Henri's furious letter to Rome on the Brossier case in which he unloaded his rancour against the La Rochefoucauld brothers, the king was again writing to his ambassador there for an entirely different purpose – to recommend La Rochefoucauld for the dignity of cardinal.

Throughout 1601, Henri's candidates for the red hat were Du Perron, Bishop of Evreux and, interestingly, La Rochefoucauld's Italian cousin, Alessandro della Mirandola, whose family loyalty to the French crown Henri considered politically valuable.[116] When Mirandola deserted to the Spaniards shortly afterwards, Henri struck him off his list, replacing him with Archbishop Villars of Vienne, followed by La Rochefoucauld.[117] But in an autograph postscript to his letter announcing this decision, we can virtually see the king changing his mind, with the result that La Rochefoucauld replaced Villars as his second choice after Du Perron: 'Since writing this letter, I have decided to place the bishop of Clermont before the archbishop of Vienne, and now inform you of my decision, despite the terms of the letter'. He offered no reasoned explanation for this change of mind, but wrote significantly that La Rochefoucauld 'has made himself worthy of my favour since his rapprochement with me'.[118] Unfortunately, we have no means of knowing whether the king was referring to some recent form of rapprochement (i.e. since the Brossier affair), or to a more gradual process of reconciliation stretching back to 1595.

From now on La Rochefoucauld's prospects of obtaining a red hat were directly dependent on the king's policy towards the papacy. After the disastrous years of Spanish domination during the League, Henri was determined to rebuild French influence in Rome, and for this Italian supporters were vital. But after Mirandola's defection in 1601, Henri's nominees for cardinal were to be exclusively French.[119] However, there was opposition to Henri's plans, and Clement VIII was in no great hurry to please him. Besides, the pope wanted to promote a French-born curial official, Seraphim-Olivieri, and pressed Henri to adopt him as an official French candidate.[120] The king was

---

116. B.N., MS. Fr. 3484, fos. 17–18, instruction to ambassador Béthune, 10 October 1601.
117. B.N., MS. Fr. 3484, fo. 30v, Henri IV to Béthune, 8 November 1601; *ibid.*, fo. 42, to same, 22 November.
118. 'Depuis ma lettre écritte Jay avisé de préférer l'Evesque de Clermont à l'Archevesque de Vienne...partant vous en escris ainsy nonobstant le contenu de ladite lettre'...'s'est rendu digne de ma recommendation depuis qu'il a raproché de moi', *ibid.*, fo. 44r.
119. On Henri's papal policy, see Bernard Barbiche, 'L'Influence française à la cour pontificale sous Henri IV', *Mélanges d'archéologie et d'histoire de l'Ecole Française de Rome* 77 (1965), pp. 277–99.
120. B.N., MS. Nouvelles acquisitions françaises 24160, fo. 38, Béthune to Henri IV, 26 August 1602; MS. Fr. 3484, fo. 127, Henri IV to Béthune, 21 September 1602.

very reluctant to do so, as it would mean dropping either Du Perron or La Rochefoucauld. But when Clement argued that if he made Seraphim a cardinal in addition to the king's nominees, the Spaniards would accuse him of creating three French cardinals, Henri yielded, and agreed to nominate Seraphim over La Rochefoucauld.[121] So it was Du Perron and Seraphim who were made cardinals in June 1604.[122] La Rochefoucauld was now, obviously, head of the king's list, but would have to wait his turn.

Despite this setback, La Rochefoucauld's return to favour at home continued rapidly. In 1602, he was briefly led to believe that Henri had designated him to succeed Cardinal d'Ossat in Rome, and would nominate him to the vacant Archbishopric of Lyon, but this rumour was quickly denied.[123] When the second edition of his *Authorité de l'Eglise* appeared in 1604, it was prefaced by a long dedicatory letter to the king, the clearest sign on La Rochefoucauld's part to date of his rapprochement with Henri. In the same year, he was one of the four ecclesiastics to be made commanders of the royal order of the Holy Ghost.[124] When a new ambassador was sent to Rome in 1605, he received instructions to press La Rochefoucauld's claims for a red hat.[125] But Clement VIII's death, and two papal elections in quick succession did not make for a prompt response. Paul V was in no more of a hurry than Clement had been, and it was not until December 1607 that La Rochefoucauld finally received the long-awaited honour.

The delay does not seem to have ruffled the new cardinal at all, for when news of his promotion arrived, he was in his diocese, 'faisant sa visite'. He only arrived at court in late March 1608 to receive his red hat from the king on Palm Sunday.[126] He was far from ungrateful to the king for an honour which placed him in the front rank of the church, as an elegant letter of thanks proves beyond doubt.[127] But without a background of personal service to the crown, political or diplomatic, he was ill at ease at court where there was no obvious role for him. And unlike him, the dominant figures in the French church, Cardinals Du Perron, Sourdis and Joyeuse, were all closely attached in

---

121. B.N., N.a.f. 24161, fo. 107, Béthune to Villeroy, secretary of state, 1 December 1603.
122. Rémy Couzard, *Une ambassade à Rome sous Henri IV* (Paris, 1901), pp. 292–3.
123. B.N., MS. Fr. 3484, fo. 164, Villeroy to Béthune, 16 January 1603, in which he denies reports Béthune had sent him from Rome in a previous letter: B.N., N.a.f. 24160, fo.136v, Béthune to Villeroy, 16 December 1602.
124. B.N., MS. Clairambault 1126, fo. 278r: 'M. l'Evesque de Clermont se trouve à la fin de la liste de ceux qui avoient esté nommés par Henri IV en 1604'.
125. B.N., MS. Fr. 17835, fo. 76, copy of instructions to the marquis d'Halincourt, June 1605.
126. B.N., MS. Italien 1264, fo. 70v–1r, Roberto Ubaldini, papal nuncio, to Cardinal Borghese, 27 March 1608.
127. Copy in B.N., Ms. Fr. 3653, fos. 21–2. An equally fulsome letter to Paul V is in A.S.V., *fondo* Borghese I, vol. 636c, fos. 19–20.

different ways to the king. Yet, because of the way in which one became a cardinal – the one rank in the church hierarchy without any pastoral dimension to it, and all the more 'political' for that reason – La Rochefoucauld became a king's man in a more real sense than he had done when he was made a bishop; his new rank placed him at the king's disposal, but without automatically specifying a role for him.

The fact that Henri IV himself had no clear role in mind for La Rochefoucauld and the latter no claim on his patronage, raises the question of the king's motives in singling him out for advancement. Predictably, the cardinal's early biographers argued that the king was struck by his piety and integrity.[128] This may be true, but is in itself probably unimportant. Clearly, on a general level, the choice was part of the king's policy of creating a party of French cardinals in Rome. But where the king's motives for promoting a Sourdis or a Du Perron are not difficult to perceive, this does not obtain in La Rochefoucauld's case. As we saw, Henri did not explicitly reveal his intentions. We can, therefore, only suppose that he was determined to bind another ex-Leaguer to him and, perhaps, advance his policy in Rome by nominating a candidate whose career and convictions were bound to win him a favourable reception there.

An equally instructive comparison might be made between La Rochefoucauld and Richelieu. When the latter became cardinal in 1622, he regarded his new rank as primarily a stepping stone to political advancement, and he immediately began to divest himself of his diocese altogether.[129] La Rochefoucauld, who found himself idle at the court of Henri IV, worried about not residing in his diocese. He sensed that henceforth residence in distant Clermont would be extremely difficult, and began looking around for a solution to this predicament. However, instead of biding his time until an arch-bishopric fell vacant – as a cardinal he might have felt entitled to one – he preferred a straightforward exchange of Clermont for the diocese of Senlis, which was within easy range of Paris and the court. Agreement was reached in 1609, and the transfers ratified by Rome in early 1610.[130] This move from one unimportant diocese to another was not a promotion, least of all for a cardinal, but it says much about his convictions on cardinals' obligations in respect of episcopal residence. Though far smaller than Clermont, Senlis was better endowed, so that La Rochefoucauld had to surrender his Abbey of St Mesmin near Orleans to his partner in the exchange, Bishop Antoine Rose of Senlis. There is some significance, too, in the identity of the two men involved in the exchange. Antoine Rose was nephew of the famous

128. Morinière, *Vray prélat*, p. 115; BSG. MS. 712, fo. 81.
129. Bergin, *Cardinal Richelieu: Power and the Pursuit of Wealth*, p. 205.
130. A.S.V., *fondo* Consistoriale, Acta Vicecancellarii 15, fo. 65, 18 February 1610.

Leaguer Bishop of Senlis, Guillaume Rose, and he had had, for this and other reasons, a difficult time of it at Senlis. With Rose happy to escape the attentions of the crown and the Paris *parlement* in faraway Clermont, and La Rochefoucauld moving close to Paris, the exchange symbolised a final playing out of some of the tensions that had divided the French episcopate since Henri IV's accession.

2

Homme d'Eglise et d'Etat

IN 1608, La Rochefoucauld was in his fiftieth year, an advanced age for his time and, by French standards, a very late one at which to become a cardinal. His episcopal activities and personal asceticism had begun to undermine his health, yet, despite numerous close encounters with death, he succeeded in wearing the red hat for longer than any French cardinal of the century. He was, in fact, merely entering upon his mid-career; the last decades of his life would be spent in very different surroundings and would be devoted to a far wider range of activities than his earlier life had been.

The transition was by no means simple. Initially, he was ill at ease at the court of Henri IV where, in general, churchmen enjoyed limited influence. Its ecclesiastical life and politics were dominated by the king's favourite, Du Perron, Archbishop of Sens and grand almoner of France since 1606. Only Joyeuse, normally resident in Rome where he held the title of 'Protector of France' could rival him in influence, partly because of his diplomatic talents, and partly because he was heir to the Joyeuse family's considerable political and ecclesiastical power in southern France. La Rochefoucauld enjoyed no such advantages; his only real card was, perhaps, his close connection with the Jesuits, and he soon seems to have struck up a close relationship with the king's recently-chosen confessor, the famous Père Coton. Henri IV had no immediate plans for him, beyond a vague desire to send him to Rome, but he was in no hurry to act upon it. La Rochefoucauld, for his part, made no attempt to hide his boredom in a letter of September 1608 to Cardinal Borghese, or his desire to depart for Rome, where he hoped to be of some use.[1] But it took another year and a European diplomatic crisis to bring this about.

In March 1609, the succession to the childless Duke of Cleves-

1. A.S.V., *fondo* Borghese III, vol. 46c, fo. 226.

Jülich became a major problem for the European powers, to which each of the numerous candidates looked for support. Religious considerations were involved, because the principality was strategically important for the survival of Catholicism in north-west Germany. Although he was a Protestant, the Catholic Habsburgs supported the Elector of Saxony, while France, England and the Dutch upheld the joint candidature of the Elector of Brandenburg and the Count Palatine of Neuburg, fearing more than anything else increased Habsburg power on the Rhine.[2] Rome, for its part, believed a Brandenburg-Neuburg succession would undermine and destroy the Counter-Reformation in the region, and inclined towards the Habsburgs.[3] Through his nuncio, Paul V objected that Henri IV's policy amounted to a promotion of heresy, a charge which the king was concerned to refute, lest the papacy succumb to Habsburg domination. He instructed his ambassador to oppose the Habsburgs' posture of defending Catholicism and to expose their real objectives — the increase of their own power and the encirclement of the Dutch.[4] The nature of the conflict, and the arguments used by the various sides, prefigure the conflicts over French foreign policy between Richelieu and the dévots during the late 1620s.[5]

To neutralise the Habsburgs and to strengthen his position, Henri IV badly needed allies in Italy, an added reason for not alienating the papacy. In late 1609, with a confrontation looming, he considered a new diplomatic offensive was needed. He usually had an able envoy in Rome in the person of Joyeuse, but he was at the time absent in France; indeed, there had been no French cardinal in Rome to put the king's case since February 1609. This proved a convenient time to fulfil his promise to send La Rochefoucauld there.

On leaving for Rome in late October 1609, La Rochefoucauld was given formal instructions relating exclusively to the Cleves-Jülich affair: Henri IV reaffirmed his determination to defend the duke's legitimate heirs and, denying that there were any religious principles involved, since the Habsburg candidate was himself Protestant,

2. See Greengrass, *France in the Age of Henry IV*, pp. 196–7; J. Michael Hayden, *France and the Estates-General of 1614* (Cambridge, 1974), ch. 3; *idem.*, 'Continuity in the France of Henry IV and Louis XIII; French Foreign Policy 1598–1615', *Journal of Modern History* 45 (1973) pp. 1–23.
3. Burkhard Roberg, 'Päpstliche Politik am Rhein: Die römische Kurie und der Jülich-Klevische Erbfolgestreit', *Rheinische Vierteljahrsblätter*, 41 (1977), pp. 63–87. See especially p. 66, n. 8, for a report on Ambassador Brèves's audience of 15 September 1609 with Paul V, where the papal attitude is clearly stated.
4. *Lettres Missives de Henri IV*, ed. Berger de Xivrey (Paris, 1843–76) vii, pp. 760–5, letter to Brèves, 31 August 1609. For the Spanish and Dutch positions, see Jonathan Israel, *The Dutch Republic and the Hispanic World 1606–1661* (Oxford, 1982), pp. 21–2.
5. William F. Church, *Richelieu and Reason of State* (Princeton, 1972) *passim*, especially pp. 197ff, J.H. Elliott, *Richelieu and Olivares* (Cambridge, 1984), pp. 97–8; Richard Bonney, *The King's Debts* (Oxford, 1981), pp. 149ff.

claimed that the Habsburgs were using religion as a cloak for expansionist ambitions. France, he insisted, had no territorial ambitions in the area, and simply desired peace, but could not achieve it single-handed: a show of good faith by others was required, too. If this were not forthcoming, Henri threatened to 'franchir le sault avec ses amis', especially if attempts were made to turn the conflict into a war of religion. This was a warning to the pope not to take refuge behind the Habsburg posture of defending religion. If the pope remained neutral, he would be in a position to mediate should armed conflict break out.[6]

Such was the mission given to La Rochefoucauld, a man with no real experience of either power politics or of diplomacy. It seems unlikely that Henri expected him to achieve a diplomatic miracle, and in all probability, he merely wished to use him to supplement the efforts of his ambassador, Savary de Brèves, in the meetings of the consistory. While the papacy might not like the character of his mission, it could only be reassured by the characterisation of La Rochefoucauld proffered by the nuncio, Ubaldini, as 'extremely retiring. . . little versed in the political arts and no great diplomat. . . and far removed from the ways of the court', and by his having Sully for an enemy and the Secretary of State, Villeroy, for a protector.[7] As part of Henri's overtures to Italian princes, the cardinal stopped in Turin and Florence, and did not arrive in Rome until mid-January 1610.[8]

Disturbing news awaited him. From what we know of hm, it would be surprising to find in him an ardent supporter of Henri IV's Cleves-Jülich policy, and there does indeed seem to have been some dispute about his attitude even before he left for Rome. It may even be that his mission was treated by the king as something of a test of his fidelity.[9] Reports certainly reached the king from Savoy, a strong supporter of Henri in this crisis, that La Rochefoucauld 'avoit parlé des affaires de Cleves au desadvantage du service de Sa Majesté'.[10] More specifically, he was supposed to have said that the king was badly advised to

---

6. B.N., Dupuy 557, fos. 101–4, copy of instruction, dated 16 October 1609. Many other copies survive, and a fragment of it was printed by Martin Philippson, *Heinrich IV und Philip III* (Berlin, 1876) iii, pp. 359–60.
7. B.N., MS. Italien 1264, fos. 373–4, letter to Borghese, 27 October 1609. The nuncio's terms were 'ritratissimo. . . poco versato nei maneggi e non gran negotiatore. . . lontano affatto del'arte della corte'. Brèves obliquely confirmed the remark about Sully and Villeroy's attitudes to him: 'la rigueur que M de Sully luy a tenue à son partement, contre vostre opinion'. B.N., MS. Fr. 18005, fo. 52, letter to Villeroy, 3 February 1610.
8. *Lettres missives*, vii, pp. 782, 790, 940, for royal letters to them.
9. B.N., MS. Fr. 17363, p. 124, La Rochefoucauld to Henri IV, 31 January 1610; 'Quand prenant congé de V.M. je le requis très humblement de surseoir le jugement de ce qui luy seroit rapporté de mes actions jusques à la cognoissance de la verité'. This phrase is too obscure and allusive to interpret fully, but it may well refer to allegations made at court, possibly by Sully and others, against La Rochefoucauld's attitude.
10. B.N., MS. Fr. 18005, fo. 52, Brèves to Villeroy, 3 February 1610. Brèves is merely repeating here what Villeroy had written to him from Paris.

assume the defence of Protestant princes, owing to the detrimental effects their success in Cleves-Jülich would have on Catholicism.[11] This was, as we saw, the pope's view, and that of those French Catholics, some of them former Leaguers, who would later be known as *dévots*. As it happens, the reports from Savoy were never properly confirmed. On being notified of them by Brèves in Rome, La Rochefoucauld wrote a categorical letter of denial to the king; he affirmed that he had argued, and would continue to argue the French case.[12] For his part, Henri IV obligingly played the 'bon prince', and replied thanking the cardinal for informing him of the rumours and asserting that he did not believe a word of them.[13]

If initially, he entertained doubts about French policy, La Rochefoucauld kept them to himself in Rome, and was soon defending Henri in consistory and in audiences.[14] The Italian Cardinal, Delfino, soon surrendered the vice-protectorship of France to him and, since Joyeuse was absent until mid-1611, La Rochefoucauld became effectively protector and, indeed, the only French cardinal in curia during Joyeuse's absence. In March 1610, replying to the cardinal's first dispatch, Villeroy restated French policy as clearly as possible – no doubt, as much to convince his correspondent as Paul V himself.[15] By then, the Prince of Condé's flight from the court to Brussels, and Henri IV's belligerence towards his Habsburg protectors, had brought Europe nearer to war.[16] In April, Paul V proposed sending legates to France and Spain, but La Rochefoucauld was instructed to reply that such a move would be an insult to France, which was not the aggressor in Cleves-Jülich, and that the pope should rather send legates to the guilty party.[17] Two months later, in June, the cardinal wrote that the pope, still concerned about the dispute, would be 'bien marry' to see Louis XIII begin his reign with a war that would be advantageous to heresy. La Rochefoucauld added that he had again stated Henri IV's views, which were still official French policy.[18] When war came later in 1610, the regency government of Marie de Medici was by then beset by problems of its own, and was in no position to pursue the late king's ambitions.[19]

La Rochefoucauld last mentioned the Cleves-Jülich affair in June

11. *Ibid.*, fos. 61–2, Brèves to Henri IV, 3 February.
12. B.N., MS. Fr. 17363, p. 124–5. The letter, a copy, is undated, but Henri's reply enables us to date it as 31 January 1610. See B.N., MS. Fr. 18005, fos. 89–90, Brèves to Villeroy, 18 February 1610.
13. B.N., MS. Fr. 17363, p. 125, undated, but probably March 1610.
14. B.N., MS. Fr. 18005, fos. 172–3, Brèves to Henri IV, 26 April 1610, for an account of La Rochefoucauld's efforts.
15. B. Institut, MS. Godefroy 492, fos. 269–70, dispatch of 16 March 1610.
16. Hayden, *France and the Estates General*, p. 38.
17. B.N., MS. Fr. 18005, fos. 172–3, Brèves to Henri IV, 26 April 1610.
18. *Ibid.*, fo. 226, letter to Marie de Medici, 21 June 1610
19. Hayden, *France and the Estates General*, pp. 43–5.

1610. His only purely diplomatic assignment and, apart from his role in the council of state after 1622, his only experience of high politics on a European scale, thus petered out inconclusively. Given his pro-papal sentiments, he is unlikely to have regretted this. Besides, Joyeuse arrived in Rome in May 1611 and, armed with wide-ranging instructions, resumed his customary diplomatic functions there.[20] If nothing else, Cleves-Jülich taught La Rochefoucauld the extent to which a cardinal, especially in Rome, had to be a king's man. And if, as Ubaldini suggested, the cardinal was a 'non gran negotiatore', it was largely because his strongly-held convictions denied him that suppleness so vital in the diplomatic arena, which made Joyeuse and Du Perron so effective.

II

Meanwhile, La Rochefoucauld had settled, happily on the whole, into the curia, where his official functions were, at least during Joyeuse's absence, extensive. But there had never been, it seems, any intention to give him wide powers to deal with French affairs generally. Brèves wrote early to Henri IV to ask whether La Rochefoucauld should be privy to all ambassadorial business but, although no answer has survived, we can assume that apart from the Jülich-Cleves affair, he received no powers, then or later, to act as an official French envoy.[21] This probably suited well enough a man who went to Rome more as a pilgrim than as a diplomat.

Shortly after his arrival, La Rochefoucauld was appointed a member of the curial 'congregations' – 'departments' of church government – of the Index and of Bishops and Regulars. It is virtually impossible to grasp the exact outlines of his role in the curia itself, since the reforms of Sixtus V had the effect of completing the transformation of most cardinals from princes and independent political figures into curial bureaucrats. The consistory, where cardinals had once been a powerful influence on papal policy, was no longer a kind of senate of the church, and did little more than ratify decisions made outside it. Politics and policy-making were, for the most part, reserved for the pope's immediate entourage, and the cardinals who represented the states of Catholic Europe. Most cardinals were nominated to congregations, where their activities were more matters of administrative routine than of high politics.[22] The congregation of Bishops and Regulars was

20. B.N., Dupuy 557, fos. 105–18, 12 April 1611.
21. B.N., MS. Fr. 18004, fo. 393v, Brèves to Henri IV, 29 November 1609.
22. See H. Outram Evennett, *The Spirit of the Counter Reformation* (Cambridge, 1968), ch. 6; Marvin R. O'Connell, *The Counter Reformation* (New York, 1974), pp. 113–16; Paolo Prodi, *Il Sovrano pontefice*, ch. 5.

essentially a tribunal for judging disputes between bishops and religious orders, and within orders themselves but, since its jurisdiction did not extend to France itself, La Rochefoucauld's role in it becomes even more difficult to gauge. However, his service in the congregation made him familiar with the problems besetting the reform of the orders, and provided him with valuable experience which he would later turn to good effect in his own attempts to reform them.

The congregation of the Index was, by contrast, altogether more important and notorious. As an Ultramontane, La Rochefoucauld was doubtless well suited to be one of its members. Its day-to-day workings are not well known, and it would doubtless be wrong to see everything it did as necessarily controversial. For example, La Rochefoucauld participated in supervising the preparation of the Roman edition of the decrees of the general councils, most notably the expurgated version of the Council of Constance, which excluded its conciliarist resolutions. This was a task which interested Jacques de Thou, the Gallican magistrate and historian, and about which he and La Rochefoucauld corresponded[23]. On the other hand, the cardinal was also proud of his role in censuring the extreme statement of papal power by the Jesuit, Becan, in an effort to stem rising Gallican feeling in France in 1612.[24] It was probably through such work, and at any rate through common membership of the congregation that he met, and became a close friend of Bellarmine, whose work he had, as we saw, long known. If posterity remembers Bellarmine chiefly as a controversialist, to contemporaries he was an equally vigorous champion of church reform, and a strong critic of both the popes and the curia for failing to promote it with all their energy. Then, as later, Bellarmine valued La Rochefoucauld's whole-hearted commitment to reform throughout the church.[25]

There is, however, one well-documented affair – the censure of de Thou's famous Histories – that does afford a glimpse of La Rochefoucauld's role in the congregation of the Index, and the dilemmas which a French Ultramontane who was also a lover of books and learning, inevitably encountered through membership of it.

The unconcealed Gallican and anti-Roman sentiments of de Thou's

23. B.N., Dupuy 812, fo. 31, La Rochefoucauld to de Thou, 23 June 1611; *ibid.*, fo. 23, to same, 29 January 1612. De Thou's letters have not survived among La Rochefoucauld's own papers.
24. B.N., MS. Fr. 18007, fo. 245, letter to Villeroy, 23 June 1612; B. Institut, Godefroy 541, fo. 32, to Marie de Medici, undated.
25. See Klaus Jaitner, 'De Officio Primario Summi Pontificis. Eine Denkschrift Kardinal Bellarmins für Papst Clemens VIII', in Erwin Gatz, ed., *Römische Kurie, kirchliche Finanzen, Vatikanisches Archiv. Studien zu Ehren von Hermann Hoberg* (Vatican City, 1979), ii, pp. 377–403. For an example of Bellarmine's collaboration with La Rochefoucauld, see X.M. Le Bachelet, 'Bellarmin et les Célestins en France', *Revue des questions historiques* 104 (1926), pp. 257–94.

work caused a considerable stir when it began to appear in 1604, and the author's friends in Rome only prevented it from being placed on the Index with considerable difficulty and vigilance, a party of cardinals being formed in 1605 to oppose any such move to ban it. But the group broke up in 1608 and, consequently, there was no one to prevent it being placed on the Index in November 1609, shortly before La Rochefoucauld arrived in Rome.[26] His dislike of Gallican ideas was no secret, but he was soon asked to lend his assistance to a move to get the decision reversed, possibly because there was some personal connection between him and de Thou. In one letter, La Rochefoucauld recalled de Thou's 'ancienne bienveillance' towards him, while the historian commissioned the cardinal in turn to hunt for rare books and manuscripts in Rome. De Thou evidently hoped the ties of friendship would prove stronger than his Ultramontanism.[27]

In fact, the curia was anxious not to offend de Thou, who seemed likely to become the next *premier président* of the Paris *parlement* and, therefore, one of the most powerful men in France. So when de Thou claimed he had not been properly heard in self-defence, the case was quickly re-opened, and entrusted to the congregation of the Index; the latter delegated La Rochefoucauld, Bellarmine and the French Jesuit Richeome to examine the Histories and to present a critique of the early books, in the light of which de Thou would be expected to revise his work.[28] The commission, which began its work in mid-1610, was in no hurry; in October, La Rochefoucauld informed de Thou that the curia was well-disposed towards him, and that matters were well in hand, a view echoed by Ambassador Brèves.[29] But de Thou's scepticism was mounting: the papacy seemed increasingly pro-Spanish, and de Thou objected to a well-known papalist such as Bellarmine having anything to do with censoring his works. Richeome was of lesser significance, so de Thou looked to La Rochefoucauld for support. But, equally, he suspected that the cardinal might have little enthusiasm for a task in which his opinions were the very opposite of his own; he was even resigned to La Rochefoucauld proving to be openly hostile.[30] In fact, the latter was more willing to help than de Thou recognised, though he believed that the censure could only be withdrawn if the Histories were revised. Within these limitations, he hoped for 'quelque bone ouverture pour mettre en plus de liberté un si bel oeuvre'.[31] According to Brèves, La Rochefoucauld would seek a rehabilitation of the Histories, but not one involving any loss to his

26. Alfred Soman, *De Thou and the Index* (Geneva, 1972), pp. 17–25.
27. B.N., Dupuy 812, fo. 19, La Rochefoucauld to de Thou, 13 October 1610.
28. Soman, *De Thou and the Index*, p. 26.
29. B.N., Dupuy 812, fo. 19, letter of 13 October; *ibid.*, fo. 150, Brèves to de Thou, 28 October.
30. B.N., Dupuy 812, fo. 154, de Thou to Brèves, 20 November 1610.
31. *Ibid.*, fo. 31, letter to de Thou, 23 June 1611.

own dignity, a condition which left him considerable leeway.[32] Finally, in early 1611, the commission produced an epitome of the Histories, which La Rochefoucauld strongly recommended to de Thou with the comment, 'ce iugement n'a esté fait à la haste'.[33] This was the most he would do, and Brèves reported him as saying the commission had been lenient. But by then, de Thou had given up all hope, convinced that Rome was behind the refusal to give him the post of *premier président* in the *parlement*. A desultory correspondence with La Rochefoucauld continued for some time, but with little hope of an acceptable compromise.[34] Increasingly worried by the resurgence of Gallican opinions in France after the assassination of Henri IV, La Rochefoucauld was probably glad to be spared a final choice over the Histories. As de Thou's friend, he had tried to moderate his own Ultramontane convictions, but this was a far cry from Du Perron's statement a few years earlier that, had he been in curia, there would have been no censure at all. Over-confident or not, this assertion highlights the gap separating two types of prelate within the French church hierarchy.

Inevitably, other tasks and responsibilities came the cardinal's way while he was in Rome. In 1612, he was appointed protector of the Cistercians in curia, a title he retained on returning to France but, although it gave him a close interest in the order, it afforded him no real power to intervene in its affairs.[35] Pierre de Bérulle also enlisted his help in securing papal confirmation of his new-founded congregation, the French Oratory, though he evidently put less faith in his diplomatic talents as such than in his prestige at Rome.[36]

But from the beginning, La Rochefoucauld's most abiding anxiety in Rome was financial. The red hat had not brought him any sudden wealth. He benefited little from royal generosity before leaving for Rome, possibly because of Sully's dislike of him. Indeed, news of his poverty reached Ambassador Brèves even before the cardinal left France; having for long clamoured for a French cardinal in curia, Brèves was now alarmed at the prospect of a penniless one. With no trace of sarcasm he wrote to Villeroy in October 1608: 'If Cardinal de La Rochefoucauld arrives here without proper means, he will harm both himself and the service of the king. Poor cardinals are no good in Rome, especially if they are French or Spanish. They must be wealthy if they are to be respected'.[37] A month later, he repeated his warning,

32. *Ibid.*, fo. 160, letter to de Thou, 20 February 1611.
33. *Ibid.*, fo. 25, letter to de Thou, 21 March [1611].
34. *Ibid.*, fos. 21, 23, 27, letters from La Rochefoucauld 1611–12.
35. B.S.G., MS. 3238, fo. 60, for the brief of nomination.
36. *Correspondance de Bérulle*, i, pp. 123, 129, 131–2, 138–9, 142–5, 153–5, 158.
37. B.N., MS. Fr. 18004, fo. 349v, letter to Villeroy, 28 October 1609; 'Si le cardinal de la Rochefoucault vient par deça necessiteux, il fera tort à soy mesme et au service du roy. Les cardinaux pauvres ne sont pas bons à Rome, particulièrement les français et les espagnols. Il fault quilz soient opulents pour estre respectez.'

adding, 'appearances are vital here'.[38] La Rochefoucauld was soon to see Brèves's point for himself. After a week in Rome, he lamented that his poverty prevented him from incurring the same expenses as other cardinals 'qui tiennent grand train et sont superbement meublez'.[39] Paul V hoped that membership of the two congregations would help to offset this, yet La Rochefoucauld's condition remained such that within six months of his arrival, he had decided to return to France.[40] He simply could not afford to live in the style his position demanded. According to one contemporary estimate, a cardinal at Rome required 8,000 *écus* or 24,000 *livres* in net annual income.[41] Marie de Medici eventually awarded him a pension of 3,000 *écus* which, although unpaid for a time, did go some way towards alleviating his distress.[42]

By 1611, increasingly impressed by La Rochefoucauld, Paul V began to take a direct hand in events, and to insist that the cardinal remain permanently in Rome. To enable him to do so without financial embarrassment, he pressed the regent to grant him the wealthy Abbey of St Arnoul de Metz. A long wrangle followed, in which the elected abbot triumphed over papal pressure, and La Rochefoucauld was merely promised a pension off St Arnoul.[43] All the time, his determination to return to France was hardening. When he first requested formal permission to return in May 1612, the pope asked Marie de Medici to refuse it.[44] But this move failed, too, and a second, firmly-worded letter from the cardinal in June 1612 won her consent. La Rochefoucauld did, however, agree to remain in Rome until the spring of 1613.[45]

Poverty was not La Rochefoucauld's only reason, nor even his major one for wishing to return home. Not without cause, he pleaded bad

38. *Ibid.*, fo. 390, to same, 29 November: 'ici l'apparence est fort necessaire'.
39. B.N., MS. Fr. 18005, fo. 32, Brèves to Henri IV, 19 January 1610. Apparently, the reason for the complaint was that he could not afford the expensive round of visits to cardinals, and the presents which accompanied them. Brèves repeated later this point to the king: *ibid.*, fo. 95, letter of 4 March 1610.
40. *Ibid.*, fo. 290v, Brèves to Marie de Medici, 19 August 1610.
41. For the position of Roman cardinals, see Wolfgang Reinhard, 'Kardinaleinkünfte und Kirchenreform', *Römische Quartalschrift* 77 (1982), pp. 157–94.
42. B.N., MS. Fr. 18005, fos. 428–9, Brèves to marquis de Puysieux, 23 December 1610; MS. Fr. 18006, fo. 62, to same, 20 February 1611.
43. The Roman correspondence for 1611 and 1612 is full of references to this question: B.N., MS. Fr. 18006, fo. 350, Brèves to Marie de Medici, 22 July 1611; *ibid.*, fo. 590, Joyeuse to same, 13 November 1611; MS. Fr. 18007, fos. 87 and 146–7, Brèves to Marie, 1 March and 12 April 1612 respectively; *ibid.*, fo. 165, Brèves to Villeroy, 12 May 1612. Other references to it in the nuncio's correspondence: B.L., Addit. MS. 8721, fo.436, Cardinal Borghese to Ubaldini, 14 September 1611; *ibid.*, fo. 443–4, to same, 29 September; Addit. MS. 8724, fo. 54, to same, 11 April 1612.
44. B.N., MS. Fr. 18007, fo. 211, Brèves to Puysieux, 8 June 1612.
45. *Ibid.*, fo. 223 letter of 29 June 1612; *ibid.*, fos. 314–15, Brèves to Marie de Medici, 27 September.

health.[46] But Ambassador Brèves also regularly reported that he was pre-occupied about his duty to reside in his diocese.[47] Bishop of Senlis since early 1610, he had yet to set foot there. The ambassador's insistence is all the more interesting since Rome teemed with non-resident bishops, a fact which should have allayed rather than aroused scruples about non-residence. The cardinal may have, in addition, been influenced by the example and writings of his friend, Bellarmine. On the other hand, he understood his duty to pope and king, and declared himself ready to spend the rest of his days in Rome, should they insist on this.[48]

In the event, La Rochefoucauld was to leave Rome in May 1613, just over three years after first arriving there. Paul V had accepted the regent's decision to allow him to leave, even if he did not abandon his efforts to have it reversed. Ironically, he succeeded just before the cardinal's actual departure, but the letters conveying the regent's change of mind failed to arrive in time. When Brèves dispatched them to Florence in an attempt to bring La Rochefoucauld back to Rome, La Rochefoucauld simply ignored them.[49] Rightly, he sensed that Marie de Medici was either weaker or more flexible than Paul V, and he preferred to answer to her. Even so, the pope kept up the pressure throughout 1613–14, hoping that if La Rochefoucauld could be persuaded to exchange his diocese for a 'good' abbey, there would be no problem of conscience to prevent him returning to Rome.[50]

La Rochefoucauld had always been personally diffident about his usefulness in Rome.[51] But as far as we can judge, the pope and his entourage were sincerely reluctant to see him leave. Even Brèves, who had feared that the cardinal's poverty would dishonour France and its king, had become an admirer, arguing that his penury was more than offset by his piety and austere lifestyle.[52] Brèves even triumphantly related Paul V's own judgement of him to Marie de Medici: 'he went on to say that the high esteem in which he was held by the entire

---

46. *Ibid.*, fo. 215, Brèves to Marie de Medici, 8 June 1612: 'sa vie aussy austère l'envieillit et le rend mal sain'.
47. *Ibid.*, fo. 87, Brèves to Marie de Medici, 1 March 1612, referring to 'sa conscience qui l'' appelle au soing de son diocèse'; *ibid.*, fo. 156, to same, 27 April, '...consciencieux comme il est, il croit tousiours ayant un evesché y debvoir la résidence'.
48. *Ibid.*, fo. 267, Brèves to Puysieux, 3 August 1612.
49. B.N. MS., Fr. 18008, fo. 321, Brèves to Puysieux, 9 June 1613; A.S.V., Nunz. Fr. 295a, fo. 98, Cardinal Borghese to Ubaldini, 6 June 1613, confidently expecting La Rochefoucauld to be back in Rome by the autumn; *ibid.*, fo. 128, to same, 2 August, expressing appreciation of the regent's decision to send the cardinal back to Rome.
50. As late as August 1614, Paul V and Cardinal Borghese were still pressing the ambassador to have La Rochefoucauld sent back to Rome: B.N., MS. Fr. 18009, fo. 252, marquis de Tresnel to Puysieux, 5 August.
51. B.N., MS. Fr. 18007, fo. 223, letter to Marie de Medici, 29 June 1612.
52. *Ibid.*, fo. 147, letter of 12 April 1612.

College of Cardinals would suffice to secure his election as Pope in a conclave, despite the fact that he was French. These were the Pope's own words'.[53] But La Rochefoucauld would never again set foot in Rome. Brèves's prediction that so long as he held a bishopric, there was little hope of re-assigning him to the curia, proved correct.[54] Once back in France, he was determined to stay; it was there, rather than in the curia, that his commitment and convictions provided greatest scope for action. Were it not for this, he might well have ended his days in the relative obscurity of Rome; whatever the opinion that Paul V and his contemporaries may have had of him, it is difficult to imagine that he would have ever have attained chair of St Peter. With his return to France, both the number and the range of his activities were to grow significantly.

III

La Rochefoucauld's journey home through Florence, Lyon and his Abbey of Tournus took him several months, and he did not reach the court until October 1613.[55] His stay there was brief as his main objective was to visit his diocese.[56] He solemnly entered Senlis on 10 November, and soon set about the task of visiting and administering it.[57] He established a special council to help him, and it provided invaluable assistance, as we shall see, in what was to be, despite La Rochefoucauld's increasingly frequent absences, a period of intensive pastoral activity.[58]

The political situation in France in late 1613-early 1614 was not such as to tempt La Rochefoucauld into court politics. The regency government of Marie de Medici was in increasing trouble, with the princes led by Condé on the verge of the revolt that would force Marie to summon what was to prove the last meeting of the Estates General

53. B.N., MS. Fr. 18008, fo. 321, letter to Marie, 9 June 1613: 'm'ayant dit de plus que la grande bonne opinion en laquelle il estoit tenu de tout le College des Cardinaux estoit suffisante en ung Conclave pour le faire eslire Pape, bien quil fust françois. Ce sont les mesmes termes qu'Elle m'a tenuz.'
54. *Ibid.*, fo. 547, Brèves to Puysieux, 27 October 1613: 'vous aurez de la peine de faire retourner en ceste cour ledict sieur cardinal si vous ne laidez à permuter son evesché, qui est ce qui l'en a faict sortir, estan prelat qui faict conscience de n'y resider'; *ibid.*, fo. 550, Brèves to Villeroy, same date: 'Il est seigneur qui est assez arresté en ses opinions, et qui a grand esgard à sa conscience'.
55. At Tournus, he founded a house for the order of *Récollets: Inventaire sommaire des archives départementales du Saône et Loire. Archives ecclésiastiques: hôpital de Tournus* (Mâcon, 1887), pp. 3, 11.
56. B.N., MS. Italien 38, fos. 124v and 127, *avvisi* from Ubaldini, 8 and 24 October 1613 respectively.
57. Senlis, Bibliothèque municipale, collection Afforty, vi, pp. 2880–1.
58. See ch. 4.

before May 1789.[59] It was as a deputy for the clergy of Senlis that La Rochefoucauld returned to Paris in October 1614.[60] Though few of those elected sympathised with the princes, the crown was, as always, apprehensive about the attitudes of the Estates.

Although only one other ecclesiastical deputy had attended the 1588 Estates General at Blois, La Rochefoucauld was, astonishingly, still the most junior of the French cardinals present at those of 1614. The bitter divisions that soon erupted between the individual estates made constructive work difficult. Marie de Medici soon cast the clergy in the difficult role of mediators, and thus relied heavily upon experienced, politically-proven cardinals like Sourdis and Du Perron who presided over the clergy's own sessions. La Rochefoucauld, presiding in their absence, had an evident distaste for the diplomatic and oratorical jousting this demanded, as well as lack of talent for it. The records of the Estates are verbose on ceremony and official delegations, but all too frequently laconic on the substance of the debates themselves. They require careful reading between the lines if one is to see just how involved La Rochefoucauld was, despite the lack of public éclat, in much of the behind the scenes work on matters of primary importance to the clergy. It was through the many delegations and sub-commissions of which he took charge that he came to influence, not only the order's deliberations, but individual members of it as well. It is no exaggeration to say that during the 1614 Estates General and the General Assembly of the Clergy which immediately followed it, he finally emerged in the consciousness of the clergy as the leading champion of reform, capitalising on experience gleaned over some thirty years. Here for the first time, he assumed a form of leadership which was to be the hallmark of his subsequent career. This can be studied under a number of headings.[61]

It was the dispute over church-state relations – a controversy that, in later years, became the clergy's most unpleasant memory of the Estates General – which was one of the principal factors which propelled La Rochefoucauld into political life. The very first article of the Third Estate's cahier demanded the enactment of a fundamental law to the effect that the king and his kingdom were subject to no external power, either spiritual or temporal; that he was answerable to God alone, to whom he owed his crown; that those holding opinions contrary to this law – which was in accordance with God's word – should be considered traitors and sworn enemies of the crown; and that

59. Hayden, *France and the Estates General of 1614*, chs. 4–5.; Bonney, *The King's Debts*, pp. 77–9.
60. A.N., G 8* 1221, no. D 48, for his act of election. He was also supposed to present the *doléances* of his clergy, but no trace of them has been found. They would no doubt have shed much light upon the state of Senlis diocese and clergy.
61. The best narrative accounts of the Estates are Hayden, *France and the Estates General*, and Pierre Blet, *Le Clergé de France et la monarchie*, 2 vols. (Rome, 1959), i, chs. 2–4.

all office- and benefice-holders should be required to assent to it before taking up their offices.[62] This comprehensively provocative article was the kind of thing an Ultramontane like La Rochefoucauld was bound to detest but, as is the way with positive loyalty tests, it also aroused the anger of the clergy as a whole. If it was the distilled essence of Gallican and *parlementaire* thought, it was also a commentary on recent French history. Since Henri IV's assassination, the *parlement* of Paris had hit out at any doctrine that seemed to justify regicide, and in practice, such anathema spread to those upholding papal claims in temporal matters. Bellarmine, Suarez, and Becan each fell foul of the *parlement* which, in 1611, forced the Parisian Jesuits to refute the theses of their foreign confrères.[63] It also backed the efforts of Edmond Richer, syndic of the faculty of theology, to restore Gallicanism as the official doctrine of the Sorbonne, and to eradicate contrary schools of thought. Richer's own *Libellus de ecclesiastica et politica potestate*, the most extreme statement of Gallican views to date by an ecclesiastic in such a key position, had been strongly condemned by special councils at Sens and Aix in 1612, although he himself remained defiant, convinced that he enjoyed public support.[64]

La Rochefoucauld, Ultramontane and pro-Jesuit, had followed these debates from Rome with a mounting sense of anxiety. In 1610, he was prepared to say to Paul V that Henri IV's assassination justified certain measures taken in self-defence, and that some church-state theories could be used for nefarious ends.[65] But the subsequent attack on Bellarmine and the Jesuits, as well as the Richer controversy, convinced him that defence had turned into attack. He concluded by 1612 that the papacy was the real target of this campaign, and played his part in relaying papal anxiety to Marie de Medici. In increasingly strong-worded and insistent letters, he attempted to provoke her into silencing Richer, whose attacks on hierarchy within the church were, he asserted, a threat to monarchy itself.[66]

62. Hayden, *France and the Estates General*, pp. 131–2, gives the text in English translation. The article also stipulated that if non-French members of an order published views contrary to the article, then its French members should be obliged to refute them – an obvious reference to the Jesuits.

63. R. Mousnier, *The Assassination of Henry IV* (London, 1973), pp. 250ff; Victor Martin, *Le Gallicanisme et la réforme catholique*, pp. 353ff; Pierre Blet, 'Jésuites et libertés gallicanes en 1611', *Archivium Historicum Societatis Jesu* 24 (1955), pp. 165–87.

64. E. Puyol, *Edmond Richer. Etude historique et critique sur la rénovation du gallicanisme au commencement du xviie siècle* (Paris, 1876) i, pp. 160ff; Edmond Préclin, 'Edmond Richer (1559–1631), sa vie, son oeuvre', *Revue d'histoire moderne* 5 (1930), pp. 241–69, 321–36; Monique Cottret, 'Edmond Richer (1559–1631): le politique et le sacré' in Henri Méchoulan, ed., *L'Etat baroque* (Paris, 1985), pp. 159–77.

65. B.N., MS. Fr. 18006, fo. 618, La Rochefoucauld to Marie de Medici, 23 December 1610: 'J'ay répresenté à San Sainteté l'obligation du parlement aux droits de la couronne, les évenements passés de fraiche mémoire, la condition présente du royaume...'

66. B.N., MS. Fr. 18007, fo. 74, La Rochefoucauld to Marie de Medici, February 1612; *ibid.*, fo. 106, [March] 1612; *ibid.*, fo. 150, 22 April 1612; *ibid.*, fo. 406, 12 November 1612.

Opinion on all sides was thus well mobilised by 1614.[67] But the clergy were hugely embarrassed by the Third Estates' article, the import of which was immediately obvious. Yet, because an outright rejection of it might be construed as disloyalty to the crown, they had to proceed carefully. In one session, they renewed the Council of Constance's declaration against tyrannicide. In full assembly, La Rochefoucauld attacked the offending article, and reminded his audience that he had participated in the papal censure of the Jesuit Becan, proof of the papacy's goodwill.[68] He was quickly entrusted with responsibility for a commission designated to draft, in reply, the clergy's own articles on a wide range of issues affecting church-state relations, 'pour regler, limiter et determiner les libertez de l'Eglise Gallicane, cas privilegiez et appellations comme d'abus'. The record is, unfortunately, silent upon the preparations and discussions that ensued. Since the clergy and the Third Estate failed to compromise, the former were determined to present their own ˙et of articles acceptable to the king. It took all their determination, as well as Du Perron's diplomatic and oratorical skills, to force a vacillating royal council to strike the offending article from the Third Estate's list, though this was not the end of the affair.[69]

While this conflict absorbed much of the clergy's time, it did not distract them entirely from their own objectives. Foremost among these was the official royal promulgation of the decrees of Trent as part of French law. To the clergy this was primarily a question of reform, but it was strongly opposed by Gallicans, especially those in the royal courts, who feared it would restore ecclesiastical administrative and legal autonomy, as well as increase papal interference in France; after decades of polemic, attitudes towards Trent had hardened into opposing views on church-state relations.[70] Gallican resistance had induced many bishops to dilute their traditional mistrust of Rome, and even to view the pope as a valuable ally in the task of reform. It was precisely this change, which was far from universal, which gave scope for leadership and initiative to men like La Rochefoucauld.[71] Even before the Estates formally met, the leaders of the clergy, with

---

67. For the political and related controversies of these years, see Denis Richet and Roger Chartier, eds., *Répresentation et vouloir politiques. Autour des états-généraux de 1614* (Paris, 1982), especially Richet's essay, 'La polémique politique en France de 1612 à 1615', pp. 151–94; Hélène Duccini, 'La Vision de l'état dans la littérature pamphlétaire au moment des états-généraux de 1614', in Méchoulan, *L'Etat baroque*, pp. 147–58.

68. *Collection des procès-verbaux des assemblées générales du clergé de France depuis l'année 1560* (Paris, 1767), ii, pp. 181–2, 187; B.N., MS. Italien 1268, fo. 401, Ubaldini to Cardinal Borghese, 30 December 1614.

69. Blet, *Le Clergé et la monarchie*, pp. 41–82; idem., 'L'Article du tiers aux états-généraux de 1614', *Revue d'histoire moderne et contemporaine* 2 (1955), pp. 81–106; Hayden, *France and the Estates General*, ch. 8.

70. The best account is still Victor Martin, *Le Gallicanisme et la réforme catholique*, who traces the arguments from the Council of Trent down to 1615.

71. Blet, *Le Clergé et la monarchie*, i, pp. 14ff.

assurances of Roman support, decided to press more vigorously than they had previously for the adoption of Trent's decrees, and to do so in the early sessions, rather than wait until later, as so often in the past, when the crown could avoid a reply by terminating the assembly.[72] But in 1614–15, differences emerged in debate. The representatives of the religious orders and the chapters demanded assurances that their liberties and privileges would continue to be protected. The bishops would have preferred to omit such a restriction, but did not dominate the assembly sufficiently to do so, and were unwilling to allow a public rift in the clergy to ruin the chances of obtaining royal acceptance of the council's decrees.[73] Even so, the more openly 'Tridentine' group were not prepared to concede so easily, and counter-attacked in debate. 'Longs et graves discours' followed and, although the protagonists are not mentioned by name, it is certain that La Rochefoucauld was one of them. Those defending a promulgation without reservations argued that it was not for the clergy to suggest that Trent's decrees threatened royal rights; if there were objections to that effect, let them come from the king, and they could deal with his reservations later. Moreover, they too held many of the traditional French views on the 'police exterieure de l'église' – the rights of the crown, ancient customs and so on – and expressed the hope that the pope would accept such diversity within the church, should the king prove unwilling to enact the council's decrees in France.[74] It was La Rochefoucauld who conveyed such arguments to the representatives of the nobility, as part of the clergy's quest for support over Trent. He declared that the clergy had always regarded the council's doctrinal decrees as absolutely binding, and pointed out that the trouble had habitually been over its disciplinary decrees, and their relation to the privileges and liberties of the French church. Such an opinion was probably representative of the bishops as a whole, as La Rochefoucauld was himself no champion of these liberties, but he did take the trouble of adding that the decrees in no way infringed French privileges, least of all those of the king. However, he went on to say that the clergy were ready to suffer limitations to the promulgation, lest the benefits to be gained from it be forfeited on the grounds that an unconditional proclamation threatened royal prerogatives.[75]

Despite support from the nobility and the regent herself, the clergy's petition failed to win royal consent; the council merely promised to consider it along with the other *cahiers* in due course.[76] But clerical pressure was not about to relax on this issue, as the General

72. *Collection des procès-verbaux*, ii, p. 113.
73. *Ibid.*, pp. 113–14.
74. *Ibid.*, pp. 114–15.
75. *Ibid.*, p. 116.
76. Blet, *Le Clergé et la monarchie*, i, pp. 124–5.

Assembly of the Clergy was scheduled to take place immediately after the Estates General ended. Because of the extensive debates in the Estates, the Assembly's scope was limited, and the question of Trent the principal item of business. The leading roles in the debates fell to Du Perron and La Rochefoucauld, as Joyeuse was on his deathbed, and Sourdis had returned to Bordeaux. When the chancellor, doubtless as a delaying tactic, suggested a conference to discuss the obstacles to a full publication of Trent's decrees, the clergy responded with alacrity, asking the cardinal-presidents to attend and, far more significantly, to 'prendre quelque bon expedient' should the ministers prove evasive.[77] It was here that La Rochefoucauld seized the initiative, holding several meetings at his residence in June and early July to find an acceptable solution. The proposal which emerged, that pending a full royal promulgation, the clergy should solemnly publish the decrees as far as their duties were concerned, did not win immediate assent.[78] The traditions of the French church made them nervous of acting independently of the crown, especially where something so controversial was involved. But if the debates of 1614–15 had done anything, it was to make them realise that their primary duty was to the church and their office, a change for which La Rochefoucauld and those close to him could take some of the credit. It was therefore symbolic that he himself should have presided the session when, on 7 July, they voted to publish and assent to the decrees themselves; he was the first to sign the resolution and the first to take the oath to observe its decrees.[79] It was also decided to hold provincial councils and diocesan synods to interpret and apply them at the lower levels of the church – a step that La Rochefoucauld had strongly commended to the deputies at the Estates General.

Both the nuncio and the pope were jubilant, though Paul V regretted the declaration on the Gallican liberties in the text.[80] La Rochefoucauld and Du Perron were warmly thanked.[81] But the most difficult hurdle, that of obtaining royal approval, had yet to be cleared. The regent was personally favourable, but knew her ministers and the *parlement* were not.[82] In their final audience, the clergy attacked boldly, inviting the king to share in the glorious deed they had just accomplished. But, in reply, Chancellor Sillery could only blame them for acting without prior royal permission. La Rochefou-

77. *Collection des procès-verbaux*, ii, pp. 240–1.
78. B.S.G., MS. 366, fo. 37, text of the proposal of the 'commissaires particuliers pour adviser à la publication du concile de Trente'.
79. *Collection des procès-verbaux*, ii, p. 243
80. B.N., MS. Italien 1269, fos. 203–8, Ubaldini to Borghese, 15 July, for a full account of events.
81. B.S.G., MS. 366, fo. 4, for papal brief to La Rochefoucauld.
82. According to Ubaldini, the *parlement* threatened to confiscate the property of the deputies in retaliation: B.N., MS. Italien 1269, fo. 204v.

cauld was incensed, and interrupted Sillery, declaring that such a rebuke was acceptable only from the king himself. Besides, he went on, the crown had been fully aware of the clergy's actions, and knew perfectly well just how their decision differed from a full royal promulgation of Trent's decrees; for that reason, no permission was required at all, as it was a simple matter of conscience. A royal publication was, he added, another matter, and the clergy firmly hoped the king would agree to one, as they considered it essential to the success of church reform. When Sillery attempted to reply to this suggestion, La Rochefoucauld again silenced him in even more peremptory fashion.[83]

The crown did not yield, however, and the clergy were left with a moral victory that expressed their own desire for reform and a measure of independence from both crown and *parlement*.[84] This was in itself significant, but failure to win royal support meant that reform would continue to be confronted with the complex pattern of exemptions, privileges and customs which frequently discouraged even the most determined reformers. The opportunity to make Trent's decrees part of the law of the land would never return, and much of La Rochefoucauld's energy was to be devoted, in his diocese and elsewhere, to dealing with the consequences of this.

Limited though it was, the clergy's decision of July 1615 was a personal triumph for La Rochefoucauld. But his advocacy of reform during the Estates General and the Assembly was not confined to the question of Trent. The 302 articles of the clergy's cahier testify to wider pre-occupations, as does the special *réglement spirituel*, an abridged programme of reform designed for immediate application. La Rochefoucauld took charge of the commission nominated to draft the general cahier, and acted as its reporter. He also undertook to draft a petition to the king, the last of its kind, for the restoration of ecclesiastical elections – a forlorn hope indeed – and to examine the question of reforming benefices and of the urgent need to improve appointments to them. When the clergy were angered by a particularly scandalous incident of trading in benefices, it was La Rochefoucauld who was asked to draft a protest to the regent.[85]

This chronicle of the debates of 1614–15 highlights the major issues confronting the French church in the early seventeenth century and, to some extent, its response to them. It is, of course, in precisely that context that La Rochefoucauld's own commitments and opinions

83. *Ibid.*, fos. 222–5, Ubaldini to Borghese, 11 August 1615.
84. Blet, *Le Clergé et la monarchie*, i, pp. 132–3.
85. The scandal involved the eviction of an abbot who had been holding a monastery *en confidence* for the Protestant duke of Sully. (*Collection des procès-verbaux*, ii, pp. 139–41, 143–6, 148, 202, 208, for references to these activities.)

have to be seen.[86] To over-dramatise his role in the proceedings would smack of hagiography, but it is clear that the assemblies afforded him, for the first time, an opportunity to acquire a measure of ascendancy over the clergy, and to use it to orient them towards the papacy and a broad vision of reform. His personal support for this and other causes was, henceforth, to make him the adviser, and virtually the conscience, of the French church in a manner that was unique for the entire century. For nearly thirty years, his Parisian residence became the habitual meeting place, in both good and bad times, of the French episcopate.

IV

Although La Rochefoucauld now retired to his diocese, where he was to reside for much of the two years following the assemblies, there were several reasons, apart from the normal appearances at court expected of a cardinal, why undisturbed residence at Senlis was increasingly problematic. The Estates General might have achieved little because of its internal divisions, but the government of Marie de Medici did not benefit much by this and, with Concini increasingly in charge, the great nobles remained as truculent as before 1614.[87] There was a political vacuum to be filled, and neither the nobles nor the old ministers of Henri IV were in a position to do it. This, as we shall see, provided considerable and unforeseen opportunities for leading ecclesiastics, of whom Richelieu was only one.[88] In addition, the clergy feared that the Gallican tendencies of 1614 would resurface, and that the government might be tempted to adopt them for its own, a possibility that provided a strong incentive for even an unpolitical figure like La Rochefoucauld to keep a close eye on the political sphere. In addition, the older generation of French cardinals was beginning to disappear. Joyeuse died in 1615; Du Perron's health began to fail thereafter, and he was to die in 1618; to the relief of many, the hot-

---

86. Earlier historians were aware of his role in 1614–15. Henri de Sponde, Bishop of Pamiers from 1626 to 1643, and continuator of Baronius's *Annales*, praised him highly for his commitment: *Annalium Ecclesiasticorum Em. Cardinalis Caesaris Baronii continuatio* (Pavia, 1682), iii, p. 596, while the eighteenth-century Gallican, Mignet was critical of both men: 'Quelque soit l'éloge que Sponde donne à ce Cardinal, son zèle ne s'étendoit point jusqu'à défendre les maximes du royaume . . . il ne doit point paroître surprenant qu'il ait témoigné tant d'ardeur à faire recevoir en France un Concile qui a autant qu'il étoit en lui, consacré tous les principes ultramontains': E. Mignet, *Histoire de la réception du concile de Trente par les divers pays d'Europe* (Amsterdam, 1756), ii, pp. 374–5.
87. Bonney, *The King's Debts*, pp. 84ff, for a succinct account of the political upheavals of these years.
88. Bergin, *Richelieu*, pp. 69ff.

tempered and unmanageable Sourdis remained in his diocese. Since 1615, there had been a Guise cardinal once again, but his dismal reputation made him incapable of filling any useful role, political or ecclesiastical.[89] The 'generation' of La Valette, Richelieu and Bérulle had not yet arrived.

These were the historical circumstances in which La Rochefoucauld came to the forefront of the French church, and began playing a part in French politics. It is not easy to pinpoint the beginnings, but early in 1617, we find him acting as mediator, presumably at the invitation of Richelieu who was then secretary of state, between the crown and the rebel princes, and using Père Joseph, Richelieu's future confidant, in the process. La Rochefoucauld evidently had little sympathy with the princes, but his suggestions that the injustice of their stance should be denounced in the name of the clergy if they did not come to their senses, does not seem to have been tried.[90] In any case, Louis XIII had Concini assassinated in April 1617, a move which led to the collapse of his ministry and to Marie de Medici's internal exile at Blois. Concini was replaced by Luynes, but three further years of political drift and uncertainty were to follow. La Rochefoucauld in no way suffered from his modest connection with Richelieu, for shortly afterwards we find him in a more characteristic role — that of ensuring that Père Coton, disgraced for advocating leniency to Marie de Medici in May 1617, would be succeeded as royal confessor by another Jesuit.[91]

Another reason for La Rochefoucauld's advancement was that the new papal nuncio, Guido di Bentivoglio, who had been instructed to press for church reform in accordance with the resolutions of 1615, found in him a very willing ally, and one who had the added advantage of being devoted to the papacy. Bentivoglio did all he could to keep La Rochefoucauld at court in 1617, especially as the 1614 cahiers were to be discussed in council; not only had the church its own case to argue, but it feared a resurrection of the dreaded Gallican article of the Third Estate.

The principal outcome of these discussions was the Assembly of Notables which met at Rouen in December 1617. As many of those invited were parlementaires, the clergy became somewhat alarmed, and sought assurances that the debates of 1614 would not be reopened

89. Bergin, 'The Decline and Fall of the House of Guise as an Ecclesiastical Dynasty', *Historical Journal* 34 (1982), pp. 781–803.
90. Steffani, *Nunziatura di Bentivoglio*, i, pp. 148–9, Bentivoglio to Borghese, 14 March 1617; *ibid.*, i, p. 160, to same 28 March; *ibid.*, i, p. 190–1, to same 11 April. See Berthold Zeller, *Louis XIII, Marie de Medici, Richelieu ministre* (Paris, 1899), pp. 162–6, on the failure of these talks.
91. *Ibid.*, i, pp. 218–19, Bentivoglio to Borghese, 9 May 1617. Other candidates included the Bishops of Aire and of Nantes, the Dominican theologian Nicolas Coëffetau, and the curé of the Parisian parish of St Paul.

nor the *tiers*'s article put on the agenda. Despite pressure from La Rochefoucauld, Bishop Gondi of Paris, Bentivoglio and Arnoux, the royal confessor, no such assurance was given, though Luynes was sympathetic to the clergy. The latter now attempted to gain control of the assembly itself, and Arnoux won a promise from Louis XIII that the presidency would be given to La Rochefoucauld. But after confirmation of this had been given to Bentivoglio, Cardinals Du Perron and Guise each pressed their own claims to the honour, Du Perron so strongly that unpleasant scenes ensued. In the end, Louis XIII appointed his brother Gaston nominal president, to be assisted by two ecclesiastics and two nobles. In fact, the presidency was assumed chiefly by Du Perron and La Rochefoucauld.[92] The latter, according to Bentivoglio, remained completely aloof from these intrigues, behaviour which led the nuncio to describe him as too much of a 'stoic' – by which he meant too detached from events – for France's condition at the time.[93]

The assembly's discussions were wide-ranging. Firm support from Luynes and the king prevented Gallican proposals unacceptable to the clergy from being carried; the article of the Third Estate was omitted from the agenda altogether.[94] But the clergy's role was by no means a negative one, as they presented issues of their own to the assembly and to the king's ministers. They were especially concerned about abuses in nominations to benefices; some of these nominations, especially of unwanted coadjutor bishops, had been on the increase in recent years, a matter Rome had long been complaining about. A better system of episcopal appointments and the question of the reform of the orders – both to become central concerns to La Rochefoucauld in coming years, as well as storng evidence that he was not an inactive president of the assembly – were also discussed.[95] But the question of Trent's decrees was not raised at all, and even Rome seemed to have forgotten this unfinished piece of business.

No sooner had the assembly ended after Christmas 1617 than work on drafting a full-scale ordinance was begun under the direction of the *parlement*'s procurator general, Mathieu Molé. The clergy were

---

92. The negotiations, as well as the clergy's fears, can be followed in the nuncio's correspondence: Steffani, *Nunziatura di Bentivoglio*, ii, pp. 1–2, Bentivoglio to Borghese, 11 October 1617; *ibid.*, ii, pp. 21–2, to same, 13 October; *ibid.*, ii, p. 26, to same, 25 October; *ibid.*, p. 77, to same, 22 November; *ibid.*, ii, pp. 92–4, Borghese to Bentivoglio, 22 November.
93. *Ibid.*, ii, pp. 108–9, letter to Borghese, 11 December.
94. *Ibid.*, ii, pp. 122–3, Bentivoglio to Borghese, 19 December. In the absence of an official record of the assembly's debates, Bentivoglio, who was present at Rouen, offers the most circumstantial account of what happened there.
95. For the text of the articles proposed for discussion, and the assembly's responses to them, see *Mémoires de Mathieu Molé*, ed. Aimé Champollion-Figeac, 4 vols. (Paris, 1855–7), i, pp. 162–212.

naturally concerned about its ecclesiastical clauses, which they demanded to see before publication. La Rochefoucauld and Arnoux were
principally involved in these attempts to ensure acceptable legislation,
assisted by bishops specially delegated for the purpose. A revealing
pointer to their attitude is the fact that they objected to royal officials
legislating for the church at all; it was Trent's decrees, and not the
great edicts of Orléans or Blois, which they wanted to form the basis of
future ecclesiastical legislation. The ordinance was eventually published in July 1618 but, when the *parlement* refused even to discuss it, it
was quickly forgotten.[96]

Little by little, and because of his ecclesiastical interests, La
Rochefoucauld was being drawn into politics. The original decision to
confer the presidency of the Rouen assembly on him is an indication of
his rapid rise to eminence since his return from Rome and, especially,
since the 1614–15 assemblies. But he still had no official position at
court, and remained intent on residing in his diocese. In early 1618,
Bentivoglio and Arnoux, with papal support, tried to alter this by
inducing the ageing Du Perron to resign his important office of grand
almoner to La Rochefoucauld; when he named his price as 9,000
livres, they found friends of La Rochefoucauld who were willing to put
up the price on his behalf. Arnoux took charge of the negotations,
which were kept secret, but evidently nothing had been settled by the
time of Du Perron's death on 5 September 1618.[97] This opened the
way for a direct royal nomination, and Louis XIII promptly gave the
office to La Rochefoucauld. There had been, it appears, other
candidates, and Puysieux, the secretary of state, reported 'quelques
brigues et poursuittes d'ailleurs assez fortes pour l'emporter', interpreting the choice of La Rochefoucauld as evidence of the king's
resolution to give major offices to deserving candidates.[98] Bentivoglio,
for his part, wrote that the cardinal had not been party to these
dealings.[99]

If the grand almoner of France was not quite a minister for
ecclesiastical affairs, he was certainly privy to all dealings at court
affecting the church. Apart from membership of the king's council,
the office was the best point from which to exert pressure on the

96. Steffani, *Nunziatura di Bentivoglio*, ii, pp. 129ff, letter to Borghese, 26 December 1617;
    ibid., ii, p. 172, to same 17 January 1618; *ibid.*, ii, p. 188, to same, 31 January; *ibid.*,
    ii, pp. 532–3, to same, 15 August; *ibid.*, iii, pp. 101–2, to same 21 September; *ibid.*,
    iii, pp. 124–5, to same 19 December. From Rome, the Rouen debates were followed
    closely and with some trepidation, especially the debates on church reform, and in fear
    that they might deviate from Trent: Ferrara, Archivio di Stato, *fondo* Bentivoglio 18/12,
    nos. 9, 16, 21, letters from Borghese to Bentivoglio, January 1618.
97. Steffani, *Nunziatura di Bentivoglio*, ii, pp. 183–4, Bentivoglio to Borghese, 17 January
    1618.
98. B.N., MS. Fr. 16051, fos. 176v–7r, letter to Archbishop Marquemont of Lyon, in
    Rome, 11 September 1618.
99. Steffani, iii, pp. 21–2, letter to Borghese, 21 September 1618; *ibid.*, iii, p. 27, n. 1,
    avviso from nuncio, 12 September; *Journal de Héroard*, ii, p. 226, 8 September 1618.

crown. As a patron of the Jesuits, La Rochefoucauld possessed the added advantage of having an avenue to the king through the royal confessor, and his relations with successive confessors were both harmonious and close. That he had no ambition to become absorbed in politics is evident from the fact that he made no effort to compete at this point with Bishop Gondi, who had recently been created the first Cardinal de Retz, for the more politically important prize of a seat in the royal council; an attempt to drive a rift between the two cardinals by insinuating that Retz's seat should have gone to La Rochefoucauld came to nothing, and Retz went on to obtain the presidency of the council.[100] La Rochefoucauld's incursions into politics around this time seem to have been confined to reconciling enemies and factions, and by far his best-known effort was the negotiation of the Treaty of Angoulême of May 1619, an abortive reconciliation between Louis XIII and Marie de Medici. He had pleaded for leniency and negotiation from the early stages of this conflict, but his mediation collapsed in the face of intense mutual suspicion, and the dispute had to be resolved by force of arms in 1620.[101]

It was characteristic of him that he spent much of his time on specifically ecclesiastical policies during these years. In 1618–19, for example, two connected conflicts re-appeared which were to figure prominently in the rest of La Rochefoucauld's career – the Richer affair (here a synonym for the Gallican-Ultramontane controversy), and the quarrel between the seculars and the regulars.

Richer, as we saw, was not silenced by the censures of 1612, and after his return from Rome in 1613, La Rochefoucauld seems to have strengthened his links with the Ultramontane doctors of the Sorbonne, of whom André du Val was the most distinguished, and who opposed Richer at every turn.[102] In addition, his appointment in 1618 as director of the College of Navarre, one of the university's most important constituent colleges, gave him a perfectly valid reason for concerning himself with its affairs.[103] He was, in any case, one of a generation of bishops who resented the university's ancient pretension to be the oracle of Christendom, and arbiter of all important doctrinal issues. Moreover, the papacy's growing ambition to be just that served to give old rivalries and suspicions a new lease of life.

The cardinal's first direct dealings with Richer date from 1619.

100. Steffani, iii, p. 42, Bentivoglio to Borghese, 10 October 1618.
101. The main sources for La Rochefoucauld's mission are in the *Négociation commencée au mois de mars de l'année 1619 avec la reine Marie de Médicis par Monsieur le comte de Béthune et continuée conjointement avec Monsieur le Cardinal de la Rochefoucauld* (Paris, 1673), documents printed from B.N., MS. Fr. 15699. The Venetian ambassador's dispatches in B.N., MS. Italien 1773, are also detailed and instructive.
102. In addition to Puyol's *Richer*, vol.ii, see Aimé-Georges Martimort, *Le Gallicanisme de Bossuet* (Paris, 1953), ch.1; *idem*, *Le Gallicanisme* (Paris, 1973), pp. 58–74, especially 71–4.
103. B.S.G., MS. 3238, fo. 64, copy of *brevet*, 10 September 1618.

Richer, by his own account, sought a reconciliation with Retz, his bishop, and offered to provide an orthodox explanation of any disputed proposition in his *Libellus*, with the exception of those on infallibility.[104] A group of theologians discussed this offer with Retz, La Rochefoucauld and the nuncio, but rejected it, demanding that Richer retract, in general terms, the heretical ideas of the *Libellus* and acknowledge the validity of the 1612 condemnations, which he had always refused to do. But Richer withdrew at this stage, a move which, according to the nuncio, infuriated La Rochefoucauld.[105]

In the two men's next encounter, it was the cardinal who took the initiative. He feared that Richerist ideas, a major feature of which was the re-valuation of the parochial clergy and their jurisdiction over their parishes, were gaining ground among the Paris clergy and thus breeding agitation against the religious orders in the capital and the Sorbonne.[106] In 1617, he had co-operated with Bentivoglio to ensure the confessorship to the king remained in Jesuit hands, especially as a leading contender for the post, the curé of St Paul in Paris, was hostile to the regulars.[107] He also opposed the efforts of the Bishop of Orléans to impose restrictions upon the activities of the regulars in his diocese in 1618.[108] Polemic and conflict continued thereafter, and he was encouraged by the papacy to act as a mediator in settling them.[109] In early 1623, when Louis XIII returned to Paris from an anti-Huguenot campaign, La Rochefoucauld, who had recently been appointed to the royal council, evidently tried to grasp the nettle by urging the king to repeat his military victories with one over Richer – schismatics being, in his view, as dangerous as heretics. An assembly was held at La Rochefoucauld's Ste Geneviève residence, which denounced Richer as a schismatic: he was to be asked to accept that the pope's legislative power was binding on all Christians and that, therefore, he could authorise regulars to confess within individual dioceses. Richelieu's intervention was sought in February 1623, as he had recently assumed the important position of provisor of the Sorbonne, but he was careful not to take such a strong line, preferring to leave the responsibility to La Rochefoucauld and others.[110]

104. Edmond Richer, *Histoire du syndicat d'Edmond Richer* (Avignon, 1753), pp. 295ff.
105. *Ibid.*, pp. 303–21.
106. For the nuncio's reports to Rome of these quarrels, A.S.V., Nunz, Fr. 63, fo. 219, Ottavio Corsini to Cardinal Ludoviso, secretary of state to Gregory XV, 21 March 1623; *ibid.*, fo. 261, to same 28 April; *ibid.*, fo. 302, to same, 16 May.
107. Steffani, *Nunziatura di Bentivoglio*, i, 221–2.
108. A.S.V., Nunz, Fr. 297, fos. 446–7, Borghese to Retz, 7 September 1619, congratulating the two cardinals on their stand, and urging them to 'far cessar ogni novità'. See Steffani, *Nunziatura di Bentivoglio*, iii, pp. 542–3.
109. Steffani, *Nunziatura di Bentivoglio*, iii, pp. 469–70, Borghese to Bentivoglio, 20 August 1619; *ibid.*, iii, pp. 510–22, Bentivoglio to Borghese, 22 September; *ibid.*, iii, p. 543.
110. Richer, *Histoire du syndicat*, pp. 342–7.

Further assemblies at Ste Geneviève now followed, at which it was agreed that the divisions of the theology faculty needed to be healed urgently, and that La Rochefoucauld should begin by summoning Richer to declare himself on the condemned propositions of the *Libellus*.[111] According to Richer, La Rochefoucauld obtained the king's permission in council for this step.[112] Richer duly appeared at Ste Geneviève on 21 March, to find the king's secretary present. He later related that La Rochefoucauld harangued him for three hours about his book, but avoided mentioning specific articles. Supple as ever, Richer reaffirmed his desire to submit to his bishop and the pope for the sake of peace, but in accordance with his earlier declarations – a position which, not unexpectedly, failed to satisfy the cardinal. Returning the following day, Richer found La Rochefoucauld in a far more hostile mood, treating him as a recognised schismatic. Deadlock followed when Richer refused to submit unless the heterodoxy of his ideas was clearly demonstrated – a virtually impossible task. Richer then muddied the waters by seeking the chancellor's help, impressing on him that his work was a defence of the rights of the crown. The chancellor requested that La Rochefoucauld leave the syndic alone. But by then, the cardinal had accepted the challenge to prove the heretical content of the *Libellus* which, with the help of a group of bishops and doctors, he spent two days examining. However, no censure was ever published, as La Rochefoucauld no doubt failed to carry a now divided council with him.[113] It would take a Richelieu, wielding greater power and using much sharper methods, to silence Richer once and for all in 1629.

Louis XIII's anti-Huguenot campaigns of the early 1620s, made possible by Luynes's conversion to the idea of a Catholic crusade, was a triumph for the church and the *dévots*, who were to dominate French politics for much of the 1620s.[114] It was a policy which La Rochefoucauld could wholeheartedly support. But it also meant that the court was frequently absent for long periods each year from Paris, and La Rochefoucauld was now too old for life on campaign. This left him valuable time to pursue his religious priorities. He held a thoroughly-prepared diocesan synod at Senlis in 1620, and became the first French bishop to follow the directives of the 1615 assembly on the formal publication of Trent's decrees at diocesan level.[115] From August 1619, he was Abbot of the Parisian monastery of Ste Geneviève, which he

---

111. B.A.V., Barb. lat. 8058, fos. 113–15, Corsini to Ludoviso, 31 March 1623.
112. *Histoire du syndicat*, pp. 348–9.
113. *Ibid.*, pp. 349–61. See also Charles Urbain, *Nicolas Coëffetau. dominicain, evêque de Marseille* (Lyon, 1894), p. 128. Coëffetau was one of those present, having taken a large part in the controversy.
114. Blet, *Le Clergé de France et la monarchie*, i. pp. 235ff.
115. See ch. 4.

undertook to reform. More significantly, he was for several years deeply involved in negotiations with Rome with a view towards a general reform of the French religious orders. And, in his capacity as grand almoner, he made strenuous efforts to regulate the religious and ecclesiastical life of the court when it was present in Paris or its environs.

V

By 1622, however, La Rochefoucauld was to be drawn once again into political life. Luynes, the royal favourite, died during the 1621 Midi campaign, while Retz, the president of the council, died in mid-August during the 1622 campaign. His death re-opened the struggle for both seats in council, and for control of it. Louis XIII had earlier promised to give Retz's place to another cardinal, but La Rochefoucauld was not the only name mentioned. In August 1622, Richelieu was only weeks away from receiving his red hat, and Marie de Medici was pushing his claims as hard as she could. Rome and its nuncio, Corsini, had no doubt that La Rochefoucauld was the man to support.[116] Avoiding the Brûlart faction that temporarily controlled the council, Corsini successfully recruited allies, including the Prince of Condé and Schomberg, then finance minister.[117] The result was that the king granted the place to La Rochefoucauld in early September 1622, while the court was still in the Midi, and La Rochefoucauld in Paris.[118]

None of the surviving evidence suggests that the cardinal took any part in these negotiations, though he may have been kept informed of them. He accepted the king's offer promptly, but made no effort to join the court at Lyon that winter.[119] It was not until the king's return to Paris in January 1623 that the question of his position in the council could be clarified. The Brûlarts insisted that Retz's presidency should not go to someone who owed his seat to their opponents, and even suggested that a cardinal in the council chamber would be a papal spy.[120] But this only provoked La Rochefoucauld into insisting that his dignity as cardinal entitled him to succeed Retz, and that anything less was an offence to his rank. Less of a politician than the more

116. A.S.V., Nunz. Fr. 58, fos. 473–4, Corsini to Cardinal Ludoviso, 14 August 1622.
117. *Ibid.*, fo. 545, Corsini to Ludoviso, 25 September.
118. B.S.G., MS. 3238, fo. 469, copy of king's letter offering place in council to La Rochefoucauld, 6 September 1622.
119. *Ibid.*, fo. 147, letter of acceptance, 18 September.
120. A.S.V., Nunz. Fr. 63, fos. 46v–7r, Corsini to Ludoviso, 21 January 1623. See also Berthold Zeller, *Richelieu et les ministres de Louis XIII de 1621 à 1624* (Paris, 1880), pp. 172–82.

diplomatic Retz, who had often prudently absented himself from council meetings rather than provoke the violent personal confrontations that were common there until Richelieu's ministry, he proved far more unbending on what he saw as a matter of principle.[121] No one, not even the Brûlarts, imagined that he was using this to secure personal control of the council, or to wrest the conduct of policy from them; only perhaps in the area of foreign policy, where the Brûlarts were slowly moving towards peace at home and opposition to the Habsburgs abroad, could a real clash of opinion be anticipated. Even the papal nuncio, suspecting that he had little intrinsic appetite for the business of government, tried to suggest that the pope bring strong pressure to bear on La Rochefoucauld's conscience to make him assiduous in attending council, and to serve the interests of the church there.[122]

It took two months to resolve the conflict, during which time La Rochefoucauld refused to attend council at all.[123] The deadlock was finally broken in his favour only when he received the support of a surprising set of allies – Marie de Medici and Richelieu. The outcome weakened the Brûlarts, whose slide towards disgrace it helped to accelerate.[124]

La Rochefoucauld was satisfied that his dignity as cardinal had been respected. He would preside in council by virtue of having precedence over its other members, princes of the blood excluded. Obviously, this did not prejudge the issue of who controlled the council's business and decisions. However, La Rochefoucauld did not wish to sit idly there, and he outlined his ideas on necessary reforms in the state – finances, office-holding, conciliar organisation, the church itself and so on – in a long, unpublished memorandum submitted to the king.[125] But with the Brûlarts, and after them La Vieuville, dominant in the council, there are few signs that his suggestions were taken seriously, and they may not have been discussed at all.

121. A.S.V., Nunz. Fr. 63, fos. 23–4, Corsini to Ludoviso, 13 January 1623; B.N., MS. Italien 1778, p. 122, Ambassador Pesaro to Venetian senate, 14 January.
122. B.A.V., Barb. lat. 8055, fo. 478, Corsini to Ludoviso, 18 December 1622: 'Ma l'esser egli tanto vuoto d'ambizione, e poco curante d'ingerirsi nei negozi, ci tiene in qualche gelosia pero sarebbe molto a proposito che Nostro Signore con un breve lo riscaldasse, anzi gl'ordinasse, che dovesse rendersi soggetto e diligente al consiglio regio e senza mai mancare assistervi di continuo; al che certo stimo io, che sia tenuta in coscienza, perche altimente nuocerebee alla chiesa mentre che senz'utile occupasse un luogo nel quale potrebbe un alto ecclesiastico profitare.'
123. B.N., MS. Italien 1778, pp. 163, 188, Pesaro to Senate, 27 January and 4 February 1623.
124. *Mémoires du cardinal de Richelieu*, ed. Société de l'Histoire de France, iii, pp. 248–9; vii, p. 250. Even the *dévot*, Michel de Marillac, who was entrusted with solving the problem, was critical of La Rochefoucauld's rigid stance, but agreed that an outcome acceptable to the church must be found, lest the cardinal lose his seat altogether: B.A.V., Barb. lat. 8058, fos. 3–5, Marillac to Corsini, 12 January 1623.
125. B.S.G., MS. 3238, fos. 167–84.

La Rochefoucauld had thus reached the pinnacle of the political system, more by accident than by design, more by conventions about places in council than by a burning ambition to enjoy such a place. Indeed, by early 1623, he was too old and infirm to meet the demands of his elevated station. Frequently too ill even to attend council, especially when the court was moving about, he had little chance of influencing policy. In 1623, he was venerable, but past his prime. It was, therefore, not long before nuncio Corsini was reporting that the king's opinion of La Rochefoucauld's value was decreasing,[126] and that Corsini himself was suggesting that, to make up for the cardinal's shortcomings, a second cardinal was increasingly necessary in council.[127] This was one of the considerations which explains Louis XIII's much-postponed and reluctant decision to admit Richelieu to his council in late April 1624.[128] At first, it was rumoured that La Rochefoucauld had actually been disgraced, but shortly afterwards he was fit enough to rejoin the court, and to preside in council.[129] Richelieu sat beside him as soon as he won his battle to take precedence over other members.[130] It was to be only a matter of time before he would eliminate La Vieuville and secure control of the council.

None of this implied much, if any, change in La Rochefoucauld's position, since he had never sought to dominate the ministry, as Richelieu manifestly did. The latter, therefore, had no grounds for trying to oust him, as the formal presidency was divorced from the reality of power in his case. It is, in fact, unclear when La Rochefoucauld surrendered the presidency to Richelieu, but it is clearly not the case that he formally retired from the council in 1624 or 1625.[131] He continued to play an increasingly intermittent political role during the late 1620s, and was one of those retained in the 1629 re-shuffle of seats in the council.[132] Indeed, Michel de Marillac, keeper of the seals

126. A.S.V., Nunz, Fr. 63, fo. 300, Corsini to Ludoviso, 16 May 1623.
127. Nunz. Fr. 60, fo. 102, Corsini to Cardinal Barberini, secretary of state to Urban VIII, 15 March 1624; *ibid.*, fo. 192, to same 28 April, reporting that the king personally favoured the Archbishop of Tours, and Corsini and the royal confessor the Archbishop of Lyon. Richelieu was admitted to council the following day.
128. *Les Papiers de Richelieu. Section politique intérieure: correspondance et papiers d'état*, ed. Pierre Grillon (Paris, 1975–, in progress), i, p. 65, 'Instructions pour le sieur Tronson', 30 April 1624.
129. A.S.V., Nunz. Fr. 401, fo. 71, Bernadino Spada, papal nuncio, to Barberini, 3 May 1624; Nunz. Fr. 61, fo. 194, 201, to same 9 May. The rumour stemmed from the fact that La Rochefoucauld was informed of Richelieu's appointment by the king's secretary, Tronson, who was frequently employed to announce the disgrace of courtiers.
130. *Papiers de Richelieu*, i, pp. 85–8; B.N., MS. Fr. 16052, fo. 294v–5r, Raymond Phélypeaux, secretary of state, to Archbishop Marquemont, in Rome, 9 May 1624.
131. This is clear from the correspondence of the papal nuncio, Spada, and from the news-sheets (*avvisi*) sent from Paris to Rome: B.L., Addit. MS. 8730, *passim*.
132. La Rochefoucauld, *Homme d'église*, Appendix 2, pp. 386–7, for the text of the *brevet*.

and leading *dévot*, described La Rochefoucauld's failure to formally resign as most uncommon ('chose particulière').[133]

When the nature of La Rochefoucauld's short presidency is grasped, it will come as no surprise that it should have left so few traces in contemporary political life. Apart from the initial controversy over the presidency question itself, Richelieu makes no mention of it in his *Mémoires*. Yet it may be appropriate to quote Richelieu, not one given to extravagant compliments unless they would serve his purposes, in support of the view expressed here of La Rochefoucauld as an unpolitical figure who strayed into politics for non-political reasons. Writing to Cardinal La Valette in 1625, he said of him: 'Je ne croy pas qu'il manque de bonne volonté en vostre endroit, mais de son naturel il est, comme vous scavez, indifferent en toutes choses, mesmes de celles qui le concernent'.[134] The presidency of the council conferred no new dimension on La Rochefoucauld's stature within the French church, which was, and continued to be, independent of it. The office of grand almoner suited his interests better, and his activities at court, insofar as they can be traced, were more marked by it than by his admittedly brief tenure of the presidency.

If only because of his age and health, La Rochefoucauld had begun to withdraw from court before 1624. Significantly, he remained grand almoner until early 1632. But his court appearances in that role became infrequent, and he probably retained the office for ecclesiastical motives of his own. Even by 1619, his absences from Senlis had begun to trouble his conscience over his duties of residence there. He temporarily accepted a compromise worked out for him by Jesuit theologians in order to overcome his scruples.[135] But by 1622, he had evidently concluded that it was not good enough to make arrangements, however adequate, for absentee administration, and he resigned the see to a handpicked successor, Nicolas Sanguin.[136]

Most important of all, it was also in 1622 — in many ways his *annus mirabilis* — that an event occurred which turned his attention away from the court, and provided him with a huge amount of new work. After three years of negotiation, the papacy finally granted him a special commission for six years to reform the main monastic orders of France. It was an undertaking that had the king's support, but even

---

133. B.S.G., MS. 741, fo. 50, for Marillac's statement.
134. *Papiers de Richelieu*, i, p. 167, letter of *c.* 20 February 1625. The subject of the letter is unknown.
135. B.S.G., MS. 366, fos. 370–1, Etienne Binet S.J. to La Rochefoucauld, 19 July 1619; *ibid.*, fo. 98, Martial Duboucherys, the cardinal's agent in Rome, to La Rochefoucauld, 20 January 1620, on Rome's acceptance of his arrangements.
136. A.S.V., Processus consistoriales 17, fos. 202–24, for the canonical enquiry *de vita et moribus* on Sanguin.

so, the task was enormous, especially for someone of his age. It would occupy most of La Rochefoucauld's time right up until his death over two decades later. For this and other reasons that we shall examine, his 'retirement' from the world of politics and diocesan administration was to be characterised by intense activity.

3

Active Retirement

I

In the final two decades or so of his life, La Rochefoucauld gradually divested himself of his various offices — his commission to reform the orders was temporary and revocable — and so was left without a hand on any of the levers in either the church or the state. No longer a bishop, he could not, for instance, attend the momentous Assemblies of the Clergy of 1625, 1635 and 1641. Nevertheless, he was more than ever involved in the affairs of the French church. This impression does not arise merely because sources are more plentiful for this period of his career. With fewer obligations of office to distract him, he could devote his time to religous affairs and, despite advancing age, enhance the position of leadership that he had built up since 1614–15. For all its limitations, that leadership was increasingly moral in character, as there was now little to buttress it apart from reputation, experience and commitment.

The most obvious sign of this, though the most difficult to convey in a general way, is the continuing stream of *ad hoc* assemblies meeting at his Ste Geneviève *hôtel* until the eve of his death, and dealing with an enormous variety of issues — theological, jurisdictional and pastoral. Many were, of course, devoted to minor and deservedly long-forgotten issues, but which, as so often, assumed symbolic importance at the time, because of the principles, such as episcopal power and ecclesiastical jurisidiction generally, they seemed to embrace. There is not much of a general nature that can be said about such gatherings, except to note the focus they provided for ecclesiastical politics and the extent to which they occupied the cardinal's time. In addition, regular assemblies met at least weekly for over twenty years to discuss the reform of the religious orders, and attracted a wide range of advisers and participants, from bishops and senior figures in the orders themselves, to other clergy and royal officials. If the reform of the orders may seem, in retrospect, a somewhat marginal issue, it was not treated in isolation from other questions of church discipline and reform. Less formal than such meetings, but of even more significance were the assemblies which dealt with questions such as relations between the French church, the crown and the papacy, as well as between the regular and secular clergy. It is these, naturally, which command attention, and which will provide much of the central thread of this chapter. They serve to show La Rochefoucauld's role at its clearest, while at the same time serving to indicate where the main limitations on his leadership lay.

It would be futile to attempt to explain here the reasons for all the tensions which ran through the French church in the first half of the seventeenth century. Yet some understanding of them is indispensable if the controversies of the 1620s and 1630s are to be intelligible. As the debates of the 1610s showed, the struggle between Gallican and Ultramontane was far from being exhausted by the events of the League, and indeed had been exacerbated by the assassination of Henri IV; they also demonstrated that Ultramontane ideas had some strong protagonists in the ranks of the upper clergy. Subsequent attempts, notably under Richelieu, to define royal power more precisely, and to raise kingship above all earthly authority, only served to exacerbate the conflict. French foreign policy, directed mainly against Habsburg Spain seemed increasingly divorced from religious considerations and hostile to the best interests of Catholicism, added further fuel to the fire, again pitting *bons français* against *bons catholiques*. And, when it came, full-scale war made financial and other demands on French society, which not even the highly-protected clergy could altogether escape.

At the same time, the French upper clergy, and particularly the episcopate, was slowly becoming more assertive, both within their dioceses and beyond them; they were more ready to protest at what they saw as infringements of their jurisdiction, whether by the papacy or by royal officials. To a certain extent, this had always been a feature of the Gallican church. But in the seventeenth century, it was reinforced by the far-reaching revaluation of the secular clergy which was, possibly, the main contribution of the French church to early modern Catholicism. The insistence of Bérulle and his followers on the superiority of the priesthood over all other conditions of Christian life led them to support episcopal authority against the regular clergy, with their age-old claims of the primacy of the *vita contemplativa* and their papal privileges guaranteeing them a large measure of independence from local bishops and church institutions. It was against this background that the long-standing quarrel between regular and secular clergy took on a new lease of life in the 1620s and 1630s.

We saw in the previous chapter that the moves made against Richer in 1619 and 1623 had not been occasioned by public controversy, as in

1612 or 1614; rather they were a pre-emptive action occasioned by fear of the damage that might be caused by the spread of Richer's ideas. By contrast, the alarum provoked by the great conflict of 1625 sprung from the fact that it erupted within the ranks of the clergy themselves, thereby exposing them to what men like La Rochefoucauld saw as virtual schism. As a full account of the events of 1625 already exists, we shall, for our present purposes, concentrate upon La Rochefoucauld's part in resolving it.[1]

The storm began when anonymous pamphlets began appearing in Paris in 1625, attacking Richelieu's anti-papal and anti-Habsburg policies: this was the moment of French intervention in the Valtelline in support of the Protestant rulers of valleys whose Catholic subjects both Spain and the papacy were attempting to protect. The pamphlets warned Louis XIII that such a policy endangered his personal salvation. If it came to the worst, the pamphleteers argued, the pope might have to take drastic measures to defend the church, making use of his right to proceed against rulers who were either heretical or persecutors of the church. More ominously, the tracts hinted at the legitimacy of revolt by the *grands* in such circumstances. This was, at the very least, to re-open the debate on papal temporal power and the independence of rulers.[2] The clergy had no desire to revive the polemics of 1614 but proved willing, when requested by Richelieu, to censure the offending pamphlets, albeit on vague and general grounds that they were outrageous, offensive and provocative, rather than because they ran counter to any clearly-defined principles or monarchical rights. The clergy then proceeded to formal approval of a censure drafted on their behalf by Bishop Etampes of Chartres, only to discover in horror on actually reading it, that Etampes had exceeded his brief and made clear, positive statements of royal absolutism, justifying the independence of secular rulers and imposing on Christians the duty to accept even tyranny passively. The censure, duly printed under the title of the *Jugement des evesques*, suggested that the clergy were now officially championing a more extreme form of Gallicanism than ever before.[3]

Not surprisingly, there was an uproar, and frantic attempts followed to reverse the censure and then replace it with a vaguer declaration of the kind originally intended. But the *parlement*, delighted with Etampes's work, was determined to see it stand as an official declaration by the clergy, enshrining the central principles of

1. Blet, *Le Clergé de France et la monarchie*, i, pp. 335—69.
2. Church, *Richelieu and Reason of State*, pp. 120—6, This remains the most comprehensive analysis of the controversies of the period from 1624 to 1635.
3. Blet, *Le Clergé et la monarchie*, i, pp. 338—41. During the session on 9 December, Etampes began reading his text, but the trusting assembly dispensed him from doing so in full, thereby implicitly giving his work their approval.

Gallicanism and divine-right monarchy. Sensing the crown's political weakness at this juncture, it was also prepared to intimidate the assembled clergy, with the result that a succession of decrees forbade the clergy from altering Etampes's text. Nevertheless, the assembly did vote a second censure in January 1626, although it had not obtained formal recognition of it from the crown by the time it disbanded, on 23 February.[4]

La Rochefoucauld had not been a member of the assembly. When the storm broke, the nuncio Spada sought his help, since a section of the assembly supported Etampes, while others feared reprisals from the *parlement*. At first, the cardinal was hesitant: he could not come to the assembly since, as a member of the council, he needed royal permission; nor did he think he could achieve much by approaching the king, feeling that his word now carried insufficient weight. However, after this initial hesitation, he agreed to speak to the king, though only if accompanied by Cardinals La Valette (president of the assembly) and Richelieu. The latter refused, pointing out the difficulties in which the clergy now found themselves in relation to the *parlement*.[5]

Once the assembly formally dissolved, the enterprising Spada continued his efforts to secure, from some or all of the bishops, a rejection of Etampes's censure. Rightly fearing that such an act 'quasi clandestino' would offend the king and further provoke an assertive *parlement*, he asked La Rochefoucauld to convene the bishops still in Paris, ostensibly to protest against the *parlement's* interference in the clergy's affairs and to have its decrees rescinded, which was in itself a formidable objective. La Rochefoucauld at first hesitated, and then agreed. His decision encouraged others to attend.[6] In the climate of the time, no one else would have dared convene them. For their part, the bishops felt safer at Ste Geneviève, where there was by now a well-established tradition of regular meetings. Twenty-eight of them attended the first gathering on 26 February. Almost immediately, La Rochefoucauld ignored the ostensible reason for their meeting: his intention was to secure a firm disavowal of Etampes which would make the clergy's position clear. After five hours of debate, all but one bishop signed an act disowning every previous declaration that purported to emanate from the clergy.[7] The next step was, logically, to restore the clergy's internal unity by having Etampes himself accept this latest move. Although invited by La Rochefoucauld, he had not

4. *Ibid.*, pp. 350–2.
5. A.S.V., Nunz. Fr. 65, fos. 51–68, Spada to Barberini, 30 January 1627.
6. *Ibid.*, fos. 113–15, Spada to Barberini, 27 February; A.N., G 8* 643F, fo. 289v, *procès-verbal* of meeting of 25 February.
7. A.N., G 8* 643F, fo. 290–3, 26 February, Unfortunately, here, too, there is no account of the actual substance of the debates.

attended the meeting on 26 February, even to defend his actions.[8] He now replied that he would attend if the disavowal of him were itself withdrawn. La Rochefoucauld countered by saying that he was merely required to say that his work did not represent the position of the French clergy as a whole and, referring directly to Etampes, went on to state in stern language his own understanding of the principle involved:

> 'it is for him to rejoin this body, should he so desire; he cannot expect it to move in his direction in order to find a common accord. For matters of religion are different from temporal affairs, where those who are in disagreement should meet each other half-way; instead, those who have strayed from the church, are obliged to go the whole way themselves in order to return to it, not for love of the church, but for their own salvation'.[9]

Such a statement is characteristic of La Rochefoucauld, and may help to explain why contemporaries felt he was no diplomat. But it failed to produce the desired result, for Etampes and two supporters refused to sign the disavowal unless the Ste Geneviève assembly proclaimed the absolute independence of the crown in temporal matters, which it had no intention of doing any more than had the official assembly.[10] Meanwhile, attempts to have the *parlement*'s decrees quashed continued, but ministers proved hostile, and Richelieu was unwilling to confront the *parlement*.[11] However, in an audience with the king on 1 March, La Rochefoucauld obtained a promise that the next session of council would deal with the case.[12] Two days later, however, the *parlement* condemned the Ste Geneviève assemblies and ordered the bishops home.[13] In response, the bishops temporarily suspended their meetings because a short royal absence from Paris made them vulnerable. But on 5 March, Etampes finally agreed to signed the act which disowned his initial censure of the anti-Richelieu pamphlets, and two days later, La Rochefoucauld re-convened the bishops, and informed them that he had explained the disavowal in council, to the satisfaction of the king, Marie de Medici

---

8. *Ibid.*, fos. 294–5, 27 February.
9. *Ibid.*, fo. 295r: 'c'est a luy de revenir au corps pour s'y joindre s'il luy plaist, et n'attendre pas que le corps puisse aller à luy pour s'accorder, parce qu'il n'en est point des affaires de la religion comme des temporelles, pour lesquelles ceux qui sont en differents doivent faire la moitié du chemin de part et d'autre, au lieu que ceux qui sont esloignez de l'Eglise doivent faire le chemin tout entier pour y revenir, non pour l'amour de l'Eglise, mais pour leur propre salut.'
10. *Ibid.*, fo. 295r-v.
11. *Mémoires de Mathieu Molé*, i, p. 352, Molé to Pierre Dupuy, 21 October 1625, where he remarks that the clergy no longer seem willing to obey either pope or king.
12. A.N., G 8* 643F, fo. 296v, 2 March.
13. B.N., MS. Dupuy 678, fos. 281–3.

and the councillors present. A formal audience was then promised to the clergy, which would allow them to present remonstrances against the actions of the *parlement*.[14]

Yet the conflict was far from over. Matters came to a head on 9 March, when the *parlement* officially served notice on individual bishops of its decree against the assemblies. They reacted by angrily denouncing this as an unwarranted interference and an attempt to exercise jurisdiction over them. The battle of ideas had become a battle for influence, with the king as arbiter. Once again, the assemblies ceased during a second brief royal absence from Paris, but La Rochefoucauld was asked to re-convene them as soon as Louis XIII returned. He agreed to do so, having first sounded out the king, who gave his permission albeit with no great enthusiasm.[15] The clergy reassembled under the cardinal's presidency, and drafted their remonstrance, which, on 13 March, La Rochefoucauld then went to present at court. But the crown continued to avoid the issue over the next few weeks, making half-promises of audiences and discussions in council. The assemblies themselves continued until late March, when they finally disbanded without ever obtaining their promised audience.[16] The crown evidently preferred to let the matter drop rather than have to decide between the clergy and the *parlement*. The clergy's only consolation was that Richelieu persuaded Etampes to write a letter of submission to the pope.

With the possible exception of those of 1639, the 1626 assemblies were the most famous of all those held at Ste Geneviève. Legally, they could not claim to be a continuation of the official assembly, and the *parlement* made strong efforts to persuade Louis XIII that bishops might not meet at all without his prior permission. La Rochefoucauld and his colleagues strongly defended their inalienable right to do so, though in practice this right was becoming more difficult to sustain. On questions of substance, the bishops were also on dangerous ground, as the king could hardly fail to relish Etampes's encomium of divine-right monarchy. Indeed, the whole dispute shows the clergy desperately trying to avoid actual discussion of Etampes's theses; they sensed that they could not hope to win any political battle which followed from an open debate on Gallican views of church-state relations.

La Rochefoucauld was, characteristically, less reticent than most on this question. The official record of the assemblies is not very helpful in providing a detailed account of his role during the crisis, and much of the work was probably undertaken by younger men, like Bishop Sanguin of Senlis, but it is quite clear that La Rochefoucauld's

14. A.N., G 8* 643F, fo. 298.
15. *Ibid.*, fos. 299–303.
16. *Ibid.*, fos. 303–15, for the records of these sessions, ending on 1 April.

willingness to receive his colleagues at Ste Geneviève and to maintain the assemblies, despite ministerial and *parlementaire* disapproval, was crucial. One revealing token of this is the refusal of La Vallette, president of the official assembly, to attend a meeting unless La Rochefoucauld was present; simply by being present, the cardinal emboldened others to attend and to defy the *parlement*. His membership of the council also proved useful, not so much for the results obtained, but because he provided some kind of direct access to the king. The *parlement*, for its part, preferred to attack other bishops, realising no doubt that an attack on La Rochefoucauld would be counter-productive. The lead that he offered in 1626 at least succeeded in preventing Etampes's views from being foisted on the clergy as the official opinion of the French church.

If Louis XIII wished to forget the whole affair, La Rochefoucauld emphatically did not. The rapid appearance of a history of the censure, which justified the *parlement*'s stance, inspired him to publish a counterblast. The whole enterprise had the support of both the French and the Flanders nuncios.[17] With the assistance of secretaries and advisers, some of them Jesuits, La Rochefoucauld composed in the second half of 1626 a long vindication of the clergy's actions which, after revision by Spada and Suffren, the king's confessor, was then printed in great secrecy in Brussels.[18] Despite Spada's resistance – he feared it would give offence – La Rochefoucauld insisted on formally presenting a copy of it to Louis XIII at Easter 1627.[19]

The *Raisons pour le desaveu* is not La Rochefoucauld's greatest work. It is more an *ad hoc* compilation than a systematic treatise, and some scholars have claimed that it was in fact written by La Rochefoucauld's Jesuit secretary, the classical scholar Jean Phélypeaux. Certainly, some of its chapters give this impression, but none of those close to La Rochefoucauld at the time of its composition ever hinted at this.[20]

17. A.S.V. Nunz, Fr. 65, fos. 211–12, Spada to Barberini, 22 June 1626. It is impossible to say which history of the affair La Rochefoucauld was attempting to refute. In compiling his refutation, Spada encouraged the cardinal to draw on a diary which the strongly Ultramontane Bishop of Angers, Charles Miron, had kept during the assembly, but as this work has been lost, one cannot determine how far La Rochefoucauld relied upon its contents.
18. B.N., MS. Italien 64, fos. 131–2, Spada to Barberini, 30 November 1626; *ibid.*, fo. 190, to same, 18 December. For the secret printing of the book: *Correspondance du nonce Giovanni Francesco di Bagno 1621–1627*, ed. Bernard de Meester (Brussels, 1938), p. 798, Bagno to Barberini, 5 December 1626; *ibid.*, p. 817, to same, 30 January 1627. See also B.L., Addit. MS. 8730, fo. 326v, *avviso* of 20 November: 'Al 13 del corrente parti da Parigi il gentilhuomo avvisato con cifra de x, che dal sr. cardinale de la Roccafocò è stato proposto a la stampa del libro *Raisons pour le desaveu*'. Despite this, the title-page bears the inscription, 'Paris 1627'.
19. A.S.V., Nunz. Fr. 302, fos. 164–5v, Spada to Barberini, 8 April 1627.
20. Because of the semi-clandestine nature of the enterprise, little is known about its authorship, and the initial intention seems to have been to publish it anonymously. See B.L., Addit, MS. 8730, fos. 326–7, *avviso* of 20 November 1626: 'La risolutione di proporre a l'opera il nome del Auctore è giunta poco aspettata a quegli stessi che havevano qualche notitia dei pensieri der sr. cardinale'.

Be that as it may, there can be no doubt whatever that the prefatory letter to the king with which the *Raisons* begin, is La Rochefoucauld's own work. His rank in both church and state obliged him, he wrote, to speak out and warn the king and the public of the dangers facing them. It was also necessary to provide a true record of the recent crisis, in order to make the church's position clear.[21] His book was accordingly directed against the 'schismatiques de ce tems', by which he meant the Gallicans. Explicitly linking the Etampes censure to the article of the Third Estate in 1614 and the oath devised by James I for English Catholics, he implied that France was treading the same path as England toward Erastianism. This was his reason, he claimed, for composing the *Raisons*.[22]

In his account of the censure, La Rochefoucauld studiously avoided pointing the finger in any particular direction. Etampes could not have intended to embarrass the clergy. Indeed, the censure was not his at all; it was a tract circulating in the clergy's name which could not possibly have obtained their approval.[23] Likewise the *parlement* acted in good faith, believing that in defending Etampes it was defending the clergy against a faction.[24] He was strenuously avoiding giving any hint, as the assembled clergy had been before him, at the ideological grounds for the controversy. Like them, he insisted that no one in France had the right to make fundamental doctrinal pronouncements or to declare, as the *parlement* frequently did, that certain unpalatable ideas could be condemned as heretical and contrary to any alleged 'sacred canons'.[25]

This last question led La Rochefoucauld to examine the doctrinal issues which had provoked the crisis, but which the clergy had striven to ignore. We have already noted the genealogy of ideas which he saw as responsible for schismatic tendencies in France. Heresy was open rebellion; schism was more insidious, as it aimed to deceive even the well-meaning. He felt compelled to state the theological principle of the unity of the church as the *summum bonum*. Unity did not preclude a reasonable diversity, but such diversity quite properly had no place in the realm of doctrine, where there could be no national variants. It was the pope alone, he affirmed, who had the right define doctrine and his whole defence of papal primacy hinged on this simple conviction.[26] This was, and would continue to be, unacceptable to many in France, even in the upper reaches of the clergy. What disturbed La Roche-

21. *Raisons*, pp. 1–5.
22. *Ibid.*, pp. 8–9, 58ff.
23. *Ibid.*, pp. 11–14, 203.
24. *Ibid.*, p. 8.
25. *Ibid.*, pp. 72ff. On this point, he quoted the works and speeches of Du Perron and Richelieu in 1614.
26. *Ibid.*, pp. 82–114.

foucauld most about French Gallicans was the facility with which they believed that everyone but themselves must be in the wrong.[27]

La Rochefoucauld also turned to the controversies that lay behind the 1625–6 crisis. In the debates over Richelieu's policies, he detected what he viewed as a dangerous tendency to employ categories such as *bons français* and *bons catholiques*, and to regard the latter as bad subjects of the king.[28] This seemed to him to separate religion and politics – which to an Ultramontane appeared to be schismatic: to be a Catholic was to be a *Roman* Catholic.[29] He defended the primacy of religion in human affairs, and rejected any double morality, public or private. Religion and politics might have different functions in a society, but La Rochefoucauld was quick to dismiss the view shared by Etampes and the *parlement* that they had 'chacune leurs limites distinguées'. If France were to accept this position, she would cut herself off from the main body of Christendom.[30] Fearing a schism grounded in a *raison d'état* derived from a mixture of Gallican and *parlementaire* maxims, La Rochefoucauld devoted much time in the *Raisons* to deflating the claims of the *bons français*. To love one's country, he replied, was a duty, not a claim to special merit.[31] He was also worried about the associated implication that ecclesiastics were politically suspect because of their special ties with Rome in its guise as a foreign power. It was one thing, he argued, for clergy not to seek royal office – they had, after all, more pressing duties to attend to – but it was quite another to wish to exclude them in principle from public life altogether.[32] Predictably, La Rochefoucauld saw this, too, as an attack on the papacy.

Curiously, perhaps, La Rochefoucauld had nothing to say about the temporal claims of the papacy. His silence can only be explained by the situation in 1626, for he would almost certainly have thought the idea of Louis XIII being deposed by the pope ludicrous and unwarranted.[33] The occasion did not, therefore, call for a statement of papal power. Instead, he urged the king to ignore the prophets of

---

27. *Ibid.*, sections xi–xii.
28. *Ibid.*, p. 138: 'non qu'il ne soit louable et du devoir des françois de maintenir les droits des Eglises de France, ceux du Roy et de l'estat: ceux en particulier qui ont été acquis à si bons titres par les mérites de nos Rois envers l'Eglise et le Saint Siège...je n'entends parler en ce lieu de l'employ de cette qualité de bons françois pour faire division entre l'Eglise de France et l'universelle, ou le Chef d'icelle.'
29. *Ibid.*, pp. 139–42, 327–34.
30. *Ibid.*, pp. 197–228, for a discussion of the refusal to receive the decrees of Trent as an example of *raison d'état*.
31. *Ibid.*, pp. 139–46.
32. *Ibid.*, pp. 155ff. During the conflict between La Rochefoucauld and the Brûlarts in 1623 over the presidency of the council, it was suggested to the king that having a cardinal in the council would mean the pope would be privy to the king's secrets. La Rochefoucauld bitterly resented this charge, and his discussion of it in the *Raisons* bears the traces.
33. *Ibid.*, pp. 319ff.

raison d'état, and imitate his ancestors' unshakable fidelity to Rome.[34]

Whatever his intentions, the *Raisons* did not rekindle the controversy. La Rochefoucauld attacked the ideas lying behind the recent crisis, while being civil to those involved in it. Even the *parlement* remained unprovoked. Only Richer thought it worthwhile to publish a detailed rebuttal, in which he restated his own views vigorously, though less provocatively than before.[35] But he, too, was ignored. La Rochefoucauld could conclude that the unity of the clergy had been restored.

Indeed, the cardinal received gratifying proof of this shortly after the publication of the *Raisons*. In mid-January 1627, the Assembly of Notables revived a proposal originally made at Rouen to consider the papal nuncio as a foreign ambassador, with whom it would be treasonable for the king's subjects to have any dealings. With Gaston d'Orléans's support, the proposal passed. Spada immediately contacted La Rochefoucauld, who denounced it as schismatic and as an intolerable attempt to separate the clergy from the papacy. He had himself been delegated by the king's council to attend the meeting of the notables, and was now slow to convene an assembly which might be viewed as a challenge to the crown. But under pressure from his friends, and with the ecclesiastical notables threatening to walk out of the Assembly of Notables altogether, he eventually did so. Unhappy at Richelieu's vague promise that the offending proposal would be suppressed later,[36] the twenty-one bishops meeting at Ste Geneviève condemned the proposal as schismatic, and renewed their threat of a walk-out if it were not withdrawn.[37] La Rochefoucauld was pleased with this challenge to the *parlementaire* notables in particular, and was commissioned to draft instructions for an envoy who would seek a royal audience. But in a manner reminiscent of 1626, no such audience was granted, and the prelates continued their meetings.[38] When the king sent a messenger to La Rochefoucauld to abandon a particular meeting, the only reply he received was that business had

34. *Ibid.*, pp. 379–80.
35. *Considérations sur un livre initutlé Raisons pour le désaveu fait par les évêques de ce royaume etc, mis en lumière sous le nom de M. François de la Rochefoucault, contre les schismatiques de ce tems, par Timothée, François catholique* (Paris, 1628).
36. A.S.V. Nunz. Fr. 302, fos. 31–32, Spada to Barberini, 1 February 1627. It is clear from Spada's report that the idea that the assembly should be convened by anyone else had not occurred to the clergy present. La Valette, acting president of the Notables, suggested to Spada that La Rochefoucauld take the initiative.
37. *Ibid.*, fos. 49–50, *procès-verbal* of 22 January: 'Fu detto e stabilito che la religione cattolica non può comportare che nasca divisione tra'l Papa, il quale è capo della Chiesa, e li membri suoi . . . tra quali il Rè è il primogenito figliulo . . . che in consequenza di cio il prohibire alli sudditi del Rè di trattare con li signori Nuntii, et altri Ministri di S. Santità è dividerli dal Papa capo della chiesa. Che con la detta qualità de capo di Chiesa, Il Papa non può esser stimato in Francia principe forestiere.'
38. *Ibid.*, fos. 53–6, *procès-verbal* of 24 January.

begun, and could not be now cut short; they would, however, merely discuss church affairs. But the king, probably stung by this reaction, held firm, while assuring the cardinal that he would support the clergy's point of view. In the end, the clergy obtained satisfaction through Richelieu's intervention.[39]

Subsequent years offered further proof that La Rochefoucauld and the Ste Geneviève assemblies were geared to defending the rights of the papacy and to keeping Gallican ideas at bay, especially among the clergy. When, in 1629, the learned and eccentric Archbishop of Rouen, François de Harlay, published an ecclesiastical history which contained frequent disparaging references to the papacy, La Roche-foucauld acted even before the nuncio could. He had an episcopal assembly at Ste Geneviève examine the work and censure parts of it. Harlay was himself then confronted with the censure and, rather surprisingly, formally disapproved of the offending passages when invited to do so.[40] La Rochefoucauld and the nuncio duly authen-ticated these declarations and forwarded them to Rome. However, it proved more difficult to persuade Harlay to write a satisfactory letter of apology of Urban VIII. And when briefs thanking both prelates were dispatched, Harley refused to accept his from La Rochefoucauld's hands.[41] Like Etampes and others before him, Harlay doubtless found the cardinal's combative Ultramontanism too much to take.

The continuity of La Rochefoucauld's vigilance in defence of the papacy is evident from events taking place a decade later. In early 1639, he found himself at the centre of a much more famous act of censure – that of Pierre Dupuy's treatise on the Gallican liberties. This was by far the most massive statement of the Gallican case yet compiled, and was backed up with a volume of *preuves* – edicts, treatises, royal declarations, decrees and so on. La Rochefoucauld convened the bishops present in Paris, had them examine the work and single out ideas deemed to be pernicious. In an unprecedented move, a formal letter was then drafted for circulation to the clergy, warning them against Dupuy's errors. Richelieu's approval of the whole proceedings was sought and obtained, despite the fact that Dupuy had published his work with his permission. At a subsequent assembly, La Rochefoucauld, whose memory was decidedly long on such matters, suggested that the matter be placed beyond all doubt by getting the

39. *Ibid.*, fos. 45–8, Spada to Barberini, 1 February. On the position and status of the papal nuncio in seventeenth-century France, see Pierre Blet, *Histoire de la représentation diplomatique du Saint-Siège* (Vatican City, 1982), pp. 373ff.; *idem.*, 'Le Nonce en France au xviie siècle. Ambassadeur et délegué apostolique', *Revue d'histoire diplomatique* 88 (1974) pp. 223–53.
40. B.S.G., MS. 366, fos. 216–17, *procès-verbal* of 17 July 1629.
41. A.S.V., Nunz. Fr. 72, fo. 17, Bagno, nuncio since 1627, to Barberini, 18 January 1630; *ibid.*, fo. 125, to same, 28 May.

Archbishop of Paris to summon a provincial council to formally censure Dupuy, as Du Perron had done in 1612 in the case of Richer.[42] Meanwhile, the letter, signed by La Rochefoucauld and twenty bishops, was dispatched to the clergy of France.[43] The *parlement* was infuriated by these moves, but a decree of the king's council prevented it from attacking La Rochefoucauld's assemblies as it had in 1626.[44] Because of its rapidity and efficiency, the Dupuy censure was later regarded by many as the high point of Ultramontane influence within the French church.

II

It should be clear that the Ste Geneviève assemblies, even though lacking well-defined status, were capable of acting as an unofficial episcopal watchdog; nor could they be easily dismissed as a private cabal, since on several occasions, they included bishops who were in disagreement with La Rochefoucauld. Indeed, it was probably their ambiguous status which enabled them to take place regularly, and act as an effective lobby. After all, the General Assembly met only every ten years, and there was clearly a need for an interim body which could speak for the church, as well as defend ecclesiastical interests.

On the other hand, there was an ever-present danger that the crown might try to use these unofficial assemblies in order to obtain money and other concessions from the church, rather than haggle with the General Assemblies, which tended to be long, expensive, tight-fisted and argumentative. The court was always tempted to bypass them, especially in its search for funds, and the clergy had reason to fear that a few court-based bishops might be used to authorise new subsidies.[45]

La Rochefoucauld was directly solicited for this purpose only once, in 1630, at the height of the Mantuan war. Richelieu and the king were absent in Piedmont, and La Rochefoucauld and the Duke of Monbazon had been requested to form a provisional council in Paris to look after the internal security of the realm.[46] It was ironic, in view of

42. B.S.G., MS. 366, fo. 246, *procès-verbal* of 9 February, which also gives an account of the delegation sent to Richelieu, whose role in the whole affair was, to say the least, ambiguous. It was probably he who prevented Archbishop Gondi from censuring a work which he wished to see remain on the market.
43. *Ibid.*, fos. 248–9, for the original manuscript text of the letter, with signatures.
44. See Gabriel Demante, 'Histoire de la publication des livres de Pierre Dupuy sur les libertés de l'église gallicane', *Bibliothèque de l'Ecole des Chartes* 5 (1843–4), pp. 585–600. Two letters from the papal nuncio, Bolognetti, describing events, are printed in H. Laemmer, *Melematum Romanorum Mantissa* (Ratisbon, 1875), pp. 467–8.
45. For the history of earlier conflicts, see L. Serbat, *Les Assemblées du clergé de France*, especially part I. In 1628, the crown succeeded in obtaining 3 million *livres* from an assembly of audit which, strictly speaking, was not empowered to make such a grant: Blet, *Le Clergé de France et la monarchie*, i, pp. 370ff.
46. B.S.G., MS. 3238, fo. 356, Louis XIII to La Rochefoucauld, 5 May 1630.

earlier royal disapproval of his assemblies, that the cardinal should now be asked to summon the bishops to discuss details of a new clerical *don gratuit* of 1.3 million *livres*. The king had already 'authorised' the contribution, and dispatched letters to the bishops of France to see that it was collected.[47] The fifteen bishops who attended quickly realised that the slightest semblance of consent on their part would enable the court and the financiers to go into action. The Bishops of Riez, Orléans and St Paul-Trois-Châteaux were sent as envoys to the king to demand that an official Assembly of the Clergy be authorised, but with no power to negotiate further or consent to royal demands. Further assemblies were held in Paris, which then empowered the deputies to express a wish to assist the king, provided he first withdrew his consent to the levy. A regular assembly of audit was overdue, and had not so far been summoned.[48] La Rochefoucauld himself petitioned Suffren, the Jesuit confessor, to beg the king to desist from his intention. Recent heavy impositions had impoverished many parishes, he claimed, and in any case, consultations with a group of theologians had led him to the conclusion that any alienation of church property required prior papal consent.[49]

This combination of argument and obstructionism seems to have worked. Negotiations dragged on all summer; the envoys corresponded with La Rochefoucauld, and messengers passed to and fro.[50] The crown, unwilling to summon an official Assembly of Clergy, finally abandoned its attempt later that summer. The principle that only such assemblies could vote subsidies had been effectively defended.

Nine years later, in 1639, La Rochefoucauld found himself in the midst of a similar, though much more explosive situation, one of the most protracted and bitter of Richelieu's ministry. War was squeezing the tax-payers, while the crown's revenues were never sufficient for its needs. It was increasingly at the mercy of its financiers, who tried to include the church in their imaginative schemes.[51]

In April 1639, an edict was published which was designed to raise six million *livres* in composition fees payable by the clergy on

---

47. *Papiers de Richelieu*, v, nos. 291–2, letters of Louis XIII to Gaston d'Orléans, *lieutenant général* of the kingdom in his absence, and the bishops of France, 6 June 1630. The king alleged that the 1628 assembly had made a promise to raise further sums, and that this was the basis of his demand in 1630.
48. B.S.G., MS. 3238, fos. 354–5, *procès-verbal* of assembly of 19 June; *Papiers de Richelieu*, v. no. 336, p. 341, Michel de Marillac, keeper of the seals, to Richelieu, 25 June.
49. B.S.G., MS. 3238, fos. 349–50, 'copie d'un mémoire donné au R.P. Suffren...en juin 1630'.
50. *Ibid.*, fo. 353, La Rochefoucauld to envoys, [...]July 1630; *ibid.*, fo. 352, envoys' reply, 20 August. *Papiers de Richelieu*, v. no. 368, pp. 363–4, Claude de Bullion, *intendant des finances*, to Richelieu, 3 July : 'M. d'Orléans estime que sans assemblée il sera très difficile de venir à bout du secours qu'on demande au Clergé'. The envoys conveyed the unwillingness of the Ste Geneviève assemblies directly to Richelieu. *ibid.*, v, no. 412, p. 408, letter of 17 July.
51. See Bonney, *King's Debts*, pp. 170ff for the crown's financial position in the late 1630s.

inalienable church property acquired since 1520. At first, those liable to pay ignored the edict, but when the financiers proceeded to wholesale sequestrations of church property, the outcry began in earnest; according to the nuncio, it reached its peak when La Rochefoucauld's benefices were seized.[52] Almost simultaneously, Richelieu's relations with Rome, which had been gradually deteriorating, reached a nadir in late 1639, when he refused to accept Ranuccio Scotti as the new, 'ordinary' nuncio to France. Rumours also circulated that he was planning a national council, and was aiming to become patriarch of a national French church. Recent incidents in Rome involving the ambassador and his servants had made Richelieu determined to make no concessions to the papacy.[53]

Inevitably there was confusion and bewilderment when the bishops assembled at Ste Geneviève on 1 December 1639. After long discussions, in which complaints were made that the council was conniving at the financiers' exactions, it was decided to seek Richelieu's protection, and to request the convocation of a General Assembly.[54] Further meetings were held that month and, when envoys were sent to see Richelieu, he promised his assistance.[55] However, he did nothing to prevent the formation, some weeks later, of a mixed commission of bishops and councillors to raise 3.5 million *livres* from the clergy.[56] Significantly, none of the bishops selected to serve on it had frequented Ste Geneviève. That Richelieu wanted money without calling a General Assembly of the Clergy became clear when, in April 1640, the king formally 'dispensed' them from holding one.[57]

The clergy did not underestimate the threat, and from March onwards, the assemblies resumed under La Rochefoucauld's presidency. On at least one occasion, he led a number of bishops in directly opposing one of Richelieu's spokesmen as he attempted to justify the latest levy, and in deploring the failure to hold an official assembly. In fact, Richelieu struck the same day as this clash, by forbidding La Rochefoucauld to hold assemblies without formal authorisation from the king.[58] A few days later, it transpired that this ban was general —

---

52. Blet, *Le Clergé de France et la monarchie*, i; pp. 478–86, for the best account.
53. There is a succinct survey of these questions by Blet in his introduction to the *Correspondance du nonce en France Ranuccio Scotti 1639–41* (Rome, 1965), pp. 7ff. Richelieu would only accept Scotti as 'extraordinary' nuncio empowered to deal with the question of peace in Europe, and was insisting that Mazarin be appointed 'ordinary' nuncio to France, with a view to securing a cardinal's hat for him.
54. *Ibid.*, p. 199. Scotti to Barberini, 2 December; Antoine Aubery, *Mémoires pour l'histoire du cardinal-duc de Richelieu* (Paris, 1660), i, p. 417. Twenty-two bishops were in attendance at Ste Geneviève.
55. Aubery, *Mémoires pour l'histoire*, i, pp. 418–19.
56. *Correspondance de Scotti*, p. 321, Scotti to Barberini, 6 January 1640.
57. Blet, *Le Clergé de France et la monarchie*, i, p. 480.
58. *Correspondance de Scotti*, p. 282, Scotti to Barberini, 30 March 1640. The nuncio's reference in this letter to the 'solita assemblea' of bishops at Ste Geneviève suggests that several had been held before this date.

the bishops might not meet anywhere.[59] Already debarred from seeing the nuncio, they were now isolated and helpless. Though in a truculent mood, they were stymied and had no option but to obey a formal royal command.

During the following months, La Rochefoucauld and his closest episcopal associates tried to have new assemblies authorised, and to pave the way for a General Assembly to remove the excessive demands being made of the clergy, as Scotti put it.[60] Richelieu desperately wanted money, but was made to realise the strength of opposition to him when attempts to win over some of his opponents failed. When he finally bowed to pressure for new assemblies, he implicitly acknowledged La Rochefoucauld's peculiar role by insisting that they should *not* take place at his residence. The Archbishop of Bourges was finally prevailed upon to convene them by an adamant Richelieu, and even then the Archbishop of Sens ironically could not be persuaded to attend them until La Rochefoucauld himself requested him to do so.[61] In fact, Richelieu had decided to revoke the financial edicts, and to permit a General Assembly for 1641.[62] The nuncio did not fail to notice that the list of deputies Richelieu wished to see elected to that assembly did not include those who had taken La Rochefoucauld's side in the recent quarrel.[63]

It will come as no surprise that La Rochefoucauld was particularly concerned during this period about the state of Franco-papal relations. Just as the first assemblies were meeting in December 1639, Richelieu began preparations for a national council – a move probably intended to intimidate both pope and nuncio. In doing so, he encouraged the episcopate to believe that they would, through a council, obtain redress of grievances against Rome, notably over the vexed question of the heavy burden on French benefices represented by annates payable to the curia. Scotti, the contested nuncio, fell into a trap laid for him on just this question, with the result that he was denied both royal audiences and all contact with the bishops.[64] However, he did contrive to keep La Rochefoucauld informed of Richelieu's schemes, and reassured Rome that the elder cardinal would always be a 'contrapunto par la sede apostolica all'istesso cardinale di Richelieu'. Scotti was over-personalising the issue, but was right about La Rochefoucauld's loyalties. In the December assemblies, which Scotti followed closely, the cardinal challenged those bishops, especially

59. *Ibid.*, p. 288, Scotti to Barberini, 6 April.
60. *Ibid.*, pp. 406, 409–10, Scotti to Barberini, 9 November 1640; 'per rimediare alli grandi assurdi sopra il clero'.
61. *Ibid.*, p. 418, Scotti to Barberini, 23 November. The Archbishop of Bourges had arued with Richelieu that their usual meeting place was at Ste Geneviève.
62. *Ibid.*, pp. 421–2, Scotti to Barberini, 23 November.
63. *Ibid.* pp. 465–6, Scotti to Barberini, 25 January 1641.
64. *Ibid.*, pp. 207–12, Scotti to Barberini, 9 and 13 December 1639. See also Blet's account of these incidents in his introduction to this volume.

Sourdis of Bordeaux, who wanted open action against Rome on the annates question. He led a number of bishops, among whom those of Sens, Beauvais and Senlis were the most active, in refusing to sign a petition to Louis XIII, asking him to seek a reduction of the annates. Richelieu did his best to prevent this opposition, because by dividing the bishops, it would make his policy towards Rome unworkable.[65] In private, La Rochefoucauld told the nuncio that the issue would disappear of its own accord if the pope undertook to reduce French annates, but he would not publicly be party to any manoeuvre directed against Rome in the name of the French clergy.[66]

La Rochefoucauld also seems to have been the only leading churchman to flout the ban on contact with Scotti. Shortly after it had been imposed, he received the nuncio warmly, regretting the reprisals against him and promising his assistance.[67] No efforts were made to have him respect the ban. Instead, Richelieu tried to warn him not to allow the nuncio to deceive him – an insinuation that he rejected indignantly.[68] Attempts to detach his closest allies on the episcopal bench – the Bishops of Senlis, Pamiers, Sens, and Beauvais – from him proved fruitless, as all declared they would attend no assembly without him.[69]

While Scotti was partly responsible for his own discomfiture, Rome did not underestimate the threat from France, and regularly recommended that he rely on trusted friends of the papacy there. La Rochefoucauld headed Cardinal Barberini's list of pro-papal clergy, and Scotti was advised to concert his defence with him.[70] A papal brief thanking him for his stance had to be presented secretly in March 1640, lest it provoke jealously, or be regarded by the council as a provocation.[71] Later, when the bishops could freely assemble again, Scotti was instructed to oppose the crown's financial expedients, 'relying on the more pious and zealous prelates, and especially on the

65. Aubery, *Mémoires pour l'histoire*, i, pp. 417–19, for the *procès-verbaux* of these assemblies, one of which was not held at Ste Geneviève because of Richelieu's insistence, and at which those present signed the formal record. Richelieu's own fears of La Rochefoucauld's influence, and the tactics needed to overcome it, are clear from his memorandum for Sourdis in *Lettres, instructions diplomatiques et papiers d'état du cardinal de Richelieu* ed. D.L.M. Avenel (Paris, 1853–77), vi, pp. 652–3, 17 December 1639.
66. *Correspondance de Scotti*, 585; *Mémoires de Montchal archevêque de Toulouse* (Rotterdam, 1718) i, pp. 54ff. Montchal was one of Richelieu's bitterest enemies during this dispute, and he was to be expelled by the cardinal from the ensuing General Assembly of the clergy in 1641.
67. *Correspondance de Scotti*, pp. 209–12, Scotti to Barberini, 13 December 1639.
68. *Ibid.*, p. 216, Scotti to Barberini, 20 December, Richelieu acted through the intermediary of Chavigny, the secretary of state for foreign affairs.
69. *Ibid.*, p. 216, note: letter from Oratorian Bertin to Scotti, *c.* 16 December. The bishops involved with those of Sens, Beauvais, Senlis and Pamiers.
70. *Ibid.*, pp. 221, 229–30, 233, 249, Barberini to Scotti, 23 December 1639, 6 and 7 January 1640.
71. *Ibid.*, p. 260, Berberini to Scotti, 14 February 1640; *ibid.*, p. 273, Scotti's reply, 9 March.

authority of cardinal de La Rochefoucauld'.[72] But the conflict abated and the cardinal's 'authority' was no longer needed.

The Ste Geneviève assemblies continued almost until La Rochefoucauld's death in February 1645, and were not only a distinctive feature of the life of the French church, but clear proof of La Rochefoucauld's unique position in its affairs. As he grew older, he was doubtless unable to organise personally what he saw as the defence of the church's interests, and it seems that many of the initiatives were taken by younger prelates – Sanguin, his successor at Senlis, Potier of Beauvais and others. But it is equally clear that without his 'autorità', which we can legitimately translate as leadership, none of this might have happened at all, or even if it had, would probably have led nowhere. Without his protection, few of them would have dared taking any risks when there was conflict with the *parlement* or the council. And only he would take the risk of giving the lead and putting into words the thoughts and complaints of many of the bishops. He was far less amenable to pressure, or to the prospects of advancement or punishment than the great majority of them. It would be wrong, however, to see him as leading an Ultramontane rump or an anti-Richelieu faction because, with the possible exception of the 1639–41 period, neither he nor the French episcopate regarded Richelieu as their enemy and oppressor. La Rochefoucauld only opposed Richelieu's designs when he saw them as an attack on clerical immunity and relations with Rome. Nor was he a firebrand who was ready to rush into action at the slightest sign of trouble. He was a cautious, conservative Ultramontane who, as we have seen, would hesitate before embarking on a course of action which might lead to a collision with the crown, whose support for his other reform projects was of great importance to him.

III

At the same time, however, La Rochefoucauld's leadership did not command universal support among the French clergy. He was far more Ultramontane than most of the bishops, and made very few apologies for being so. Bérulle alluded quite clearly to this when he referred to a French bishop in 1629 as 'learned and virtuous, but with a reputation of being entirely of the same mind as cardinal de La Rochefoucauld, and of being dominated by the Jesuits'.[73] La Rochefoucauld was quick to spot conspiracy and schism where others might not, or were more

72. *Ibid.*, p. 435, Barberini to Scotti, 17 December 1640, 'valendosi de prelati maggiormente pii et più zelanti, e dell' autorita del signore cardinale de Rochefoucauld'.
73. *Correspondance de Bérulle*, iii, p. 494, Bérulle to Richelieu, 27 June 1629; 'docte et vertueus, mais il est en la réputation publique d'estre tout dans les sentimens du cardinal de la Rochefoucault, et en la main des Jésuites'.

tolerant. And in the major conflicts, at least from that of 1626 onwards, there were always dissenters among the episcopate who, whether out of principle or self-interest, found his zeal in defending papal interests excessive. But there is another factor, to which we must now turn, which prevented him from winning the confidence of a broader spectrum of the French clergy: his long-standing defence of the regular clergy against their critics.

We have already noted the main reasons for the revival of the quarrel between the secular and regular clergy in the early seventeenth century. The question of papal authority, which was the foundation of the orders' privileges, had always been central to it, but the nature and extent of episcopal authority was an increasingly passionate issue in the French church. The Council of Trent had nearly foundered altogether by attempting to delimit papal and episcopal authority, and in the end had taken refuge in studied evasion and ambiguity.[74] The French church, because of Gallican traditions, tended to maximise episcopal power at the expense of that of the papacy. Arguably, attempts at reform in the early seventeenth century strengthened rather than weakened this pre-disposition. Bishops were angered at papal support for the regulars against their ordinances, and few dioceses were entirely free of some form of conflict. If Ultramontane views appealed to many bishops in the face of secular intervention and the refusal to accept Trent's legislation, the attitude of the papacy (and the regulars) probably serve to dampen their attractiveness.[75] Like many other bishops, La Rochefoucauld insisted, in his own Senlis statutes, on members of the orders having prior episcopal permission before they could perform religious or pastoral functions in his diocese. This may make his strong defence of the regulars difficult to explain but, as far as we can judge, his statutes were not intended as an expression of militant episcopalism; the loss of his episcopal archives makes it impossible to tell how much actual conflict there may have been in Clermont and Senlis.[76] Besides, the Jesuits were increasingly the spokesmen for the religious orders, and tact or deference was not always their dominant characteristic in controversy. It was largely through his close connection with the Jesuits that La Rochefoucauld was drawn into the conflict.

Even before his critique of the Bishops of Paris and Orléans between 1618 and 1623, La Rochefoucauld was well known as a defender of the regulars. But it was in 1625–6, at the same times as the Etampes

74. See Hubert Jedin, *Geschichte des Konzils von Trient*, iv, part ii (Freiburg-im-Breisgau, 1975); there is a brief summary of the Tridentine debates in A.D. Wright, *The Counter-Reformation* (London, 1982), pp. 103–4.
75. Charles de Chesneau, *Le Père Yves de Paris et son temps* (Meaux, 1946–8), i, ch. 1.
76. B.S.G., MS. 3238, fos. 209–10, memorandum in the hand of Etienne Binet, S.J., one of La Rochefoucauld's advisers at Senlis, on the limits of episcopal authority over regulars. This suggests that the cardinal was looking for an acceptable solution within his own diocese.

censure, that he became publicly identified in this role. He was involved in 1625 in what was known as the Louytre affair, which only gradually came to centre on the regulars. Initially, the question was whether a papal-judge delegate, Etienne Louytre, could act against a recalcitrant bishop protecting a group of Carmelites who were in turn defying their superiors.[77] As Louytre was merely dean of a chapter, the bishops of the 1625 assembly indignantly rejected his right to place an interdict on one of their members, and forced him to apologise for doing so. During its discussions, however, the assembly was informed of widespread insubordination by the regulars to the bishops. Tempers rose sharply, and the clergy drafted a long *règlement* subjecting the regulars to rigorous episcopal control. La Rochefoucauld did not attend the assembly, but was concerned insofar as the offending Louytre had received his papal commission through him and Cardinal La Valette. Naturally enough, the assembly asked him to dissociate himself from Louytre, although there is no evidence that he did. He was all the more unlikely to have agreed with the assembly as Cardinal Barberini, who was then on a mission to France, was insisting that a delegate could use papal powers against a bishop; and he would have had little difficulty in accepting the papal request, contained in special briefs dispatched to him and La Vallette, that the Louytre censure and the *règlement* be withdrawn.[78] In due course, the assembly modified its assertions, and did so under the influence of prelates close to La Rochefoucauld.

At the same time, the cardinal became even more directly involved in another celebrated controversy – the Santarelli affair. When the Jesuit Santarelli's *Tractatus de haeresi* appeared in early 1626, the *parlement* pounced on it, forcing the French Jesuits to disown this extreme papalist statement and, more menacingly, to accept whatever censure the Paris theology faculty might pass on it. The old battles resumed within the faculty, and in April 1626, André du Val and the Ultramontanes failed to prevent hastily-convened assemblies from drafting a detailed censure, which inevitably meant a positive assertion of the opposite, Gallican view.[79] Desperate, the nuncio Spada sought but failed to obtain Richelieu's help – the latter seems to have have been pleased to see the Jesuits suffer for their audacity.[80] At the same

---

77. For the background to this affair, see Michel Houssaye, *La Vie du cardinal de Bérulle* (Paris, 1872–5), ii, *passim*; Blet, *Le Clergé de France et la monarchie*, i, pp. 296ff.
78. Blet, *Le Clergé de France et la monarchie*, i, pp. 310ff.
79. See Victor Martin, *Le Gallicanisme politique et le clergé de France*, pp. 163ff, for the background to this dispute.
80. In December 1625, Richelieu issued a remarkable warning to the new royal confessor, Jean Suffren: 'Faites que vos pères se rendent soumis en ce qui se doit aux ordinaires, qui sont les puissances légitimes establies par l'Eglise...que vos superieurs prennent soigneusement garde, je vous prie, qu'aucuns de vostre compagnie ne fassent imprimer des livres contenant de mauvaises maximes contre les justes règles des Etats': *Les Papiers de Richelieu*, i, p. 239.

time, the Jesuits were being criticised by the learned abbé de St Cyran, whose attack on them revealed him as a champion of episcopal authority as well as of rigorous religious standards.[81]

As might be expected, Urban VIII spoke of schism in France, and of the faculty turning into a dangerous Gallican stronghold. He criticised the French Jesuits for surrendering so easily and demanded a revocation of the censure.[82] In May 1626, the Jesuit general, Vitelleschi, directed his members to take their lead from Spada and La Rochefoucauld.[83] Spada was obviously the more active of the two men, and La Rochefoucauld's involvement in the early stages of the controversy is hard to pinpoint. But his encounters with Richer had alerted him to the danger of a Gallican faculty that would be a natural ally of the *parlement*. Even before Vitelleschi's letter arrived, he had begun to exert himself. When the Jesuits complained to Louis XIII in March 1626 of the *parlement*'s vindictiveness, it was he who presented their petition for redress.[84] With Richelieu unhelpful, Spada relied on La Rochefoucauld to present the papal position in council. He went to council on the day on which the faculty was due to censure Santarelli but was not invited to attend council — Richelieu knew the sort of thing he would say.[85] During these weeks, frequent meetings of Ultramontane members of the faculty occurred at Ste Geneviève, and Archbishop Harlay later denounced La Rochefoucauld to Louis XIII for plotting with them to reverse the faculty's decision.[86]

The court spent much of 1626 in western France, so that La Rochefoucauld and the Ultramontanes achieved little, but they remained determined to remove the censure from the faculty's registers. Pressure produced a decree of the royal council reserving cognisance of the issue to itself, but both the *parlement* and the faculty ignored it, as it had been issued from Nantes.[87] A further, though partial victory, was the decision to allow those doctors who were members of the orders to return to the faculty's assemblies, from which they had been excluded during the act of censure.[88] But Richelieu, who was provisor of the Sorbonne, was in no hurry to go any further. La Rochefoucauld and Marillac both attempted to

81. Jean Orcibal, *Jean Duvergier de Hauranne, abbé de Saint-Cyran, et son temps* [*Les Origines du Jansenisme*, ii] (Louvain-Paris, 1947), pp. 260ff.
82. Cardinal Marquemont to Louis XIII, Rome, March 1626, in J.M. Prat, *Recherches historiques et critiques sur la compagnie de Jésus en France* (Lyon, 1876–8), v, pp. 466–70.
83. Vitelleschi to French provincial superiors, 5 May 1626, in Henri Fouqueray, *Histoire de la compagnie de Jésus en France* (Paris, 1910–25), iv, pp. 188–9.
84. Prat, *Recherches*, v, pp. 475–9, Ignace Armand S.J. to Vitelleschi, 26 March.
85. B.N., MS. Italien 64, fos. 20–7, Spada to Barberini, 10 April.
86. B.N., MS. Italien 65, fo. 212, Spada to Barberini, 22 June. It was the king himself who confirmed Harlay's denunciation of the cardinal to him.
87. *Collectio iudiciorum de novis erroribus*, ed. Charles du Plessis d'Argentré (Paris, 1728), ii, pp. 222–3.
88. *Ibid.*, p. 223.

maintain pressure on him, and La Rochefoucauld seems to have attended council more assiduously during the second phase of the conflict (November 1626 to February 1627).[89] The pressure finally told and, on instructions from Richelieu, the faculty revoked the censure on 2 January.[90] The following month was hectic, as faculty decisions had to be confirmed by its next assembly. Du Val wished to see La Rochefoucauld pressurise the faculty by holding assemblies at Ste Geneviève, but it is not clear that he did so.[91] With the original censure revoked, Rome was determined there should not be another, however vague, while Richelieu believed that something was necessary in order to placate the *parlement* and the faculty. But the council's decision to entrust the drafting of a new censure to a group of prelates, betrays the hand of La Rochefoucauld, Marillac and Spada whose clear intention it was that the whole affair be buried quietly.[92]

The Santarelli case thus ended, like the Etampes censure, on a note of ambiguity. The regulars and Ultramontanes may have won some tactical victories, but they were nevertheless the real losers. The faculty had moved a step closer to its Gallican declaration of 1664, while the Ultramontanes realised how shaky their position was: they could only hold on by avoiding open discussion of the central issues and by confining the debate to questions of form and procedure; even Du Val could only air his views publicly by modifying them considerably.

In his *Raisons pour le desaveu*, composed during the Santarelli affair, La Rochefoucauld linked the latter to the Etampes controversy, though not explicitly to St Cyran's attacks, seeing the common Gallican enemy at work in both. The *Raisons* also contained a strong defence of the place of the orders in the church, with two chapters being particularly fulsome in their praise of the Jesuits.[93] There was no sign of concession or compromise in such views.

With the 1625–7 controversies proving inconclusive, renewed disputes were virtually inevitable. The bishops grew more militant and, after 1625, came to appreciate the value of collective action. This became clear for all to see in the conflicts of 1630–3, the last in which La Rochefoucauld seems to have played a part. This time the conflict originated in England, where the Jesuits refused to accept the

89. B.N., MS. Italien 64, fo. 190, Spada to Barberini, 18 December 1626; *ibid.*, fo. 132, to same, 10 November; fo. 203, undated memorandum on case; *ibid.*, fo. 209, Spada to Barberini, 22 February 1627.
90. *Collectio iudiciorum*, ii, p. 251.
91. A.S.V., Nunz. Fr. 416, fo. 196, unsigned and undated *billet* to La Rochefoucauld, probably from du Val.
92. *Collectio iudiciorum*, ii, p. 225; B.N., MS. Italien 64, fo. 211, Spada to Barberini, 22 February 1627.
93. *Raisons*, pp. 171–96. Indeed, in an appendix to the work, a number of documents relating to the Santarelli case are published.

authority of the Apostolic Delegate, Richard Smith, who arrived in France under Richelieu's protection, and looked to the bishops to defend his cause. They did so all the more willingly as the English regulars had impugned episcopal authority, openly asserting that a church could function without bishops at all, and that the religious life was superior to all other conditions. Crucial issues seemed to be at stakes, and passions were inflamed all the more easily, as some of the best propagandists of the age took part.[94]

The flames were kindled in mid-1631 by the circulation of attacks on Smith, allegedly by Jesuits. The bishops were quickly drawn into the dispute, rejecting papal efforts at mediation as too biased towards the regulars. Rumours of censures, book-burnings and a national council spread. Meetings were held at Ste Geneviève to enable La Rochefoucauld to restore peace. But by October 1631, according to the nuncio Bichi, La Rochefoucauld was so concerned at a schism provoked by the bishops that he had no success; by now tempers had risen too much for a simple compromise to be acceptable. Even Richelieu failed to impose silence on the participants. Rival assemblies met, and thundered against each other. Knowing where La Rochefoucauld's sympathies lay, at least in this instance, the bishops ceased to assemble at Ste Geneviève, removing themselves from any influence he might have had on their declarations.[95]

The departure of the court to Lorraine in early 1632 restored La Rochefoucauld to the centre stage. Before leaving, the king attempted, but to no avail, to impose silence on both parties. Châteauneuf, the keeper of the seals, was inundated with requests from the bishops for a free hand to deal once and for all with the regulars: the opportunity seemed too good to miss.[96] Angry at being abandoned by the papacy, the bishops questioned the latter's right to grant privileges that were prejudicial to episcopal authority. Realising where events were heading, Richelieu and the king ordered the bishops home, but this move, too, was ignored, the bishops even sending a delegation to plead their case in Lorraine.[97]

La Rochefoucauld then intervened, on 29 March 1632, with a full blast of his own – an open letter to the king warning him of the danger of schism and reminding him that he had both the power and the duty of maintaining unity in both church and state. With the connivance of

94. See Orcibal, *St Cyran et son temps*, pp. 335ff; Chesneau, *Le Père Yves de Paris*, i, pp. 34ff.
95. A.S.V., Nunz. Fr. 74, fos. 151–5, Bichi, papal nuncio, to Barberini, 7 June 1631; *ibid.*, fos. 161–2, Barberini to Bichi, 12 July; *ibid.*, fos. 174–5, Bichi to Barberini, 24 July; Nunz. Fr. 74A, fo. 21, Barberini to Bichi, 21 July; *ibid.*, fos. 159–60, Bichi to Barberini, 28 October; *ibid.*, fo. 164v, to same, 5 November; Nunz. Fr. 76, fos. 222–5, to same, 9 September 1632.
96. A.A.E., Mems et docs., France 802, fo. 64, 19 March; *ibid.*, fo. 77, 27 March.
97. A.S.V., Nunz. Fr. 76, fos. 222–3, Bichi to Barberini, 9 September 1632.

ecclesiastics whom he did not name, that unity was now threatened.[98]

In fact, this initiative of his took place with Richelieu's prior knowledge, for a few days earlier his confident, Père Joseph, had approached La Rochefoucauld with a view to ending the conflict.[99] Richelieu doubtless hoped to divide the bishops, thus facilitating more decisive royal action later. The open letter to Louis XIII was accompanied by a private one to Père Joseph, expressing confidence in the king's resolution.[100] This augured badly for the bishops, as Père Joseph was a strong advocate of the regulars' position. At any rate, La Rochefoucauld's next step was to summon, with royal approval, an assembly of doctors of theology to examine the signs of schism. Three of them agreed with the cardinal's own diagnosis, and asked the king to impose silence while a settlement was negotiated; the fourth expressed reservations favourable to the bishops.[101] Simultaneously, a group of regulars assembled by Père Joseph conceded that episcopal permission was necessary before they could preach or confess, but they did so on the virtually impossible condition that the papacy would agree to this.[102] This only led to further controversy, since the bishops wanted to force the regulars to agree to their concession without any such reservation. Further assemblies were held by both sides, and deadlock ensued.

La Rochefoucauld's initiative thus failed. His letter and the *avis* of the doctors both annoyed the bishops and isolated him further. In the Sorbonne's assemblies, the bishops abetted reprisals against the doctors concerned, but for the moment, they and La Rochefoucauld were secure behind royal protection.[103] The principal episcopal leaders, Toulouse, Bordeaux and Beauvais, demanded important concessions from the orders, and regarded La Rochefoucauld's mediation as dangerous to their cause, emboldening the orders as it did to remain obstinate.[104] Potier of Beauvais, usually so close to the cardinal, insisted that he be excluded from all further discussions, while Sourdis argued that the *avis* had been extorted unwillingly from

---

98. B.S.G., MS. 3238, fos. 331–2, letter to Louis XIII. He enclosed a memorandum on the affair for the king, but no trace of it has survived.
99. A.A.E., Mems. et docs., France 804, fo. 86, La Rochefoucauld to Richelieu, 29 March: 'Je prends occasion sur ce que le R.P. Joseph me dit il y a quelques jours de vostre part d'écrire au Roy et à vous sur mesme suiet duquel vous scaves mieux que moy le mal et le remède.'
100. B.L., MS. Egerton 1673, p. 358.
101. B.S.G.. MS. 3238, fos. 246–7, *avis* dated 2 April. The doctors agreeing with La Rochefoucauld were well-known Ultramontanes: Du Val, Isambert and Cornet.
102. Chesneau, *Le Père Yves de Paris*, i, p. 81. The phrase used was 'sub beneplacito Apostolicae Sedis'.
103. A.S.V., Nunz. Fr. 76, fos. 222–5, Bichi's report on the quarrel, 9 September 1632.
104. *Ibid.*, fos. 227–8, for a statement of the bishops' demands: that the regulars condemn their anti-Smith publications, accept that they could only preach with episcopal licence, and that this licence could be withdrawn at episcopal discretion.

the doctors.[105] Potier later added that if some of the bishops had their way and were to reassemble at Ste Geneviève, La Rochefoucauld and his friends would be enabled to prevent any action at all against the regulars.[106]

A rational solution to the quarrel between the seculars and the regulars was probably impossible in the religious climate of the early 1630s. La Rochefoucauld was held in high respect by both sides, but his mediation was not even-handed. If he failed to resolve the quarrel, he did a great deal to save the regulars from the full brunt of the bishops' onslaught, at a time when the regulars did not have many friends. His action served to divide the episcopate, and to secure a vital measure of powerful protection for the orders. Most of all, the disputes show the isolation of La Rochefoucauld from all but a handful of like-minded Ultramontanes in a matter that increasingly pre-occupied the upper clergy. Many of them blamed him for deserting the episcopal cause and for allowing himself to be led by the Jesuits. Archbishop Harlay for one complained bitterly in 1633 of the immunity enjoyed by the regulars, and of La Rochefoucauld's assistance to their cause: 'Les religieux traitent de leurs affaires comme il leur plait; quand l'alarme est au camp, le tocsin sonne à Sainte Geneviève'.[107]

Of course, it is by now hardly necessary to point out that the obvious additional clue to La Rochefoucauld's defence of the regulars is indisputably his closeness to the Jesuits. It is here that his involvement in the controversies of the last decades of his career leads us back, finally and briefly, to biography. La Rochefoucauld was a man of strong commitments and strong loyalties, as we shall see again in later chapters, and his loyalty to the Jesuits was among the strongest of them all. As Bishop of Clermont, he engineered their return there after the edict of 1603. When he was made a cardinal in 1607, the Jesuit general asked him to assume the role of protector of the order; although he declined the title, he replied that he would prefer to serve the Society in a humbler fashion.[108] There can be no doubt that he did so, and both then and later he did much to endow Jesuit houses financially, and support their teaching and pastoral activities. This was a natural corollary to the extensive use he made of their services in his successive dioceses. The College of Clermont and the Paris Jesuits generally also experienced patronage and endowment at his hands, notably around 1605 and again in 1637.[109] In both 1617 and 1625, he was intrumental in ensuring that the new royal confessor would be a Jesuit, a post that was essential to the order's survival in a hostile

105. A.A.E., Mems, et docs., France 804, fo. 196, Sourdis to Richelieu, 15 June 1632.
106. *Ibid.*, fos. 216–17, Potier to Richelieu, 28 June.
107. Quoted in Chesneau, *Le Père Yves de Paris*, i, 136.
108. A.R.S.I., Francia, Epistolae Generalium 2, fo. 211, Vitelleschi to La Rochefoucauld, 11 December 1607; *ibid.*, Gallia 35, unfoliated, La Rochefoucauld's reply.

environment.[110] Ten years later, in 1635, he went even further, and requested papal permission to lay aside his rank of cardinal in order to end his days as a simple member of the order. At seventy-seven, he could hardly expect to live much longer, and he may have felt a need for a kind of retirement distinguished by total withdrawal from church affairs, but it must be said that we know nothing of the background to this extraordinary request. Perhaps the difficulties he experienced in reforming the religious orders and the endless disputes to which it give rise, drove him to seek a final refuge. It appears that the Jesuit general obtained the consent of Cardinal Barberini, but repeated requests failed to move Urban VIII, who decided that neither the cardinal's age nor his station made such a change appropriate. No doubt, the pope had a keener appreciation than those around him of the reaction which such a concession might provoke. Instead, Vitelleschi was empowered to permit La Rochefoucauld to take Jesuit vows on his deathbed and to be buried in a Jesuit habit.[111]

Despite Urban VIII's refusal of his request, La Rochefoucauld was virtually a Jesuit cardinal in his last years. His confessor and director of conscience had both been Jesuits for many years, and a some point he may have formally bound himself not to take any important decision without consulting them in advance. The consequences of this worried some of his advisers, especially where decisions concerning the other orders were concerned, but he adhered to his resolution.[112] It seems, therefore, entirely fitting that, at the end of an immensely long career, he should, in his testament, have left his books and his heart to his *alma mater*, the College of Clermont.[113] In the words of a motto he would have understood, *finis coronat opus*.

109. For his patronage of the Auvergne houses, see Fouqueray, *Histoire de la compagnie de Jésus en France*, iii. pp. 57–60. For Paris: A.R.S.I., Francia 36–7, fos. 173–83, documents relating to houses bought and refurbished in Paris around 1605 and later by La Rochefoucauld, and then given to the college; A.N., M 241, unfoliated, Louis XIII to La Rochefoucauld, 14 October 1621, giving permission to 'incorporate' a number of benefices in favour of the Jesuits; B.N., MS. Latin 9758, fos. 169–70.
110. B.L., Addit. MS. 8730, fos. 164–5, *avviso* of 2 January 1626.
111. Rouvier, *Vita*, pp. 87–8, Vitelleschi to Etienne Binet, S.J., 12 September 1636. This is the only source of Vitelleschi's letter, of which no manuscript copy appears to have survived. Rouvier declared that he published it 'nullo mutato auspice'.
112. B.S.G., MS. 3281, fo. 80, François Boulard, prior of Ste Geneviève, to Charles Faure, coadjutor-abbot of the monastery, 9 May 1636: 'Monseigneur le Cardinal veut communiquer les affaires que scaves au PP. Bony et Royer, et luy ay dit que ce seroit tout gaster. . .il m'a fait responce. . .que pour l'asseurance de sa conscience il ne pouvoir rien faire sans leur communiquer'.
113. B.S.G., MS. 745, for the text of La Rochefoucauld's will and the various codicils to it.

4

The Bishop as Reformer

I

LA ROCHEFOUCAULD'S episcopal career spanned nearly forty years, a length of service not wholly uncommon in a time when preferment came at an early age. The reputation he gained as a bishop led some contemporaries and biographers, as well as later historians, to refer to him as mentioned earlier as the Charles Borromeo of France. But the meaning of this title, which was also attributed to other reformers besides the cardinal, has never been wholly clear. It is difficult to tell whether it is to be taken as signifying that he was directly dependent on Borromeo, or that he was the French church's equivalent of Milan's reforming archishop.[1] It is of more significance for our purposes that La Rochefoucauld was one of the most distinguished of that neglected and largely unstudied first generation of post-Tridentine reformers in France whose labours, often incomplete or unsuccessful as they were, laid the foundations for the far better-known generations that followed them.[2] There have, of course, been exceptions in this chronicle of neglect: it is striking that Louis Cognet, in a brief but authoritative survey of the seventeenth-century French church, actually took La Rochefoucauld as both model and yardstick with which to evaluate this first generation of churchmen, using his successes and failures as an index of what was possible in the years following the wars of religion.[3]

Study of La Rochefoucauld as bishop is beset by some severe

1 See Pual Broutin, *La Réforme pastorale en France au xviie siècle*, 2 vols. (Brussels, 1956). See Above, p. 14, n. 22.
2. There are brief attempts to rescue them from oblivion in Marc Venard, 'France: le xvie siècle' in *Dictionnaire d'histoire et de géographie ecclésiastiques*, xviii, cols. 51–78; Robert Sauzet, in *Histoire des catholiques en France*, ed. François Lebrun (Toulouse, 1980), pp. 94ff.
3. *History of the Church*, ed. Hubert Jedin (London, 1980), vi, ch. 1, especially pp. 20–1. The original German edition of this work was published in 1970.

difficulties. The virtual disappearance of his episcopal archives at both Clermont and Senlis is the most serious of these, especially in view of recent advances in the study of early modern French Catholicism, based mainly on intensive study of episcopal and other archives. We are, therefore, vouchsafed only episodic, fragmentary glimpses of his actual work as a bishop. But we should miss the opportunity of seeing the essential continuity of his career if we were to pass over these decades in silence on such grounds alone. Some important non-archival sources have survived — books, synodal statutes, directives, acts of foundation and so on — though even these are not especially abundant. Works of this kind, as well as the archival sources that we do possess, enable us to study his views upon the clerical estate, and the requirements of reform among both clergy and laity. Indeed, the 'realism' that characterises these 'literary' sources, especially his *Estat ecclésiastique*, with their diagnosis of the state of the church, compensates in no small measure for the paucity of archival material. They also enjoy the positive merit of affording a direct insight into the mind of a major reformer — a feature which is rare in studies that draw heavily or exclusively on archival records. La Rochefoucauld's *Estat ecclésiastique*, conceived as an instrument of reform, incorporated ten years of action and reflection. His statutes, directives and consultations with advisers, show him attempting to match his ideas to the realities of his diocese, even though we cannot learn from this type of document how successful his labours were.

It can be said at the outset that La Rochefoucauld stands firmly in the mainstream of post-Tridentine thought on church reform, and that he played a prominent part in the French church's principal contribution to the Counter-Reformation — the ideal of the clergy.[4] This new ideal was initially forged in Italy and Spain, mostly in the wake of the Council of Trent. France produced relatively few new ideas after Clichtove and the early sixteenth-century humanists.[5] It is clear that in the late sixteenth century, *dévots* and reformers alike were heavily dependent upon works imported and translated from Italian and Spanish: new French editions of writers like John of the Cross, Teresa of Avila, Luis de Granada and others appeared almost every year, while original French authors of any real stature were infrequent until well into the next century.[6]

Yet we possess an unusual but valuable document with which to trace some of the origins and stimuli to La Rochefoucauld's reforming

---

4. See the recent judgement of him by Robert Sauzet: 'son oeuvre...exposant un idéal clérical tout tridentin' (*Histoire des catholiques en France*, p. 126.)
5. For earlier French developments, see Jean-Pierre Massaut, *Josse Clichtove, l'humanisme et la réforme du clergé*, (Paris, 1968) vol. ii.
6. This is clear from Jean Dagens, *Bibliographie chronologique de la littérature de la spiritualité et de ses sources 1500–1601* (Paris, 1952).

activity – a catalogue of his books made in 1621. This is not a full inventory of his library, but rather a list of the books he kept, presumably for regular consultation, in his private oratory.[7] The date of the catalogue, of course, makes it impossible to say what precisely he was reading in the 1580s and 1590s, but it leaves no doubt as to his strong and abiding interest in reformist spirituality. We find in it all the great sixteenth-century religious authors. There are no fewer than twenty-six volumes of Luis de Granada, the Spaniard who exercised such influence on Borromeo and his Italian contemporaries, and who has been described as 'un des théologiens espagnols du seizième siècle qui ont eu le plus d'influence en France'.[8] The cardinal's collection also contains lives of Borromeo himself, as well as his *Acta Ecclesiae Mediolanensis*, that indispensable handbook for generations of Catholic reformers. Louis de Blois and François de Sales, another alumnus of the College of Clermont, are both well represented. There are also a large number of small, unknown works of a traditional devotional and historical kind. Works of controversy and of ecclesiastical history, born of the religious divisions of the age, also figure very prominently: the anti-Huguenot polemics of Du Perron and Jean Bodin, the histories of Baronius and Henri de Sponde, and no fewer than ten volumes of Bellarmine. Such a collection faithfully reflects La Rochefoucauld's abiding interest in the defence and the reform of the church, and it comes as no surprise that his own major works, both of which appeared in 1597, deal with just these questions.

The *Authorité de l'Eglise* need not detain us long. Written in defence of the church and drawing heavily on Bellarmine, it placed the emphasis very clearly on the authority of the infallible church as the basis and foundation of truth. But, apart from polemic against the Protestant churches, the book also reflected its author's acute concern for the future of the French church at the end of the religious wars. Recent conversions in 1596–7 gave him grounds for cautious hope, and his conclusion served as a kind of preamble to the more interesting *Estat ecclésiastique*, the final chapters of which also returned, despite the very different content of the book, to these same themes of hope and survival.[9]

La Rochefoucauld's passionate defence of the church, which included many harsh words for the Protestant reformers, did not blind him to its defects. His *Estat ecclésiastique*, addressed to the clergy of Clermont diocese, constantly denounced the clergy for bringing the

7. B.S.G., MS. 2131, fos.6–22. The document is dated 12 August 1621, and the books are simply described as belonging to 'Monseigneur'. That this refers to La Rochefoucauld is clear from his letter of 15 August 1621 to his secretary, Desbois, asking him to send him the inventory: B.S.G. MS. 3238, fo.530.
8. Jean Quéniart, *Les Hommes, l'église et dieu dans la France du xviii*ᵉ *siècle*, p. 72.
9. *Auctorité de l'église*, pp. 474–5; *Estate ecclésiastique*, bk. iv, chs. 18–20.

church into its present state. His was not, of course, the only voice raised against abuses at this time, but we must examine what he singled out for criticism if we are to understand the remedies he went on to propose. The *Estat*, in which he admitted that he had himself achieved very little as bishop, brought together the experience of ten years of an active episcopate, and illustrated his resolve to persevere in his efforts at reform. It is a treatise upon the clergy, as seen through the eyes of an ex-Leaguer and reforming bishop. Although it has often been referred to by historians, it has not so far received the close study it deserves as a comprehensive introduction to the early phase of the 'renaissance religieuse' of the seventeenth century.

For La Rochefoucauld, reform should never lose sight of the multiple causes of the church's deplorable state. Although he was a harsh critic of clerical failings, he did not believe that these were the only source of the current malaise, and he provided his own reading of ecclesiastical history in order to explain how the church had become entangled in the concerns and values of secular society.[10] Like most reformers, both Protestant and Catholic, he considered the early church to be the golden age of religion – a time when the church, existing as it did on the margins of Greco-Roman society, was able to preserve its purity. The decline in its primitive fervour had brought in its train an increasing reliance on the secular power to defend its authority. Since the time of Constantine, the church and the 'world' had become co-terminous; the values of each were inextricably confused in men's minds; indeed, the 'world' was now inside the church itself. The church had, accordingly, never completed its mission of Christianising the 'world'.[11] Proof of this abounded. The present state of the church bore witness to the ways in which its great wealth and endowments had made it a prime target for the ambitions of individuals and families. Secular rulers had not been slow to lay their hands on the church, and they had all too frequently enjoyed the support or collusion of churchmen too weak to resist. La Rochefoucauld lamented that, while in ordinary life men were careful as to whom they selected for office, they had come to regard the church as a suitable career even for the least endowed, both intellectually and physically, of their children.[12] Such careerism had led to the thoughtless plundering of benefices, with the smallest of them becoming so impoverished that they could attract only destitute and unworthy ecclesiastics.[13]

The most significant result of this pattern of behaviour was the church's loss of autonomy, especially in the choice of personnel. La Rochefoucauld deplored the way in which rulers had defied canon law,

10. *Estat*, pp. 67–8.
11. *Ibid.*, pp. 253, 297–9.
12. *Ibid.*, pp. 89–91.
13. *Ibid.*, pp. 201–2.

arrogating rights to nominate to benefices and abolishing elections.[14]
With nominations to lesser benefices in the hands of lay patrons,
chapters and monasteries, well-intentioned bishops were powerless,
and the episcopal right to scrutinise all candidates for orders was
difficult to use effectively. As he admitted, the reintroduction of strict
standards would lead to vacant parishes, and this was an even greater
evil.[15] Clerics who had not been ordained priests could obtain parish
benefices in order to draw their revenues, and put in vicars to perform
their duties for them.[16] La Rochefoucauld had the lowest opinion of
these vicars: they were illiterate vagrants, ordained in some other
diocese, and perpetually on the lookout for a benefice of their own.
Such anarchy, which made it easy to subvert what remained of
episcopal power over both the clergy and the laity, was destructive of
both order and hierarchy in the church.[17] Here, as throughout the
Estat, La Rochefoucauld might quote the Bible and the Fathers of the
Church, but what he wrote was both a close commentary on the
general condition of the late sixteenth-century French church, and of
the diocese of Clermont in particular.

If these were abuses that La Rochefoucauld considered common to
the whole church, there were others that were particularly endemic in
France. He devoted considerable attention to them, as part of his effort
to inform and reform the clergy. Indeed, in more than one case, he
ceased quoting his usual biblical or patristic authorities altogether –
the abuses were too recent for that to make much sense – and took
pains to cite and explain recent papal pronouncements, with some of
his examples coming from his own diocese of Clermont.

Although simony was not a uniquely French vice, he alleged that it
had reached alarming proportions in that country. The religious wars,
which had seen many benefices fall into lay hands, aggravated the
situation, and the clergy were now so accustomed to purchasing
benefices that they considered it perfectly normal and acceptable. In
such circumstances, it was not surprising that they tried to recoup
their losses by demanding money for performing religious services[18]
Remedying this was an urgent priority of reform for La Rochefoucauld.
By contrast, the *confidence*, the practice whereby a cleric nominally held
a benefice in trust for a layman who drew its revenues, seemed to him
to be peculiarly French. What dismayed him most was that its

14. *Ibid.*, pp. 355ff, 702.
15. *Ibid.*, pp. 317–18.
16. These men were often ordained in very undemanding conditions. For evidence that large
    numbers of men from the Auvergne went to Avignon in the sixteenth century to seek
    ordination, see Marc Venard, 'Pour une sociologie du clergé au xvi^c siècle: recherches sur
    le recrutement sacerdotal dans la province d'Avignon', *Annales: économies, sociétés,
    civilisations* (1968), p. 1006.
17. *Estat*, pp. 241–2.
18. *Ibid.*, pp. 168–91.

illegality was so generally ignored, and he thus went to great lengths to explain to his readers just why it was so objectionable, citing and commenting on recent papal condemnations.[19]

Simony and *confidence* might be symptoms of the dominance of worldly values within the church, but La Rochefoucauld recognised that both required clerical connivance to work at all. Some of his harshest words were accordingly reserved for a clergy so ignorant of the dignity of their state and calling as to permit such abuses. The church was not the innocent, protesting victim of lay tyranny; the clergy were principally responsible for its pitiful state.[20] It was dishonest to claim that lay hostility was directed at the church, and not at its unworthy pastors. To pretend otherwise was to defend not the church, but rather clerical privilege. He went on to launch a scathing attack on the exercise of church authority in a manner directly contradictory to Christ's teaching: church censures — even excommunication — had become objects of derision from their over-use by clergy pursuing personal ambitions or antipathies.[21] Grasping and arrogant clerics had forgotten that the real end of authority in the church was the service of the people.[22] The French clergy, he concluded, were an only too faithful reflection of the society in which they lived.

There were many other abuses that La Rochefoucauld described as essentially clerical, but the single most important problem he identified was neither an abuse nor a vice. It was the 'prodigious ignorance' of the clergy which both Protestant and Catholic reformers everywhere were discovering to their dismay, and which they agreed to be the principal enemy of true religion. La Rochefoucauld's discussion of it is of particular interest, as it precedes the well-publicised discoveries of later French missionaries and reformers.[23] It is also the main bridge linking diagnosis and prognosis in his thought.

La Rochefoucauld saw clerical ignorance everywhere, and claimed as late as 1597 that it could still destroy the church. The problem was intractable — men might change their way of life and embrace devotion, but the obstacle that ignorance constituted to an effective ministry could not be so easily eliminated.[24] Ignorant clergy could not preach, catechise, teach, or refute heresy, and all of these tasks were

19. *Ibid.*, pp. 192–200. The most recent of these condemnations had been made by Sixtus V (1585–90).
20. *Ibid.*, pp. 742, 744–5.
21. *Ibid.*, pp. 663–6.
22. In respect of the *confidence*, La Rochefoucauld accused the clergy of often taking the initiative, as part of their search for more than one benefice at a time.
23. *Ibid.*, p. 297. For the phenomenon in general, see Jean-Claude Dhôtel, *Les Origines du catechisme moderne* (Paris, 1967), part ii; also the more recent synthesis, not confined to religious considerations, by Roger Chartier in *Histoire de la France urbaine*, ed. Georges Duby (Paris, 1981), iii, pp. 243ff.
24. *Estat*, pp. 301–7, especially 304.

essential to their role; still less did they possess the qualities required for a proper use of the confessional, which was becoming increasingly important for the reform of the laity.[25] The cumulative effects on the laity of an ignorant clergy were only too plain to see: parishoners despised their pastors; superstitious practices flourished; religious practice waned, and communion was taken less frequently.[26] La Rochefoucauld never tired of asserting that sin was very much and very often a question of ignorance, and that the ignorance of the laity was an inevitable consequence of that of the clergy; the ignorance which excused the one, accused the other.[27] In a moment of bitterness, he even wondered whether it would be better if they were not Christians at all, so badly did they serve the church.[28] Such views must be seen as part of the post-Tridentine church's efforts to reorient itself towards a more active cure of souls; it was this which gave importance and urgency to the crusade against what was seen as unforgivable clerical ignorance.

The persistance of abuses and the successes of the Protestant reformers made it necessary to think again about the priesthood and the role of the clergy in the church.[29] On the theological front, the reformers had attacked a clerical tradition that was excessively levitical – too confined, that is, to performing acts of worship – and this attack was far-reaching enough to warrant a new statement on the nature of the priesthood as an indispensable preamble to any serious attempt at Catholic reform. The classic response, that of Pierre de Bérulle and his disciples, did not crystallise until the early to middle decades of the seventeenth century.[30] La Rochefoucauld's work may lack the theological or mystical profundity to be found in that of a Bérulle or a St Cyran, but it nevertheless offers a comprehensive portrait of a reformed clergy which later generations were to draw upon.[31]

25. *Ibid.*, pp. 301–2, 344–6, 352–6.
26. *Ibid.*, pp. 506ff, 537.
27. *Ibid.*, pp. 372–3.
28. *Ibid.*, p. 500: 'Parmy tant de personnes ecclésiastiques qui prennent le nom, je ne dy pas de prestres, mais de simpels chrétiens, il y a fort peu qui soient et vrays chrétiens et dignes du nom de Jésus Christ. Et ne scay à la vérité lequel des deux seroit moins tolérable: ou qu'ils ne creussent point en Jésus Christ, ou bien qu'ayans receu de luy le don de la foy, ils s'employent si mal et sans doute à leur damnation.'
29. *Ibid.*, pp. 347–8: 'aussi devons-nous attribuer principalement le grand progrez et la longue durée des hérésies en ceste Europe, et particulièrement en la France, à l'ignorance des pasteurs qui n'ont peu par leur doctrine chasser les loups hors de leur bergerie'.
30. See Michel Dupuy, *Bérulle et le sacerdoce* (Paris, 1969); Michael Arneth, *Das Ringen um Geist und Form der Priesterbildung im Säkularklerus des 17 Jahrhunderts* (Würzburg, 1970).
31. The anonymous editor of the 1651 edition of the *Estat*, who promised a complete edition of all the cardinal's works, wrote in his preface: 'Vous verrez les obligations que vous avez d'entrer dans les sentiments que vous va proposer Monseigneur le Cardinal de la Rochefoucauld, puisque ce ne sont pas ceux d'un docteur particulier, mais ceux de toute l'église'.

Over the years, historians have devoted much attention to the new post-Tridentine ideal of the bishop as pastor. Early reformers like Borromeo and Paleotti found Trent's decrees a rather narrow basis for a spirituality suitable to the new pastoral ideal, and felt that they needed more than decrees and sanctions to motivate them. Writers like Luis de Granada found themselves being called upon to develop an 'episcopal' spirituality.[32] It was soon realised that something similar was needed for the even more neglected secular clergy. However, historians have devoted relatively little attention to this problem of developing a 'sacerdotal' spirituality in the post-Tridentine period. This is surprising, as Trent's decrees fell far short of providing a well-defined model of the priest. Most of the work remained to be done, and post-Tridentine writers found earlier ideas of relatively limited value.[33] Once again, Borromeo helped to lead the way, and his *Acta Ecclesiae Mediolanensis* exercised great influence throughout Europe.[34] But the classic synthesis was provided by the *école française*, which in due course found institutional embodiment in the seminary-trained clergy of the eighteenth century. Yet it is not sufficiently realised how halting and protracted this process was.[35] Above all, it would be anachronistic to assume that the standards and objectives of the eighteenth century were already those of the early seventeenth. The merit of La Rochefoucauld's *Estat* is that it is one of the first systematic attempts at such reflection in France; and to examine its ideas is to look at a neglected phase of post-Tridentine reform.[36]

The long section entitled 'de la religion' with which the *Estat* began, was designed as an introduction to La Rochefoucauld's ideas on

32. See Hubert Jedin, 'Das Bischofsideal der katholischen Reformation', in his *Kirche des Glaubens, Kirche der Geschichte. Gesammelte Aufsätze* (Freiburg, 1966). This pioneering essay was first published in 1942. Also valuable is Paolo Prodi, *Il Cardinale Gabriele Paleotti*, ii, ch. 1. For a comprehensive survey of subsequent work, see Bruno Maria Bosatra, 'Ancora sul "vescovo ideale" della riforma cattolica. I lineamenti del pastore tridentino-borromaico', *Scuola Cattolica* 112 (1984), pp. 517–79.

33. This is well brought out by Massaut, *Josse Clichtove, l'humanisme et la réforme du clergé*, ii, pp. 109–364. There are useful comments in H. Jedin, 'Le Concile de Trente a-t-il formé l'image-modèle du prêtre?', in *Sacerdoce et célibat. Etudes doctrinales et historiques*, ed. Joseph Coppens (Louvain, 1970), pp. 11–31.

34. See Leon-E. Halkin, 'La Formation du clergé catholique après le concile de Trente', in *Miscellanea Historiae Ecclesiasticae*, ed. Derek Baker (Louvain, 1970), iii, pp. 109–24; A. Degert, 'Saint Charles Borromée et le clergé français', *Bulletin de Littérature Ecclésiastique*, 4 ser., 4 (1912), pp. 145–59, 193–213; and the works by Darricau and Broutin already cited above.

35. The bibliography is immense, but different aspects of the subject may be followed up in: A. Degert, *Histoire des séminaires français jusqu'à la Révolution*, 2 vols. (Paris, 1912); Bernard Plongeron, *La Vie quotidienne du clergé français au xviii* siècle (Paris, 1974); Quéniart, *Les Hommes, l'église et dieu*; Timothy Tackett, *Priest and Parish in Eighteenth-Century France: A Social and Political Study of the Curés in a Diocese of Dauphiné 1750–1791* (Princeton, 1977), especially chs. 2–3, 6; Philip T. Hoffman, *Church and Community in the Diocese of Lyon 1500–1789*, chs. 3–5.

36. Dupuy, *Bérulle et le sacerdoce*, p. 71, sees La Rochefoucauld as a precursor of Bérulle.

the clergy. The church, he argued, must reflect the order to be found in God's universe, and for that reason it had to be ordered and hierarchical.[37] Ideas of hierarchy enjoyed a renaissance in the late sixteenth century, and later became central to Bérulle's ideas of the priesthood.[38] La Rochefoucauld was much less explicit about them, but he saw the value of such concepts in restoring internal order to the church, as well as in defending the ecclesiastical order against the levelling tendencies of the Reformation, expressed in the notion of the priesthood of all believers. An ordered church guaranteed the autonomy of the clergy as a separate estate, and expressed this through the medium of canon law. Like any estate, it was defined by its privileges and exemptions, and these were therefore indispensable to its survival; no member of the clergy might rightfully trade or surrender them.[39] As to the form that this self-government should take, La Rochefoucauld was categorical: within his diocese, the bishop was the divinely-appointed ruler, without partners or equals. To him alone belonged the right to ordain the clergy, to examine, visit, and correct them.[40] All of this may smack of reaction, but La Rochefoucauld consistently viewed the service of the faithful as the only possible *raison d'être* of the privileges enjoyed by the clergy; only a truly worthy clergy could justify such privileges. The problem he defined in 1597 was that the juridical armature of the ecclesiastical state lacked a corresponding social reality: the *Estat* was written to show how this could be remedied.

As we have seen, La Rochefoucauld saw the office of bishop as essential to reform. As one who alone possessed the fullness of the sacrament of orders, the bishop was literally the gateway to the clerical state. It was in the light of such considerations that he deployed his ideas on two concepts of central importance to that state: mission and vocation. His interpretation is traditional insofar as he rejects the Protestant reformers' claim that a vocation may come directly from God, without any necessary mediation by the church. For him, a genuine vocation required public approval, expressed through the sacrament of orders, for without this safeguard, there was no way of keeping intruders or the self-appointed at bay. For this reason, mission – being 'sent' by the church, as the Apostles had been sent by Christ – and vocation were inseparable.[41] Yet La Rochefoucauld also strongly insisted on the idea of vocation to the ecclesiastical state as

37. *Estat*, pp. 1–10, 19–26, 30–6, 57–8.
38. See the brief remarks by Michel Dupuy, 'Hiérarchie', *Dictionnaire de spiritualité*, vii, cols. 441–51.
39. *Estat*, pp. 699–706. See H. Jedin, 'Mittelälterliche Würzeln des Klerikalismus', in his *Kirche des Glaubens, Kirche der Geschichte*, ii, p. 331.
40. *Estat*, p. 702: 'Car Dieu a voulu que le gouvernement de l'Eglise appartint aux Evesques, et non aux princes séculiers; lesquels s'ils sont fidèles à son Eglise, Il a voulu qu'ils fussent obéissans aux gens de l'Eglise.'
41. *Ibid.*, bk. ii, chs. 13, 15.

such; rejecting the reformers' theses did not mean outlawing the notion of vocation as a subjectively-felt calling from God. On the contrary, this aspect had to be emphasised in order to effect the transition from the priest as a liturgical functionary to the priest as pastor. Aptitude for certain functions was secondary to a sense of vocation, which required a distinctive way of life, behaviour, and spirituality. Of course, the church reserved the right to test all individual vocations and, if a man was found suitable, he entered the ecclesiastical state by what La Rochefoucauld, measuring his words carefully, described as the 'grand et droit chemin de la vocation légitime'.[42]

This scrutiny of vocations belonged by right to the bishop, and La Rochefoucauld admitted that episcopal negligence had greatly contributed to the abysmal standards among the clergy. As a direct warning to those of his own diocese, he wrote that he would nominate no one to a benefice 'who lacked satisfactory testimony from people who were either well-known or of considerable standing, as to his age, behaviour, family, education and religion, and even of his material resources'.[43] Elsewhere he added that one of the resolutions that he had taken at Clermont was always to conduct such a scrutiny personally, rather than leaving it to lesser officials.[44]

Following the decrees of Trent, La Rochefoucauld viewed the question of vocation in terms of the church's real needs, which he judged to be chiefly pastoral; candidates must be fit for the corresponding duties and way of life. He disdained the clerical 'proletariat', so numerous in Clermont, which exercised no real ministry, but was paid to recite the office and say masses for the dead.[45] The church had more pressing needs than that of perfecting the plain chant: such concerns were quite legitimate in the religious orders, precisely because their vocation was of a different kind.[46]

Of course, to be effective, the boundaries of La Rochefoucauld's ecclesiastical state had to be socially as well as legally defined. Like other contemporary reformers, he believed the reform of the clergy to consist at least partly in their being separated from the laity, so

---

42. *Ibid.*, pp. 74–80.
43. *Ibid.*, p. 82, 'qui n'eust suffisante attestation, de personnes cogneues ou de notable qualité, de son âge, vie, race, institution, et religion, et mesme de ses moyens'.
44. *Ibid.*, p 62: 'après avoir diligemment recherché en moy-mesme tous les moyens que je pourrais avoir de luy [church] apporter quelque secours en son extrême et presque deplorée necessite: rien ne m'a semblé plus digne du soing d'un pasteur, et plus pressé de prompt remède, que l'instruction, la correction et l'entière réformation, s'il se pouvoit, de ceux qui se présentent pour y entrer'.
45. *Ibid.*, p. 479. For the high proportion of such clergy in Clermont until the eighteenth century, see Abel Poitrineau, *Le Diocèse de Clermont*, pp. 145–7; Louise Welter, 'Les Communautés de prêtres dans le diocèse de Clermont du xiiie au xviiie siècle', *Revue d'histoire de l'église de France* 35 (1949), pp. 7–32.
46. *Estat*, p 490.

emphasising the social differences between them. Theologically, the vocation to offer Christ's sacrifice in the Mass had the effect of consecrating the clergy entirely to God, and it was this that set them apart from ordinary men. But a real social separation was equally necessary, for only if extricated from materialism and secular ambitions, could they ever acquire the detachment and social distance required for pastoral effectiveness.[47] In this context, La Rochefoucauld dwelt at length on the 'honour' and 'dignity' of the clergy, but he did so in order to confront them with their elevated calling and responsibilities, rather than with its attendant privileges.[48] The more separate the clergy, the more inescapable the nature and duties of their state would appear to them, thus leaving them with fewer excuses for negligence. In turn, the laity might legitimately expect higher standards from a separated clergy, and reform would be stimulated by their rising expectations.

The question of clerical celibacy was an obvious test-case for La Rochefoucauld's theme of a separated clergy. He was unequivocal on this controversial point – a genuine vocation to the priesthood necessarily implied a vocation to a life of celibacy. Christianity, he claimed, was not a 'social' religion like those of Greece or Rome, and all notions of hereditary priesthood were alien to it.[49] Far from being an intolerable burden, celibacy liberated the clergy from the onus of raising families, with its concomitant threat to the autonomy of the ecclesiastical state. However, celibacy should only be embraced after mature reflection, and he agreed that not everyone was suited to it.[50] The detachment that it offered was not merely a practical advantage or a social fact, but was to be transmuted into a spiritual value in its own right. Along with the notion of poverty as detachment from material things, it was one of the values most developed by later Catholic reformers.

But by poverty, La Rochefoucauld did not mean utter destitution. Predictably, he found it 'mal séant' for the clergy to have to work or beg for their living; their state called for detachment from such activities. Bishops might need some knowledge of secular affairs in order to administer their dioceses, but a bare minimum should suffice for the ordinary clergy. Whatever wealth came their way should be used with great modesty and restraint. Even when unavoidably involved in 'secular' affairs, the clergy should be clearly and easily distinguishable by their spiritual outlook.[51] And it goes without saying that La Rochefoucauld insisted upon the most easily recognised symbols of clerical separation – the tonsure and the soutane – which

47. *Ibid.*, p. 725.
48. *Ibid.*, p. 574.
49. *Ibid.*, p. 84ff.
50. *Ibid.*, pp. 124–5.
51. *Ibid.*, p. 623ff.

must be visible at all times.[52] None of this need be taken as implying scorn for the rest of humanity. He was a great admirer of the religous orders, but did not share their claim to be the perfect 'way' to salvation, nor did he subscribe to their elitism in regarding all outsiders, the secular clergy included, as virtually beyond saving. Given his idea of what the ecclesiastical state should be, he simply believed that many secular activities were intolerable, even scandalous, in the clergy. His yardstick was not some notionally 'perfect' state, but the church's pastoral needs.

These needs were the basis of the demands La Rochefoucauld made of the clergy, demands which were very much in tune with the efforts of Catholic reformers generally to orient the church towards a more positive pastoral role. This did not mean replacing worship and the sacraments with preaching and instruction, but it was clearly necessary to redress the balance after the ravages of Protestantism.[53] In particular, the sacraments had to be integrated into a wider pastoral structure which would prove capable of providing an intelligent understanding of them, thereby eliminating many of the almost magical ideas that surrounded them at the time. Only if Christians were properly educated in their religion, could the sacraments play their rightful role in church life; if barely or poorly understood, they easily became assimilated to magical practices.[54] They might hold pride of place in the economy of grace, but in practice, to be effecitive, they had to come after knowledge and instruction.[55] La Rochefoucauld insisted on the clergy's duty towards the faithful, to celebrate mass regularly and lead their parish in performing man's basic obligation to worship God, and for this to be effective an informed laity was required.[56] This is one of the many examples where he saw the reform of both clergy and laity as two sides of the same coin.

The duty to preach was, perhaps surprisingly, quite central to his view of the clerical ministry.[57] If even Borromeo and his contemporaries were dismayed at its neglect, and even more so at their own personal lack of preparation and inability to preach, it is not difficult to appreciate what La Rochefoucauld was demanding of the clergy of backward Clermont.[58] Yet he scarcely even attempted to prove the necessity for the clergy to preach. While characteristically afraid of

---

52. *Ibid.*, pp. 268, 276.
53. *Ibid.*, pp. 318–19: 'les offices principaux d'un homme d'Eglise sont, d'annoncer au peuple la parole de Dieu, d'enseigner les commandements, de reprendre les fautes, de refuter les erreurs et hérésies, qui sont contraires à la vraye doctrine, d'administrer les sacrements...de prier et sacrifier pour le peuple'. The order in whch these duties are ranked is noteworthy.
54. *Ibid.*, p. 506ff.
55. *Ibid.*, bk. iii. ch. 9.
56. *Ibid.*, pp. 512–16, 537–8, 545–9.
57. See n. 51, above; also *Estat*, bk. iii, ch. 4.
58. See Prodi, *Il Cardinale Gabriele Paleotti*, ii, pp. 77ff, 99ff.

scripture in the vernacular, he assumed that scripture would still be the basis of all preaching. The clergy must be familiar with it, especially with its controversial passages. He regarded laziness, fear, and the desire to flatter the great as the main reasons which prevented them from preaching as they should. They perverted God's word, and silence was preferable.[59] He saw the reform of preaching as starting with the exclusion of all secular matters from the pulpit; the clergy should not be a medium for the government, landlords, local officials, and so on.[60]

Preaching and the refutation of heresy were, if not identical, at least inseparable in La Rochefoucauld's mind.[61] Both demanded a theological culture enjoyed by but a few clergy of his time, and least of all by those serving in parishes. It was therefore natural, even easy, for him to assume that the religion of the laity derived entirely from that of the clergy. If sin was largely a question of ignorance, genuine religion reposed on knowledge of the true faith. He made this clear in his treatment of confession, the sacrament which he saw as pre-eminently suitable for awakening and enlightening men's consciences, and without which reform would make no progress. Preaching and instruction were one-sided, impersonal exercises; only through the discipline of regular confession could real progress be made, and men made aware of their sinfulness.[62] Confession, leading to the 'culpabilisation' of consciences, was to be the lynch-pin of Catholic reform throughout Europe.[63] But this, too, made heavy demands of the clergy. Not only were they to administer the sacrament in a new, more positive fashion, but they were themselves to be subjected to a new penitential regime – something they were as slow to embrace as were the laity. For La Rochefoucauld, the proper administration of the sacrament was essential to reformed religion based on regular devotional practice, and designed to produce concrete results among individuals. This 'souci d'efficacité', as it has been called, derived largely from the methods of self-examination enunciated by the *devotio moderna*, but above all by Ignatius Loyola's *Spiritual Exercises*, with which La Rochefoucauld was certainly familiar, and which inspired a pastoral philosophy that was more individualist and activist than that of the medieval church. The subsequent development of manuals of pastoral theology, casuistry and confessional practice shows that La Rochefoucauld's pre-occupations were shared by later reformers until

59. *Estat*, bk. iii, chs. 4–7.
60. *Ibid.*, pp. 316–17.
61. *Ibid.*, pp. 320ff, 345–9.
62. *Ibid.*, pp. 352–66.
63. This thesis has been developed by Jean Delumeau. For his recent, most comprehensive statement of it, see his *Le Péché et la peur. La culpabilisation en occident, xiii^x – xviii^x siècles* (Paris, 1983).

they became the common coin of what is usually referred to as Tridentine Catholicism[64]. He was fully aware of the demands which this type of ministry made of the clergy, on both the human and doctrinal levels. Prudence, insight, and other associated virtues were needed in dealing with individuals, while the rudiments of moral theology and casuisty were equally indispensable.[65] And only a clergy clearly removed from secular affairs would be accepted by their parishoners in the delicate role of confessors.

Thus far, we have only considered what might be called the sociology of La Rochefoucauld's view the ecclesiastical state – its visible exterior as expressed by the clergy's way of life and occupations. Its spirituality, a much more important innovation, also deserves scrutiny. La Rochefoucauld was acutely aware that, to be complete, his vision of the clergy required an appropriate spirituality, and that this also needed to be extensive, covering not merely the clergy's functions and duties, but above all their state in life. Here lay the novelty of his work, as of later generations of French reformers.

Historically, there had been no spirituality specifically conceived for the secular clergy. Medieval spirituality had been largely the creation of the religious orders, and as such was built around their vows and rule, rather than around the priesthood itself, since many of their members were not priests at all. It was dominated by the idea of withdrawal from the world in order to pursue the *vita contemplativa*. The orders tended to believe that it was impossible for seculars, given their involvement in the affairs of the world, to attain a genuine spiritual life. Medieval treatises on the clergy tended to deal with their office, but remained silent on matters of spirituality.[66] The new orders of the sixteenth century, particularly the Jesuits, represented something of an advance by combining a spirituality with intense activity in the world – something which partly explains their attractiveness to many people at the time. However, there were limits here too, and when Bérulle, to take an illuminating example, decided not to become a Jesuit in 1602, it was because they seemed to him to be regulars first, and priests second; the regeneration of the secular clergy that he dreamed of could not be achieved with models derived from the orders.[67] It would require a spirituality based on the priesthood itself, and the great achievement of Bérulle and his followers was to create

64. Delumea, *Le Catholicisme entre Luther et Voltaire* (Paris, 1971), pp. 256ff; Quéniart, *Les Hommes, l'église et dieu*, pp. 91–167. For a very different interpretation of these trends, see John Bossy, *Christianity in the West* (Oxford, 1985), part ii.
65. *Estat*, pp. 356ff, 362.
66. See Francis Rapp, *L'Eglise et la vie religieuse en Occident à la fin du moyen age* (Paris, 1971), pp. 124–5; W.A. Pantin, *The English Church in the Fourteenth Century* (Cambridge, 1955), ch. 9.
67. Dupuy *Bérulle et le sacerdoce*, pp. 59–60.

one.[68] But before that, La Rochefoucauld, who had doubtless learned from his Jesuit teachers that action and spirituality could be combined, had perceived the different nature of the secular clergy's needs and set about finding a solution to them.

Given the standards he set for the clergy, the purpose of the new sacerdotal spirituality, apart from developing personal piety, was to inculcate the attitudes essential to the ecclesiastical state. The growth of such attitudes would be proof that the appropriate behaviour and way of life were being accepted and internalised. La Rochefoucauld gave numerous examples of this. We saw earlier how he treated vocation in relation to the principle of hierarchy. But he also postulates humility and obedience as fundamental clerical virtues, enabling priests to accept episcopal authority as well as their own subordinate position in the church hierarchy.[69] Similarly, celibacy was not merely an external constraint imposed on those taking orders. Through the virtue of continence, it could be internalised and transmuted into a positive spiritual value.[70] Other virtues, such as detachment, poverty and modesty, were to be the interior equivalents of the clergy's external separation from the world. When put together, this spectrum of attitudes formed a spiritual portrait of La Rochefoucauld's reformed clergy, with the ecclesiastical state finding its logical fulfilment in a sacerdotal spirituality.

Prayer was to be the ultimate source and constant vehicle of this spirituality. La Rochefoucauld was writing at a time when, according to Lucien Febvre, a minor spiritual revolution was taking place in France.[71] Whole sections of society began to pray, methodically and systematically. Theirs was not the customary liturgical or oral prayer, but rather the more recent forms of interior, mental prayer best expressed by the *devotio moderna* and, especially, the *Spiritual Exercises*. Such prayer was, indeed, relatively novel, but it may be doubted how extensively it was practiced outside a *dévot* élite. It is, however, significant that La Rochefoucauld devoted much of the *Estat* to the place of prayer in the life of the clergy, and to explaining its newest forms to them; he did so to such an extent, that one commentator has written of him 'transforming his work into a treatise on prayer'.[72] La Rochefoucauld was eminently clear in his approach from the outset — 'l'oraison est l'appuy principal de tout le reste des fonctions de cet estat'.[73] The clergy should consider even the highest stages of interior

68. J. Choné, 'La Spiritualité sacerdotale', *XVII Siècle* 62–3 (1964), pp. 126–8.
69. *Estat*, bk. ii, ch. 15, 'De la vocation et de l'obeyssance'.
70. *Ibid.*, pp. 124–39.
71. Lucien Febvre, 'Aspects méconnus d'un renouveau religieux en France entre 1590 et 1620', *Annales: économies, sociétés, civilisations* (1958), pp. 639–50.
72. Choné, 'La Spiritualité sacerdotale', p. 123.
73. *Estat*, pp. 379–80.

prayer accessible to them — something earlier generations would have thought impossible. They might lack the advantages of the cloistered orders, but La Rochefoucauld insisted that their activities should not be dismissed as so many distractions that made attentiveness to God impossible; they should, instead, turn regularly to God in prayer. This kind of prayer required a revolution within the clergy, and was possible only if they developed attitudes of penance, humility, and openness towards God. To La Rochefoucauld and, later, to the *école française*, the priest was pre-eminently a man of payer, and therefore an acceptable mediator between God and men. The relationship between prayer and the ecclesiastical state was reciprocal. It oriented man towards God, but it was also the indispensable vehicle for the development of sacerdotal spirituality.[74] It was not just one ecclesiastical activity among others: it was their essence. La Rochefoucauld was perfectly logical in concluding that the clergy could only be transformed by prayer. In this sphere of reform, means and ends were indistinguishable.

II

It is clear that La Rochefoucauld was describing an ecclesiastical utopia that existed nowhere in his own time, and one which would only gradually and partially become a reality during the next century and a half, when it was most completely embodied in the seminary-trained French clergy. It was to be the French church's principal contribution to the Counter-Reformation. From having had to look to other European countries for ideas and inspiration in the late sixteenth and early seventeenth centuries, it gradually became, in its turn, a model for them to follow. La Rochefoucauld's work, which is known to have influenced Bérulle and which was reprinted in 1604, 1628, and 1651, dates from the crucial early phase of this transformation. However, what his *Estat* does not reveal is the means and institutions he envisaged for the reform of the clergy; its format may have precluded the offering of such blueprints, but one is entitled to ask just how he hoped to implement his vision. What was he trying to achieve as a bishop, and what were his methods?

In retrospect, it may appear obvious that only a properly-trained seminary clergy could begin to meet La Rochefoucauld's standards, and that he should have sought to develop the necessary institutions. But such a conclusion would be simplistic, for it would not take account of the slow and confused process this proved to be in the

---

74. *Ibid.*, bk. iii, chs. 12, 14–32 are entirely devoted to explaining the different forms of prayer, and the attitudes they require.

French church generally. Like his contemporaries, La Rochefoucauld might have been groping his way towards better institutions, but he did not have much to build upon. The Council of Trent's decree on seminaries was far less clear and specific than is usually imagined, and subsequent interpretations of it differed widely.[75] Even when the classic 'Tridentine' seminary finally took root over a century later, programmes, methods, and objectives still varied considerably. Practical ideas on its functions and aims were slow to evolve, not least because the ideal of the clergy itself developed over time. There were practical problems, too. The few seminaries founded in France after Trent quickly foundered, and even wealthy prelates like Lorraine and Joyeuse found it difficult to put them on a sound financial footing. The existing benefice-holders tenaciously resisted, often through appeals to the royal courts, all efforts to make them contribute to the establishment of a seminary.[76] It is hardly surprising, therefore, that La Rochefoucauld, the incumbent of an impoverished see, had few hopes of succeeding where wealthier bishops had failed. Success or failure in founding a seminary is thus not a realistic yardstick with which to assess the record of early seventeenth-century reformers. Besides, even those seminaries which did exist took in only a handful of aspiring priests for many decades.[77]

The surviving evidence does show that La Rochefoucauld at least kept pace with his most advanced contemporaries in the French church. In the *Estat*, he wrote of his determination to examine personally all candidates for orders, but he recognised that this was only a first step. From an early date, he seems to have used the Jesuit colleges in the Auvergne for the purpose of receiving ordinands in the weeks before their ordination, instructing them in their duties, and giving them the bare rudiments of a spiritual formation.[78] This was almost certainly one reason why he opposed the Jesuits' expulsion in 1595 and worked so hard for their restoration after 1603. It is of interest that, in 1640, when he enquired of Vincent de Paul, one of the major figures in the seminary movement, about the functions of his Paris seminary, the answer disclosed that these differed hardly at all from what he had himself been attempting to do through the Jesuit colleges in Clermont.[79] Evidence from around the same time, when the cardinal was no longer a bishop, may serve to illustrate the

75. A. Michel, *Les Decrets du concile de Trente* (Paris, 1938), pp. 501–5, for the text with commentary; Degert, *Histoire des séminaires français*, i, ch. 1; Halkin, 'La Formation du clergé catholique après le concile de Trente', pp. 109ff.
76. Degert, *Histoire des séminaires*, i, chs. 3–5.
77. See the brief remarks in Queniart, *Les Hommes, l'église et dieu*, pp. 52ff. By way of example, see the experiences of Richelieu with his small seminary at Luçon: L. Lacroix, *Richelieu à Luçon. Sa jeunesse, son épiscopat* (Paris, 1890), pp. 93ff.
78. Rouvier, *Vita*, pp. 15–16.
79. B.S.G. MS., 3238, fo. 283, reply to La Rochefoucauld's questions about the functions of his seminary.

continuity of his approach. In 1639, he founded an annuity of 1,300 *livres* for the Jesuits of Montferrand

> in order to instruct the clergy and other ecclesiastics who may have need of it, in the affairs of their profession. . .and to carefully ensure that those clerics of the said diocese who are to be later admitted to holy orders shall be examined not only in respect of their knowledge, but especially of their manner of behaviour and habits, and finally that they be taught free of charge about the greatness and excellence of the sacred character that they are seeking after, of its exercises and uses, as of the devotion and purity required in order to receive it properly.[80]

At a distance of forty years, it is not hard to see in these carefully measured phrases echoes of the ideas of the *Estat*. Shortly before his death, he tried to persuade the reformed canons-regular of Ste Geneviève in Paris to open a seminary for the secular clergy, and to take their place alongside the Jesuits, Oratorians, and Lazarists, although nothing came of his proposal.[81]

Clearly, this limited type of seminary could of itself achieve little, even if it did attempt to reach all those about to take orders. Above all, it had no answer to the problem of the existing clergy. Other methods had to be employed, the most important of which was the pastoral visitation, an institution largely neglected by late medieval bishops, but which revived strongly with the development of the 'pastoral' ideal of the bishop after Trent. Such visitations allowed bishops to gauge for themselves the 'prodigious ignorance' of both clergy and laity and, consequently, the extent of the task facing them. Visitation records have recently been fruitfully used by historians of religious practice and change, and this makes their disappearance at Clermont and Senlis – a fate by no means confined to these two dioceses – particularly regrettable.[82] It is, however, clear that La Rochefoucauld took his duty to visit seriously. With its 850 parishes, some of them extremely

---

80. *Ibid.*, fo. 291, contract dated 27 May 1639, 'pour enseigner aux curez et autres ecclésiastiques qui en auront besoin, les choses de leur profession. . .par une exacte précaution que les clecs dudit diocèse qui par cy après sont promeus aux ordres sacrés, soint non seulement examinez en leur doctrine, mais encore particulièrement reconnus en leurs habitudes et inclinations, et soint de plus charitablement instruits de la grandeur et excéllence du sainct caractère qu'ils postulent, des exercices et usages d'iceluy, et de la dévotion et pureté requise pour dignement le recevoir quelques jours auparavant'.
81. B.S.G. MS. 3263, fo. 302, Charles Faure to François Blanchart, 2 July 1644.
82. The number of works based on such sources has grown rapidly since Gabriel Le Bras's *Etudes de sociologie religieuse*, 2 vols. (Paris 1955–6). For a fine synthesis of research, as well as a discussion of methodological issues, see Dominique Julia, 'La Réforme post-tridentine en France d'après les procès-verbaux des visites pastorales: ordres et résistance', in *La Società religiosa nell'età moderna* (Naples, 1973), pp. 311–433. Among more recent works, see Robert Sauzet, *Les Visites pastorales dans le diocèse de Chartres pendant la première moitié du xvii* siècle (Rome, 1975); Sauzet, *Contre-Réforme et réforme catholique en Bas-Languedoc. Le diocèse de Nîmes au xvii* siècle.

remote, Clermont was large enough to tax even the most energetic bishop.[83] In the *Estat*, he referred to visitation as a normal part of his activities. In his 1599 statutes, he bade his clergy furnish at future synods information that he did not have time to collect while on his rounds of the diocese, and his statutes at both Clermont and Senlis refer to books distributed by him during visitations.[84] From a later source, it emerges that he also employed special *procureurs* at Clermont, possibly because of the size of the diocese, and that these were required to report in particular on the administration of the sacraments and instruction through the catechism.[85] Senlis was, of course smaller but, despite growing demands on his time, he seems to have managed annual visitations after his return from Rome in 1613, making it a point, when on such tours, to perform at least part of the bishop's own pastoral ministry – preaching and administering the sacraments.[86] This kind of visitation had an immediacy that the practice was to lose later in France, when it became a somewhat bureaucratic routine involving the clergy and their distant superior. It appears that La Rochefoucauld did keep records of his visitations, and that he consulted them before making a subsequent visit in order to determine to what extent his previous ordinances had taken effect. His *Avertissements pour les curés de Senlis* of 1618 were explicitly based upon a comparison of the records, a striking early instance of the methodical search for results so typical of later French reformers. He is also known to have attempted to enforce clerical residence at Senlis while on visitation, obliging canons who also held parishes to chose between their prebend and their parish.[87] He also tried to act against absentee *curés* who employed vicars to stand in for them, though with what success it is impossible to say.[88]

While short, occasional, visitations might enlighten bishops about the state of their dioceses and help to restore their control over the clergy, they were certainly less effective as a means of improving clergy incapable of instructing their own parishioners. One post-Tridentine

83. A document relating to only one of his visitations in Clermont has survived: A.D. Puy-de-Dôme, 1 G 979.
84. *Statuts renouvelez par le R.P. François de la Rochefoucault evesque de Clairmont* (Clermont, 1599), pp. 6, 18–20; *Avertissements pour les curés de Senlis* (2nd ed. Paris, 1638), pp. 6, 48.
85. B.S.G. MS. 3238, fo. 308, letter of 23 Sept 1638 to Bishop d'Estaing of Clermont, protesting about the suppression of the *procureurs*, and explaining why he had found them useful.
86. B.S.G., MS. 366, fo. 306v, biographical memoir on La Rochefoucauld by his long-standing friend, the famous Jesuit, Jacques Sirmond. The same claim appears in Desbois, *Biographie*, p. 47.
87. B.S.G., MS. 366, fo. 306v.
88. Charles Jaulnay, *Histoire ou annales de chacun evesque de Senlis* (Paris, 1648), p. 631. Jaulnay was a member of La Rochefoucauld's diocesan council, and perhaps one of his diocesan vicars.

answer to the problem was to promote systematic and methodical misions, under active episcopal sponsorship, in contrast to the predominantly urban missions of the medieval friars which rarely touched rural areas.[89] This was another reason La Rochefoucauld cultivated the religious orders – the Jesuits obviously, but also the Capuchins and the Récollets[90] – who were the only experienced missionaries available at the time. At Senlis, he used the Jesuits extensively to catechise villages.[91] No contemporary sources survive for Clermont, but detailed provisions that he made late in his career for missions there, makes his appreciation of their value perfectly clear.[92] Missions were initially founded by him in 1637–8, but he soon expressed dissatisfaction with these because not all parishes of the districts concerned had been covered, nor had provision been made for the annual repetition of them.[93] A second act of foundation in 1639 clearly enunciated the missionaries' task – the simultaneous reform of both clergy and laity.[94] The reports addressed to him reveal that the missionaries did indeed spend most of their time instructing the clergy and acting as itinerant seminaries.[95] If this was the state of the Clermont diocese around 1640, it had doubtless been far worse fifty years previously. At Senlis, a smaller diocese and a clergy of somewhat better quality enabled La Rochefoucauld to vary his methods of instruction still further. He instituted regular ecclesiastical conferences, which were to become a feature of the French church, and some of these met at his own residence; others involved the better educated clergy instructing the more ignorant. This was an area in which his episcopal council, partly composed of regulars, seems to have been especially active.[96]

These were some of the principal means employed by La Rochefoucauld to improve both clergy and faithful. However, they tell us

89. The fullest study is that of Charles Berthelot du Chesnay, *Les Missions de Saint Jean Eudes* (Paris, 1967); see also the methodological remarks in Delumeau, *Catholicism*, pp. 189–94.

90. See the endowments, some of them testamentary, that he made in favour of these two orders in the diocese of Clermont, specifically to enable them to carry on their missions and catechising activities: B.S.G., MS. 3238, fos. 277, 293–5, 301.

91. B.S.G., MS. 3249, fo. 333, Etienne Charlet to La Rochefoucauld, 1 August 1618; *ibid.*, fo. 338, Christophe Nevèle to same, 12 February 1621, expressing the hope that the cardinal 'me fera *encores* la grace d'aller catéchiser ès villages de vostre evesché' (italics mine).

92. The original acts of foundation, dating from March 1636 have not survived, but Bishop d'Estaing's directives are in A.D. Puy-de-Dôme 1 G 1626, fos. 55–6.

93. B.S.G., MS. 3238, fos. 305, 308v.

94. *Ibid.*, fos. 291–2, contract of 27 May 1639. This second act of foundation was prepared with considerable care, and only signed after successive drafts had been circulated to Bishop d'Estaing, who was opposed to the Jesuits, and to the cardinal's advisers, all of whom had important comments to make.

95. B.S.G., MS. 3249, fos. 341, 345, 349, 356.

96. B.S.G., MS. 366, fo. 306v; Rouvier, *Vita*, p. 36.

little about his immediate objectives, nor the problems he encountered. There are two other types of source which may supply some answers here.

The first is a set of consultations between La Rochefoucauld and his council at Senlis. Government by council was characteristic of La Rochefoucauld's method, and we may assume that the practice dates from his Clermont days.[97] While the consultations do not say what decisions he took, they reveal the issues which concerned him, and the various lines of action open to him. Above all, they show an extraordinary concern with the correct and official practice of the church as the basis of his decisions, particularly as expressed in the decrees of Trent; in some cases, he even sent to Rome for advice.[98] As the consultations deal with matters where he encountered difficulties or resistance, they give some idea of the problem of enforcing Tridentine reforms, even after the 1615 declaration he had sponsored.

Several papers record consultations about the nature of episcopal control over religious orders within the diocese, particularly in relation to female orders; because many of them were not centralised, they were bound, in theory at least, to acknowledge the bishop as their normal superior. As we shall see later, this was the kind of problem that no reforming bishop could ignore, and it was one that caused endless trouble in numerous dioceses. La Rochefoucauld viewed the issue as much as a question of reform as one of authority. When, as invariably happened, the orders claimed exemption, the cardinal's council advised him to counter by acting as papal delegate, as he was clearly entitled to do under the decrees of Trent. But his advisers had to concede that, since Trent was not part of French law, there was little he could do in the case of an *appel comme d'abus* against him.[99] The problem of schoolteachers also received much attention. La Rochefoucauld's initial query makes it clear that, while attempting to establish more schools, the church also claimed the right to choose teachers. Having consulted the relevant royal edicts, his council declared that the right to nominate was his, and the fact that it had been usurped by secular judges during the League did not invalidate his title.[100] But in a separate memorandum, other advisers took a different view, and claimed that the civil law did not recognise La Rochefoucauld's claim.[101] This was precisely the kind of confused situation, in which church law contradicted civil law, that made the cardinal and fellow-

97. Jaulnay, *Histoire de chacun evesque*, p. 636; Rouveir, *Vita*, p. 36.
98. B.S.G., MS. 366, fo. 102, Cardinal Verallo to La Rochefoucauld, 4 September 1621.
99. *Ibid.*, fos. 104, 329, 354, 358–9, 378; MS. 3238, fos. 209–11. For difficulties throughout Europe in respect of female religious orders, see Wright, *The Counter-Reformation*, p. 47.
100. B.S.G., MS. 366, fos. 366–7, memorandum of 3 August 1619.
101. *Ibid.*, fo. 368.

reformers desire a royal reception of Trent's decrees. A further problem was how the clergy should react to pressure from secular officials to publish 'choses profanes' from the pulpit and to keep parish registers as a civil duty, especially when this pressure was accompanied by threats to seize their property.[102] Again, there were differences among his advisers, but the feeling was general that there was no legal basis for resisting officials, especially over the question of parish registers, as the clergy could not regard this as a purely ecclesiastical matter until and unless Trent's decrees became law in France.[103] But on the question of announcing 'choses profanes' from the pulpit, the cardinal tired of procrastination, and openly forbade all such announcements in his 1620 statutes.[104]

Examples such as these point to a bishop clearly anxious to expand the scope of his activities, but frequently faced with jurisdictional problems when attempting to do so. Such questions of law in fact bring us to the last source for La Rochefoucauld's episcopal activity – his synods and statutes. Trent had envisaged that triennial provincial councils and annual diocesan synods would be revived and used as instruments of religious regeneration. A few councils were indeed held in France in the aftermath of Trent, but they quickly became rare, while synods were not held regularly in most dioceses until the seventeenth century. La Rochefoucauld, for his part, referred in the *Estat* to his Clermont synods and, in his statutes of 1599, went further by obliging his clergy to attend 'les synodes de chaque année'.[105] That these regular synods have left no legislative trace in print is an indication that he regarded them as instruments of reform rather than mere legislative organs. His custom of regularly assembling the Senlis clergy, which was possible because of the smallness of the diocese, may be a natural extension of this practice, in which case the difference between assemblies and formal synods loses some of its significance. His Clermont statutes made it quite clear that even vicars serving in parishes were obliged to attend synods 'pour restablir. . . les choses spirituelles en quelque meilleure forme'.[106] Above all, they permitted him to bring direct pressure to bear on the clergy, and to learn more about the state of his diocese.[107] But his most important and interesting synod was that of 1620 in Senlis. The 1615 Assembly of Clergy had recommended the holding of provincial councils and synods to implement at local level its acceptance of Trent's decrees. As

102. *Ibid.*, fos. 356v, 366.
103. *Ibid.*, fo. 358v.
104. *Statuts synodaux de Senlis (1620)*, in *Actes de la province ecclésiastique de Reims*, ed. Thomas-J. Goujet (Reims, 1842–4), iii, p. 696.
105. *Statuts*, p. 18.
106. *Ibid.*, pp. 17–18.
107. *Ibid.*, pp. 18 19, for the subjects on which the clergy were to report to him.

hopes of a royal acceptance of the decrees faded, even Rome began to put its faith in unilateral action by the clergy.[108] But few bishops responded, and the crown feared that such actions might spark off Huguenot discontent.[109] La Rochefoucauld's own metropolitan at Reims, Cardinal Louis de Guise, was one of those least interested in observing the assembly's injunction. La Rochefoucauld clearly became impatient with such delay, but did not immediately try to jump the gun. This was no doubt the reason for the appearance in 1618 of his interesting and comprehensive *Avertissements pour les curés de Senlis* which, although couched in less formal language, are virtually a set of synodal statutes. But, some time after that, he turned to his council for advice, and was told what he no doubt wished to hear – that it was his duty to hold a synod at which he would publicly announce the reception of Trent's decrees in his diocese.[110] He did so in October 1620 in a well-planned synod, and with the same reservations about Gallican liberties and the king's prerogatives as had been expressed in the 1615 declaration.[111] The cardinal was aware that he was the first bishop to take such an initiative, and one of his early biographers claimed he was pessimistic about his example being followed by others.[112]

Despite such prolonged synodal activity, one would search in vain for a detailed recapitulation of Trent's decrees in the cardinal's Clermont or Senlis statutes: for him, it was enough to declare that the council's decrees were henceforth binding in his diocese. Synodal statutes were intended to deal with immediate problems of reform, and would be followed up by the bishop's personal activity. Thus, whatever the nature of his indebtedness to Borromeo, La Rochefoucauld was certainly not an encylopaedic legislator in the Borromean mould. It is only to his printed statutes, the *Institutio* prepared for the Clermont clergy in 1608, and the *Avertissements* of 1618, that we can look for statements of his immediate objectives and difficulties as a reforming bishop.[113]

Reform had to begin with the restoration of ecclesiastical authority – the bishop's in his diocese, the *curé*'s in his parish; the anarchy caused by competing authorities had to be eliminated. As a first step,

108. Archivio di Stato, Ferrara, *fondo* Bentivoglio 18/11, no. 165, for instructions issued to nuncio Bentivoglio, 22 August 1617.
109. Martin, *Le Gallicanisme et la réforme catholique*, p. 394.
110. B.S.G., MS. 366, fo. 358v.
111. *Statuts*, pp. 693–4; 'pour m'acquitter de la promesse faicte avec serment, après en avoir differé jusqu'à présent l'éxécution, par l'advis de plusieurs personnes ecclésiastiques... je fais la déclaration conformément au contenu dudict article [of 1615] que ledict concile de Trente est par nous receu dans ce diocèse'.
112. Rouvier, *Vita*, pp. 44–5.
113. The *Institutio* was a short manual for the use of confessors and preachers in the Clermont diocese.

La Rochefoucauld tried to regulate the movements of his clergy. Only with express episcopal permission might external clergy exercise any ministry in another parish; if that permission were not produced, a *curé* might refuse all facilities.[114] Visitations could only be conducted by episcopal nominees, and not by dignitaries or chapters with traditional claims to do so.[115] At Clermont, even the parish clergy were required to obtain a licence to preach and to hear confessions, a clear indication of his low opinion of their ability; only *in extremis* might an unlicensed priest hear confession.[116] Of course, these were pastoral functions that had been the near monopoly of the religious orders, but while La Rochefoucauld was clear about his continuing need of the orders, he also intended to keep them in check. A number of statutes were designed to oblige them to seek episcopal licence to preach, catechise, or conduct any ministry outside their own churches.[117] La Rochefoucauld even wished to be kept informed about regulars residing temporarily in his diocese[118]. All these measures fit in well with what we know of his determination to enforce proper religious enclosure; the orders would be set apart, while the seculars would become masters in their own parishes.

If the clergy regained control of their parishes, it would be thanks to the bishop. This, in turn, would render them more vulnerable to pressure from him to discharge their duties responsibly rather than farm them out to miserably-paid vicars. La Rochefoucauld thus felt entitled to demand continual residence from them, although it may be doubted whether he was more successful than other reformers in this respect.[119] He reiterated his decrees in Clermont in 1607, and threatened action by his *official* against offenders. While he did admit some legitimate grounds for absence, he made every effort to limit its effects by refusing permission until the incumbent had nominated a vicar adjudged capable by La Rochefoucauld himself.[120] One of his collaborators at Senlis reported that this was one of his chief concerns when visiting parishes, as some offending clerics discovered to their cost.[121]

Naturally, the *curé*'s control of his parish embraced the faithful as a whole. Even in his statutes the cardinal never treated this question

---

114. *Statuts* (Clermont), pp. 13–14; *Statuts* (Senlis), p. 695.
115. *Statuts* (Clermont), p. 13.
116. *Ibid.*, pp. 22–3.
117. *Ibid.*, p. 23–4; *Statuts* (Senlis), p. 695.
118. *Statuts* (Senlis), p. 697.
119. *Statuts* (Clermont), pp. 4–5; *Statuts* (Senlis), pp. 694–5, 698.
120. 'Extraicts des registres de l'officialité': appendix to the 1608 edition of the Clermont statutes, pp. 25–6.
121. Jaulnay, *Histoire de chacun evesque*, p. 631: 'j'en parle comme ayant assisté plusieurs fois, mais davantage que pourront répliquer plusieurs curez qui se déchargent de leurs fonctions sur des vicaires'.

independently of the pastoral obligations it involved, and the elevated character of the vocation it implied.[122] Within the parish, Christian life was to be centred wholly upon the sacraments, the chief duty of the clergy being their proper preparation and administration. La Rochefoucauld's statutes abounded in directives about this. Interestingly, he enjoined his clergy to respect local customs and manuals, and warned them against introducing unjustified changes which might merely upset people.[123] He insisted, not surprisingly,that the clergy's main task was the constant and methodical instruction of their charges, for without this the sacraments would be of little value to those taking them:

> They shall make known and frequently repeat the catechism to their parishioners, telling them that without this kind of belief, they cannot either obtain their salvation through taking the sacraments or be held to be true christians. . .above all lest some people remain ignorant of the articles of faith which everyone must know if he is to be justified and saved.[124]

Here, in a different format, we meet again La Rochefoucauld's familiar themes of knowledge and true religion. With parents often ignorant, and schoolteachers either little better or of unreliable opinions, the clergy's duty to catechise was unmistakable. To be more effective at it, he even recommended that their own meditations should be based on the catechism.[125] He urged the holding of Sunday Schools for the instruction of both old and young. It was not, he claimed, a matter of turning the faithful into theologians – it would suffice if they grasped the sense of what was being explained to them.[126] Preaching itself should, he held, be a least partly catechetical, and he required sections of the catechism to be read and explained during the Sunday mass.[127] Clearly, a true Catholic was one who believed in specific doctrines rather than one who merely attended religious services.

In the *Estat*, La Rochefoucauld had diagnosed the neglect of the sacraments as a major symptom of religious decline, and in his statutes he urged upon his clergy the need to reverse this pattern. Baptism,

---

122. *Statuts* (Clermont), p. 3: 'le nom et charge d'un pasteur luy doivent apprendre que son soing et travail ne peuvent avoir autres limites que celles mesmes que la muable condition des choses humaines a posé à l'estat de l'Eglise durant le cours de son pélérinage et combat sur terre.'
123. *Statuts* (Senlis), p. 695; *Avertissements pour les curés de Senis*, p. 48.
124. *Avertissements*, pp. 5–6, 'ils feront scavoir et le répéteront souvent à leur paroissiens; que sans ceste créance, ils ne peuvent recevoir les sacrements à leur salut, ny estre tenus pour vrays chrestiens. . .de crainte que quelques uns n'ignorent surtout les articles de la foy que chacun est obligé nécessairement de scavoir pour estre justifié et sauvé'.
125. *Ibid.*, p. 8.
126. *Ibid.*, pp. 6–7, 11.
127. *Statuts* (Senlis), p. 696.

confirmation, and extreme unction were no less important for being received only once, as they represented milestones in the Christian life. Penance and communion were, of course, essential sacraments, and La Rochefoucauld unhesitatingly recommended more frequent reception of them than was usual for his time.[128] Predictably, he devoted much attention to confession, and to defining the clergy's duty in relation to it. They were to ascertain and improve their parishoners' religion; they should patiently help the weak and ignorant, while demanding a serious attempt at improvement; they should prepare them for confession from the pulpit, especially before the great church feast-days. La Rochefoucauld was not a moral rigorist in the field of penance, for he considered, as did Richelieu, attrition (sorrow for sin based on fear of divine punishment) sufficient to obtain forgiveness for sin, although agreeing that contrition (genuine sorrow for offending a loving God) was the nobler motive in a penitent.[129] In the *Insititutio* of 1608, the problem of examining penitents was treated in considerable detail: given that a person's age, sex, and station in life were the main sources of sin, confessors should ascertain these, assess the gravity of offices committed, and treat their penitents accordingly.[130] It is hardly surprising that he insisted on allowing only some of his Clermont clergy to hear confessions.

Marriage, at once social institution and sacrament, gave Catholic reformers immense trouble; it was also the subject of much juris-dictional conflict, especially in France where secular courts had made considerable inroads on ecclesiastical authority, and took a much tougher line in defending parents' rights to determine their children's marriages.[131] Abuses abounded, and the post-Tridentine church was determined to restore order. At Clermont, the problem of clandestine marriages was serious enough for La Rochefoucauld to demand that his clergy bring lists of such marriages to his synods, along with the names of the clergy involved.[132] At Senlis, he apparently had to seek papal dispensations for numerous marriages.[133] Stipulations that no

128. *Ibid.*, p. 695: 'Qu'ils veillent à faire approcher plus fréquemment leurs paroissiens avec plus de respect des sacrements de pénitence et d'eucharistie, faisant tout leur possible pour que la pluspart le fassent tous les mois, et les autres au moins aux quatre festes solenelles.' This kind of approach would be later attacked as 'laxist' by Jansenists, and it makes La Rochefoucauld's alleged hostility to Jansenism, and especially to Antoine Arnauld's *De la Fréquente Communion*, entirely credible: see the *Mémoires du père René Rapin sur l'église et le jansénisme*, ed L. Aubineau (Paris, 1865), i, p. 88.
129. *Avertissements*, pp. 14–34.
130. *Institutio*, fos. 20–1.
131. See Michel, *Les Decrets du concile de Trente*, pp. 506–84; Gabriel Le Bras, 'Mariage', in *Dictionnaire de Théologie Catholique*, ix, cols. 2229ff; René Pillorget, *La Tige et le rameau. Familles anglaise et française, xvi–xviiie siècles* (Paris, 1979), ch. 1; Wright, *The Counter-Reformation*, pp. 55–6.
132. *Statuts*, p. 19.
133. Deshois, *Biographie*, pp. 47–8.

betrothals take place in private houses or in churches after sunset may now strike us as amusing or farcical, but they certainly indicate the type of problem bishops encountered. La Rochefoucauld insisted that all betrothals take place before a priest, or be certified by a notary; only then might the marriage banns be published in the presence of the assembled parish on Sundays. Outsiders might only be married by presenting a letter of freedom from their own *curé*.[134]

This study of La Rochefoucauld's efforts to 'Christianise' his flock and expand his clergy's ministry may be appropriately rounded off with reference to death and dying. He was concerned at what he viewed as superstitious practices and beliefs about death, and was consequently at pains to explain the nature and function of the sacrament for the dying, extreme unction.[135] Superstition would be eradicated if the clergy integrated the care of the sick and the dying into their ministry by giving spiritual advice and preparing people to face death as a Christian should. For their part, the dying should remain content with ordinary medical care and refuse charms of any kind whatever.[136] Success in such an endeavour, as in many others, represented, on a number of levels, what reformers like La Roche-foucauld were aiming at – the eradication of superstition; the education of the faithful to think of life and death in purely Christian terms; the integration of death into a satisfactory sacramental system; and the extension of the clergy's ministry into every corner of human existence. La Rochefoucauld's generation came nowhere near achieving this happy state, but it is no exaggeration to say that such an ideal encapsulated the essence of the *pastorale* of the post-Tridentine reform.

134. *Statuts* (Senlis), pp. 696–7; *Institutio*, fos. 12–14.
135. *Statuts* (Senlis), p. 696; *Avertissements*, pp. 41, 43–6.
136. *Avertissements*, pp. 41–2, 47.

5

Grand Almoner of France

LA ROCHEFOUCAULD held the title of Grand Almoner from the death of Du Perron in September 1618 until February 1632 when, after much haggling over benefices and compensation, he resigned it to Richelieu's brother, Alphonse, Cardinal of Lyon.[1] As its name suggests, it was one of the great offices of the crown, and its holder was always listed first in the official *états* of the royal household.[2] But any claims it might have had to an ancient pedigree were belied by the facts. It was only in the previous century that the late-medieval king's almoner assumed the title of Grand Almoner of France, and only in the seventeenth that the title was held by a succession of distinguished cardinals.[3] It never really fulfilled its potential as an unofficial ministry for ecclesiastical affairs because, while still enlarging its scope, it was already being affected by the general tendency of great offices of the crown to lose their significance and to become gilded, well-endowed court sinecures. Indeed, there was some hint of this at the time of La Rochefoucauld's appointment, as it was believed at court that the king would pass him over and appoint instead his own natural brother, the unconsecrated Bishop of Metz, purely in order to induce him to

---

1. B.S.G., MS. 3238, fo. 347, royal *brevet* allowing La Rochefoucauld to retain pensions and privileges in case of resignation, 8 December 1631; *ibid.*, fo. 345, act of resignation by La Rochefoucauld, 6 February 1632; *ibid.*, fos. 337–41, articles agreed by La Rochefoucauld and the Cardinal of Lyon, 8 February 1632. For the negotiations, see *ibid.*, fo. 231, 'mémoire fait par Monseigneur en october 1631'; *Les Papiers de Richelieu*, vi, pp. 685–7, Claude de Bullion to Richelieu, 27 November 1631; *ibid.*, pp. 710–11, same to same, 8 December 1631.
2. E. Griselle, *Etat de la maison du roi Louis XIII* (Paris, 1912), p. 1.
3. See Guillaume Mollat, 'L'Aumônier du roi de France du xiii au xv siècle', *Comptes-Rendus des séances de l'Académie des Inscriptions et Belles-Lettres* (1939), pp. 514–25; Michel Portal, 'Le Grand aumonier de France jusqu'à la fin du xviie siécle', *Revue de l'assistance publique* 29 (1954), pp. 291–306.

remain in the ecclesiastical state.[4] The cardinal later complained strongly, as we shall see, that his authority was wholly insufficient for several of the responsibilities attached to the office.[5] Those who had pressed La Rochefoucauld's candidacy on Louis XIII welcomed his appointment principally because it placed a reputable and influential churchman near the king; the functions of the office interested them much less than its potential usefulness in ecclesiastical politics. La Rochefoucauld was doubtless not blind to that either, but he soon demonstrated that he was just as concerned with its duties; he was not one to let an office entrusted to him sink to the level of a sinecure in the pursuit of other interests. He came to it with several ideas of how it could be exercised, and soon found that it offered some constructive outlets for his commitment to reform. Indeed, in the years before his withdrawal from court and his immersion in the reform of the orders, he proved to be one of the most active and enterprising grand almoners of the century. In this, the ill-defined nature of the office gave considerable scope for action, both official and unofficial: much depended on the ability and willingness of the holder to make the best use of it. It is regrettable that there is no satisfactory study of the origins, growth and attributions of this office, because its archives only date from the eighteenth century, by which time it had already suffered considerable decline.

The very title of 'grand almoner' suggests that its holder was a kind of minister of public assistance, whose principal function was to dispense and supervise royal charity. By tradition, his authority covered, in the first instance, the hospices and sick houses of royal foundation, and he bore overall responsibility for their administration. La Rochefoucauld assumed office at a time of confused transition, when the crown was attempting to gain a measure of supervisory control over all the charitable institutions of the kingdom. Of course, most of these were not royal, but private foundations, with administrators appointed by descendants of the founders, and serving personnel who were usually religious observing the Augustinian rule. By the late Middle Ages, bishops and other church bodies had gained control of most of them, but not always with beneficial results. The coveted post of administrator was gradually converted into a benefice, thus becoming part of the ecclesiastical spoils system. Bishops claimed the right of visitation and the supervision of accounts.

But they soon found opponents, particularly in the growing towns, where ecclesiastical negligence and insensitivity to changing needs led to efforts to wrest control from them. These efforts were initially directed at financial mastery of the charities, and by the early

4. Archivio di Stato, Ferrara, *fondo* Bentivoglio 18/38, fo. 76, *avviso* of 29 August 1618.
5. B.S.G., MS. 3238, fos. 183–90, 6 August 1632.

seventeenth century, the bishops were experiencing difficulty in even attending, or being represented at, the annual auditing of accounts. Control had by then slipped from their hands, and appeals to the crown rarely improved matters, as the crown was intent upon establishing its own authority. Indeed, it began using the grand almoner for just this purpose. In judging disputes, its tactic was to expand the notion of royal foundation by employing that of royal protection; its aim initially was to see that ecclesiastical administrators were replaced by laymen proposed by the towns. It had other aims, too, and Henry IV in particular was keen to see hospices used at least in part as refuges for invalided soldiers. With this in mind, he established in 1606 the royal commission known as the *chambre de charité chrétienne*.[6]

The church was less than enamoured with this drift towards secularisation. The Council of Trent had insisted upon ecclesiastical control and administration of charitable institutions, although its decrees contained few new ideas on the problem and contributed little to the actual reform of the institutions.[7] In France, where its decrees were not law, the administrators easily played off bishops and and grand almoners against each other in order to prevent any close supervision. Yet, by reference to abuses which inevitably continued, the crown and the towns were each able to extend their control further.[8]

La Rochefoucauld liked the growth of secular control no more than Du Perron had before him. But as holder of a royal office, he faced the same dilemma: he had to accept that few reforms had been implemented, and that the conflict of jurisdictions was partly responsible for this. Determined to promote reform, he opted to work through an extension of royal authority. To some extent, Du Perron had shown the way in 1612 by replacing Henry IV's *chambre de charité* with a more ambitious *chambre de la généralle réformation des hôpitaux et maladeries*, from which the marshals of France were pointedly excluded. He also tried to restore the grand almoner's personal authority by working through a team of grand vicars, something La Rochefoucauld retained after him.[9] The latter was, if anything, more involved than Du Perron in the workings of the new *chambre*.[10] Under his direction, it pursued

6. The foregoing is based heavily upon Geneviève Voitel-Grenon, *La Chambre de la généralle réformation des hôpitaux et maladeries de France 1612–1676* (thesis, Ecole des Chartes, 1973). I am grateful to Bernard Barbiche for bringing this thesis to my attention, and particularly to the author for allowing me to read and quote from it.
7. Jean Imbert, 'Les Préscriptions hospitalières du concile de Trente et leur diffusion en France', *Revue d'histoire de l'église de France* 42 (1956), pp. 5–28.
8. See Roger Doucet, *Les Institutions de France au xvi⁰ siècle*, 2 vols. (Paris, 1948), ii, pp. 807–10.
9. Voitel-Grenon, *La Chambre*, pp. 51ff.
10. He sought to appoint grand vicars in every diocese in France, a move which does not appear to have been envisaged by Du Perron: B.S.G., MS. 3238, fo. 555, circular letter of 1 June 1621, for the purpose of selecting suitable local candidates.

the extension of royal rights, by invoking all earlier judgements, however obscure or ambiguous, in the king's or the grand almoner's favour.[11] But he discovered in 1626 that not all of the changes made over the previous fourteen years had been well received. The marshals and soldiers, who resented Du Perron's moves, had not given up hope, and petitioned both the Estates General of 1614 and the Assembly of Notables of 1626 for places in the hospices. The clergy attending the second of these assemblies asked La Rochefoucauld to bring the soldiers' claims to the king's attention, but he stubbornly refused despite Richelieu's support for their demands.[12] They then petitioned the nobles at the assembly for the return of Henry IV's *chambre*, and received their backing. But it was enough, in La Rochefoucauld's view, that invalided soldiers should be placed in monasteries as lay brothers or draw pensions off them, without being allowed to invade the hospices too. So again, he proved unyielding, and this, the most serious challenge to his grand almonership, subsided.[13] Although pursuing royal interests, there were, clearly, limits to the degree of secularisation he would countenance.

But La Rochefoucauld did not confine himself to continuing the policies of his predecessor. At a time when he was increasingly engaged in reforming the orders, it is hardly surprising that he should have attempted something similar for the charitable institutions by reforming their personnel.[14] However important administrative improvements might be, problems of reform would remain since the institutions' personnel were religious observing the rule of St Augustine. Yet they, too, were adept at playing him off against the bishops whenever he attempted to change their habits. It may be that La Rochefoucauld hoped that an attempt at internal religious reform would lessen the pressure to secularise the institutions. At any rate, soon after taking office, he embarked on a major, and for a royal official surprising, initiative – he renounced his direct spiritual authority over the institutions and transferred it to the bishops in the interests of effective control and reform. He secured Louis XIII's approval for this step in December 1620 and, through the king, that of Gregory XV in May 1622.[15] La Rochefoucauld promptly circularised the bishops with copies of the papal bull, urging them to visit and reform the

11. Voitel-Grenon, *La Chambre*, pp. 140, 176.
12. *Les Papiers de Richelieu*, i, p. 350, Richelieu to Michel de Marillac, early June 1626.
13. See Jeanne Petit, *L'Assemblée des Notables de 1626–1627* (Paris, 1936), pp. 163–7.
14. For example: B.S.G., MS. 3249, fo. 294, undated letter recommending him to commence the reform of the *Hôtel-Dieu* at Rouen by separating its male and female inmates, a major source of scandal; MS. 3238, fo. 382, minute of letter concerning administration of Le Mans *Hôtel-Dieu*, 25 May 1629; MS. 366, fo. 104, for the rebuilding of the *hôpital* at Crépy, 20 November 1621.
15. B.N., MS. Fr. 17364, p. 525, Louis XIII to Ambassador Sillery, 2 May 1622; B.S.G., MS. 3238, fos. 204–6, printed text of the bull.

communities, regardless of their traditional claims to exemption from episcopal authority. Simultaneously, he announced the appointment of grand vicars of his own in every diocese to enforce his authority in respect of the temporalities of the institutions, which was not affected by the change; in particular, they were to assist at the auditing of accounts, so as to prevent collusion between local authorities and royal officials.[16] His determination to get reform moving is also evident from the care with which he had earlier begun to select his grand vicars.[17]

Of course, La Rochefoucauld's strategy was in itself no guarantee of successful reform. Much now depended upon the individual bishop's use of his newly acquired authority, and only detailed local studies could tell to what extent the cardinal's intentions became reality. It seems, for example, that bishops and La Rochefoucauld's grand vicars did not always see eye to eye, and these disagreements led him to circularise the bishops again in 1628 in order to reiterate his policy. He had, he claimed, earlier defined their respective areas of authority, and conflict could be avoided by respecting that definition. The source of such conflicts is not entirely clear but, according to La Rochefoucauld, they concerned differences of authority in regard to spiritual functions performed within the institutions, and some bishops may have objected to the presence of external ecclesiastical officials like the grand vicars.[18] On the other hand, there is evidence that some bishops were glad of La Rochefoucauld's regulations and support for their own attempts to counter the malpractices of local and royal officials.[19]

La Rochefoucauld also felt that other aspects of his responsibility for the charitable institutions required further clarification. Some time after his appointment, he obtained royal permission to assemble a commission of senior councillors of state to work on a wide-ranging ordinance. This was duly drafted, but neither the *parlement* nor the *grand conseil* would register it, which would have made it legally enforceable. However, La Rochefoucauld later claimed that both he and the *chambre de réformation* had observed its terms as far as possible. One of its major clauses fitted in well with his contemporary concern for the reform of ecclesiastical benefices – the stipulation that hospices and sick-houses should no longer be granted as benefices, but that their 'title' and revenues should be given to the person actually administering them. By 1631, he was able to claim that he no longer

16. B.S.G., MS. 3238, fos. 206v–7, printed circular dated only '1622'.
17. For example: B.S.G., MS. 3249, fo. 336, Michel Rabardeau, S.J., reporting to La Rochefoucauld on his enquiries in the Bourges diocese, 14 December 1620; *ibid.*, fo. 285, Cauchon, vicar for Reims, to La Rochefoucauld, 11 February 1620.
18. *Ibid.*, fos. 199–202, circular of 28 February 1628.
19. For example: B.S.G., MS. 3249, fo. 141, Bishop of Tréguier to La Rochefoucauld, 24 June 1622.

had the unpleasant duty of 'presenting' to the king for nomination to such positions individuals who would treat them merely as revenue-yielding benefices.[20] We cannot verify the truth of this claim, but if it is accurate, then La Rochefoucauld had made progress.

II

These issues all fell within the well-defined and generally accepted sphere of the grand almoner's authority. But there were others which did not, where clarity and definition were still largely absent. Among them was the idea that the grand almoner was the 'bishop of the court'. While the title suggests what was implied, there was no agreement in 1618 as to what this might mean in practice, and La Rochefoucauld soon found himself in conflict with the Bishop of Paris (archbishop after 1622) who claimed to be *curé* of the court'. La Rochefoucauld was, by his own later account, clearly dissatisfied with the situation, and soon attempted to find answers for himself. The court was still peripatetic, and could scarcely come under the authority of any one bishop. Besides, it had always claimed exemption from local bishops. Its ecclesiastical and religious life was also far too confused for La Rochefoucauld's liking. Courtiers employed their own chaplains and confessors, and the personnel of the king's chapel and the royal preachers were numerous and largely uncontrolled. Subject to no superior, their ecclesiastical status was dubious; with discipline lax or non-existent, it was not surprising that many clerics took refuge at court, without holding any official position there.[21]

It was not in La Rochefoucauld's nature to tolerate such confusion. In his attempts to impose a measure of order, he enjoyed the king's goodwill. Since Henry IV's death, the rather easy-going and licentious atmosphere of the court had begun to change.[22] Louis XIII was shy, devout and scrupulous, and reformers like Coton, Bérulle, Du Perron and La Rochefoucauld had both his and Marie de Medici's approval.

20. The facts of this paragraph are derived from B.S.G., MS. 3238, fos. 150–1, 'Estat de ce qui a esté changé par Monsieur le cardinal de La Rochefoucauld ayant esté pourveu de la charge de grand aumosnier'. Composed just before he resigned his office in early 1632, this document contains much valuable information about his administration and reform of the charitable institutions. It provides a synopsis of some of the articles of the *règlement*, the text of which has not been preserved.
21. Paragraph based on B.S.G., MS. 3238, fos. 183–90, 'Mémoire pour la charge de grand aumosnier de France', dated 6 August 1632. This long and informative memorandum was probably composed by La Rochefoucauld as a review of his activities and as a guide to his successor, Alphonse de Richelieu.
22. Victor-Lucien Tapié, *La Politique extérieure de la France et le début de la guerre de trente ans* (Paris, 1934), p. 324, 'peut-être n'a-t-on pas sufisamment souligné ce changement. Il ne pouvait manquer de se faire sentir ses effets, à la longue, jusqu'à dans la politique générale.' See also, M. Magendie, *La Politesse mondaine et les théories de l'honnêteté, en France au xviie siècle de 1600 à 1660*, 2 vols. (Paris n.d.), i, part 1.

La Rochefoucauld's first step was to try to establish what being 'bishop of the court' meant. He consulted experts, had older treatises examined and books sent for, even from Italy.[23] He then drafted a document which has, unfortunately, been lost, and which he submitted to the pope for his approval.[24] He in turn referred it to two cardinals for study, but they were not satisfied with the basis of La Rochefoucauld's claims, and asked for further clarification. His Roman correspondent, Cardinal Bonsi, told him not to count on a positive response from Rome, possibly because his claims for episcopal authority at court were too great for the curia's liking, but to go ahead and exercise his office as he saw fit.[25] This, indeed, is what he seems to have attempted. In 1625, when Henrietta Maria was about to marry the future Charles I of England, La Rochefoucauld wrote to Rome that he did not think that, as grand almoner, he required any special permission to marry the princess: he had been assured some years earlier by a commission of theologians that it came within the scope of his functions as bishop of the court; this authority, he continued, allowed him to act independently of the local bishop, even if he happened to be Archbishop of Paris.[26]

But a royal marriage is not a satisfactory test of La Rochefoucauld's policies. It was in trying to regulate the daily religious life of the court that he encountered the greatest resistance. His aim was to exercise normal episcopal authority over the administration of the sacraments, preaching, and the provision to benefices such as the parishes and priories throughout France that were of royal foundation. But during his years in office, he found that his authority as grand almoner was simply inadequate for this purpose. Too many categories of court clergy – almoners, royal *prédicateurs* and so on – escaped his jurisdiction altogether. He also lamented the fact that at court the grand almoner's powers had to be exercised personally, and could not be delegated to a grand vicar; when other obligations kept him from the court, his authority virtually lapsed. After several years of effort, he finally concluded that the expression 'bishop of the court' was an empty honour devoid of any real substance. He argued that since most grand almoners were likely to be bishops with other obligations which would occupy their time and keep them away from the court, they would never be in a position to effect the necessary 'réduction à l'obéissance'; the only sensible solution to this impasse was, as in the

23. B.S.G., MS. 366, fos. 370, 374.
24. *Ibid.*, fo. 98, Martial Doubochery to La Rochefoucauld, Rome, 20 January 1620, for the receipt of the lost memorandum.
25. *Ibid.*, fo. 94, letter of 19 January 1620.
26. A.S.V., Nunz. Fr. 62, fo. 95, for the text of his memorandum. For a subsequent discussion by La Rochefoucauld's advisers concerning the marriage: B.S.G., MS. 3238, fos. 233–4. The second Cardinal de Retz was incensed by his uncle's failure to prevent La Rochefoucauld from conducting the marriage: *Oeuvres du cardinal de Retz*, ed. Marie-Thérèse Hipp and Michel Pernot (Paris, 1984), p. 183.

case of the charitable insititutions, to transfer spiritual jurisdiction over the court to the bishop in whose diocese the court happened to be resident.[27]

La Rochefoucauld also recorded his regret, when he came to resigning his office, that his authority was no stronger in other areas nominally under his charge. He was expected to supervise the *Collège royal*, but he found conditions there unsatisfactory, and some of its professors less than worthy of their exalted rank. He also found the whole University of Paris 'en extrême nécéssité d'une puissante authorité pour la restablir, principalement en ce qui concerne la piété et les moeurs', but was forced to confess his own powerlessness to do anything about it.[28] However, he did make strenuous attempts to reform one of its major – and most distinguished – colleges, that of Navarre, responsibility for which lay with him as a result of a royal *brevet de direction* he had received shortly after becoming grand almoner in 1618.[29]

III

In view of his pessimistic conclusions, it was perhaps just as well for La Rochefoucauld that his role as grand almoner was not exhausted by his formal duties, and that its ambiguous contours gave him other, more positive outlets for his interests. The whole question of nominations to church benefices was one that he had always considered to be acutely important. Because there were no clear rules or patterns for nomination to benefices in the king's gift, it was always possible, depending on the character of the king and his entourage, that an influential and strongly motivated grand almoner might acquire some formal role in the exercise of this royal prerogative. Under Louis XIV, nominations partly became matters of administrative routine, dealt with by the 'ministre de la feuille' – the 'feuille' being the list of those awaiting nomination to benefices. But by then its holder was the royal confessor rather than the grand almoner, evidence of the latter's decline in importance.[30] Even this type of rudimentary bureaucracy, which by no means eliminated political intrigue, did not exist under Louis XIII, when nominations were still 'political' in the full sense. Because of

27. B.S.G., MS. 3238, fos. 183–90.
28. *Ibid.*, fos. 186–7.
29. *Ibid.*, fos. 253–6, *règlement* for running of the college; *ibid.*, fos. 471–4, articles and letters patent for union of colleges of Tournai and Navarre, with purpose of establishing a society of theologians like that of the Sorbonne, 1638. La Rochefoucauld explicitly retained the direction of the College when he resigned as grand almoner, on the grounds that it had been given him by virtue of a separate *brevet*.
30. See Norman Ravitch, *Sword and Mitre. Government and Episcopacy in France and England in the Age of Aristocracy* (The Hague, 1966), pp. 57ff; Georges Guitton, *Le Père de La Chaize confesseur de Louis XIV*, 2 vols. (Paris, 1959), i, ch. 10, 'Autour de la feuille des bénéfices'.

this, and because of the crown's predictable unwillingness to restore elections, church reformers realised that the presence of ecclesiastics near the king was vital, if they were to influence his choices and obstruct unsatisfactory ones. La Rochefoucauld fully shared this view, and was to use his office to secure better nominations, especially of bishops.

At present, very little is known about episcopal nominations under Henry IV and Louis XIII. Except for the occasional *cas célèbre*, the documentation is very thin, and must therefore be treated with caution. What is clearly evident, however, is the absence of any kind of 'system'.[31] Even a rumour that a bishop was seriously ill sufficed to set off a frenetic scramble in the king's entourage, as families and clientèles struggled to maintain and, where possible, to improve their position.[32] The exclusive right to nominate candidates to the pope for approval might belong to the king, but he frequently ended up confirming other people's choices or arrangements; in many cases, benefices changed hands like secular offices, through acts of resignation. Bishops and abbots would seek to obtain the successor of their choice by having them appointed coadjutors during their lifetime. Certain nomination rights had been alienated in the previous century to individuals or members of the royal family.[33] As La Rochefoucauld himself once confessed, reformers were wary of becoming involved in so openly political and explosive and arena.[34] The king's confessor was, in theory at least, the best placed to influence royal decisions, but he also ran the risk, and it was by no means negligible, that he would offend the powerful and lose the king's favour.

Although unproven, it is usually claimed that the quality of the French episcopate improved under Henry IV. Certainly, the pluralism of the previous century disappeared completely with the Cardinal de Joyeuse. But Rome remained less than happy with some royal decisions, and in 1611 Paul V strongly urged the new regent, Marie de Medici, to nominate worthy candidates.[35] Nothing especially new emerged from the Estates General of 1614 which, it will be recalled,

---

31. Michel Péronnet, *Les Evêques de l'ancienne France*, 2 vols. (Lille, 1978) is much more informative on the eighteenth than on the seventeenth century.
32. For numerous examples of this, see *Les Papiers de Richelieu*, vols. i–vi. *passim.*
33. Under Louis XIII, for example, Marie de Medici could 'present' to the king her choices for all the Breton bishoprics, as well as for Clermont and St Flour. Gaston d'Orléans could nominate to numerous benefices, but not the episcopal sees, in his apanage of Orléans and Chartres; contemporaries, who may not have been aware of this, assumed episcopal nominations there were in his gift: B.S.G., MS. 3249, fo. 202, Nicolas de Netz to La Rochefoucauld, 19 August 1630: 'Le Roy m'ayant fait l'honneur de me nommer à l'évesché d'Orléans lorsque j'y pensois le moins, croyant que la nomination en appartenoit à Monsieur frère du Roy à cause de son apanage'.
34. Rome, Corsini Library, MS. 713, fo. 238, copy of letter to Jean Arnoux, S.J., 16 November 1621.
35. Ludwig von Pastor, *History of the Popes*, (London, 1937), xxvi, pp. 464–6, for the text of the brief.

asked La Rochefoucauld to draft a petition to the king for the
restoration of elections. The Assembly of Notables of 1617 went
further, suggesting the establishment of a council to advise the king
on nominations, 'pour le décharge de sa conscience'. There were also
complaints against the flood of coadjutors being forced on bishops who
had no need whatever of them.[36] The abortive reform edict of July
1618 confined itself to proposing that bishops submit a slate of worthy
candidates to the king for preferment at the end of their provincial
councils; it also promised an end to coadjutorships and expectancies.[37]

La Rochefoucauld, who had participated in all of these debates, thus
became grand almoner at a time when serious reform suggestions were
in the air, even at court. His main concern was to see much greater
care exercised in the choice of bishops, without which reform at
diocesan level stood little chance of success. It was also known that,
since Concini's fall in April 1617, Louis XIII had expressed his desire
to choose worthy bishops. But such promises were, under the circumstances, difficult to honour. Procedures for adequately informing the
king did not really exist, and there were all kinds of reasons for not
wishing to offend families and factions in search of high church office.
With the aid of successive royal confessors, La Rochefoucauld
attempted to ensure that the king's nominations would be made with
as much knowledge as was possible about the calibre of the candidates.
We can assume that much of this work was done orally and infor-
mally; with episcopal nominations averaging no more than five a
year, it is hardly surprising to find few traces of such activity in
the records.

That La Rochefoucauld's standards were high was already well
known. Consulted by Ubaldini in 1615 about a coadjutor recently
nominated to Noyon, he gave a devastatingly negative report, undeterred by the fact that the nominee was brother to a president in the
parlement of Paris.[38] Such severity would not win him friends at court,
and might even prevent him from having any say as grand almoner in
episcopal appointments. In 1621, we still find him complaining
strongly about a particularly scandalous nomination to Coutances, and
of others made since then.[39] The papacy, still struggling to have the
canonical enquiry 'de vie et de moeurs' into royal nominees conducted
exclusively by the nuncio, and unhappy about progress towards the
reform of episcopal nominations, valued La Rochefoucauld's co-
operation and consistency. Shortly after his election, the energetic

36. Steffani, *Nunziatura di Bentivoglio*, ii, p. 129; *Mémoires de Mathieu Molé*, i, p. 194.
37. B.N., MS. Dupuy 35, fo. 5v.
38. B.N., MS. Italian 1269, fos. 249–52, Ubaldini to Borghese, 27 September 1615.
39. Rome, Corsini Library, MS. 713, fo. 240, La Rochefoucauld to Arnoux, 16 November
    1621.

Gregory XV urged him to see to it that vacant benefices were filled and nominees promptly sent to Rome for their bulls of provision.[40]

In practice, the most pressing problem encountered by La Rochefoucauld after his appointment as grand almoner seems to have been that of episcopal coadjutorships, which guaranteed succession rights for those who secured them, and were easily wrested from the crown in times of political weakness. There was a steady flow of such nominations each year during the 1610s, and the papacy became increasingly exasperated by the importunity of the French court.[41] It had high hopes that the resolutions of the Assembly at Rouen in 1617 would rectify matters; the king himself approved of these, but the hopes were disappointed.[42] Rome frequently reminded its nuncio to take a firm stand, and it supplied him in 1618 with a list of recent coadjutorships to assist in the struggle to stem the flow of royal largesse; it was feared that virtually all bishoprics would end up being filled in advance by coadjutors.[43] The king was embarrassed when reminded of his earlier promises. In mid-1619, at the same time that he became personally interested in the reform of the orders, he commissioned La Rochefoucauld, Retz, Arnoux and Bishop L'Estang of Carcassonne to investigate problems relating to current episcopal nominations. They considered three cases, and in each they recommended the appointment of suffragans to perform the episcopal functions, because of the age or incapacity of the incumbent bishop. And, in a challenge to the practice of nominating coadjutors, they reminded the king that the question of whether the suffragans should eventually succeed to the dioceses in question was entirely secondary, and should not influence his decisions.[44] Shortly afterwards, La Rochefoucauld was able to inform the nuncio that the king had again resolved to make worthy nominations henceforth, and asked him to ensure that the pope would himself take a harder line in rejecting those who were manifestly unsuitable for the mitre.[45] Judging by La

40. B.S.G., MS. 3248, fo. 607, Cardinal Ludoviso to La Rochefoucauld, 13 March 1622; B.A.V., Barb. lat 7952, fo. 17, La Rochefoucauld's reply, 30 April.
41. Archivio di Stato, Ferrara, *fondo* Bentivoglio 18/11, no. 100, Borghese to Bentivoglio, 29 May 1617; *ibid.*, no. 221, to same 19 October 1617; Steffani, *Nunziatura di Bentivoglio*, i, pp. 507–8, for the nuncio's account of his efforts to secure better nominations.
42. Archivio di Stato, Ferrara, *fondo* Bentivoglio 18/12, no. 71, Borghese to Bentivoglio, 18 March 1618; Steffani, *Nunziatura di Bentivoglio*, ii, p. 331, Bentivoglio to Borghese, 14 April 1618; *ibid.*, p. 339, to same, 25 April; *ibid.*, pp. 538–9, to same 15 August.
43. The list is in Archivio di Stato, Ferrara, *fondo* Bentivoglio 18/12, no. 198; it was sent to the nuncio in July 1618: *ibid.*, no. 197, Borghese to nuncio, 8 July. The frequency of the requests for coadjutorships can be seen from the letters from Cardinal des Ursins in Rome to the French court: B.N., MS. Fr. 18011, fos. 55, 93, 132, 254, 281, 304, 316, 336; MS. Fr. 18012, fos. 20–1, 106, 226, 334.
44. B.S.G., MS. 3238, fos. 343–4, for the record of their deliberations, 1 September 1619.
45. Steffani, *Nunziatura di Bentivoglio*, iii, p. 501, Bentivoglio to Borghese, 11 September 1619.

Rochefoucauld's own account, this problem was not solved rapidly.

If La Rochefoucauld's initial influence on episcopal nominations appears limited, and our account of it sketchy, this is largely because the notion of the royal *conseil de conscience* as then conceived was in an early stage of development. It was not until 1643 that such a council, with a well defined membership, met regularly to discuss candidates for benefices and make recommendations to the crown. Before that, it was more a question of advice being sought by the king in certain cases only, and 'pour la décharge de sa conscience'. Such advice was only requested when the king himself had doubts, and wished to know whether he could in conscience make a nomination he suspected to be unworthy. His personal attitude depended on who had access to him, and could bring most influence to bear. La Rochefoucauld explained this succinctly to Richelieu in October 1631 towards the end of his term in office:

> 'So far I have not actually proposed anyone to the king for vacant bishoprics. The weight of the responsibility and my own weakness are what have restrained me in these matters. When the king has commanded me to do something, it has been my practice to take advice from people I judged suitable for the purpose, in order to protect his conscience and reputation. I then reported it to His Majesty, who might otherwise have attributed his own ignorance on such occasions to lack of good advice.[46]

Clearly, the *conseil* still functioned in a very limited way, and then only to exclude the undersirable. Indeed, there is no evidence that La Rochefoucauld either tried to, or succeeded in placing men of his own choosing on the episcopal bench. The surviving sources suggest that he gradually became the king's regular *conseil* in the above limited sense of the term. Even a man as determined as La Rochefoucauld to improve nominations found himself placed in an invidious and isolated position at court, as is illustrated by a significant incident from 1621–2.

The last Guise cardinal, Louis III de Lorraine, entered the church simply to preserve the family's collection of benefices, which included the see of Reims and a string of great abbeys like Cluny, St Denis and Corbie.[47] Even after becoming a cardinal in 1615, he remained restless

---

46. *Papiers de Richelieu*, vi, p. 621, 14 October 1631, 'Je n'ay jusques à présent proposé aucunes personnes pour les évêchés. La grandeur de la charge et la foiblesse de mon jugement m'aiant deu contenir en ce sujet, et quand il a pleu au Roy de m'y faire quelque commandement, je l'ay emploié à prendre avis de personnes que j'ay estimé le pouvoir, à la décharge de sa conscience et de sa réputation, et en ay fait rapport à Sa Majesté, laquelle nous eut reproché ne sçavoir, manque de bon conseil en ces occasions'.
47. What follows is based on my article, 'The Decline and Fall of the House of Guise as an Ecclesiastical Dynasty', *Historical Journal* 25 (1982), pp. 781–803, especially 792ff.

and troublesome; he quarrelled with the duc de Guise, his brother, partly because the latter would not let him have a share of the Joyeuse benefices which also fell into Guise hands in 1615. When Louis died suddenly in mid-1621, nothing had been decided in respect of his benefices, though the Guise family were determined to ensure that the duc's seven-year old son would step into his uncle's shoes.

Louis XIII was on campaign in southern France when informed by his confessor, Jean Arnoux, of the affair and its implications. He quickly turned for advice to La Rochefoucauld, who had remained in Paris. This presented the cardinal with a delicate task, as he himself had strong family ties to the Guises. He assembled a group of theologians and personally endorsed their firm refusal to allow Guise to retain Reims, Cluny and the other abbeys. It was now the Guises's turn to besiege the king, and they convinced him that La Rochefoucauld was being unreasonable over this; they promised to convene a second assembly which would give a more balanced opinion, and this it duly did, although it was one which La Rochefoucauld, naturally, did not endorse. Comparing the two recommendations, Louis XIII was troubled by the discrepancies between them, and told Arnoux to inform the cardinal that he wanted his personal opinion above all: 'he was anxious to have your opinion above all others, in order to be sure whether he could in conscience make a decision one way or the other, and that your silence appeared suspicious to him.'

La Rochefoucauld chose to speak clearly and unequivocally against Guise demands.[48] It was, he said, a question of whether the service of God and of souls should be set aside to please powerful individuals. It angered him to see an archbishopric and five abbeys – 'ces épouvantables charges', as he described them – going to a child incapable of governing himself, let alone others. To insert special clauses in the *brevets de nomination* to the effect that, if the young Guise could not have them immediately, they would be 'reserved' for him for later, was a clear case of *confidence*. Proposing him as coadjutor to the abbot of Cluny was equally intolerable, and the recently-elected abbot should be confirmed without delay, so that the order could be properly governed and reformed. Nor should any Guise candidate for Reims be considered, lest an arrangement smacking of *confidence* follow such an appointment. He relented somewhat by conceding that if Guise 'honour' required it, the young heir might be given those benefices which did not involve the cure of souls, and in conclusion, wrote that he attached great importance to the king's decision, since the consultations left no excuse for uninformed or precipitate action. If the right decision were not taken, future reform would be all the more

48. Rome, Corsini Library MS. 713, fos. 238–42, copy of letter to Arnoux, 16 November 1621.

difficult; a bad precedent set in a major case would make it hard to refuse similar concessions to others later. He also pointed out that the king's prerogative entailed a heavy responsibility before God and that, surrounded as he was by people who generally obtained benefices 'sur injustes demandes', the king could only save his soul 'par bon conseil des personnes qui puissent décharger sa conscience'.

While recognising that the line he took was severe, La Rochefoucauld wrote that 'ma response est nettement comme Sa Maiesté la désire'. This may have been so, but it did not settle the matter. There was a change of confessor in December 1621, and Louis XIII postponed his decision until his return to Paris in early 1622. Gaspar Ségueran, the new confessor, did not feel strong enough to support La Rochefoucauld in the last phase of the drama, and the resourceful duchesse de Guise succeeded in excluding the cardinal altogether from the final negotiations, which were brought to a conclusion by Ségueran, with the assistance of La Rochefoucauld's friend, the Sorbonne theologian André Du Val. Nevertheless, La Rochefoucauld did win a moral victory of sorts, for Guise had at least to part with Reims and Cluny, leaving his son with five major abbeys for his sustenance.[49]

While untypical of the general run of royal nominations, the Guise affair does reveal the difficulties and pressures facing anyone intent on improving nomination procedures in the French church. While political considerations may have enabled the Guises to retain most of their benefices in 1622, La Rochefoucauld was not damaged by the conflict. His appointment to the royal council followed in September 1622, and this probably enhanced his ability to act as the king's *conseil de conscience*. Once again, the evidence is scattered and fragmentary, but it all points in the same direction: La Rochefoucauld's own surviving papers contain a number of memoranda prepared for him by his advisers on dubious or unknown candidates for the mitre.[50] Curiously, his role emerges clearest of all in the discussions that followed Archbishop Marquemont of Lyon's request in 1624 that he be allowed to return from Rome to his diocese; the king's ministers obviously wished him to remain at his post. Always well-informed, Marquemont wrote that the king wanted 'l'avis de Monsieur le Cardinal de La Rochefoucault et d'autres personnes qu'Elle [Sa Majesté] a choisis pour conseil de conscience, ou ledict Cardinal tout seul.'[51] Marquemont also saw that his best chance of a recall lay with La Rochefoucauld, who had once been in a similar position, but confessed that if the cardinal agreed with the ministers, that would satisfy

---

49. Bergin 'Decline and Fall of Guise Ecclesiastical Dynasty', pp. 797−9.
50. B.S.G., MS. 366, fos. 374−5; MS, 3238, fos. 183−90; MS. 3249, fo. 340.
51. B.N., MS. Fr. 16052, fo. 253, Marquemont to Phélypeaux, secretary of state, 16 April 1624.

his conscience.[52] Two months later, the secretary of state conveyed the council's refusal to the archbishop and, to underline the responsible nature of the decision, added:

> Cardinal La Rochefoucauld, who is quite scrupulous and severe where questions of conscience are concerned, also took the general view, recognizing that the service of the king and of the public was a valid discharge for your conscience in the sight of God, especially as your suffragan bishops and grand vicars can stand in for you.[53]

Apart from underlining the importance of La Rochefoucauld's judgement, this delay also suggests that he conducted his own enquiry about the state of the diocese of Lyon. It is equally significant that when, in the following year, Marquemont tried again to leave Rome, he wrote directly, albeit without effect, to La Rochefoucauld.[54] There is no evidence that Louis XIII ever had a properly constituted *conseil de conscience*, but Marquemont was aware that La Rochefoucauld, acting alone, partially filled such a role.

Further evidence shows that La Rochefoucauld, although increasingly absent from court, retained considerable influence over nominations after 1624. In December 1625, Richelieu proposed Henri de Sponde for the see of Pamiers, but La Rochefoucauld, for reasons that remain unclear, opposed him. Richelieu only got his way by using the nuncio as an intermediary with the cardinal.[55] The following year, Béthune, French ambassador in Rome, canvassed his son's claim to Lyon, and then to Bayonne, which the king seemed disposed to grant to him, until La Rochefoucauld objected that the son was too young. In doing so, he apparently created a scene in council, but did succeed in frustrating Béthune's ambitions.[56] The same year,

52. *Ibid.*, fos. 280–1, letter to Louis XIII, 6 May.
53. 'Monsieur le Cardinal de La Rochefoucauld qui est assez délicat et sevère en matière de conscience, s'est aussy rendu aux voeux communs, et a reconnu que le service de Sa Majesté et du public estoit une dispense et une décharge valable envers Dieu pour vostre conscience, puisque vos suffragans et grans vicaires peuvent suppléer.' *Ibid.*, fo. 327, Phélypeaux to Marquemont, 6 June.
54. B.S.G., MS. 3249, fo. 124, letter of 26 August 1625.
55. B.L. Addit. MS. 8730, fo. 138, *avviso* of 19 December 1625: 'trovandosi vacante il vescovado di Pamia (*sic*)...il sign. Card de Richelieu aiuta per la nominatione de la persona di M de Sponde che si trova a Roma, ma perche'l sign. Card de la Roccafocò vi fa qualche oppositione, la cosa perche resti sospesa. Richelieu m'ha pregato far uffici, come da me, col Card Rocchefoucault per che desista dall'oppositione. Io ho promesso parlarne'. Although the author of these *avvisi* remains unknown, the most probable candidate is the nuncio, Spada. Sponde eventually got Pamiers: *ibid.*, fo. 157, 16 January 1626.
56. *Ibid.*, fo. 321v. *avviso* of 23 October 1626: '[Béthune] si duoli assai, che'l sr cardinale de la Roccafocò habbia strepitato col Rè e col consiglio sopra l'età del'abbate di Bettunes'. For Béthune's earlier petition for Lyon, and his complaint that Bayonne really was beyond the pale of civilisation: B.N. MS. Fr. 3678, fos. 108–9, letter to Phélypeaux, 4 November 1626.

when Richelieu wished to give the see of Toulon to his well-known protégé and pamphleteer, Mathieu de Morgues, there was immediate opposition. Richelieu promptly informed the nuncio that de Morgues would only receive Toulon if La Rochefoucauld gave his consent. But on being asked about the nomination, the latter replied that 'the king had not mentioned it to him, as he was in the habit of doing for all the others, and that if he had, he would have rejected de Morgues'. What subsequently happened is unclear, but de Morgues never received Toulon. He felt Richelieu had let him down, and certainly regarded La Rochefoucauld, whose pro-Jesuit Ultramontanism he attacked, as responsible for his defeat.[57] Also in 1626, La Rochefoucauld was warned by his grand vicar of the need for vigilance in the case of Reims where he obviously feared a Guise comeback in the form of a request from the ailing archbishop for a coadjutor in the person of the youthful son of the duc de Guise. The move was evidently stopped, but in 1628 the young Guise had his way after the archbishop's death.[58] By that date, evidence of La Rochefoucauld's continuing influence over nominations has all but disappeared. He might still be grand almoner, but the infrequency of his visits to court must have precluded any regular say in ecclesiastical affairs. Even so, a letter to Richelieu in October 1631, shortly before he was to resign his office, suggests that the king or Richelieu had continued to seek his advice about candidates for the mitre.[59]

La Rochefoucauld's claim in 1626 that the king consulted him on *all* episcopal nominations may be exaggerated, or possibly misreported, especially in view of his own later statement to Richelieu that such consultations were occasional. But there is no denying the use he made of his grand almonership. It is equally clear that Richelieu, once he had established his hold on power, was keen to control episcopal nominations. He seems to have successfully warned off the royal confessor as early as 1625 from intervening in such matters.[60] But this certainly did not account for La Rochefoucauld and, as the incidents from 1625–6 suggest, it may have taken Richelieu several years to secure the control he wished. Indeed, it may not be far-fetched to

57. A.S.V., Nunz. Fr. 65, fos. 213–15, Spada to Barberini, 22 June 1626; *ibid.*, fo. 352, to same, 3 November 1626.
58. B.S.G., MS. 3249, fo. 287, Jean Frizon to La Rochefoucauld, 11 April 1626. See Bergin, 'Decline and Fall of the Guise Ecclesiastical Dynasty', p. 800.
59. *Les Papiers de Richelieu*, vi, p. 621, La Rochefoucauld to Richelieu, October 1631.
60. *Ibid.*, i, p. 239, [late 1625]: 'N'ayez point l'ambition de disposer des éveschez et abbayes, estant chose qui doit dépendre immediatement du Roy, ainsy que toutes les autres grâces; à moins que vous ne seussiez quelques raisons qui vous obligeassent en conscience de parler pour empescher que les grandes charges de l'Eglise fussent remplies par des personnes indignes de les posséder'. Several years later, in 1628, Suffren wrote to Richelieu: 'La crainte que j'ay qu'on ne m'embarque en ces matières bénéficiales comme mes prédécesseurs s'y estoient laissés porter, me fait d'estre réservé': Bibliothèque de l'Institut, collection Godefroy 15, fo. 394.

suggest that one reason he persuaded La Rochefoucauld to resign his office in favour of his brother, Alphonse, in 1632, was to ensure that he would not be faced by a grand almoner claiming to be the guardian of the king's conscience. In any event, there is no doubt that La Rochefoucauld's years in that office helped establish the case for such a guardian, and were an important step on the road towards a formal *conseil de conscience*, as well as a contribution to the reform of the episcopate.

6

The Reform of the Old Orders and the Origins of La Rochefoucauld's Commission of 1622

I

WITH A FEW distinguished exceptions, the old orders do not figure prominently in the historiography of the French Counter-Reformation. This may be because there are few genuine successes to record, or because the chronicle of failed reforms constitutes a depressing chapter of the Counter-Reformation that is best forgotten. Clearly the newer orders, both male and female, were more sensitive to contemporary religious and social needs, and proved more attractive to those entering the religious life out of a sense of calling. Orders like the Jesuits, Capuchins, Oratorians, Lazarists and Eudists among the male societies, and the Ursulines, Carmelites and *Visitandines* among the female, dominate the historical accounts, sometimes to the point where the Counter-Reformation seems little more than the history of their birth and expansion.

But none of this demonstrates that the older orders were unsuited to the needs of the age. On the contrary, there is abundant evidence that, if reformed, they could act as centres of religious revival, and attract individuals of outstanding character and ability. The earliest stirrings of the French Counter-Reformation during the 1590s and 1600s owed much to reformed houses of old orders like the Benedictines, Carthusians and Carmelites, and many of the forty or so religious houses founded in Paris between 1600 and 1640 belonged to the old orders.[1] Thereafter, the Maurists, Port Royal and the Cistercian Strict

---

1. See Jean Dagens, *Bérulle et les origines de la restauration catholique* (Paris, 1952); Roland Mousnier, *Paris capitale au temps de Richelieu et de Mazarin* (Paris, 1978).

Observance were proof of their continuing attractiveness and of the positive role the orders could play in the French church.[2] To ignore the old orders because they contributed less than those of recent foundation is to neglect an important dimension of the Counter-Reformation. There was not a single figure of any importance in the French church of the time who did not devote some of his energy to the reform of the old orders. To regard them as survivors from an earlier age is to miss the point; the real question facing contemporaries was how to reform them and revive their original observance.

The reform of the orders was perhaps the single most difficult problem facing the Counter-Reformation church, and its limited success is not altogether surprising. Given the size, numbers, wealth and structure of the orders, it could scarcely have been otherwise. The worse abuses denounced by generations of reformers flourished among them – the misuse of considerable power and wealth, the neglect of spiritual and pastoral responsibility, the endless quest for benefices, and so on. No active bishop could even begin to reform his diocese without confronting the orders settled in it: their extensive possessions, their numerous and widely-scattered benefices and, above all, their claim to exercise a pastoral ministry independently of episcopal control made sure of that. Monastic and diocesan reform were thus inextricable, and some of the bitterest conflicts of the century were between bishops and monastic houses. The reform of the orders was thus an essential item on the agenda of church reform generally, not a peripheral addendum to it or the preserve of the orders themselves.[3] It was an important test of the intentions and priorities of the papacy, the French crown, the episcopate and the orders. There were, of course, major obstacles besetting reform, but success depended crucially on the ability of these parties to work together effectively. However, harmonious co-operation of this kind was notoriously difficult to achieve, which helps to explain the wide discrepancy in the results of efforts at reform in the post-Tridentine church.

A late-comer to monastic reform, the French church had its own peculiar problems, which obviously conditioned the approaches to reform taken there. Unless we examine these problems, we shall not understand why it was decided in 1622 to set aside normal procedures for reform, and to introduce, with full royal support, an extraordinary papal commission to deal with the embarrassing problems posed by the old orders. After briefly sketching the condition of the orders, we shall turn our attention to the negotiations that led to the 1622

2. For the record of the Maurists in Lorraine, see G. Michaux, 'Les Professions dans la congrégation de Saint-Vanne et Saint-Hydulphe', *Annales de l'Est* 27 (1975), pp. 63–78.
3. For the question of their reform in La Rochefoucauld's own diocese of Clermont, see Louise Welter, *La Réforme ecclésiastique*, chs. 4, 5, 9, 11, 14.

decision, as the arguments deployed then provide the best insights into the minds of those who were directly concerned with promoting reform among the orders.

II

Like most of Europe, France had had its observant reform movements well before the seventeenth century. The most recent of these had preceded the Council of Trent, especially at the turn of the sixteenth century.[4] They merit some attention here, because the similarities with events that took place a century later are striking. Both the episcopate and the observant movements among the orders looked to the crown as the only effecitve agent of reform, and obtained its support from the early 1490s onwards. This support culminated in the wide-ranging commission given by both pope and king to the principal royal minister, Cardinal d'Amboise, to implement reforms among the monastic and mendicant orders. The orders were forbidden to claim privilege or exemption against him or his delegates. Like his Spanish counterpart Cisneros, who received similar powers from the pope, Amboise favoured the formation of observant congregations within the orders, with their own superiors, visitors and general chapters. His reform measures were often published as decrees of the royal council, and he did not hesitate to wield his authority as royal minister when his powers as papal commissioner appeared inadequate.[5] However, both the scope and the success of his measures proved more limited than in Spain, where the majority of religious houses joined the reformed congregations, and could elect their own abbots on a regular basis.[6] In contrast, the French crown continued to extend rather than limit its practice of giving abbeys *in commendam* to ecclesiastics or even laymen. After the Concordat of Bologna (1516), the *commende* was gradually applied to most of France's monastic establishments. A century later, it was still a major stumbling-block in the way of reform.[7]

4. Francis Rapp, *L'Eglise et la vie religieuse en occident à la fin du moyen age* (Paris, 1971), pp. 216ff; H.O. Evennett, *The Spirit of the Counter Reformation* (Cambridge, 1968), ch. 4; Hubert Jedin, 'Zur Vorgeschichte der Regularenreform, Trid. Sess. XXV' *Römische Quartalschrift* 44 (1936), pp. 231ff.
5. On Amboise, see Pierre Imbart de la Tour, *Les Origines de la réforme*, (Paris, 1946), ii, pp. 488ff. On the observant movements, see the special number devoted to them by the *Revue d'histoire de l'église de France* 65, no. 174 (1979), as well as the classic A. Renaudet, *Préréforme et humanisme à Paris pendant les premières guerres d'Italie 1495–1517* (Paris, 1916) and Jean-Pierre Massaut, *Josse Clichtove, l'humanisme et la réforme du clergé*.
6. There is an extensive account of the Spanish reforms in José Garcia Oro, *La Reforma de los religiosos españoles en tiempo de los reyes católicos* (Valladolid, 1969).
7. See R.J. Knecht, 'The Concordat of 1516: a Reassessment' *University of Birmingham Historical Journal* 9 (1963), pp. 16–32; Pierre Blet, 'Le Concordat de Bologne et la réforme tridentine', *Gregorianum* 45 (1964), pp. 241–79.

Most of Amboise's congregations survived throughout the sixteenth century, but the reform movement itself gradually lost momentum. His congregations ceased to be genuinely observant, but survived out of a desire to preserve the rights and privileges acquired during the reform period. Later reformers would nearly always find in them adversaries of new reforms. The crown's commitment to reform also proved short-lived, as its refusal to curtail the *commende* suggests. In contrast, reform proved more lasting in Spain because the crown remained committed to eliminating abuses, even in the face of curial malpractices against which the Spanish church was less well protected than that of France. Accompanying the Abbot of Cîteaux to Spain in 1603–4, Barthélemy Joly noted the splendour, wealth and discipline of the monasteries they visited, even if his truculent nationalism prevented him from indulging in comparisons unflattering to the French orders.[8]

The French Wars of Religion erupted just as the Counter-Reformation was, with the termination of the Council of Trent, entering a new phase. They ensured that the time-scale of reform in France would differ from that of Catholic Europe, something which makes historical comparison difficult. Few of the earlier reforms survived the wars. A Benedictine 'congrégation des exempts' was formed shortly after Trent, attracting a sizeable membership; but it seemed more intent on escaping from possible episcopal control than in genuine reform, and it began to break up as early as the 1580s.[9] A series of able abbots of Cîteaux made only modest headway in trying to improve observance in their French houses, while Cluny attempted scarcely anything during the long tenure of its Guise abbots (1528–1622).[10] If one is to believe foreign observers, the French orders remained in a much worse state than in other Catholic countries for many decades to come.[11]

It would be pointless to attempt to catalogue here the familiar lamentations, many of which changed little over the centuries, of both reformers and critics of the French old orders. It will suffice to examine a few central issues which contributed significantly to the emergence

8. L. Barrau-Dihigo, ed., 'Voyage de Barthélemy Joly en Espagne, 1603–4', *Revue hispanique* 20 (1909), pp. 459ff.

9. U. Berlière, 'La Congrégation bénédictine des exempts de France' *Revue Bénédictine* 14 (1897), pp. 398ff.

10. On Cîteaux see, Polycarpe Zakar, *Histoire de la stricte observance de l'ordre cistercien depuis ses débuts jusqu'au généralat du cardinal de Richelieu* (Rome, 1966) chs. 1–2; Louis J. Lekai, *The Rise of the Cistercian Strict Observance in Seventeenth Century France* (Washington, D.C., 1968), chs. 1–2. On Cluny, see J.A. Bergin, 'The Decline and Fall of the House of Guise as an Ecclesiastical Dynasty', *Historical Journal* 25 (1982), pp. 783, 785, 790, 796–800; G. Charvin, 'L'Abbaye et l'ordre de Cluny de la fin du xve au début du xviie siècle', *Revue Mabillon* 43 (1953), pp. 85–117; 44 (1954), pp. 6–29, 105–32.

11. The correspondence of the papal nuncios, little of which has been published for the late sixteenth or early seventeenth century, abounds with references to the orders.

by the 1610s of the conviction that effective reform could only be achieved through extraordinary measures.

As indicated earlier, the growth of the *commende* seriously hampered efforts at reform. During the sixteenth century, a hard-pressed monarchy used its right of appointment to hundreds of abbeys and priories as a valuable source of patronage. The leading churchmen, royal servants and the court aristocracy generally, benefited enormously from this, especially when the crown was weak. The accumulation of several benefices by a single individual or family became common, and some of the most spectacular collections belonged to cardinals like Guise, Bourbon or Joyeuse, or even to royal princes like Condé, Conty or Soissons. Cluny, which as head of an order should have escaped the *commende*, was in Guise hands for almost a century. Only Cîteaux and some of its leading houses seem to have consistently escaped it.[12] The abbeys held by these men usually had many subordinate houses of their own, which by increasing their patronage powers, extended the impact of the *commende* downwards through the orders.

The effects of the *commende* were wide-ranging. Commendators usually claimed the right to receive and profess new members, to appoint to monastic offices and to nominate to outside benefices in the abbey's gift – all prized sources of patronage, whose impact on the monastic regime is easily imagined. The religious wars introduced a major new complaint against the *commende*. Widespread destruction made it urgently necessary to undertake expensive building and repair work, without which any trace of monastic life might disappear altogether. But commendators were generally reluctant in the early seventeenth century to contribute sums corresponding to their share of the revenues, and individual monasteries were rarely powerful enough to oblige them to do so. Moreover, the general absence of an agreed and equitable division of monastic revenues between commendator and community, a problem as old as the *commende*, continued to bedevil relations between the two sides. Consequently, it was all too often impossible to effect repairs to the 'claustral' buildings (chapel, chapter, dormitory, refectory, infirmary, etc.) indispensable for normal community life.[13] Canonical visitors inspecting religious houses in several regions of France during the early seventeenth century still commented on the appalling physical state of many of them, which had the effct of postponing plans for their reform.[14] For

---

12. See the references in n. 10, above.
13. See Guy Lemarchand, 'Les Monastères de Haute-Normandie, essai de bilan économique', *Annales historiques de la révolution française*, 37 (1965), pp. 4ff, for some useful material on the seventeenth century.
14. For example: report by Jean Darnault to Cardinal Givry on the *exempts* of Aquitaine and Occitanie, June 1607, in U. Berlière and J.B. Kaiser, 'Le Cardinal de Givry et les Bénédictins', *Revue Bénédictine* 42 (1930), pp. 257–67; Louis J. Lekai, 'Moral and Material Status of the French Cistercian Abbeys in the Seventeenth Century', *Analecta Cisterciensia* 19 (1963), pp. 199ff.

that reason, it was not uncommon for some of these houses to be offered by their members to reform movements in the hope that the latter would shoulder the financial burden. Unsolved problems like these fuelled the existing animus against the *commende*.

The *commende* was, however, not the source of every evil in the monastic world; reform was possible, as we shall see, without its abolition. The monastic world itself had undergone internal change. The religious wars accelerated the abandonment of enclosed, community life that was already widespread since the later Middle Ages. Common property and revenues tended to be divided up into individual prebends or 'places'. Monastic offices like those of prior, sacristan or steward, had frequently become benefices which could be acquired, exchanged and passed on to others, usually to members of one's own family, like church benefices generally. Revenues assigned to these offices became part of their incumbents' personal prebends, for which they largely ceased to be accountable. As a result, most monasteries were administered and controlled by a small oligarchy of office-holders drawn mostly from the better-off local families, and with a strong interest in preserving the status quo; their families could thus count on placing younger sons and daughters in a relatively convenient and undemanding environment. It was the combined resistance of office-holders and local notables that reformers often found the most difficult to overcome.[15] This was particularly the case, it appears, among the Benedictines, the Augustinian canons-regular and most female orders, since they did not possess a corporate structure; among them, each house was a tiny self-governing republic firmly anchored in local society.[16] Membership was strictly controlled through the system of 'places', which served to maintain the value of individual prebends.

Finally, the orders were past masters at using the complex system of legal appeals, either to the royal courts or to Rome, available to them, and which usually proved more than an adequate cushion against superiors, bishops or reformers. The cornerstone of the whole system was the long-established and contentious *appel comme d'abus* to a royal court against an alleged abuse of power by an ecclesiastical authority or tribunal. As clear definitions of what constituted such an abuse were lacking, the *appel* proved to be an admirably flexible instrument of self-defence. Seventeenth-century magistrates, despite their dislike of monastic 'disorders', did not lightly sacrifice the opportunities it afforded to erode ecclesiastical jurisdiction. The only effective method

15. René Pillorget, 'Réforme monastique et conflits de rupture dans quelques localités de la France méridionale au xvii siècle', *Revue historique* 252 (1975), pp. 77–106, for some striking illustrations of this.
16. For an examination of these issues in the context of the reform of a single abbey, see J.A. Bergin, 'Ways and Means of Monastic Reform in Seventeenth-Century France: St Denis de Reims 1630–1633', *Catholic Historical Review* 72 (1986), pp. 14–32.

of overriding an *appel comme d'abus* was to secure the support of the royal council – an impossibility for all but a well-placed few. Reformers, and not just of the orders, held the *appel* to be a major scourge of the French church, one which reminded them of their dependence on the crown. Moreover, since the decrees of the Council of Trent were not part of French law, bishops were unable to counteract the *appel* by availing of the right enshrined in the decrees to visit and reform monasteries as delegates of the papacy. Moreover, the papal curia was not averse to upholding appeals to it from the orders, especially against external interference. Since their privileges and exemptions originated in papal grants, the curia was merely defending its own conception of papal power by accepting appeals for its intervention and protection. As La Rochefoucauld would repeatedly discover, not even the Counter-Reformation papacy would refrain from putting the defence of privilege above the pursuit of reform.

III

The first stirrings of reform were visible among the French orders by the 1590s. Most of them were supported by Clement VIII, whose otherwise undistinguished pontificate has an impressive record in the field of monastic reform.[17] The Feuillant congregation emerged within the Cistercian order in the 1580s and 1590s, while the same order's future 'strict observance' began to take root in the daughter houses of Clairvaux after 1600.[18] In 1596, Clement VIII laid down guidelines for the revival of the Benedictine 'congrégation des exempts'; but some of its leading members despaired of its will to reform and obtained permission to launch their own reform in 1603 under the name of the 'société de Bretagne'.[19] Similarly, a small observant movement among the Mathurins or *Trinitaires* obtained papal approval in 1601.[20] On the other hand, Cluny was still in Guise hands and therefore leaderless, with the leading reform movement among the Benedictines still confined to Lorraine.

To a large extent, these efforts at reform sought to revive older forms of observance. This was a common feature of reform movements, but in the sixteenth and seventeenth centuries it was reinforced by

17. Ludwig von Pastor, *History of the Popes*, (London, 1933), xxiii, pp. 148ff. See in particular, Clement's instructions to his emissaries throughout Europe in Klaus Jaitner, ed., *Die Hauptinstruktionen Clemens' VIII für die Nuntien und Legaten an die Europäischen Fürstenhofen 1592–1605*, 2 vols. (Tübingen, 1984).
18. Lekai, *Rise of Strict Observance*, pp. 27ff; Zakar, *Histoire*, ch. 1.
19. Berlière, 'Congrégation bénédictine des exempts', p. 403.
20. Paul Deslandres, *L'Ordre des trinitaires pour le rachat des captifs*, 2 vols. (Toulouse-Paris, 1903), i, pp. 227ff.

powerful nostalgia for the early church.[21] As the orders were not quite as old as the church itself, this sentiment engendered veneration of their own original forms of observance. A primary objective was to restore common life in all its aspects, with the necessary suppression of many individual and collective privileges, even if they were based on concessions by the papacy; there was also strong pressure, especially among female orders, to revert to strict rules of monastic enclosure, and to limit casual intercourse with outsiders.[22] But the most visible symbol of reformed observance was the celebration of the divine office and the full monastic liturgy and, to a lesser extent, the practice of manual labour. The Maurists were not alone in attaching importance to study and learning, while the reformed Cistercians emphasised pentitential discipline.[23] But reform among the older orders cannot be viewed merely as a simple return *ad fontes*. Most of them borrowed something from the newer orders, although not without resistance and controversy. Systematic mental prayer and examination of conscience, regular reading in private and in common, as well as variations on the Spiritual Exercises of Ignatius Loyola were among the most important new practices, and profoundly affected the nature and balance of monastic observance.[24] These borrowings were best exemplified in attempts to create special houses of novitiate, in which those seeking admission to the monastic life – called novices – would undergo a thorough grounding in spirituality and religious observance.[25]

The novitiates were only one of several organisational features of reform movements. Since the late Middle Ages, these movements had tended to assume a congregational structure which, by enabling them to choose their own superiors and officials, largely exempted them from subordination to their traditional superiors within the orders. This development was especially likely where a reform stood little chance of winning over an entire order to its cause, or where it feared

21. Gerhart B. Ladner, *The Idea of Reform* (Cambridge, Mass., 1959) is the classic study. For seventeenth century variations on it, see Bruno Neveu, 'Archéolatrie et modernité dans le savoir ecclésiastique au xviiᵉ siècle' *XVII Siècle*, 33 (1981), pp. 169–84; idem., 'L'Erudition ecclésiastique du xviiᵉ siècle et la nostalgie de l'antiquité chrétienne', in *Religion and Humanism*, ed. K.G. Robbins (Oxford, 1981), pp. 195–225, for the intellectual dimensions of this phenomenon.
22. The celebrated 'journée du guichet' of 1609 at the Cistercian convent of Port Royal, when the young Abbess, Angélique Arnauld, refused entry to the cloister to her own family, is the best-known and most quoted instance of this. See Louis Cognet, *La Réforme de Port-Royal* (Paris, 1950).
23. Dominique Julia, 'Les Bénédictins et l'enseignement aux xviiᵉ et xviiiᵉ siècles', in *Sous la règle de Saint Benoît. Structures monastiques et sociétés en France du moyen âge à l'époque moderne* (Geneva, 1982), pp. 345–400; Lekai, *Rise of Cistercian Strict Observance*, ch. 13.
24. P.W. Janssen, *Les Origines de la réforme des Carmes en France au xviiᵉ siècle* (The Hague, 1963), pp. 79–83.
25. Robert Lemoine, *L'Epoque moderne, 1563–1789. Le monde des religieux* [*Histoire du droit et des institutions de l'église en occident*, vol. xv, part ii] (Paris, n.d.), pp. 7–10, for a brief conspectus.

that the order's superiors would attempt to eliminate it altogether.[26] There could also be political reasons for this, as in Spain and Italy, where reformers and rulers alike were anxious to lessen their dependence on superiors resident abroad; this happened especially within Cluny and Cîteaux, both of which were governed by French abbots-general.[27] More generally, reform movements tended to dislike superiors and officials who were elected for life or who held their positions as benefices guaranteeing life-tenure. Wherever possible, they attempted to undermine their status as benefices by insisting that such offices 'belonged' to communities, and not to the individuals holding them; consequently, they insisted on a rotation of offices, usually by election. But they were also convinced that even superiors-general and other leading officials should be elected, so as to guarantee a responsible exercise of authority. Among orders like Cluny and Cîteaux, which were strongly attached to very different traditions, such objectives seemed profoundly disruptive.

La Rochefoucauld, as we shall see, inherited many of these objectives when he became papal commissioner for the reform of the orders in 1622, and his efforts to apply them produced widely contrasting results. Meanwhile, French reform movements seemed to be making painfully slow progress, confined to the margins of orders which they had little hope of converting. This increased the temptation to create autonomous, self-governing, observant congregations, a move which invariably produced conflict and squabbling within the orders. In keeping with tradition, many of the French reform movements appealed directly to the crown to defend them against their orders. In 1606, the general of the 'exempts', Dom Isaye Jaunay, appealed publicly to Henry IV to protect the nascent 'société de Bretagne'.[28] In the following year a similar, though indirect, call was made to the king to enforce Clement VIII's constitutions for the 'exempts' themselves.[29] Henry seemed more interested in promoting a new congregation being founded by the 'royal' Abbey of St Denis from among its dependent houses, but which Dom Jaunay denounced as an anti-congregation both hostile to genuine reform, and dangerous

26. *Ibid.*, especially book 1, chs. 1–4 for a survey covering the whole of Europe.
27. See the remarks of A.D. Wright, 'The Religious Life in the Spain of Philip II and Philip III', in *Monks, Hermits and the Ascetic Tradition*, ed. W.J. Sheils [*Studies in Church History*, vol. xxiv] (Oxford, 1985), pp. 251–74; A.W. Lovett, *Early Habsburg Spain 1517–1598* (Oxford 1986), pp. 280–1.
28. *Remonstrance au très-chrestien roy de France et de Navarre Henry III sur la réformation nécessaire et ja ordonnée par Sa Majesté estre faicte en l'Ordre de St Benoist*, (Paris, 1606). No trace, however, has been found of any royal directives for reform by Henry IV.
29. By Jean Darnault, visitor of the *exempts*, to Cardinal Givry, 2 June 1607, asking him to intercede with Paul V to put pressure on the king: Berlière and Kaiser, 'Givry et les Bénédictins', p. 262.

because it enjoyed royal protection.[30] Rome was slow to respond to the king's enthusiasm, and may well have harboured similar suspicions of St Denis.[31]

This suggests that Henry IV's attitude to reform was at least erratic; while he extended his protection to individual houses, he never attempted to evolve a conscious policy towards the reform of the orders as a whole. Indeed, it was not until a few months after his death that the first important royal decision concerning a reform was taken: in September 1610, the Benedictine reform of St Vanne of Verdun, to be known late in France as that of St Maur, received permission to establish itself without restrictions within the kingdom.[32] In contrast to Henry IV, both Marie de Medici and Louis XIII were far closer to the *dévot* and reformist circles of Paris, and the gradual change which came over the court after 1610 could not but favour the cause of reform. But this potential advantage for the reformists was offset by the crown's weakness and the political instability of the 1610s.

The 1610s proved to be a confused and often troubled decade for reform movements. Orders like the Augustinian canons-regular and Cluny remained virtually untouched by currents of reform. A few examples will help to show why many reformers favoured more radical measures by 1620. When Louis Petit succeeded his uncle as general of the Mathurins in 1612, he quickly destroyed the amicable relations that had existed between the observants and the previous general. For the next thirty years, he pursued an unremitting vendetta against them, to the displeasure of the papacy which proved quite incapable of restraining him.[33] In 1613 efforts to introduce an Italian-inspired reform among the Celestines, a branch of the Benedictine order, quickly ran into opposition, and the affair dragged on for five years. The French houses claimed to be independent of their Italian general, and that their privileges were part of the precious 'gallican liberties'. They also found their own provincial superior too rigorous in enforcing reform, and the opposition removed him from office and even imprisoned him for a time. They repeatedly foiled the efforts of the crown and of the papacy (which employed specially-delegated commissioners including several French cardinals), to restore peace and secure acceptance of the reform. Significantly, when the conflict

30. Berlière, 'Congrégation des exempts', p. 403; Berlière and Kaiser, 'Givry et les Bénédictins', pp. 348–9, prior and monks of St Denis to Givry, 26 October 1607; *ibid.*, pp. 358–9, Jaunay to Givry, 30 November 1608. Givry was official protector in Rome of the *Exempts*.
31. Both Henry IV and Louis XIII had to repeat the initial request for confirmation: B.N., MS. Fr. 3542, fo. 9, Henry IV to Brèves, 6 January 1609; *ibid.*, fo. 26, Louis XIII to Brèves, 1 September 1610.
32. E. Martène, *Histoire de la congrégation de St Maur*, ed. G. Charvin, (Paris, 1928), i, p. 9.
33. Delandres, *L'Ordre des trinitaires*, i, pp. 231ff. See ch. 10 below.

was temporarily resolved in 1618, reform had become such a divisive issue that it had to be shelved purely in the interests of internal peace.[34] Three years later, in late 1621, the Spanish-born general of the Cordeliers initiated a reform of his order in France at Louis XIII's invitiation. But the Paris house lodged an *appel comme d'abus* to *parlement* against his measures, which it viewed as an absolutist attack upon its traditions and privileges. When the court accepted the appeal, the general and papal nuncio had to work hard to secure the support of the royal council. The affair became a *cas célèbre* when some of the general's opponents launched an armed attack on him at night, from which he narrowly escaped with his life. A compromise was finally worked out between the council and the *parlement*, which permitted the general to exercise his office in France provided he obtained letters patent which would have to be registered by the *parlement* before his actions could be deemed valid. When the court came to registering the ensuing patents, it asserted that foreign generals – and they were numerous – could exercise no jurisdiction over their French subjects without following identical procedures.[35] Such nationalism was not new – it was also practised by the Spanish crown – and made the task of foreign generals in France all the more difficult.

The Cordeliers affair was, of course, an extreme case. If incidents of this kind were not daily occurrences, they were frequent enough to highlight the problem of reforming the orders, more particularly the legal and political restraints on reform arising from the interplay of national antagonisms, traditional privileges and complex jurisdictional rivalries. They also sharpened contemporary awareness of the gap separating the orders in France from those of Catholic Europe generally, an awareness that the religious orders recently imported from abroad did much to foster. It was against this background that calls for extraordinary measures to deal with the orders began to be heard.

IV

It would be futile to attempt to pinpoint with any accuracy the emergence of this conviction, which must have always been felt in some measure by frustrated reformers. An initial, if partial, instance of

34. X.M. Le Bachelet, 'Robert Bellarmin et les Célestins en France', *Revue des questions historiques* 104 (1926), pp. 257–94, for a full account.
35. Account based on the correspondence of the nuncio, Corsini: B.A.V., Barberini latini 8055, fos. 5, 23, 33, 49, 57, 94, 120–2, 149–52, letters to Cardinal Ludoviso, papal secretary of state, February–March 1622. The *appel comme d'abus* and related documents are in B.N., MS. 500 Colbert 159, fos. 238–41, 245–6, 250–1.

it can be detected in late 1613, soon after the reform of St Vanne, which had been gradually establishing itself in France, gained control of the Paris College of Cluny. Its *procureur* was Dom Laurent Bénard, the real founder of the French Maurists, and his objective was to use the college, where the brightest young members of the order studied, to form a whole new generation of reformed Cluniac and Benedictine leaders.[36] Almost immediately, he turned his attention to the powerful neighbouring Abbey of St Germain-des-Près, then part of the old congregation of Chezal-Benoît. But anticipating stiff opposition there, he appealed, through the leading *dévots* at court, to the protection of the Regent, Marie de Medici, who agreed to petition the pope for a special commission for Cardinals Joyeuse and La Rochefoucauld to oversee the reform.[37] The papacy's initial reaction was promising, but there followed a long delay in preparing the commission.[38] Marie de Medici approached Paul V personally in May 1614, recommending the project and, significantly, expressing a desire to see St Germain become the centre of a general reform of the French Benedictines, as St Vanne had for those of Lorraine. She even suggested that the two commissioners be given powers to initiate this process, and the right to co-opt others to assist them.[39] Paul V acquiesced this time, and a brief of commission − which has not survived − was sent to Joyeuse and La Rochefoucauld, as well as to Cardinal Sourdis and the Bishop of Amiens.[40] By mid-1614, however, political unrest and the summoning of the Estates General effectively shelved the project.

The Estates General nevertheless provided a useful forum for a broader discussion of church reform than that normally provided by the clergy's ten-yearly General Assemblies, which traditionally contented themselves with calls to the crown to enforce the terms of the great sixteenth-century ordinances of Orléans, Blois and Moulins.[41] The clergy of 1614 thought in similar terms, but the growing influence of a more energetic reform party turned them increasingly, as we saw, towards the decrees of Trent as the proper basis of reform. Royal acceptance of the decrees would, for example, have enabled bishops to visit and reform religious houses that claimed exemption from their authority, to enforce strict cloister where necessary and to compel independent houses to join observant congregations; it might

36. Martène, *St Maur*, i, pp. 11−15.
37. *Ibid.*, pp. 23−7.
38. B.N., MS. Italien 1267, fos. 421−2, Ubaldini to Cardinal Borghese, 21 November 1613. In his reply, Borghese stated the pope was ready to play his part in reform: A.S.V., Nunz Fr. 295a, fos. 182−3, 22 December 1613. Ubaldini's letters shed no light on the subsequent delay.
39. Martène, *St Maur*, i, pp. 23−6, for the text of the letter.
40. No trace has been found of this brief, which Martène refers to.
41. *Recueil des actes du clergé*, xiii, cols. 1146, 1154−6 (1595),, cols. 1170, 1181−2 (1606).

even have reduced interference by the secular courts in issues of reform.[42] The clergy's *cahier* duly listed their demands – the abolition or, at least, the modification of the *commende*, the tightening of religious discipline, the revival of study among the orders, and the reduction of secular interference in religious and monastic affairs. In the case of the huge Benedictine order, they urged individual houses to join either St Vanne or Chezal-Benoît as a first step towards eventual reform.[43] Most of these points were reiterated in the *règlement spirituel* submitted to the crown by the clergy at the end of the Estates and designed for immediate implementation.[44]

It is obvious that the representatives of the French clergy were still thinking along conventional lines in 1614. They were not yet ready to demand more drastic measures, doubtless because they continued to believe in royal acceptance of the Tridentine decrees. However, their proposals for the Benedictines is noteworthy, and may have originated in a pamphlet published during the Estates General, with a view to influencing their discussions. The *Avis à Messieurs des Estats pour restablir l'ordre de Saint Benoît* was anonymous, but we can see in it the hand of Dom Bénard. He discussed the problems raised by the *commende*, arguing that without a fixed and realistic division of revenues between monks and abbots, improvements were impossible. He conceded that reform was a matter of conscience, but argued that once it had begun, reformed and unreformed monks should form distinct communities inhabiting different houses, so as to reduce conflict to a minimum. The unreformed houses would be forbidden to receive or profess new members, thereby enabling the reform to gradually take over all the order's houses. He concluded with a direct appeal to the deputies at Estates General:

> And because it is pointless to make good laws and regulations unless there are qualified, powerful and zealous men who will see to their enforcement, the cardinals and prelates are asked to nominate to the king commissioners chosen from their ranks, in order to implement these articles or others which he may approve for this purpose.[45]

But circumstances were not propitious for such an initiative in 1614, nor is there any evidence that the clergy's leaders approached

42. For the making of the Tridentine decrees, see Jedin 'Zur Vorgeschichte der Regularenreform', pp. 231ff; *idem.*, *Geschichte des Konzils von Trient* (Freiburg-im-Breisgau), iv, pt. 2, chs. 7–8.
43. *Recueil des actes*, xiii, cols. 1288ff.
44. *Ibid.*, cols.1351ff.
45. 'Et par ce les bonnes loix et réglemens se font en vain, s'il n'y a personnes qualifiées, puissantes et zélées qui les facent observer, Messieurs les Cardinaux et Prélats sont nommément suppliez de présenter d'entre eux des commissaires à Sa Majesté pour faire exécuter ces articles, ou autres qu'elle aura agrée à la fin que dessus.' This text figures in the 'Advis vii'. The pamphlet is unpaginated.

Marie de Medici with such a proposal. The latter bore a striking resemblance to that put forward the previous year for St Germain. Nevertheless, the Estates General did arouse expectations that they could not fulfill, as is clear from a violently-worded pamphlet, the *Anatipophile Bénédictin*, published in early 1615, which made bolder suggestions for the reform of the Benedictines – the introduction of study, mental prayer and novitiates for training those seeking admission to vows; the grouping of houses into three congregations; and more adventurously, the election of a kind of watchdog committee from the three congregations to ensure that each of them would remain observant.[46] It would be years before some of these suggestions would be taken seriously; they fell on decidedly stony ground in 1615, when the crown was only interested in arresting the author and publisher of the tract.

In concrete terms, the clergy gained little from the Estates Geneal. The crown would not publish Trent's decrees, and both the *cahier* and the *règlement spirituel* were referred to the council for discussion at a later date.[47] Marie de Medici's ageing ministers had little time or taste for innovation in times of political instability. The reform of the orders does not appear to have been raised again until the Assembly of Notables met at Rouen in late 1617. Little is known about the substance of their debates, but criticism of the *commende*, of episcopal coadjutorships, and of grants of pensions off monastic revenues, led to a proposal for a royal commission of prelates to undertake a wide-ranging reform of the orders.[48] Reports that Louis XIII was planning a general reform reached Rome, where they were welcomed.[49] In another pamphlet from 1618, Dom Bénard implicitly confirmed that such a move had been contemplated, and even claimed that the king had promised to abolish the *commende* among the Benedictines.[50] This, too, proved premature, as Louis XIII was soon far too distracted by political events to honour whatever promises he may have made at Rouen.

It was not until July 1619, during another lull in the political turmoil, that the matter of the orders was raised again. What is noteworthy is that this time, the debate occurred in the king's immediate entourage, with the initiative coming from a group of

46. *Anatipophile Bénédictin aux pieds du Roy et de la Royne pour la réformation de l'Ordre de St Benoist en ce Royaume, par un père du noviciat de l'observance réformée* (1615), pp. 80ff.
47. See Blet, *Le Clergé de France et la monarchie*, i, ch. 4.
48. *Mémoires de Mathieu Molé*, i, pp. 174ff, 194. One of its proposed functions would be to advise on the appointment of abbots in future.
49. B.N., MS. Fr. 18012, fo. 253, Archbishop Marquemont of Lyon to Louis XIII, 24 April 1618.
50. *Remerciements des Bénédictins au Roy Très-Chrestien Louys XIII de France et de Navarre sur la proposition faicte par S.M. en l'Assemblée de Rouen de remettre les Abbayes en régularité* (n.p., n.d.).

dévots and reformers that included the first Cardinal de Retz, Arnoux, the royal confessor, Michel de Marillac, the future keeper of the seals and, above all, La Rochefoucauld. We saw in earlier chapters the role the latter played in the 1614 and 1617 debates on reform, and how his appointment as grand almoner in September 1618 had placed him in the forefront of ecclesiatical politics. It is no exaggeration to say that the most far-reaching, if unforeseeable, consequence of that involvement, both for himself and for the French church, was the extraordinary commission for the reform of the orders which was first seriously proposed in 1619, but which did not materialise until 1622.

V

The traditional account of the origins of that commission does scant justice either to the issues or the individuals concerned. Briefly, it claims that the pious Louis XIII was scandalised by the behaviour of the Benedictine monks of the great Abbey of Marmoutiers when he attended religious services there in July 1619; on enquiring how this state of affairs could be improved, La Rochefoucauld and others took the opportunity to explain their ideas on reform and to secure the backing of an impressionable and well-meaning monarch.[51] No evidence for this edifying tale exists, and the papal nuncio, Bentivoglio, who actually resided at Marmoutier during this time, and who is the principal source for the negotiations that begin in 1619, makes no mention of it. The surviving sources tell a different, far more interesting story, even if the exact sequence of events remains obscure in places. Despite this, they enable us to place the negotiations for the commission firmly in the context of the reform movement then developing within the French church.

The presence of the court at Tours in July 1619 was occasioned by the short-lived reconciliation between Louis XIII and Marie de Medici, which La Rochefoucauld had helped to negotiate a few months earlier.[52] It was, therefore, probably as reward for his services that the king offered him the Parisian Abbey of Ste Geneviève *in commendam* when its abbot, Bishop Brichantau of Laon, died on 13 July. The *brevet* granting the abbey was dated 15 July, and Louis promptly ordered the *procureur général* of the *parlement* of Paris to prevent an election of a successor-abbot to Brichantau by the canons of Ste Geneviève until he had made a firm decision.[53] This was a curious gesture by the king, as

51. See the version of it in G. de La Rochefoucauld, *Homme d'Eglise*, p. 196, and Morinière, *Vray prélat*, pp. 146–7.
52. See Pierre Chevallier, *Louis XIII, roi cornélien* (Paris, 1979), pp. 215–17.
53. *Mémoires de Molé*, i, p. 220.

Ste Geneviève still enjoyed the right to elect its abbots; indeed, sensing that it might be under threat, its canons had already elected Brichantau's younger brother, Philibert, as abbot, on condition that he become a canon-regular himself.[54]

La Rochefoucauld seems to have been embarrassed, as well he might, by the king's generosity. He had held two abbeys *in commendam* to date, but as a critic of benefice-hunting practices in the French church, he was reluctant to take responsibility for placing a great abbey *in commendam* for the first time. A further complication arose from the fact that he was related to the Brichantau family, and that he agreed to press the young abbot-elect's claims when approached by his family. But Louis XIII proved adamant.[55] La Rochefoucauld had to yield, but with the provision that after his death, Ste Geneviève should return to electing its abbots.[56]

Although the royal *brevet* was dated 15 July,[57] La Rochefoucauld's final acceptance only came later in the month.[58] There is no independent evidence that Louis XIII initially offered him Ste Geneviève on condition that he reform it, but there is no doubting that La Rochefoucauld eventually made some such reform a condition of his acceptance. By then, however, the Ste Geneviève affair had provided a starting point for a much broader discussion of the whole question of reforming the orders. La Rochefoucauld's central role in the ensuing negotiations thus stems from a mixture of private and general concerns.

The nuncio Bentivoglio reported on 30 July 1619 that the main protagonists, La Rochefoucauld, Retz and Arnoux had already won the support of the king's all-powerful favourite, the duc de Luynes, for sweeping reforms. At the king's request, discussions then followed with an unnamed 'person of known zeal and integrity', possibly Marillac. They recommended that the king petition the pope to commission several people to conduct the reform, that the commissioners receive full royal backing for their efforts and that, to achieve swift, effective results, opportunities for appeal and evasion by the orders be curtailed.[59] Discussions then took place in the royal council, but resolutions were slow to emerge: the issue of reform gave rise to elaborate written proposals, which had to be weighed and considered. At the same time La Rochefoucauld and some of his

---

54. *Gallia Christiana*, vii, col. 774. Philibert de Brichantau succeeded his brother as Bishop of Laon.
55. B.S.G., MS. 611, fo. 53v; Abbé Oroux, *Histoire ecclésiastique de la cour*, ii, p. 351; La Rochefoucauld, *Homme d'église*, pp. 175–7.
56. B.S.G., MS. 621, fos. 579–80, text of papal bull.
57. *Ibid.*, fos. 581–8, text of the *brevet*.
58. This emerges from his letters to his secretary, Desbois, dated 27 and 31 July: B.S.G., MS. 3275, fos. 606, 607.
59. *Nunziatura di Bentivoglio*, iii, pp. 412–13, Bentivoglio to Borghese, 30 July.

colleagues were involved in discussing ways to improve the quality of episcopal nominations. The reform of the orders was not being considered in isolation.[60]

Only two of the memoranda submitted to the council survive, and they merit closer attention for the light they shed on the proposals that were later put to Rome. The first paper suggested that La Rochefoucauld be given a special commission for reform and that, advised by a council, he should begin work among the canons-regular. It recommended the sending of visitors to individual monasteries to ascertain their attitudes to reform. The order could be divided into provinces, each with its own novitiate and house of studies run by reformed canons; the unreformed *anciens* could be relegated to designated houses, and forbidden to receive or profess new members. Reformed houses could form their own congregations and become independent of external authorities. Having started with the canons-regular, the commissioner might then apply the same methods to other orders, especially if their superiors were French; as for those with foreign generals, the writer confessed that 'il est plus difficile d'y remédier'. Not forgetting that the ultimate objective was spiritual, he recommended the introduction of such modern practices as meditation, spiritual exercises, regular examination of conscience and spiritual conferences. He also demanded a clear division of revenues between abbots and communities, and concluded by insisting on the need for full royal support for the venture and that the ordinary courts should not be allowed to interfere in any way with the reforms – 'car sans cela il ne se peut rien faire'.[61]

The second memorandum repeated some of these points, while adding some bolder suggestions. Given that the number of actual pro-reform religious were few and isolated, they could best be employed at organising within their own orders general seminaries, in which they would train others who would in turn take charge of smaller provincial seminaries, attendance at which would be compulsory for all new members of the orders,. Reform would thus spread outwards from its initial narrow base. A council for reform, with power to hear all appeals in the last resort, also appeared indispensable to success.[62]

These and other proposals were submitted to the royal council by 'personnes très habiles'.[63] It is evident from these two memoranda that

---

60. B.S.G., MS. 3238, fos. 343–4, memorandum to king, 1 September.
61. B.S.G., MS. 607, fos. 70–1, 'avis par articles touchant la réformation des réguliers de France'. This and the following document are in the form of copies made by the late seventeenth century historian of Ste Geneviève, Claude du Molinet. But he omitted them from the final version of his history (MS. 611), which historians have used in the past; MS. 607 is an earlier draft of MS. 611.
62. *Ibid.*, fos. 72–3.
63. *Ibid.*, fo. 73r.

their authors were close to, or possibly inspired by, La Rochefoucauld. The influence of Dom Bénard can again be sensed in some of the ideas which were more far-reaching than anything adumbrated so far.[64] It will come as no surprise that the abolition of the *commende* was called for, and even less that the crown was not seriously ready to patronise reform at the cost of losing so valuable a fount of patronage.

By September 1619, clear proposals had begun to emerge. The king had even selected a group of commissioners – six of whom would be councillors of state or members of the *parlement* – whom the pope would be asked to approve.[65] But doubts immediately arose about the likely papal reaction to such a request, and the king quickly agreed to an alternative proposal: there would be two commissions, one wholly ecclesiastical and invested with papal authority, the other a mixed body of ecclesiastics and laymen, chosen by the king, whose purpose would be to add the stamp of royal authority to the policies of the papal commission. The proposed list of ecclesiastical commissioners included some of the most experienced bishops and members of religious orders of the early seventeenth-century church.[66] This change of strategy was probably instigated by La Rochefoucauld and Retz, both of whom were sensitive to Roman fears of lay involvement in religious matters. They also pressed the nuncio for Rome's reaction, but the curia, while expressing satisfaction that its own promptings were at last being heeded, was content to await the arrival of formal proposals.[67]

Instructions were finally dispatched to the French ambassador, the marquis de Coeuvres, in October or November 1619. In covering letters to him and the pope, Louis XIII defended his decision to request extraordinary powers to reform France's religious houses, both mendicant and monastic, male and female. The proposed commission would sit for six years; it could request the assistance of whomsoever it saw fit, and might judge without further appeal all cases arising out of reform. The *appel comme d'abus* would thus become inapplicable, and the king promised his full support to the commission.[68] The

---

64. *Advis pour la réforme et nourriture des religieux à qui Sa Majesté voudroit donner les abbayes de leur ordre.* This document is printed after the *Remerciement des Bénédictins* cited above, n. 50.
65. *Nunziatura di Bentivoglio*, iii, p. 500, Bentivoglio to Borghese, 11 September. The nuncio does not supply the names of the proposed commissioners.
66. *Ibid.*, p. 515, to same, 15 September. The commissioners were Retz, president of the council, La Rochefoucauld. Archbishop Marquemont of Lyon, Charles Miron, former Bishop of Angers, Bishop L'Estang of Carcassonne, Jean Arnoux S.J., Honoré Champigny, a Capuchin, dom Veny d'Arbouze, grand prior of Cluny, Dom Bénard, and Dom Adam Ogier, a Carthusian.
67. B.S.G., MS. 3249, fo. 128, Marquemont to La Rochefoucauld, 29 October 1619.
68. B.N., MS. Fr. 17364, pp. 225–6, undated copy of king's letter to Coeuvres. His letter to the pope exists only in the form of a 'supplicatio' translated into Italian: Ferrara, Archivio di Stato, *fondo* Bentivoglio 18/14, no. 7, no date.

instructions sent to Coeuvres, of which the text has been lost, repeated these points, and tried to parry the objections that the curia could be expected to raise. They also provide an interesting insight into contemporary perceptions of the respective priorities of the curia and of the French crown and church. Extraordinary measures, it was asserted, could no longer be avoided in France, given the repeated failure of traditional methods in the face of escape routes like the *appel comme d'abus*. Neither the decrees of Trent nor the jurisdiction of the Roman congregation of regulars were recognised in France. By the terms of the Concordat of Bologna, all appeals to Rome from France had to be referred to judges-delegate within France, a practice which, it was no secret, opened the door to further appeals. The existing arrangements were thus quite inadequate, and it would be best to take energetic measures while the king was personally favourable to them. It was also hinted that a commission nominated and removable by the papacy was surely preferable to independent royal action should the curia prove unwilling to co-operate. Furthermore, all the proposed commissioners were friends of Rome, and the very existence of the commission would constitute an acknowledgement that final authority for reform lay with the papacy. The only purpose of the second, royal, commission was to ensure the efficacy of reform.[69] The range and detail of these arguments show that no effort was being spared to make the French case an impregnable one, but they also imply that extreme reticence was anticipated in the curia.

The pope's initial response to these proposals was to refer them to a congregation of cardinals. Coeuvres, who was heartily loathed in Rome for his arrogance, raised the question in consistory on 3 January 1620, and offered to clear up any difficulties that might arise. However, the ageing Paul V was content to await the cardinals' report. Three days later, Coeuvres wrote that they were well-disposed to the petition and that Rome accepted the principle behind it. The idea of a parallel royal commission also appeared to win favour, although he added that there was reluctance to deny the right of appeal to Rome against its decisions — the curia would not want its hands tied so tightly.[70]

But Couevres's illusions were shattered within a week. Under pressure from the orders, especially from the mendicant generals who were usually based in Rome, the cardinals concluded that the proposed commission would split the orders within France, and that the resulting factions would refuse obedience to legitimate superiors and would expend their energies on litigation. Other means would have to

69. B.S.G., MS. 611, fos. 56–9, a detailed *résumé* of the instruction made by Claude du Molinet.
70. B.N., MS. Fr. 18014, fos. 5–6, Coeuvres to Louis XIII, 3 January 1620.

be tried. Coeuvres himself professed not to be unduly perturbed by these reports. Paul V, who Coeuvres knew to dislike the provisions for the limitation of appeals, had not yet made his decision.[71]

The ambassador's optimism was again misplaced. Two weeks later, on 20 January, Cardinal Borghese communicated to Bentivoglio his uncle's response to the French plan. Paul V rejected the need for a general reform, holding that at least some orders were in a healthy state. Coeuvres seems to have offered to limit the commission to the Benedictines, but Paul found even that excessive, given the order's size in France. He believed that the orders themselves were the best judges of necessary reforms, and he pledged his support for those conducted 'secondo il modo canonico'. The nuncio, who would understand the dangers inherent in limiting appeals to Rome, was to explain that this 'negativa libera e assoluta' was the pope's own decision. A special brief explaining the refusal and urging him to accept it was to be sent to La Rochefoucauld, already perceived as the champion of exceptional measures.[72]

The gap between the crown and the papacy could hardly have been wider, yet neither Louis XIII nor La Rochefoucauld was prepared to drop their scheme so readily. Even before learning of the pope's decision, the king had written a firm letter to Coeuvres: his resolution was unchanged, the proposed commissioners were excellent men, and the curia's arguments did not impress him. Coeuvres was, therefore, to pursue the negotiations.[73] When Bentivoglio's turn came to explain the papal refusal, he encountered a stubborn unwillingness to believe that so worthy a project could be dismissed so comprehensively, and was taken aback by the force of French dismay. The king openly showed his displeasure, and twice sent him to confer with La Rochefoucauld and Arnoux, both of whom demanded detailed explanations.[74] La Rochefoucauld counter-attacked with further arguments. Experience showed that 'il modo canonico' bore no fruit in France and must give way to extraordinary measures; the papacy must accept that there was no intention whatever of dimishing its authority or jurisdiction, for which all the necessary guarantees would be given. Giving

---

71. *Ibid.*, fo. 13, letter to Puysieux, secretary of state, 11 January.
72. A.S.V., Nunz Fr. 299, fos. 12–17, Borghese to Bentivoglio, 20 January. A truncated version of this letter was published in *Nunziatura di Bentivoglio*, iv, pp. 116–18, and a contemporary copy of it in Zakar, *Histoire*, doc. no. 5. No trace of the brief sent to La Rochefoucauld has survived.
73. B.N., MS. Fr. 17364, p. 273, undated copy of king's letter, but probably late January or early February 1620.
74. *Nunziatura di Bentivoglio*, iv, pp. 140–1, Bentivoglio to Borghese, 26 February 1620. See *ibid.*, p. 169: 'Il cardinale della Rochefoucault, particolarmente, si riscaldò assai nella matiera, come quello che vi ha la piu parte d'ogni altro: onde io fu costretto di esporgli appieno tutte le ragioni scrittemi da V.S. Illma, ch'egli volse ventilar meco tutte con grande esatezza.'

voice to his own Ultramontane convictions, he even claimed that the commission might prove a turning point in the affairs of the French church, enabling it to regain control of its affairs and to circumvent the execrable *appel comme d'abus*. The pope need not fear creating a precedent, since Spain, the country most likely to exploit one, possessed religious orders of exemplary discipline. In any case, similar concessions had been made in the past – to Amboise, for example. France, he asserted, would accept whatever strings the papacy might attach, if only reform itself could be launched. He begged the nuncio to argue strongly for reform, and informed him that Marillac would be sent as special envoy for this matter in place of the unsuitable Coeuvres.[75] If La Rochefoucauld's arguments were anything to judge by, French determination had been strengthened rather than weakened by the papacy's response.

Throughout 1620, Bentivoglio remained under steady pressure from La Rochefoucauld, Arnoux and possibly Marillac, to induce the pope to change his mind.[76] But the nuncio moderated his earlier support for the French proposals, and confined himself to repeating his instructions from Rome. He did have some success in persuading the French of the depth of curial opposition with the result that Marillac's mission was cancelled, lest he suffer the indignity of returning empty-handed from Rome.[77] However, a new French offensive was launched in July 1620, using Coeuvres and the French assistant to the Jesuit general, Christophe Balthazar.[78] The king made it clear he expected results this time.[79] If the proposals were essentially the same as before, they had also been modified to meet Roman misgivings, particularly the foreign generals' concern about the effects of a commission on the unity of their orders.[80] The pope referred the proposals to the same congregation of cardinals. This time, they appeared to Coeuvres less categorical: the proposals seemed reasonable enough, apart from that for a standing tribunal to judge appeals in France; admitting the need to do something about the French orders, the cardinals were never-

75. *Ibid.*, iv, pp. 168–72, Bentivoglio to Borghese, 25 March 1620.
76. *Ibid.*, iv, p. 173, second letter to Borghese, 25 March; *ibid.*, 441–2, to same, 20 October 1620.
77. A.S.V., Nunz Fr. 299, fo. 32, Borghese to Bentivoglio, 11 April 1620; *ibid.*, fo. 43–4, to same, 6 June; *Nunziatura di Bentivoglio*, iv, pp. 219, 235, 245–6, nuncio to Borghese, 6 and 20 May.
78. *Nunziatura di Bentivoglio*, iv, p. 309, Bentivoglio to Borghese, 1 July 1620. Balthazar was well-known to La Rochefoucauld, having served in senior positions within his order in France.
79. B.N., MS. Fr. 17364, p. 325, undated letter to Coeuvres, but probably late July 1620. This dating seems confirmed by Borghese's letter of 23 August to Bentivoglio, referring to Balthazar's mission: 'non ha ancora parlato della riforma delli regolari': Ferrara, Archivio di Stato, *fondo* Bentivoglio 18/20, no. 139.
80. B.S.G., MS. 611, fos. 59–60, résumé of the instructions.

theless nervous about approving the new proposals.[81] But it soon became apparent that while the curia did not wish to give a flat refusal, it was in no hurry to make up its mind. La Rochefoucauld himself continued to put pressure on Rome in late 1620, but had made no progress by the time of Paul V's death in January 1621.[82]

His successor Gregory XV reigned only two years, but in that time he did much to revive the flagging papal leadership of Counter-Reformation.[83] His instructions to the new papal nuncio, Ottavio Corsini, in April 1621, show that he had considered the request put to his predecessor, but that he had not yet made his decision. In them, he informed Corsini that the French case had been motivated by the appalling state of the orders, implying that it was not as objectionable to him as to his predecessor.[84] The papacy was moving closer to the French position, even though Corsini was given no brief, either then or later, to negotiate on the issue.

The election of a new pope was traditionally the time to press for concessions refused by his predecessor. But the French waited for a change of ambassadors in mid-1621 before making a new approach to the curia, especially as the new ambassador, Cardinal Sourdis, was, despite his personal eccentricities, a more suitable negotiator than the swaggering Coeuvres.[85] But unlike Coeuvres, Sourdis made no mention of his efforts in his letters to court. It is ironic, therefore, that when the affair of the Cordeliers reform was at its height in March 1622, Corsini, who may have been unaware of Sourdis's instructions, suggested to Cardinal Ludoviso that it might be worth reviving the proposals once put to Paul V, as he could see no other way around the opposition to reform, especially from the *parlement*.[86]

In fact, Corsini's letter had not reached Rome before Gregory XV finally granted the French request. His decision receives no more than a laconic, uninformative reference in Sourdis's correspondence.[87] So apart from the pope's personal desire to promote reform, we are denied

81. B.N., MS. Fr. 18014, fo. 382, Coeuvres to Puysieux, 27 August 1620.
82. *Nunziatura di Bentivoglio*, iv, p. 480, 487, Bentivoglio to Borghese, 1 December 1620; B.N. MS. Fr. 18014, fo. 675v, Coeuvres to Puysieux, early December. One of Borghese's last instructions to the nuncio made it clear that no concessions were in the offing: Ferrara, Archivio di Stato, *fondo* Bentivoglio 18/15, fo. 399, 10 January 1621.
83. See H. Jedin, ed., *History of the Church*, v, pp. 615ff.
84. A.S.V., Nunz Fr. 57, fos. 1/–19. Extracts from this instruction in Zakar, *Histoire*, doc. no. 7.
85. No trace of Sourdis's instructions on this question has been found, but he refers to them in a letter to Louis XIII on 2 June 1621: B.N., MS. Fr. 18016, fo. 159.
86. B.A.V., Barberini latini 8055, fos. 149–52, letter to Cardinal Ludoviso, 22 March.
87. B.N., MS. Fr. 18018, fo. 218v, letter to Puysieux, 9 April. He says here that he was also writing to La Rochefoucauld about the commission but the letter, which would almost certainly have been more informative, has not survived.

any contemporary explanation of the curia's change of heart after years of tenacious refusal.

VI

If the brief of commission granted on 8 April 1622 was largely what the French had pressed for, it too was not without its surprises.[88] Undoubtedly the most important of these was that it was given to La Rochefoucauld personally, despite the fact that both he and the king had always envisaged a group of commissioners. This move may well result from papal fears of Gallicanism – the pope could count on La Rochefoucauld's well-known Ultramontanism to prevent any undesirable consequences of the commission. A single commissioner may also have been regarded as posing less of a threat than a group, which would inevitably acquire a corporate identity. Secondly, the commission was confined to the Benedictines, Augustinian canons, Cluny and Cîteaux. No explanation was offered for the choice of these four orders, which admittedly comprised the majority of French religious houses, but clearly the resistance of the mendicant orders in the early stages of negotiations had been successful, and their possible need for reform been quietly put to one side. The general reform of all the orders as first envisaged in mid-1619 would thus be much less comprehensive in scope. The commission itself was to run for six years, and the commissioner was allowed to form a council of prelates and religious of his own choice to assist him. He was also empowered to visit and reform the orders, regardless of whether their houses were independent or members of older congregations; none, not even houses claiming direct subordination to the papacy itself, could claim any ground for exemption against him. His powers to restore observance, erect new congregations, change statutes and establish new constitutions for the orders were impressive. Against opposition, he could employ the full panoply of ecclesiastical censures, including excommunication. The pope also declared that appeals against the commissioner's decisions should not be allowed to suspend the operation of those decisions while the case was being judged. This clause proved to be one of the most controversial during the 1630s since, to La Rochefoucauld's annoyance, neither the crown nor the papacy proved willing to enforce it literally. The brief also explicitly declared the benefices belonging to the orders to be out of bounds to the commissioner; he could not interfere with them without express

---

88. The full text, based on the original minute from the Vatican Archives, is printed in Zakar, *Histoire*, doc. no. 9. Numerous copies of it have survived in manuscript and in print in French libraries and archives.

papal consent. The curia's fiscal interests were deeply tied up with them, and no reform-minded pope would be allowed to go too far in sacrificing them, as La Rochefoucauld would realise in due course. Finally, he was invited to submit serious problems to Rome for consideration.

Louix XIII received the brief in May 1622 while campaigning against the Huguenots in southern France, so it was not until mid-June that the indispensable letters-patent activating the commission were ready for his signature; without them no papal commission possessed legal validity in France.[89] That apart, the main purpose of the patents was to establish the institutional *pièce maîtresse* of the reform, the royal commission of prelates, councillors of state and *maîtres des requêtes* which would handle the 'temporal' aspects of reform, support the commissioner, and judge all appeals arising from his decisions. For these purposes, the commission would have the force of conciliar *arrêts*.[90] The patents ended with a formal order to the *parlements* and other royal courts not to accept or judge any appeals made to them against La Rochefoucauld; to do so would constitute interference in matters reserved exclusively to the royal commissioners, who were entitled to evoke all such appeals before themselves. As La Rochefoucauld had always wanted, this amounted to setting aside the *appel comme d'abus*. The freedom of action given to the commissioner was, it scarcely needs saying, extensive. Although he had some undisclosed criticisms to make about its terms, he was soon so immersed in the enormous task assigned to him that no real amendment was ever made to it.[91]

It had taken nearly three years of hard bargaining to persuade the papacy to fall in with French attitudes towards the orders. The major paradox of the negotiations was the reversal of roles that they produced. For years, Rome had admonished and besought the French crown and church to take the question of the orders seriously. When, however, they finally grasped the nettle, they produced ideas which went far beyond anything Rome had envisaged. It was driven back on the defensive, and the gap was only bridged by a newly-elected, short-

89. The copy of the patents used here is the printed one found in B.S.G., MS. 3240, fos. 6–9. The royal commissioners were Retz, Archbishop Hébert of Bourges, Bish⌐ , Sanguin of Senlis and Miron of Angers; councillors of state Châteauneuf, Roissy, Jeannin, Marillac and Aligre; and *maîtres des requêtes* Lefevre de Lezeau and La Poterie.

90. The history of the various organs of the royal council, and that of the *conseil privé* in particular, is confused for this period, but the original minutes of the decrees issued by the commissioners are to found among those of the *conseil* in the V⁶ series in the *Archives Nationales*.

91. B.A.V., Barberini latini 7952, fo. 18, La Rochefoucauld to Cardinal Ludoviso, 20 June 1622. This letter does not specify the actual criticisms, which were listed in a separate memorandum which has not been found. In view of La Rochefoucauld's later experiences as commissioner, particularly in relation to appeals against his ordinances, it would have been interesting to know what he saw as the brief's shortcomings.

lived pope. On the French side, church leaders were fortunate that over these few years, Louis XIII developed a strong personal commitment to reform; without it, the negotiations in Rome might have died a quick death.

The commission opened a new chapter in the history of the major orders in France, and set a number of patterns for future reforms. La Rochefoucauld had, as we shall see, strong convictions about the shape that reform should take in every order, and his efforts to realise them formed common themes that, as the remaining chapters will show, would recur throughout the history of his commission.

7

The Reform of the Canons-Regular. I: Beginnings

IF LA ROCHEFOUCAULD is best remembered for his attempts to reform the old orders, this is due in large part to his endeavours with the Augustinian canons-regular. The proceedings of his successive papal and royal commission for their reform stretched in an unbroken chain from 1622 to 1639, far longer than for any other order, and La Rochefoucauld's involvement with the order's affairs absorbed a great deal of his time during those years. Although the reform has rarely received more than passing references from historians of the seventeenth-century French church, it has produced a massive documentary legacy which, in addition to its own intrinsic interest, enables us to observe at close hand the cardinal's objectives and *modus operandi* in tackling the reform, not just of the canons-regular, but of the other orders, too.

More interesting perhaps than the success or failure of La Roche-foucauld's policies for the canons-regular is the fact that, unlike the other orders he dealt with, he had to create a reform movement virtually from scratch, and develop a set of institutions to ensure its permanence. In sharp contrast to Cluny, Cîteaux and the Mathurins, the canons-regular were an order without corporate structure or central institutions. Each house was a small, self-governing republic usually dominated by a small group of comfortably ensconced *officiers* drawn from local notable families. In church law, the 'natural' superiors of such houses were the bishops, but their authority was usually more theoretical than real. The order experienced the full effects of the *commende*, which only served to exaggerate the isolation of individual monasteries and root them even more firmly in local society. This very amorphousness was to be the single most important factor in shaping La Rochefoucauld's approach to reform: an order without a centre could not be reformed or 'captured' from the outside (like Cluny or Cîteaux), nor could there be any real centre until a reasonable number of houses had been painstakingly reformed one by one.[1] Admittedly, a few older congregations like St Victor, Val des Ecoliers and St Ruf still survived, but they were no longer genuinely observant. St Victor, for example, was based on the famous Paris abbey of the same name, but by 1622 its eight member-houses went their separate ways, regardless of bishops or their own superiors. Congregations of this type were kept alive by little more than their privileges and traditions, which they would defend with a vigour which belied their otherwise moribund condition.[2]

Small, isolated reform movements had begun to emerge before 1622, but the obstacles were enormous and progress corresponding-ly limited. Philippe Gallet (1576–1654) prior of the Abbey of Toussaints at Angers, had long entertained hopes of founding an observant congregation in Touraine, but was still confined to fighting opposition within his own abbey.[3] Further south, the young Abbot of Chancelade in Périgord, Alain de Solminihac (1593–1659), had just discovered his vocation as a reformer, but had made even less progress by 1622 than Gallet.[4] La Rochefoucauld would have long and tortuous dealings with both men, but in the early days, they and their abbeys were too remote to be either a help or a hindrance to him – in sharp contrast to his diocese of Senlis and abbey of Ste Geneviève.

He had been intermittently associated with the modest reform that had been developed at St Vincent de Senlis since 1615. Its younger members attempted to adopt a reformed observance, but lack of interest in such 'nouveautés' among the prior, *officiers* and benefice-holders made for slow progress. When the reform group appealed to their bishop for protection in 1615, he responded with a surprise visitation, as a result of which he deposed the prior.[5] But his own appointee proved a disappointment, and La Rochefoucauld's continued protection remained indispensable. The future seemed safe when, in 1617, a chapter presided over by the cardinal elected as prior the most prominent of the reformers, Robert Baudouin (1590–1639). Although few in number for many years, the Senlis group was both purposeful and energetic.[6] From its members were to come the principal agents of

1. For a more detailed examination of these questions in the context of the reform of a single abbey, see J.A. Bergin, 'Ways and Means of Monastic Reform in Seventeenth-century France: St Denis de Reims 1630–1633', *Catholic Historical Review* 72 (1986), pp. 14–32.
2. On St Victor, see Fourrier Bonnard, *Histoire de l'abbaye royale et de l'ordre des chanoines réguliers de St Victor de Paris*, 2 vols. (Paris, n.d.), ii, chs. 1–3, 5. The *parlement* of Paris had even called for the reform of St Victor in 1619, permitting the prior to call in outside, secular help should he need it in enforcing obedience on his canons: B.S.G., MS. 3243, fo. 13, copy of decree of 27 February 1619.
3. B.S.G., MS. 611, fo. 92r, Claude du Molinet's manuscript history of the Ste Geneviève reform.
4. Eugène Sol, *Le Vénérable Alain de Solminihac* (Cahors, 1928), chs. 1–4.
5. B.S.G., MS. 621, fos. 497–510, first petition to La Rochefoucauld for help, with detailed denunciation of abuses at St Vincent.
6. B.S.G., MS. 611, fos. 31–4, 42–5.

La Rochefoucauld's reforms; their later influence on him would be so extensive that it is worth pausing at this point to consider them and their approach to reform.

The group was especially fortunate to produce a leader of considerable spiritual and physical energy. Born near Paris in 1594, Charles Faure entered St Vincent in 1613 for quite conventional reasons. Educated by the Jesuits at La Flèche, he took the habit, it seems, in deference to his recently widowed mother. Small and frail-looking, he initially evinced neither much interest in, nor aptitude for, the reformed observance. Indeed, the reformers even voted to debar him from taking vows, only to find themselves overruled by the commendatory abbot, a family friend. In Faure's case, the exercise of this much-criticised prerogative bore unanticipated fruit, for he very soon emerged as a leader whom even older reformers such as Baudouin were to accept unreservedly; his will-power and clear vision quickly won, and long retained, their full support. In 1616, he and his companions decided that true reform required learning, and went off to Paris to study philosophy and theology. There they benefited from contact with the abrasive Adrien Bourdoise, a leading figure in the movement for the reform of the secular clergy and founder of the seminary of St Nicolas du Chardonnet. Faure himself was ordained by La Rochefoucauld in 1619. By then, he was novice-master at St Vincent, where he was beginning to implement his own ideas on reform. These, too, would have a direct bearing on La Rochefoucauld's future undertakings.[7]

Fundamental to Faure's group was the need to revive the novitiate, and make it the engine of reform – the equivalent for the regulars of the later seminaries for the secular clergy. Its purpose was to provide the moral and spiritual formation which would lay the foundations of an enduring religious observance. Thus, only those over sixteen and with some schooling should be admitted as novices; none should be accepted who were 'presented' by parents or relatives in the traditional manner, especially if the latter were paying for their keep, a stipulation designed to remove external pressure for the admission of novices to vows. Only a genuinely observant community could achieve such a goal, which made it imperative to eliminate the small oligarchy of *officiers* that tended to facilitate such pressure and perpetuate family dominance of monastic houses. To this end, monastic offices were to be stripped of their status as benefices, and rotated through a system of triennial elections, starting with the prior, who should be subject

7. *Ibid.*, fos. 37–9. The only full biography of Faure is that F. A. Chartonnet, *La Vie du révérend père Charles Faure, abbé de Sainte Geneviève, où l'on voit l'histoire des chanoines réguliers de la congrégation de France* (Paris, 1698), while the only modern study of any value is the brief notice by Louis Cognet in *DHGE*, xvi, cols. 714–19. Cognet pointed to the lack of a serious critical study of Faure's career and influence, especially as a spiritual writer and director of conscience.

to episcopal approval. Those holding benefices outside the walls –
parishes, chaplaincies and so on – should either reside in them, or else
surrender them and return to their monastery; they should also be
obliged to render a detailed account of their stewardship and hand over
surplus income to their community. Similar accountability was to be
demanded of holders of monastic offices. Neither category should
be allowed to regard monies at their disposal as prebends for their
own personal use.[8]

The problem of how to deal with 'dependent' benefices like parishes
was, in some ways, the issue which perplexed Faure and his friends
most. In 1616, their own prior had offered them benefices, in the hope
of neutralising reform altogether. They had refused, and undertaken
never to accept a benefice in the future. Faure himself concluded that
the canons-regular should abandon benefice-holding entirely, and
appoint vicars from the secular clergy to those benefices they controlled, but some of his associates were less convinced, feeling that
parish service was an established and legitimate tradition of their
order. A compromise was reached: pastoral traditions would be
maintained, but benefices would be given only to those with genuine
vocations. All hoped that an effective reform would eliminate the
benefice-hunting so typical of many entering monasteries under the
existing regime.[9] This problem, which bore so closely on general
church reform at parochial level, was not, in the event, so easily
solved, and would exercise Faure for many years.

Objectives like those that Faure and his colleagues set themselves
required a thorough spiritual and moral training of new recruits. The
early years at St Vincent had already shown that tenacious resistance
could be expected from the numerous vested interests that had
accumulated over time. La Rochefoucauld's continuing protection
thus proved indispensable for the survival and growth of the reform. In
fact, a modest attempt at expansion occurred before 1622, when at the
request of its abbot and the Archbishop of Rouen, a small group was
sent from Senlis to the Norman abbey of Eu to introduce its canons to
the reformed observance. After promising beginnings, the prior and
other *officiers* opposed the experiment, and not even the archbishop's
support could prevent Faure from withdrawing in defeat in 1623. He
had upset local conventions by refusing, among other things, to
profess the novices at Eu, whom he found unfit for reform, despite
strong pressure from their families. Neither canons nor families were
ready for such innovation. At Clairefontaine in diocese of Chartres,
another Senlis group had greater hopes of success, as they received

8. B.S.G., MS. 621, fos. 519–38, draft statutes presented to La Rochefoucauld for his
   approval in May 1614.
9. B.S.G., MS. 611, fos. 34v–5v; Chartonnet, *Vie de Charles Faure*, pp. 107–8.

control of the abbey's affairs and one of them became prior. But the resident canons proved unenthusiastic about adopting reform for themselves. There was no open confrontation, but this fruitless venture was also ended abruptly and without much regret in 1624 when La Rochefoucauld needed men to reform Ste Geneviève[10] The lessons of these failures were not lost upon the reformers, and made them extremely cautious about all forms of uncontrolled expansion. Theirs would be a prudent, planned and piecemeal reform.

La Rochefoucauld, as we saw, accepted Ste Geneviève from Louis XIII on condition that he reform it. But he seems to have few pre-conceived ideas of how this might be done. As the abbey's first commendator, he was careful to humour its canons, who were doubtless apprehensive about so much talk about reform which took no account of them.[11] In mid-1620, he had persuaded them to talk to an *ad hoc* council he had convened, and by August they had agreed to a set of rules which demanded of them little more than a bare minimum of regular observance. One rule was even devised to appeal to their self-interest by reserving all future benefices for those embracing reform![12] In March 1621, La Rochefoucauld obtained royal approval for his statutes; patents were issued which stated that monastic offices would lose their status as benefices and stipulated that Ste Geneviève should return to elected abbots after La Rochefoucauld's death.[13] His efforts to restore observance by strengthening the prior's authority, eliminating private property and imposing a minimum of common life, continued throughout 1621.[14] He insisted on novices being professed or dismissed after a year's novitiate and, as abbot, he retained strict control of nominations to benefices and offices, requiring the prior to consult him on all important problems.[15] Yet little progress had been made by June 1622, when his commission for the whole order came into force; henceforth, reform of the abbey would be closely tied to that of the order.

10. B.S.G., MS. 611, fos. 66v–9v (Eu); *ibid.*, fos. 78r–9v (Clairefontaine).
11. This emerges from La Rochefoucauld's letters to the prior and canons after his nomination as abbot in August 1619: B.S.G., MS. 3238, fos. 73, 74, 75, 89, 90, 537. He did not personally take possession of the abbey until January 1620: MS. 621, fos. 589–92, act dated 7 January.
12. B.S.G., MS. 621, fos. 593–4, 'résultat d'une assemblée faicte en présence de Monseigneur...avec responce des religieux de l'abbaye de Sainte Geneviève pour l'acceptation de la communauté, en l'année 1620'.
13. *Ibid.*, fos. 603–10, text of royal letters, March 1621; *ibid.*, fos. 647–50, new patents to the same effect, February 1622.
14. See *Documents inédits pour servir à l'histoire du christianisme en orient*, ed. A Rabbath (Paris, n.d.), i, p. 335, Jean de La Bretesche S.J. to Christophe Balthazar S.J., 21 September 1621: 'Hier inopinément M. le cardinal m'appella pour voir et décider, avec quelques autres, les points de la réforme de son abbaye'.
15. B.S.G., MS. 621, fos. 617–22, 'advis du conseil sur plusieurs poincts pour l'administration du spirituel et temporel de l'abbaye de Sainte Geneviève', 25 October 1621.

II

Nothing in what La Rochefoucauld had attempted so far as bishop or
as abbot pre-determined his approach to the reform of the order as a
whole once he had become papal commissioner. Having waited and
argued for years for that commission, La Rochefoucauld was anxious
not to waste further time. In August 1622, he summoned three well-
known regulars to Ste Geneviève to advise him. Nobody came armed
with blueprints for reform, and it was merely decided to establish an
advisory council that would meet weekly at the cardinal's residence.
An enlarged council, attended by some of the royal commissioners,
met in September, but took no decisions either. However, La
Rochefoucauld did accept the suggestion that he should begin his
reform by reviving the congregation of St Victor, the only institutional base available to him, and by having a new superior-general
elected. Delegates from St Victor's member-houses discussed reform at
Ste Geneviève in early September, and only one of them objected to
what La Rochefoucauld was planning. He ignored the protest, and
Didier de Saint-Germain, prior of St Victor, was elected general on 10
October.[16] His election was quickly ratified by St Victor, and a week
later the congregation's superiors complied with an order to bring
written reports on the state of their houses to La Rochefoucauld's
council.[17]

The commissioner thus appeared to be pushing forward vigorously,
using existing institutions. But determined not to place all his hopes
on St Victor, he summoned representatives of fourteen abbeys located
near Paris for discussions on 30 October. Few appeared, and he was
obliged to postpone the assembly for some weeks. But most of those
who did attend on 21 November gave non-committal replies when
queried on their attitude to his commission and reform: they wanted
time to reflect, to consult their superiors, episcopal and abbatial. The
lack of enthusiasm was unmistakable.[18] Worse soon followed: conflict with St Victor also blew up in November 1622, when La
Rochefoucauld proposed that his council discuss the question of
benefice-holding by canons-regular. Convinced, as we saw, that it was
the root of innumerable abuses, Faure and Baudouin urged that
benefices be given exclusively to secular clergy, and added, tactlessly,
that the results of the existing system were plain to see in the case of St
Victor. Saint-Germain defended his congregation, but the council
resolved, while making an exception for St Victor itself, to incorporate

16. B.N., MS. Fr. 24080, pp. 223–5, 'Mémorial de St Victor', written by Jean de
    Toulouse, who succeeded St Germain as prior of his abbey, and who assisted at the Ste
    Geneviève meetings; B.S.G., MS. 611, fos. 74–5.
17. B.S.G., MS. 622, fos. 44–73; B.N., MS. Fr 24080, p. 227, 17 and 26 October.
18. B.S.G., MS. 622, fos. 78–91, for statements by the houses concerned.

Faure's views in a forthcoming ordinance. Saint-Germain, however, was adamant that a vital tradition was being abandoned, and warned La Rochefoucauld that many houses would resort to *appels comme d'abus* against a decree along these lines. Exasperated, the cardinal replied that anyone mentioning this execrable practice was not welcome at Ste Geneviève, and at this, Saint-Germain walked out, never to return.[19] Thereafter, St Victor progressively dissociated itself from La Rochefoucauld's reform, and gradually became a focus of hostility to it. The experiment of using existing institutions as vehicles for reform thus ended abruptly, leaving La Rochefoucauld to search for an alternative base of operations.

Setbacks like this made La Rochefoucauld realise the difficult task he faced. His commission gave him wide powers to act, but the orders concerned seemed reticent and slow to respond. His anxiety to press on is evident from the resolutions adopted on 30 November 1622. The council itself would become a permanent institution; the cardinal could delegate others to visit and reform abbeys on his behalf; he could group the latter into congregations, excommunicate opponents and disregard appeals he considered unfounded.[20] This decree highlights the importance of his council to La Rochefoucauld. Most members of the council, which frequently met weekly during the 1620s and 1630s, were from recent or reformed orders, and this had a considerable bearing on the cardinal's whole approach to questions of reform and observance. As no one attended *ex officio*, membership varied somewhat, but it is clear that La Rochefoucauld could draw upon the experience of some of the outstanding regulars of his day.[21] Celebrated figures like the Feuillant Eustache de St Paul and the Carthusian, Adam Ogier, attended regularly; there were always one or two Jesuits, notably Etienne Binet; one or more royal commissioners attended for important deliberations.

After months of work and consultation, La Rochefoucauld was ready by March 1623 to begin publishing the essential items of his reform programme. First came a set of general ordinances for the restoration of observance in all four orders subject to his commission. He declared his intention of founding several regional congregations in the orders, each of which would possess its own superiors and officials. These congregations would be characterised by a full return to community life and observance, based on the three vows of poverty, chastity and obedience; exemptions and privileges militating against them would be suppressed. Once the observance appropriate for each order had

---

19. B.N., MS. Fr. 24080, pp. 227–32, 21 November, for the most detailed account of this episode.
20. B.S.G., MS. 611, fo. 77r, 30 November 1622.
21. See n. 14, above, for just one instance of this practice.

been worked out, he would conduct formal visitations of the monasteries concerned, whose members would be obliged to declare either for or against the reform. As a result of these declarations, reformed and unreformed communities would be formed in each house; the unreformed would be denied a voice in their order's affairs, and especially the right to receive and profess new members.[22]

Clearly La Rochefoucauld had plans for reform well in hand by early 1623, and could count on a number of allies, but as yet there was no institutional basis for action. Ste Geneviève itself remained unreformed; ony the Senlis group seemed committed to reform, as their efforts at Eu and Clairefontaine showed. They, in turn, came to realise how dependent they were on the commissioner's authority. After the short-lived St Victor experiment, their influence grew, with Faure and Baudouin regularly attending his council. They were the obvious, indeed the only, instruments for realising the new 'congrégation de Paris' which the cardinal also unveiled in March 1623. In what was essentially a declaration of intent, he announced that the new congregation would consist of forty named monasteries from several dioceses around Paris. Until they could be actually reformed, they were to be considered as 'virtual' members of the congregation, which was given the exclusive right to reform them.[23] The immediate purpose of this declaration was to launch a systematic visitation of the forty houses, and it comes as no surprise that the visitors commissioned for the purpose were Faure and Baudouin. But, before sending them on their way, La Rochefoucauld attempted to clarify his view of the order's future – and that of others too – in France as a whole. Would the planned 'congrégation de Paris' become a 'congrégation de France'? In a published *Avertissement*, which was probably the result of discussions, and perhaps of disagreements in his council, he explained that, after establishing Paris-based congregations in the various orders, he would use the bishops and their delegates to found similar ones throughout France. He took care to add that this was not intended to create divisions within the orders: future congregations would remain united to each other.[24] This statement was an attempt at pragmatism, as general reform, radiating from a single centre, seemed impossible then. But it was also studiously ambiguous as to

22. *Articles faits par l'ordonnance de Monseigneur le cardinal de la Rochefoucault, grand aumosnier de France, pour le restablissement de l'observance regulière ès monastères qui en ont besoin ès ordres de Sainct Augustin, S. Benoist, Clugny et Cisteaux* (Paris, 1623).
23. B.S.G., MS. 622, fos. 116–25, 11 March 1623; MS. 611, fos. 82–3.
24. B.S.G., MS. 3240, fos. 48–9, 'et parceque le mot congrégations pourroit donner opinion que l'on eut eu dessein de faire quelque sorte de division dans les ordres, on fait savoir que ce terme de congrégations ne désigne autre chose que dénote celuy de Provinces, lequel ne fait aucune division en chacun ordre...toutes les congrégations ou provinces conservans entre elles l'unité'.

the kind of unity envisaged, an ambiguity that was, as we shall see, not easily resolved.

To a certain extent, this kind of proclamation was an academic exercise, albeit one which later proved troublesome. Meanwhile, Faure and Baudouin visited all of the forty monasteries of the phantom congregation between April and July 1623. The welcome they received, the conditions they observed, and the attitudes towards reform they encountered, could hardly have been more diverse. In some cases, their mission was rejected point-blank, usually by priors and *officiers*. At Eu, the prior predictably claimed that reform was quite unnecessary; at Provins, angry canons forced Baudouin to beat a hasty retreat, and local people advised him not to persist. Elsewhere the usual reaction was to request time to consider the proposed reform, and to consult the bishop and the abbot, before giving a formal reply. Faure soon tired of this standard answer, which he regarded as a deliberate evasion of the obligation on individuals and communities to declare where they themselves stood on the question of reform. Only once or twice did an entire community express readiness to adopt the reform; in a few others, they promised to turn over the house to reformers from outside on condition that satisfactory financial arrangements be made for themselves. The visitors found many abbeys in a such a poor state of repair that reform would have to be preceded by expensive refurbishment, something it would be virtually impossible to oblige either canons or commendators to undertake. One or two houses had no members at all, only revenue-drawing commendators, but elsewhere numbers varied from one to around twenty. The visitors were rarely noticed by the bishops, except at Châlons-sur-Marne, where the reforming Cosme Clausse sent along his grand vicars to accompany them in urging reform on the local canons. But it was the final act of each visitation that was, both then and later, the most controversial – a formal proclamation from La Rochefoucauld of an indefinite ban on receiving and professing new members without his express permission under threat of the ecclesiastical censures contained in his papal commission. The importance of this ban, and the intent that lay behind it were clear to all – loss of independence, the arrival of outsiders – and its proclamation gave rise to strong protest and rejection in nearly every abbey visited.[25]

The visitation records gave La Rochefoucauld's council food for thought. They made it clear that the goodwill and human resources required for reform were in short supply; even the well-disposed were totally ignorant of what a reformed observance might be, and required instruction. The Senlis group remained tiny. Its experiences at Eu and Clairefontaine showed that *réformés* could be neutralised by a sullen

25. B.S.G., MS. 622, fos. 134–381, for the records of their visitations.

majority of *anciens*, and that simple bi-lateral agreements for reform could be reneged upon unless backed up by the kind of authority that La Rochefoucauld wielded.

La Rochefoucauld took a number of decisions in the light of 1623 visitations. A council meeting on 19 July ordained that those canons favourable to the reform should be transferred for further instruction to Senlis or Ste Geneviève, which were designated as the congregation's sole novitiates. The ban on receiving or professing novices elsewhere was to be maintained in full, and novices sent to Paris or Senlis would have to be supported by their monastery of origin.[26]

A few days later, La Rochefoucauld published his 'articles particuliers' specifically for the canons-regular. They were analogous to those he prepared for each of the other orders to be reformed. He still envisaged the creation of several congregations governed by triennially-elected generals, who would themselves appoint other superiors and officials on a temporary, revocable basis. External benefices would be given to vicars from the secular clergy, a move which would require special papal consent since La Rochefoucauld's brief excluded him from interfering with benefices. Each congregation would have its central novitiate, to which only those showing signs of a genuine vocation would be admitted, and where they would be maintained at the congregation's expense, independently of parents or relatives. Once he had taken vows, a member might be assigned to any monastery of the general's choice.[27]

For the canons-regular, this programme contained some important innovations, in which the influence of Senlis as well as the attitudes of La Rochefoucauld and his council are apparent. The ending of the venerable tradition of 'belonging' to the monastery of one's profession – 'monastic stability' as it was called – was a radical step, but there seemed no other solution to the problems it generated.[28] Along with clauses about the temporary tenure of offices and centralised novitiates, the programme also reflects the experience of the newer orders, and the conviction that the older ones must to some extent follow their example. As a whole, it constituted a conscious attempt to jolt hitherto independent houses out of the entrenchment that had made them at one and the same time prey to local interests and supporters of them. Ending stability was central to La Rochefoucauld's policy, as was the removal of control of recruitment from local houses through the creation of centralised novitiates. These novitiates themselves can be seen as an extension of La Rochefoucauld's earlier views upon the

---

26. B.S.G., MS. 622, fos. 431–6, council meeting and decisions of 19 July 1623.
27. B.S.G., MS. 622, fos. 422–31, 23 July 1623.
28. Monastic stability was the custom whereby a monk or canon was permanently attached to the monastery in which he had been professed, and from which he could not normally be readily or unwillingly transferred.

training of the secular clergy. The reform of benefice-holding was designed to close off avenues of escape from community life and observance, and to discourage the ambitious. That the novelty of this programme did not go unchallenged by traditionalists within the order is evident from an exchange of pamphlets in 1624.[29]

Problems of recruitment and training continued to engage La Rochefoucauld's attention in the early days of his commission, and in October 1623 he published a further set of regulations as a basis for future practice. He declared that henceforth he would not accept the argument, which had been widely used during Faure and Baudouin's visitations, that regulars were under no obligation in conscience to embrace an unfamiliar, reformed observance; when questioned by his delegates, everyone was bound to declare himself either for or against it. On the basis of their statements, two communities would be formed in every house; the observants would be given spiritual and temporal control of their house, while the unreformed *anciens* would be allowed to live on 'jusqu'à ce qu'il plaise à Dieu d'en disposer'. The purpose of the novitiate was clearly stated – 'pour rendre l'observance susdite perpetuelle à l'avenir et supprimer quant et quant le désordre passé'. Only observant superiors might, therefore, accept new entrants. Given the urgency of reform, La Rochefoucauld reiterated earlier declarations that the first congregations, for the canons-regular and the other orders in his charge, should be established in Paris, and which 'pourroit servir de modèle pour toutes les autres qui seront cy-après érigées en tous lesdits ordres par toute l'estendue de ce Royaume'.[30]

Of La Rochefoucauld's two projected novitiates, Ste Geneviève was still unreformed in late 1623, and in no way fit to play the part he assigned to it. His patience, however, was wearing thin. On 1 April 1624, he finally summoned its canons to declare themselves for or against reform; only a quarter of them accepted unreservedly, the rest were either too old, too uninterested, or too hostile. A few days later, his council advised him to import reform from the outside, but before taking this advice, and anticipating trouble from the well-connected canons, La Rochefoucauld sought and obtained the king's support for such a move.[31] His caution was justified by the canons' prompt *appel*

29. See the *Examen d'une apologie pour les chanoines réguliers de St Augustin* (Paris, 1624). This anonymous work is a reply to an earlier pamphlet published at Reims, but now lost. From the reforms that it defends, one can deduce the nature of the attack on La Rochefoucauld's proposals in the original *Apologie*.
30. B.S.G., MS. 611, fos. 86–90, 'règlement pour la reception à l'habit ès ordres de S Benoist, Cluny, S Augustin et Cisteaux', 12 October 1623.
31. B.S.G., MS. 3247, fo. 85, letter to Gaspar Segueran, confessor to Louis XIII, 14 April 1624. From this letter, it appears the cardinal had already asked for a squad of archers, in case of armed resistance! The king refused this, but promised full support should there be resistance. B.S.G., MS. 3242, fos. 45–9.

comme d'abus against his action, and this was to prove to be the first major test for the canons-regular of the provisions of his 1622 commission. The case went to the royal commissioners, who quashed the appeal, warned the *parlement* not to interfere, and allowed La Rochefoucauld to proceed.[32] On 28 April, accompanied by the commissioners and an impressive retinue, he installed twelve canons from Senlis under Faure at Ste Geneviève. Its residents did not dare protest openly, but Faure's community remained for some time entirely dependent on the cardinal's protection, having no official status within the abbey.[33] La Rochefoucauld himself proceded cautiously, and only gradually transferred internal control of its affairs from the *anciens* to the reformed community.[34]

III

This initial phase of La Rochefoucauld's commission has been treated at some length, because of the problems it serves to highlight. For all his impressive-sounding powers, it proved extremely difficult for him to achieve anything during these years. Establishing a bridgehead of reform in an order so lacking in structure was no easy matter. Besides, his commission depended for its effectiveness on a desire for reform which seemed conspicuously absent. The reform of Ste Geneviève was an important breakthrough, but it owed as much to La Rochefoucauld's position as abbot and president of the king's council as it did to his brief as reform commissioner, and it remained for a time an extremely fragile achievement. Moreover, if it demonstrated that the Senlis group needed him, it showed even more clearly that he needed them. Above all, the legislation and proclamations of these early years provided the foundations for reform, and subsequent debate and controversy would frequently turn on the 'true' intentions of La Rochefoucauld's early ordinances.

The first examples of what must have been welcome episcopal initiative date from the same year as the reform of Ste Geneviève. Bishop Etampes of Chartres appealed to La Rochefoucauld to reform St Jean-la-Vallée and when he received no formal reply, went directly to Faure, who was still a semi-independent agent at Senlis, and obtained a promise of support from him. Etampes himself visited the abbey, deposed its prior and *officiers*, and installed the Senlis reform. When the *anciens* recovered from the shock, they appealed *comme d'abus*, but

32. B.S.G., MS. 622, fos. 566–9, decree and commission for La Rochefoucauld, 25 April 1624.
33. B.S.G., MS. 3242, fos. 53–4; B.N., MS. Fr. 24080, pp. 269–70, for the view from St Victor.
34. B.S.G., MS. 622, fos. 616–17, 634–6; MS. 623, fos. 64–6, 72–3.

the vigilant royal commissioners disallowed their appeal.[35] Later that year, Etampes also invoked the cardinal's commission to reform the Abbey of Chéron, and to declare it part of the new congregation.[36] In both cases, La Rochefoucauld's authority proved necessary to maintain the reform, as that of Etampes would hardly have prevented the *anciens* from undoing his work. Other petitions reached the cardinal in 1624 but he lacked the manpower to do more than to acknowledge them formally as a first step towards reform.

Nevertheless, these modest beginnings were enough to convince him that reform was acquiring some momentum, and he proceeded to establish his 'congrégation de Paris' on a formal footing in December 1624, incorporating into it the forty abbeys visited the previous year.[37] Such an action, intended to safeguard the future, was not as quixotic as it may seem – it kept up the pressure on the order, and bore witness to his determination to stick to the task. It soon attracted attention, both positive and negative. In 1625, the Bishops of Senlis and Chartres declared that all the canons-regular of their dioceses should henceforth consider themselves subject to reform.[38] The 1625 Assembly of the Clergy, with its parallel meetings at Ste Geneviève, probably provided other bishops with their first taste of La Rochefoucauld's reforms, and may explain the growing episcopal interest and co-operation of subsequent years. But it was also in 1625 that St Victor abandoned any attempt to promote reform; already concerned by the possible threat from neighbouring Ste Geneviève, it dissolved its own congregation and placed itself under the protection of the Archbishop of Paris, advising its former members to take similar precautions. Such behaviour, coupled with an invitation to Archbishop Gondi to visit the abbey, was a clear warning to La Rochefoucauld not to interfere.[39]

The cardinal and his advisers were undeterred. Installed at Ste Geneviève, the influence of Faure and his Senlis group on La Rochefoucauld grew apace. Faure in particular had a keen sense of the institutional requirements for the survival of reform. In 1626, he submitted a memorandum to La Rochefoucauld on the future of the congregation, which then comprised only four member-houses, two of

---

35. B.S.G., MS. 622, fos. 528–39; MS. 611, fos. 93v–5v.
36. B.S.G., MS. 622, fos. 590–1; MS. 623, fos. 42–5; Chartonnet, *Vie de Charles Faure*, p. 168ff
37. B.S.G., MS. 3242, fos. 60–2, 3 December 1624.
38. B.S.G., MS. 611, fo. 124v.
39. B.S.G., MS. 623, fos. 68–71, act of dissolution, 5 December 1625; B.N., MS. Fr. 24080, pp. 271ff, 311ff, 329, for a detailed account of St Victor's internal problems, and growing fear of Ste Geneviève. When St Victor defied La Rochefoucauld in 1633 by attempting to reconstitute its congregation, it claimed that notice of the 1625 action had never been formally served on its member-houses, so that the congregation had not been legally dissolved. See below, p. 188.

which – St Jean-la-Vallée and Chéron of Chartres – were barely hanging on. But there were already more requests for reform than could be met, and he felt that this pressure would increase; the time had come to put the reform on its feet by electing a superior-general. La Rochefoucauld should not allow his congregation to fall apart like St Victor's, since only a well-structured authority, under a general, could effectively break down traditions of independence, and weld together a unified congregation. He highlighted the difficulties to be faced by reminding La Rochefoucauld that his ban on receiving and professing novices was being entirely ignored.[40]

La Rochefoucauld's immediate response was to seek new letters-patent confirming an eventual return to elected abbots at Ste Geneviève, and allowing him to select a coadjutor-abbot during his lifetime. The king agreed in November 1626, but the *parlement* did not register the patents until July 1627, and the *grand conseil* not until 1630, despite renewed requests from Louis XIII.[41] It was this unforeseen delay which probably made it impossible for La Rochefoucauld to implement Faure's advice at this time, especially as his own commission was due to expire in 1628. Yet this did not prevent Faure from acting as unofficial superior of the reformed canons who, in August 1628, empowered him to take, on their behalf, whatever steps he considered necessary for the advancement of the reform.[42] He proved extremely active during these years, continually visiting the reformed abbeys, and engaging in long and exacting negotiations for the reform of others. At Senlis, it was he who admitted novices to take vows; at Ste Geneviève, he personally supervised the novices, and even taught some theology. In 1626, he founded a *séminaire des enfants* at Senlis, designed to educate young boys and to prepare those with a vocation for their entry into the religious life.[43] The following year, he appears to have persuaded La Rochefoucauld to establish a similar institution at Ste Geneviève, but the latter changed his mind under pressure from the Jesuits, who doubtless feared that it might compete with their Collège de Clermont.[44]

40. B.S.G., MS. 3250, fos. 59–60, memorandum of 26 November 1626. Faure also outlined his ideas on the proper establishment of novitiates: *ibid.*, fo. 277.
41. B.S.G., MS. 623, fos. 110–13v, text of patents; fos. 114–15, registration by the *parlement*, 2 July 1627; fos. 119–20, king to *grand conseil*; fos. 120–1, second letter from king, 3 October 1629; fos. 376–7, decree of registration, 11 March 1630.
42. B.S.G., MS. 611, fos. 166–8.
43. *Ibid.*, fos. 142–6.
44. B.S.G., MS. 3266, fo. 28, Robert Baudouin to Faure, 9 May 1627, stating that a seminary at Ste Geneviève was a matter of urgency. On the reverse of this letter is a note by François Boulart: 'En 1627, le r.p. Faure proposa à Son Eminence d'establir un séminaire à Sainte Geneviève pour les eslever de sa main, en avoir plus grand nombre et pour plusieurs autres considérations très importantes. Son Eminence y donna les mains, mais les pp. Jésuites l'empeschèrent.'

IV

During La Rochefoucauld's first commission, relations were established with two other reformers, Gallet of Angers and Solminihac of Chancelade. Because of the disputes with them that arose later, and their impact on the reform movement, it is essential to comprehend the tenor of these initial contacts.

As we have seen, neither Gallet nor Solminihac had made much progress by 1622. Two years later, Gallet and his followers first expressed interest in La Rochefoucauld's reform, and the cardinal replied by sending them copies of his ordinances to date and asking them to declare their position. Their answer was one of acceptance, coupled with an appeal for his protection against the anti-reform canons at Toussaints; they also expressed a desire to see the reform expand into Anjou.[45] Gallet's reading of La Rochefoucauld's ordinances convinced him that this was the best way to achieve his 'congrégation de Touraine'. A visit to Ste Geneviève in 1625 further fuelled his enthusiasm for the task ahead, which was soon facilitated by a generous settlement with the commendator of Toussaints.[46] But it soon became apparent that Ste Geneviève had given him no mandate to pursue his designs; within months he was complaining of a lack of support, of a failure to answer his letters, and of receiving no instructions 'pour la visite de la congrégation de Touraine'.[47] Clearly, Gallet saw himself as a reformer in his own right, the equal or partner, not the agent of Ste Geneviève. Both then and later, La Rochefoucauld was inclined to accept this premise, and lend his authority as commissioner to Gallet's plans. But there was growing opposition, which La Rochefoucauld could not ignore, to autonomous undertakings from Faure. By 1625–6, Faure firmly believed that there should be a single 'congrégation de France', and was dismayed by the idea of separate provinces with their own observances and customs; it seemed to him to run counter to the cardinal's warning in 1623 against division within the order. He felt that Gallet merely wished to plough his own furrow, using La Rochefoucauld's commission because it suited him; he also seemed bent on founding a congregation before effecting reform, when the converse was called for. In employing such arguments, Faure assumed he was interpreting La Rochefoucauld's intentions correctly, when he was in fact revealing a significant ambiguity in them, and adopting a more rigid, one-dimensional view

45. B.S.G., MS. 3250, fo. 61, petition to La Rochefoucauld, 1634; *ibid.*, fo. 63, 'déliberation capitulaire' of Toussaints, 14 September 1624; MS. 3266, fo. 4, Gallet to La Rochefoucauld, 19 October 1624; MS. 622, fos. 598–600, pro-reform canons to La Rochefoucauld, same date.
46. B.S.G., MS. 623, fos. 74–9, agreement of 19 January 1626.
47. B.S.G., MS. 3266, fo. 66, Gallet to La Rochefoucauld, 10 May 1625.

than La Rochefoucauld had meant to convey. Gallet certainly thought that Faure was turning the cardinal against him, and strongly denied any ambition to 'faire bande à part'. He found the ban on novices, which was extended to Toussaints, unfair and hard to stomach, while his failure to respect it only served to increase distrust of him at Ste Geneviève, where his view on the need to increase numbers was seen as wilful disregard of the crucial principle of central novitiates. These skirmishes between Gallet and Faure raised the important question of whether reform should be uniform, expanding outwards from a single centre, or whether La Rochefoucauld's commission should serve as an umbrella to bring together and promote independent reforms in some more generous spirit. The cardinal tended towards the second view, but was vulnerable to suggestions that an unco-ordinated approach would create permanent division. It was also difficult for him in practice to rely on Faure and his followers without adopting some of their arguments.[48]

Gallet, doubtless sensing La Rochefoucauld's underlying sympathy, frequently pressed him to settle the dispute with Ste Geneviève. But the cardinal remained undecided for several years. This, apparently, prevented Gallet from considering offers to reform other abbeys in western France.[49] On the other hand, Ste Geneviève was quite content to employ Gallet in the hazardous reform of St Pierre de Rillé, near Rennes, where, acting as La Rochefoucauld's delegate, his knowledge of local conditions and attitudes proved invaluable.[50] The opportunities denied him only seemed to make Gallet the more determined to press for an independent congregation, and it was in that spirit that he consistently championed Solminihac against Ste Geneviève in 1627–8, when the Abbot of Chancelade was seeking royal support for his proposed 'congrégation de Guyenne'.[51] Surprisingly, Gallet became convinced, in early 1629, that a single congregation might after all be the best vehicle for reform, despite his dislike of Faure's policy of withdrawal from parochial work.[52] In November 1629, he and his canons formally petitioned La Rochefoucauld for admission to his congregation.[53] The cardinal first consulted Ste Geneviève, which objected on several grounds and wished, in any case, to impose

48. The foregoing points are raised in Gallet's letters to La Rochefoucauld, Faure and Baudouin in B.S.G., MS. 3266, fos. 8, 10, 11, 21, 24, 26, 41, 66, 107.
49. The Abbey of Montfort frequently asked Gallet to transmit its desire for reform to La Rochefoucauld: B.S.G., MS. 3266, fos. 83, 311, 315, 350, Gallet's interesting letters on the possibilities of reform there.
50. *Ibid.*, fos. 126, 219, 221, 227, letters to Faure and others, 1628–9.
51. *Ibid.*, fos. 126, 169, 282, letters defending Solminihac, 1628–9. For Solminihac's efforts, see *Alain de Solminihac. Lettres et documents*, ed. Eugène Sol (Cahors, 1930), pp. 69, 73–4.
52. B.S.G., MS. 611, fos. 196–7.
53. B.S.G., MS. 623, fos. 342–5, letter of 13 November.

stringent conditions, but he ignored their arguments, and admitted Toussaints without conditions.[54] However, this decision simply drew a veil over misunderstandings and conflicting intentions, suspending rather than resolving the arguments involved. In May 1630, La Rochefoucauld was reported as saying that Toussaints should be allowed to 'travailler à part'.[55]

With Solminihac, actual contact was limited in the early years. He personally discovered the reform at Senlis, but then adopted a stricter observance at Chancelade, and remained convinced thereafter that his version of reform was superior to that of Ste Geneviève.[56] Strong-willed and with little time for others' weaknesses, he believed that La Rochefoucauld could achieve little in the south-west, where a separate congregation was called for.[57] But once again, although the cardinal esteemed him highly, he could not bring himself to underwrite his plans. There is no evidence that it was he who prevented Solminihac's projected congregation from gaining royal support in 1628. There was as yet no basis for a break between the two men.

La Rochefoucauld's first commission duly ended in 1628. It might seem that he had achieved little during the previous six years. Yet he lacked resources and allies, and these could not be conjured into existence overnight.[58] He was also discovering how difficult it was to secure the combined consent to reform of bishops, abbots and canons, without which any attempt at change might misfire, and to impose the tough demands of Ste Geneviève, especially with respect to the receiving and professing of novices. Yet it would be misguided to write off these years as unproductive. Faure provided a balanced perspective in a letter to Solminihac in 1627:

> We are making progress more in terms of the numbers of recruits than of houses, which we are in no hurry to take over. Ste Geneviève is firmly ours, we have two houses at Chartres and St Vincent of Senlis, as well as another we are seeking to reform. Everything is going well and in accordance with religious principles.[59]

54. B.S.G., MS. 3250, fos. 65, 67; MS. 623, fos. 348–51, 'délibération capitulaire' of Ste Geneviève, 21 November; MS. 3238, fo. 420, act of admission, 28 November.
55. B.S.G., MS. 3266, fo. 347, Boulart to Faure, 18 May.
56. See Sol, *Le Vénérable Alain de Solminihac*, pp. 30ff.
57. *Lettres et documents*, pp. 47–8, Jaubert de Barrault, Bishop of Bazas, to Solminihac, 27 May 1625. The bishop was also a close friend of La Rochefoucauld, and frequently served as intermediary between the two men.
58. In his 'relazione finale' of 1624, the departing nuncio, Corsini, wrote that the slow progress of La Rochefoucauld's reforms was not surprising, given the appalling state of the orders: A.S.V. Nunz. Fr. 63, fo. 521v.
59. 'Nous advançons grâce au nombre de personnes, non tant en maisons que nous voulons si tost accepter. Cette maison nous est assurée, deux à Chartres et puis St Vincent, et une autre que de présent nous entreprenons. Tout va asses bien et religieusement.' *Lettres et documents*, pp. 59–60, letter of 5 August.

When La Rochefoucauld's commission was renewed in 1628 for a further three years, he had reformed only five monasteries in all.[60] Yet his new powers enabled him to pursue a growing number of projects that were already under way, or had been temporarily shelved. The growth of the congregation meant increasingly that the details of reform were becoming routine, to be handled by Faure and others, with the cardinal's council acting as the essential linch-pin and clearing-house. This evolving division of labour often produced friction, and the ageing La Rochefoucauld was often slow to adjust to it, seeming at times to believe that the Génovéfains, as they were now called, were not always keeping him fully informed; they, in turn, feared the influence of some of his personal advisers, especially the Jesuits, on his plans. How the traditional rivalry of the orders might jeopardise their plans, and set La Rochefoucauld's entourage at cross purposes, can be seen from a major reform in the late 1620s.

The Parisian priory of Ste Cathérine, a member of the congregation of Val-des-Ecoliers which was no longer observant, was coveted by many orders, not least the Jesuits, but both its prior and the congregation's general preferred a link with Ste Geneviève.[61] When approached by them, Faure decided to act without informing La Rochefoucauld, fearing that the Jesuits and others on his council might stifle the project.[62] A contract signed on 1 April 1628 provided for the establishment of a reformed community of Génovéfains, who would, however, become part of Val-des-Ecoliers.[63] Faure accepted this and other unfavourable terms in order to secure a foothold in the congregation, and in the hope of extending the reform to its other houses later. The commendator gave his approval, and letters-patent were duly requested.[64] Quite accidentally, these were issued on the very same day as the royal letters for La Rochefoucauld's second papal commission. The cardinal discovered what Faure had done and procured a copy of the contract. His council predictably pounced on its obvious departures from established Génovéfain practice, and La Rochefoucauld himself rounded on Faure.[65] In the event, Faure's self-defence proved convincing, and the commissioner admitted he had been mistaken to attack him. Ironically, La Rochefoucauld was himself acting independently of Faure, and had already sought a special papal commission to reform the Val-des-Ecoliers congregation as a whole; fearing the jealousy of the other orders, and the dangers of

---

60. B.S.G., MS. 623, fos. 152–9, text of brief, 16 February 1628; *ibid.*, fos. 192–6, royal letters-patent, 4 April.
61. As early as December 1622, La Rochefoucauld had attempted to discuss his reform with them, but without success: B.S.G., MS. 622, fos. 92–3.
62. B.S.G., MS. 611, fos. 177–8; Chartonnet, *Vie de Charles Faure*, p. 268ff.
63. B.S.G., MS. 623, fos. 177–86.
64. *Ibid.*, fo. 191, act of ratification; fos. 198–201, patents dated 3 April.
65. B.S.G., MS. 611, fos. 177–81; MS. 3250, fo. 280, undated apologia by Faure which seems to relate to this incident.

interference from the *parlement*, he was anxious to act from a position of strength. The resulting commission, issued in June 1628, gave him what he sought, the ensuing negotiations went much more favourably for Ste Geneviève, and Faure's original concessions could be dropped. Finally, in April 1629, Ste Cathérine was occupied without incident by a Génovéfain community.[66] La Rochefoucauld's prudence proved to be well-founded, for other Val-des-Ecoliers abbeys blamed their general strongly for surrendering such as important house, and in May 1629, their general chapter drafted new reform statutes and promptly appealed *comme d'abus* to the *parlement*. Once again, the royal commissioners quickly closed this escape route, summoning the parties before them and upholding La Rochefoucauld's reform.[67] Ste Cathérine remained in his congregation, and by 1633 had become one of its central novitiates.[68]

For all its attendant confusion, this kind of success showed that reform was gathering momentum, despite the congregation's limited resources. The Ste Cathérine affair actually strengthened Faure's position, and soon afterwards, La Rochefoucauld appointed him visitor and superior of the reformed houses, with wide powers.[69] Results gradually began to show, as the number of reformed houses increased during the second commission. If it is impossible to detect a single uniform pattern in all this, since the motives and positions of the different parties in individual cases varied considerably, a sample of cases may serve to illustrate some at least of the features and *dramatis personae* involved in reform.

In 1629, the canons of St Martin de Nevers appealed to the distant congregation rather than submit to the reform that their bishop had, for ten years, been vainly attempting to impose on them. The prior and sub-prior personally embraced the reform, while the remainder vacated the abbey by retiring to their benefices outside. Far from taking umbrage at this, the bishop welcomed the breakthrough, and insisted on installing the Génovéfains himself at St Martin.[70]

St Pierre de Rillé, near Rennes, was among the first to petition for

66. B.S.G., MS. 623, fos. 220–6, papal brief, 6 July 1628; fos. 227–9, letters-patent, 23 October. La Rochefoucauld also took the precaution of seeking royal support for his action: MS. 3238, fo. 383, letter to Suffren, royal confessor, 19 March 1629. The negotiations and 'prise de possession' can be followed in A.N., LL 1457, *actes capitulaires* of Ste Cathérine.
67. B.S.G., MS. 611, fos. 182–6. This was a common enough tactic when opponents of reform were anxious to be seen to put their own house in order, and La Rochefoucauld was no stranger to it in the other orders he dealt with.
68. B.S.G., MS. 624, fos. 405–8, La Rochefoucauld's ordinance, 11 August 1632.
69. B.S.G., MS. 3242, fos. 113–14; MS. 623, fos. 280–4, two acts dated 4 May 1629. Interestingly, Ste Geneviève itself was excluded from Faure's jurisdiction; La Rochefoucauld reserved full control of the abbey's affairs to himself.
70. B.S.G., MS. 3250, fo. 576, Bishop of Nevers to La Rochefoucauld, 12 July 1629. The official acts of the reform are in MS. 623, fos. 306–11, 318–25, 336–41. The Génovéfains took possession in November 1629.

reform, and Baudouin found it in good order during his visitation in May 1628.[71] Pressed by the prior, he left some Génovéfains behind there, and one of them actually became prior; little difficulty was anticipated in having the change ratified by the abbot and the Bishop of Rennes. But within months, attitudes had altered so sharply that Faure petitioned La Rochefoucauld for permission to withdraw his canons provisionally.[72] A contract to enable the Génovéfains to reform the abbey was eventually signed, but by then the Bishop of Rennes was supporting those *anciens* of Rillé who opposed the proposed change. He insisted on an episcopal visitation of the abbey, saying he would not tolerate anything that diminished his canonical rights. But the Génovéfains won the support of the town council and, more significantly, the *parlement* of Rennes, and with their help, triumphed over the bishop and the *anciens*.[73] The peculiar circumstances of this reform and the attitudes of those involved, even among some of the Génovéfains themselves, made Rillé a source of trouble in subsequent years. It was also, as we shall see, not the only example of how wounded episcopal pride could obstruct efforts at reform. It may even be that La Rochefoucauld's relations generally with certain members of the French episcopate were adversely affected by such incidents.

Many other requests for reform were submitted to La Rochefoucauld by canons, bishops, and commendators in the late 1620s and early 1630s. But as he rarely had a full-sized community ready to place in the houses concerned, he often had to postpone action indefinitely. A crucial feature of his reform was that the canons petitioning him to reform their monasteries rarely wished to embrace it for themselves, doubtless because Ste Geneviève insisted that they return to the novitiate before deciding on whether to accept them, a condition that probably offended the great majority. Furthermore, past experience made the congregation reluctant to send a handful of its members to an abbey for the purpose of reforming the community there. In twenty years, there was not a single example of a whole community embracing reform for itself as distinct from 'accepting' it for its abbey. Thus, with only isolated individuals willing to enter the reform, progress could not but be slow; the supply of men needed to form new communities lagged far behind the demand. In 1628 alone, six petitions for reform

71. B.S.G., MS. 3266, fo. 65, Marchant, prior of Rillé, to Faure, 7 December 1627, referring to his earlier request for reform; *ibid.*, fos. 85, 89 and 95, Baudouin to Faure, 27 and 30 May, 8 June 1628. In the last of these letters, he reported the bishop's favourable reaction.
72. B.S.G., MS. 3250, fo. 121, letter of 19 November 1628.
73. The correspondence relating to this reform is extensive: B.S.G., MS. 3266, fos. 175, 201, 207, 209, 228, 231, 288, 302, letters from Jean Thomas, Génovéfain prior; *ibid.*, fos. 219, 221, 227, letters from Philippe Gallet, whom La Rochefoucauld had entrusted with the difficult task of placating the bishop and the *anciens*, and of making a peaceful reform possible.

were received, two of them from the Archbishops of Sens and Reims.[74] But many had to be turned down or shelved, partly because the 'claustral' buildings necessary for a reformed observance, were either non-existent or in ruins. Moreover, if the congregation also had to pay substantial pensions to the *anciens* as the price of entry to an abbey, its own community there might not then have adequate revenues, let alone be able to conduct extensive repairs or rebuilding. In some cases, petitions for reform were not followed up for over ten years.[75] By 1632, when it held its first general chapter, the congregation numbered only ten houses.

At no time between 1622 and 1645 did the wind of reform sweep through the Augustinian monasteries: indifference was common, and could easily turn to hostility. If a party to discussions on reform became disgruntled for any reason, its determined opposition could all but exclude further progress. Génovéfain conditions were not infrequently unacceptable to bishops, commendators or monastic *officiers*. Priors and *officiers*, for example, resented the reformers' animus against holding offices as benefices. But it was the ban on novices in monasteries officially visited by La Rochefoucauld's delegates which engendered the strongest resistance, reinforced as it usually was by offended local interests.[76]

Over the years, the cardinal regarded the general evasion of his ban by individual monasteries as the severest threat to his work, because it perpetuated the old régime. In 1631, he won an important victory in a test case that he and Faure took to the royal commissioners. Their decree, known as the *arrêt des Deux-Amants* from the name of the priory involved, ordered a strict enforcement of the ordinances on novitiates published in 1623, and commanded the recalcitrant novices of Deux-Amants either to enter an approved novitiate or return home to their families.[77] La Rochefoucauld was to make liberal use of this decree, even to the extent of serving notice of it on the families of novices when he invoked it – a telling indication of the problems he faced.[78]

It was also during his second commission that La Rochefoucauld made significant contact with Solminihac. In 1630, he commissioned him to visit the Augustinian monasteries of five dioceses in the south-west, with powers to impose his ban on novices, and to award pensions to those uninterested in reform.[79] This assignment he performed later

74. B.S.G., MS. 623, fos. 242–8 (Sens), MS. 611, fo. 176 (Reims).
75. A fuller catalogue of these petitions can be found in B.S.G., MSS. 623–4.
76. See René Pillorget, 'Réforme monastique et conflits de rupture dans quelques localités de la France méridionale au xviie siècle' *Revue historique* 253 (1975), pp. 77–106, for some striking parallels to the difficulties encountered by La Rochefoucauld.
77. B.S.G., MS. 624, fos. 29–34, decree of 11 February.
78. La Rochefoucauld twice invoked the decree in April–May 1631: *ibid.*, fos. 91–2, 95.
79. B.S.G., MS. 623, fos. 372–5, commission of 21 January 1630.

in the year, but he confined himself to the first two clauses of his brief. The houses he visited were, if anything, in a more appalling state than those of northern France several years earlier, although Solminihac's severity of judgement makes straightforward comparison risky. The religious wars, notably those of the 1620s, had ruined many of them, destroying surviving vestiges of community life. Their canons were ignorant, but knew how to evade episcopal attentions by pleading direct subordination to Rome itself. Only one abbey, St Gérald de Limoges, actively sought reform.[80] Solminihac reported to La Rochefoucauld in early 1632, but no decisions followed, except that Solminihac could continue his activities as the cardinal's delegate. Nor was there any talk at that time of incorporating the few abbeys Solminihac had himself reformed into the Paris-based congregation.[81] He duly completed the reform of St Gérald within about a year, but acted with the cardinal's authority at each stage.[82] For the time being, he had little hope of establishing his 'congrégation de Guyenne'.[83]

Meanwhile, La Rochefoucauld finally approached Rome for papal recognition of his congregation as an independent entity, as well as for a return to elected abbots at Ste Geneviève after his death. As soon as it became clear, in early 1630, that the *grand conseil* would at last ratify the patents of 1626 to this effect, Louis XIII was asked to instruct the new ambassador in Rome, Brassac, to petition Urban VIII. This was also to include a request for a coadjutor-abbot elected triennially during the cardinal's lifetime, and a stipulation that offices in the congregation's abbeys would lose their status as benefices.[84] As such concessions would certainly involve financial compensation to the curia, La Rochefoucauld employed a *banquier expéditionnaire* and his Roman 'solicitor', one Marchant, to conduct parallel discussions with curial officials.[85] Marchant received detailed instructions, especially on offices and benefices, in April 1630, but both he and Brassac needed further prodding before negotiations really got under way in

---

80. *Ibid.*, fos. 448–520; MS. 624, fos. 15–22, for the visitation records.
81. B.S.G., MS. 3243, fo. 236, Solminihac to La Rochefoucauld, 20 May 1632.
82. B.S.G., MS. 3250, fo. 164, Solminihac to La Rochefoucauld, 28 October 1632; *ibid.*, fo. 193, La Rochefoucauld's reply; MS. 3243, fo. 238, Solminihac to La Rochefoucauld, 4 June 1633; *ibid.*, fo. 242, confirmation of reform contract by La Rochefoucauld, 14 August 1633.
83. The Bishop of Limoges would not deal with him in any other capacity than as La Rochefoucauld's delegate: *Lettres et documents*, p. 133, Limoges to Solminihac, 19 November 1632.
84. B.S.G., MS. 3277, fo. 1, king's letter to Urban VIII, 13 February; MS. 3238, fo. 249, La Rochefoucauld to Brassac, 12 April, recalling the terms of the royal letter.
85. B.S.G., MS. 3250, fo. 134, certificate from Lhuillier, the *banquier expéditionnaire*, that he had instructed Marchant to conduct negotiations in curia, 30 April.

August 1630, when a new petition had to be drafted and presented.[86] It was the first time that La Rochefoucauld approached the curia with a serious demand as reformer of the canons-regular, and the negotiations may be regarded as something of a test case of its priorities and attitudes towards reform.

The pope responded well when approached by Brassac in August 1630, but the preliminary negotiations in curia, especially with datary officials, had to take their normal course.[87] Following the example of their superior, the cardinal-datarius, officials stated frankly their determination not to allow the interests of reform to involve financial loss to themselves. When they enquired if the cardinal intended suppressing benefices only within Ste Geneviève or in the congregation as a whole, the irritated La Rochefoucauld instructed Marchant to reply that reform, if genuine, must mean that monastic offices should no longer be obtainable as benefices, given that such practices were the ruin of proper observance. He did, however, exclude parishes from this category.[88] This kind of problem delayed the presentation of a formal petition to Urban VIII until May 1631, when he referred the matter to an *ad hoc* commission; he was not about to ride roughshod over his officials' financial interests. At its first sitting, the commission threw out the petition, the datarius proving deaf to appeals about the survival of the reform. When Marchant tried to assure him that one of the indemnities demanded by officials would be covered, he replied that it had never been paid from France.[89] This setback led La Rochefoucauld to modify his petition, and so initiate another round of negotiations. But nothing had been achieved by early 1632, when the cardinal decided to convene the first general chapter of his congregation with a view to electing a general and voting its statutes.[90]

In normal circumstances, La Rochefoucauld would probably have wished to postpone a general chapter until Rome had reached a decision. But the prospect of further indefinite delay there raised the possibility of a weakened reform movement in France, and made him

---

86. B.S.G., MS. 3238, fo. 250, La Rochefoucauld to Marchant, 10 May, referring to 'un mémoire bien ample' which seems not to have survived; MS. 3250, fo. 155, Brassac to La Rochefoucauld, 20 July; MS. 3238, fo. 248, Bouthillier, secretary of state, to La Rochefoucauld, Lyon 26 August, informing him the king had written a second time to Brassac and sending him a copy of the letter which has not have survived; MS. 3277, fos. 2–3, La Rochefoucauld to Marchant, 9 August.
87. B.S.G., MS. 3250, fo. 153, Brassac to La Rochefoucauld, 17 August.
88. *Ibid.*, fo. 133r, Marchant to Lhuillier, 14 September; *ibid.*, fo. 147, to La Rochefoucauld, 12 October; *ibid.*, fo. 133r–v, for La Rochefoucauld's reactions to the curia's position and queries.
89. *Ibid.*, fo. 151, Marchant to La Rochefoucauld, 7 June 1631.
90. *Ibid.*, fo. 161, La Rochefoucauld to Marchant, 6 June 1631; *ibid.*, fo. 149–50, Marchant's reply, 16 August.

listen to calls for a general chapter from the congregation's leaders in early 1632. Faure, in particular, stressed the urgency of electing a general with adequate powers of government, and deplored the lack of internal unity.[91] La Rochefoucauld evidently agreed, but what Faure probably did not anticipate was that he would invite Gallet and Solminihac, thereby making the event more an estates general of the reform movement than a narrowly-conceived chapter of the congregation.[92] The alarm spread rapidly within Ste Geneviève where, notwithstanding La Rochefoucauld's gesture of 1629, Gallet had never been accepted as a genuine member of the congregation, and was believed to be in league with a number of other dissidents.[93] There had, of course, never been any question of Solminihac's membership, as he would have himself conceded, so the cardinal's invitation to him seemed especially perverse. Finally, his request that delegates bring proposals on the future of the reform suggested that he viewed the chapter as rather more than a legislative organ of his congregation.

Most of the delegates – though not Solminihac, who did not attend – arrived before the opening date of 15 May 1632, and the struggle for La Rochefoucauld's favour began immediately. Faure and the congregation's leaders were against Gallet's being allowed to attend at all, and repeated their view that, despite the cardinal's decision, Toussaints was still not genuinely a member, having never observed any of the congregation's basic rules. They deplored the factiousness evident in some of the proposals being made to La Rochefoucauld, and warned him that the congregation might collapse if Gallet, the prior of Rillé, and others not mentioned by name were allowed to influence policy. Reform, based on unity of practice and outlook, still needed careful nursing. Given the evident lack of unity, they now argued, it would be better to postpone electing a general and drafting statutes.[94] It appears that opposition attacks were directed primarily against Faure, the presumed architect of Génovéfain exclusiveness; unfortunately, the surviving sources are too biased to unveil the arguments of the opposition in any but a vague and hostile manner.[95]

These highly-charged discussions obliged La Rochefoucauld to

91. B.S.G., MS. 705, fos. 51–3, memorandum from Faure, no date, lamenting the parlous state of the congregation's affairs, and the lack of internal discipline.

92. B.S.G., MS. 624, fos. 305–9v, decision of council to summon chapter, 17 April; *ibid.*, fos. 309v–10v, summons of chapter for 15 May by La Rochefoucauld, 21 April.

93. B.S.G., MS. 3276, fo. 373, François Boulart (secretary to La Rochefoucauld) to Faure, 24 April, announcing the cardinal's decision, and requesting him to hurry back to Paris 'pour prévoir à tous les désordres qui pourroient estre en ladite assemblée'.

94. The Génovéfains' views are made in a series of memoranda submitted to the cardinal: MS. 3250, fos. 79–80, 85–6, 87–8, 88–9.

95. B.S.G., MS. 612, fos. 36–46 gives extensive coverage of these controversies, but it is a Génovéfain account which shows no sympathy for the opposition, whose memoranda have not been preserved.

postpone the opening of the chapter until 23 May and he allowed Gallet to attend after all. He put the delegates to work in commissions, drafting articles on the training of novices, the exercise of office, the election of a general, the question of Toussaints' membership, and so on. However, when the debate on Toussaints finally began, he declared that Gallet and his followers had failed to meet the normal conditions of entry to the congregation.[96] Immensely relieved, Faure and the Génovéfains regained the initiative. When, on 26 May, La Rochefoucauld postponed the election of a general until negotiations had been completed in Rome, the chapter ceased to serve any practical purpose, and the delegates were sent home with an exhortation from La Rochefoucauld to extend the reform, but 'sans sindiquer leurs actions, ny se mesler du gouvernement'.[97] The warning was clear to all, and represented a hard-won, if somewhat pyrrhic, victory for Faure and Ste Geneviève.

In reality, the debate was by no means over. La Rochefoucauld made it clear that he did not think that the fate of Gallet and Toussaints and, therefore, the future course of the reform had been settled, by retaining Gallet in Paris for further discussions with his council.[98] Although Gallet's idea of a congregation in western France was supported by the Jesuits, despite predictable opposition from Faure, Baudouin and others, it failed to win the assent of either the cardinal or his council during successive deliberations in June, September and November 1632.[99] The frequency with which La Rochefoucauld returned to these issues is proof enough that he did not share all the views of his closest collaborators in Paris.[100] Yet by November he was ready to announce that neither Toussaints nor Chancelade would be empowered to launch their own congregations, and that central novitiates were needed for the whole of France.[101]

The 1632 debates, while inconclusive in the short term, were important for the future history of La Rochefoucauld's reform. They confirmed his congregation's own predilection for strong central government, and its suspicion of independent reformers and their motives. La Rochefoucauld might rally to these views when obliged to

---

96. *Ibid.*, fos. 39v–43.
97. *Ibid.*, fos. 43–4.
98. B.S.G., MS. 3276, fo. 408, Jean Thomas to canons of Rillé, 13 June 1632: 'On débat fort et ferme, sçavoir s'il [Gallet] sera de la congrégation ou non. Monseigneur l'a retenu icy pour cest effect, et nous attendons du jour à autre la décision du procès. Il n'y a point encores de vicaire général, ny de visitteur ny procureur scindicq nommez, mais Monseigneur a proposé de faire au plustost'.
99. B.S.G., MS. 3250, fos. 113–14, memorandum from Etienne Binet on Gallet and Solminihac, 11 November.
100. The Génovéfain view is re-stated in memoranda dated June, September and November 1632: B.S.G., MS. 3250, fos. 93, 94, 95, 100–1, 433–6, 445–7.
101. B.S.G., MS. 624, fos. 449–50, resolution dated 18 November.

make a choice, but there were no assurances that he would adhere strictly to them.

V

The year 1632, however, was not spent purely in controversy. Despite the difficulties in Rome and in the general chapter, the reform was gathering pace. Negotiations for the reform of no less than twenty-five houses were brought to various stages of completion between 1629 and 1634. But reform by contract, royal decree, and commissioner's ordinance was inherently slow and laborious. Despite all the effort deployed, the congregation counted only twelve member-houses by 1634. Yet, as it showed two years earlier, it continued to prefer such piecemeal advance to a more open-door policy of welcoming all those who professed an interest in reform. The shortage of men still seems to have been acute, although we lack the information necessary to see more precisely how this affected the congregation's decisions.[102] At the same time, the reform became a more structured affair. La Rochefoucauld made Faure its vicar general in 1633, while the younger, more supple, François Boulart had become prior of Ste Geneviève the previous year, and did much to ease relations between the cardinal and Faure.[103]

The same heterogeneity is evident in the different individual reforms occurring in the early 1630s. It was increasingly appreciated by bishops, abbots, and canons that La Rochefoucauld's commission had the great advantage of full papal and royal authority behind it, enabling him to guarantee agreements for reform in a way that no one else could. Given the framework for reform was legal, the crucial step was the contract for reform, which had to be negotiated step by step in order to satisfy all parties. The most notable reform of these years, that of St Denis de Reims, produced a staggering amount of paperwork. Promoted from the beginning by the commendator, the reform was finally completed in August 1633, when the royal commissioner, François de Verthamon, handed over the abbey buildings to a Génovéfain community.[104] In 1632, after a lapse of ten years, the

---

102. The manpower problem is frequently mentioned in internal Génovéfain correspondence. The only set of figures available concerns the *séminaire* of Senlis. Between 1626 and 1648, it admitted a total of 481 pupils; of the 382 entering between 1626 and 1643, 133 (34.9%) went on to become novices and take vows in the congregation: B.S.G., MS. 720, fos. 4–11, 'enfans du séminaire St Vincent de Senlis', 1626–49. There is no comparable information for the novitiates at Ste Geneviève and Ste Cathérine.

103. B.S.G., MS. 3242, fo. 192, 25 September 1632 (Boulart); MS. 625, fos. 68–71, 28 March 1633 (Faure).

104. See Bergin, 'Ways and Means of Monastic Reform', pp. 14–32, for a detailed study of this reform, and an analysis of many of the problems typically faced by the cardinal and the congregation.

reform returned to Eu.[105] St Ambroise de Bourges was secured with the archbishop's assistance, despite both resistance from its abbot and the powerful prince of Condé, and Baudouin's fears that it would be a source of unending trouble; there were attempts to turn it over instead, first to the Feuillants and then to Solminihac. Ignoring Génovéfain scepticism, La Rochefoucauld triumphed by using the archbishop as his delegate. But a climate of distrust lingered for some time, and, at one point, the reformed community only survived thanks to the protection of the royal intendant.[106] When the canons of St Loup at Troyes appealed *comme d'abus* against their bishop's attempt to conduct a visitation, the only way he could find out of this familiar impasse was to approach La Rochefoucauld. The appeal was quashed, and the parties sent before the royal commissioners, a move which opened the way for reform with the cardinal soon publishing the necessary ordinance. Verthamon, one of his closest allies and councillors among the royal commission, was again chosen to enforce it and to settle all the 'temporal' questions involved.[107]

Differences with Gallet and Solminihac also persisted. The latter was the more determined, and obtained La Rochefoucauld's consent to reform two abbeys in the south-west. But when he contracted independently with the young abbé Olier to reform his Abbey of Pebrac in Auvergne, La Rochefoucauld stepped in to frustrate him.[108] He and Gallet argued before the cardinal's council in April 1633, with Jesuit support, that Ste Geneviève's limited resources justified separate 'provinces' in the west and south-west. Once again, the council upheld the Génovéfain policy of a single congregation under one general.[109] La Rochefoucauld also accepted the need for swift action to prevent permanent division, and discussions towards an immediate incorporation of Toussaints.[110] Gallet, Solminihac and Baudouin met at his request in Angers in May 1633 but, although Baudouin was more flexible than Faure, the parties were as divided as ever on basic

105. B.S.G., MS. 624, fos. 287–92, La Rochefoucauld's reform ordinance, 28 March.
106. Official acts in B.S.G., MS. 625, fos. 96–103, 357–8; MS. 626, fos. 160–71; correspondence in MS. 3278, fos. 44; 109, 115, 123, 198; MS. 3279, fos. 112, 145, 163, 182. Baudouin's views are in *ibid.*, fo. 181, letter to Faure, 25 April 1634. The initial petition for reform was made by the archbishop: MS. 3250, fo. 613, letter to Faure, 27 August 1629.
107. B.S.G., MS. 624, fos. 273–5; MS. 625, fos. 80–1; MS. 612, fos. 148–54; MS. 3250, fo. 612, undated letter from Bishop of Troyes to Faure.
108. *Lettres et documents*, p. 117, Vincent de Paul to Solminihac, 23 August 1633; *ibid.*, pp. 124–5, Olier to Solminihac, 1 June 1634; *ibid.*, pp. 126–7. Archbishop Barrault of Arles (ex-bishop of Bazas) to Solminihac, 21 September 1634: 'J'avois prié Mons. le Cardinal de surseoir à ne rien ordonner sur cette affaire que vous n'eussies auparavant esté ouÿ ou envoyé les motifs de vostre procedure, mais je n'ay pas eu asses de crédit auprès de luy pour obtenir cela'. The abbé Olier in question is the celebrated founder of the St Sulpice seminary and reformer of the French secular clergy.
109. B.S.G., MS. 612, fos. 91v–93: 'il a semblé bon à Monseigneur le cardinal de ne faire qu'une seule congrégation en France de l'ordre de S. Augustin'.
110. B.S.G., MS. 625, fos. 138–9, council meeting, 3 May.

issues.[111] When the cardinal upheld Baudouin's argument that unity of observance and outlook should come before all else, negotiations petered out inconclusively, but without a final break between the parties.[112]

A more serious long-term problem had also begun to loom for La Rochefoucauld by 1633, one that was to bedevil his last years: the matter of appeals to French courts against his commission and, more worryingly, to the pope. He firmly believed that appeals should not possess supensive effect while a case was pending, and that this was enshrined in the terms of his commission. Whether this was indeed what the pope and king had actually intended, in practice appeals did become suspensive, and 'ordinary' jurisprudential rules re-asserted themselves. Since the congregation was not always strong enough to prevent this, appeals invariably prolonged the process of reform considerably. La Rochefoucauld directly addressed the problem in his *Déclaration à Monsieur le garde des sceaux* of May 1632. While expressing satisfaction with the crown's continuing support for reform, he regretted that the provisions for short-circuiting the loathed *appel comme d'abus* were not being fully enforced; only where he had clearly acted *ultra vires* should appeals be heard, otherwise litigation would be endless. He had, after all, been commissioned 'pour réformer, non pour plaider'.[113]

That La Rochefoucauld's fears were not imaginary became clear in 1633, when St Victor's attempt to revive its congregation developed into a full-scale conflict.[114] To La Rochefoucauld and Faure this move was part of an attempt to avoid reform: by definition, a congregation *should* be observant. Bishop Sanguin of Senlis, one of the royal commissioners, persuaded the cardinal to ban all assemblies planned by St Victor and, although he appears to have accepted that the abbey itself was in good order, he formally dissolved its congregation. Visitation and reform of the houses was the next logical step, but St Victor's powerful connections – its abbot was Archbishop Harlay of Rouen, who had never got on with La Rochefoucauld – was an inducement to caution. In dissolving its congregation, the cardinal incorporated four of its members into his own, and commissioned Faure to visit

111. B.S.G., MS. 3250, fo. 206, La Rochefoucauld to Gallet, 19 May; MS. 3278, fo. 138, Gallet to Faure, 10 June; *ibid.*, fo. 140, Baudouin to La Rochefoucauld, same date; *ibid.*, fo. 137, Baudouin to Faure, same date. Gallet and Baudouin give discrepant accounts of the talks.
112. B.S.G., MS. 3278, fo. 184, Gallet to Baudouin, 22 July; *ibid.*, fo. 182, to Boulart, 13 July.
113. B.S.G., MS. 624, fos. 339–40, declaration of 6 May 1632.
114. *Ibid.*, fos. 413–16, petition from St Victor to the *parlement*, in which it is claimed the congregation had never been dissolved. The petition was not directed against La Rochefoucauld specifically, yet he could not ignore it.

them.[115] One, La Victoire of Senlis, flatly refused to admit him, and rapidly obtained a decree from the king's council sending its case before the *parlement*.[116] Although La Rochefoucauld had no difficulty overturning this decision since it was in clear contravention of his commission,[117] he was far more worried by La Victoire's appeal to Rome 'en première instance' against the excommunication they had allegedly incurred for repeatedly flouting the ban on receiving novices. La Rochefoucauld's unhappy experiences of appeals to Rome by other orders made him apprehensive about the curia's handling of the first significant appeal from the canons-regular.

Rome's decision to delegate French judges to hear the appeal was just what La Rochefoucauld had most feared, infringing as it did a fundamental aspect of his commission.[118] This turned to indignation when, in August 1633, he was cited in person to appeal as defendant before an official of the Bishop of Laon, who was handling the case.[119] Through Faure, he presented a long, irate remonstrance to Louis XIII, who again obliged him with a decree quashing the papal rescript as having been wrongfully obtained, and delegating Verthamon to judge the issue.[120] However, the latter's goodwill and readiness to compromise did not suffice to resolve the increasingly bitter conflict.[121]

La Rochefoucauld might take comfort in the king's continuing support for his measures, but was much less assured of the curia's support. He let it be known in Rome in November 1633 that he would not contemplate another commission unless the rescript of St

---

115. B.S.G., MS. 625, fos. 104–7, ban on assemblies and summons to priors of four Victorine houses to answers before his council, 8 April 1633; *ibid.*, fos. 118–20, resolution to suppress congregation of St Victor, 26 April; *ibid.*, fos. 140–5, act of suppression, 9 May; *ibid.*, fos. 146–51, commission to Faure, 28 May. The view from St Victor is given by Jean de Toulouse in B.N., MS. Fr. 24080, pp. 453–5.

116. B.S.G., MS. 3243, fos. 94–5, Faure's *procès-verbal*, 10 June; MS. 625, fos. 204–8, decree of council, 23 June. Bishop Sanguin's pressure to act against La Victoire, which was in his diocese, is apparent from MS. 3250, fos. 374–5, letter to Faure, 26 April; *ibid.*, fos. 209–10, undated memorandum; MS. 3263, fo. 832, undated letter from Faure to Boulart, admitting he has had to fall in with Sanguin's wishes. As always, Jean de Toulouse saw Faure himself as the villain of the piece: B.N., MS. Fr. 24080, p. 456.

117. B.S.G., MS. 625, fos. 216–19, council decree of 8 July, delegating Verthamon to judge the case on behalf of the royal commission.

118. B.S.G., MS. 625, fos. 162–5, papal rescript delegating Bishops of Laon, Noyon and Beauvais, collectively or individually, or any one of their *officiaux*, to judge the appeal.

119. B.S.G., MS. 3242, fos. 219–20; MS. 3277, fo. 41, Boulart to Faure, 23 August; B.N., MS. Fr. 24080, pp. 467–8; Morinière, *Vray prélat*, pp. 646–50, for a summary of La Rochefoucauld's views, especially on the indignity, as he saw it, of an official issuing a summons to a cardinal who had been acting as a papal commissioner, an issue on which he was notoriously sensitive.

120. B.S.G., MS. 3243, fos. 74–5, undated petition to *conseil privé* from Faure; MS. 625, fos. 359–69, decree and commission to Verthamon, 19 September.

121. B.N., MS. Fr. 24080, pp. 470–2; B.S.G., MS. 3263, fo. 462, Faure to Boulart, 2 December 1633.

Victor were revoked as evidence of Rome's support for him.[122] Later, he claimed that uncritical acceptance of appeals would undermine his commission and destroy the reform itself, and even enable other orders to annex abbeys belonging to canons-regular.[123] Rome's reply was not encouraging, the curia insisting that it was standard practice to accept such appeals and appoint judges-delegate.[124] Interpretations of the exigencies of reform could not have differed more: what was perfectly routine ('il modo canonico') to one party, was viewed as disastrous by the other. The congregation's own envoys, who arrived in Rome in late 1633, advised La Rochefoucauld to concentrate on stiffening the terms of his next commission rather than making isolated demands, and opined that, in any case, one decree of the king's council was worth more than a hatful of papal bulls.[125] This was manifestly simplistic, and it would have taken more than one appeal to make the cardinal abandon the Ultramontanism of a lifetime.

In the event, the papal rescript was revoked in March 1634, but by then La Victoire had launched a second appeal to Rome, and obtained a second rescript in July 1634; this time, it was Faure who was cited as defendant.[126] All of this proved too much for La Rochefoucauld, who predictably feared a return to the endless tit-for-tat appeals of the years before 1622. He complained again to the king, threatening to resign his commission if the new rescript were implemented. Once again, he had his way, with the council reserving to the royal commissioners all cases arising from the reform.[127] The whole episode was a clear warning to La Rochefoucauld that attitudes in Rome had changed, while reassuring him of the crown's continuing support.

Meanwhile, the curia proved no less reluctant to grant his requests for the congregation and for his abbey, although it is not clear if this was connected to St Victor's opposition. Ambassador Brassac's return to Rome in early 1632 permitted a resumption of negotiations but, despite the cardinal's persistence, the curia was slow to respond.[128] Datary officials were adamant, even when the congregation decided

122. B.S.G., MS. 3278, fo. 288, Boulart to Esprit and Barbier, 8 November. The two canons had only recently arrived in Rome to pursue negotiations for the confirmation of the congregation.
123. *Ibid.*, fo. 286, Boulart to Esprit and Barbier, 20 November. La Rochefoucauld's views and instructions have to be pieced together from this correspondence.
124. B.S.G., MS. 3277, fos. 86–7, Esprit and Barbier to Faure, 18 December.
125. B.S.G., MS. 3279, fo. 6, letter to Boulart, 6 January 1634.
126. B.S.G., MS. 3243, fo. 117, for text of second rescript. MS. 3279, fo. 139, Esprit and Barbier to Boulart, 13 March.
127. B.S.G., MS. 3243, fo. 118.
128. B.S.G., MS. 624, fos. 267–8, Louis XIII to Brassac, 3 February 1632; MS, 3238, fos. 411–15, 'mémoire pour l'affaire de l'abbé de S Geneviesve envoyé à M. de Brassac', 12 April; *ibid.*, fo. 249, La Rochefoucauld to Brassac, 12 April; *ibid.*, fo. 258, La Rochefoucauld to Marchant, 16 July; MS. 3250, fo. 145, Marchant to La Rochefoucauld, 13 March.

to establish an annuity to the capital value of 10,000 *livres* as compensation for financial loss.[129] The situation was sufficiently worrying by mid-1633 for La Rochefoucauld to agree that the congregation must now send its own envoys to Rome to protect its interests, rather than relying on benevolent outsiders.[130] Two canons, Claude Esprit and Gabriel Barbier, left for Rome in September, only to be told on their arrival that Urban VIII himself had said that if requests like La Rochefoucauld's were granted, they would bring financial ruin upon the curia.[131] Cardinal Barberini was willing to help, but he had limited influence over the pope and the datarius. Esprit and Barbier were under pressure from Paris to obtain results. For some reason, La Rochefoucauld suspected that Richelieu and his brother might instruct the new ambassador, Noailles, to oppose his request.[132] Then, in late 1633, he fell dangerously ill, and panic seized Ste Geneviève: if he died before anything had been settled and a commendator – possibly Richelieu himself, given his appetite for benefices – received the abbey, the congregation might break up, and the reform come to grief.[133]

The envoys presented a new petition to the datarius in November 1633, which was only transmitted to the pope after datary officials had been satisfied by the financial compensation Ste Geneviève was ready to offer them.[134] This took months but, by the time news arrived of the cardinal's recovery in February 1634, Urban had finally granted the request and work on drafting the bull – another occasion for protracted haggling – was under way.[135] The bull, dispatched in April 1634, conceded what La Rochefoucauld had been seeking since early 1630 – the restoration of an elective abbacy at Ste Geneviève, the suppression of offices as benefices, the formal establishment of the

---

129. B.S.G., MS. 3250, fo. 143, Marchant to La Rochefoucauld, 23 October 1633; *ibid.*, fo. 142, to Desbois, the cardinal's secretary, same date.
130. B.S.G., MS. 3278, fo. 168, Boulart to Faure, 9 July 1633; MS. 3277, fo. 32, same to same, 18 August, announcing La Rochefoucauld's and the congregation's decision. At first, it was decided to send Faure himself, but Etienne Binet dissuaded the cardinal from doing so.
131. B.S.G., MS. 3277, fo. 337, letter to Faure, 5 November 1633; MS. 3250, fo. 221, Marchant to Lhuillier, 8 October; *ibid.*, fo. 300, same to same, no date.
132. B.S.G., MS. 3278, fos. 286, 320, letters from Boulart, 20 November and 5 December 1633 respectively. La Rochefoucauld did not himself reveal the grounds of his suspicion.
133. B.S.G., MS. 3277, fo. 20, letter from Faure and others, 3 January 1634; *ibid.*, fo. 22, from Boulart, same date.
134. *Ibid.*, fo. 92, Esprit and Barbier to Boulart, 4 December 1633; *ibid.*, fo. 141, to Faure, 12 December; MS. 3279, fo. 6, to Boulart, 1 January 1634; MS. 3278, fo. 26, to Boulart, 16 January. The Pope himself agreed fully with this method of dealing with the case.
135. B.S.G., MS. 3278, fo. 19, Esprit and Barbier to La Rochefoucauld, 28 January 1634; *ibid.*, fo. 18, to Boulart, 29 January; MS. 3279, fo. 61, to La Rochefoucauld, 10 February; *ibid.*, fos. 70–1, to Boulart, 13 February.

congregation and, with it, the right to make its own statutes in future
without prior reference to Rome. The time and money that this had
demanded were considerable — Boulart later calculated the 1634
concessions had cost nearly 13,000 *livres* in fees.[136]

Whatever the delay and expense involved, La Rochefoucauld could
regard the bull as a vital step towards a permanent reform. It would
now enter a new phase, one in which his own role as commissioner
might be less vital. Yet the attitude displayed in Rome, by both
Urban VIII and his officials, was not reassuring. The old conflict of
reform versus curial interests — the benefice-system with its financial
spin-offs — had again been played out in microcosm. While La Rochefoucauld had obtained satisfaction, the grudging manner in which it
had been granted provided more evidence that the Barberini pontificate had not inherited the predilection for reform of its predecessor.

---

136. B.S.G., MS. 3279, fo. 201, undated note. His exact total was 4,262 *écus*, much of
which went on establishing an annuity of 1,500 *livres*.

8

The Reform of the Canons-Regular II: Consolidation and Survival

I

THE PAPAL BULL of 1634 had taken years to materialise, but it was a crucial breakthrough which afforded La Rochefoucauld's reform the public recognition which enabled it to shed its 'exceptional' quality.

For his part, La Rochefoucauld realised that the papal grant had to be given additional sanction, if his congregation was to be placed on a firm institutional footing within the French church and state. Once the *grand conseil* had registered the bull in August 1635, a plenary session of his council set 17 October as the date for the election of a coadjutor-abbot for Ste Geneviève, and a superior general for the congregation.[1] The result was a foregone conclusion: Charles Faure was elected to both posts for the statutory three years.[2] But La Rochefoucauld was not content with that, and insisted on drafting a new charter for the congregation, a matter which had previously been discussed at the 1634 general chapter, though without result. He set his council to work on one in November 1634, and it produced a set of recommendations in early March 1635, which were quickly incorporated into his wide-ranging *Sentence pour la réforme* published later that month.[3] The next and final step was to secure formal royal approval of both the papal bull and the *Sentence*, which, for reasons that

---

1. B.S.G., MS. 626, fos. 340–3, decree of registration, 23 August; MS. 612, fos. 154–5, for a report of the council's discussions on 9 September.
2. B.S.G., MS. 626, fos. 450–9v, *procès-verbal* of Faure's election. He received fifteen votes out of nineteen. See MS. 612, fos. 155–9.
3. B.S.G., MS. 612, fo. 199, for the council's *avis* of 1 March 1635.

remain obscure, was delayed until May 1636.[4] In its decree, the king's council confirmed the cardinal's reforms and required full observance of the *Sentence*. Interestingly, it took pains to discourage any kind of 'réforme sauvage'.[5] La Rochefoucauld was the sole, official reformer of the order, and reform had to run along the path mapped out by him.

The *Sentence* was not yet another set of statutes, but guidelines for future reform. Its detailed specifications for reform summarised existing practice, and need no commentary here. But La Rochefoucauld also laid down certain principles of general importance. He reiterated his belief that both pope and king had always intended reform to embrace the entire order within France, and that it was not a voluntary affair limited to a handful of abbeys to which the occasional soul seeking a stricter observance might withdraw. A single, identical reform appeared both necessary and desirable, and to survive, it must possess a congregational structure. Therefore, all Augustinian houses should consider themselves virtual 'members' of the 'congrégation de France' as it would be called henceforth. To it their eventual reform was exclusively reserved; its general, assistants and visitors would have wide powers to reform them, even employing delegates on their own authority where necessary.[6] The cardinal even touched on the vexed question of the *commende*, urging an equitable division of monastic revenues as essential to reform. Furthermore, he insisted on commendators renouncing all claims to authority in spiritual matters over reformed communities; where a commendator personally opted for the reform, he could exercise as a 'regular' abbot only such spiritual authority as the congregation might allow him, and he would, among other things, be obliged to turn over his abbatial revenues to the abbey chest. Such severe terms were hardly designed to precipitate a rush by commendators to join the reform, but the cardinal considered them necessary for its independence. He also maintained the ban on novices, but realising that a general ban throughout France served no purpose, he explicitly declared it to apply only to those abbeys which had had notice of it served on them – this being the usual prelude to reform. The *Sentence* ended with an exhortation to the order as a whole to welcome and promote reform.[7]

Despite his great age – he was seventy-seven in 1635 – poor health, and frequent brushes with death, La Rochefoucauld's determination to

---

4. This obscurity is largely due to the disappearance of the principal manuscript sources for 1635–6. Unspecified difficulties with the ordinance, which demanded additional examination, are alluded to by François Boulart in a letter to Charles Faure: B.S.G., MS. 3280, fo. 219, 21 July 1635; and by Verthamon to Faure: MS. 3251, fo. 12, undated.
5. The text of the council's decree is printed with the *Sentence pour la réforme* cited in n. 7, below.
6. Until this juncture, only La Rochefoucauld, as papal commissioner, possessed such powers of delegation.
7. *Sentence pour la réforme des chanoines réguliers de St Augustin, portant règlement pour la réformation dudit ordre, et l'union de tous les monastères d'iceluy à la congrégation de France* (Paris, 1636).

see the reform expand was as strong as ever. A suggestion from his council in 1635 that the future papal commissions be granted to the congregation's general was not taken seriously, and La Rochefoucauld's commission was prolonged for three years in 1631, for two in both 1634 and 1636, and for one in 1638. These shorter terms were not signs of diminishing papal approval of his actions; it was, apparently, common practice in Rome by the 1630s to shorten the duration of 'graces' of all kinds.[8] And as we shall see, even the failure to renew his commission in 1639 did not prevent him from promoting reform and effectively protecting its interests.

By 1635, less than 5 per cent of the French houses of canons-regular had been reformed, so the task facing La Rochefoucauld remained enormous. Nor was he to be assisted by any sudden access of enthusiasm inside the order, which left him to pursue reform by the same prosaic methods of negotiation and contract. Hopes for its future rested with a new generation of canons trained in the congregation's novitiates and houses of study. But this, too, made for slow progress. The congregation possessed only three novitiates until 1637, when the addition of Nanterre improved matters.[9] Besides, the relatively strict standards it applied to new recruits meant that there was frequently a shortage of the manpower needed to establish observant communities in new abbeys. It is little wonder that the waiting-list of monasteries to be reformed lengthened throughout the 1630s, with petitions from impatient bishops, abbots and unreformed abbeys filling the correspondence of the congregation's leaders.

Relatively standardised procedures for reform had been established by the 1630s. Because they help to explain the measured pace of the congregation's growth, it may be appropriate to outline them approximately here, always bearing in mind that the possible variations were numerous, and that no single reform can be regarded as truly representative.[10]

After the initial decrees and visitations of 1622–3, it became La Rochefoucauld's basic rule not to take action unless he had received a formal petition, whether from the commendatory abbot, the local bishop or the canons themselves, to reform a monastery. La Rochefoucauld was not inhibited by petitions submitted by a minority of canons, since pro-reform minorities were always in the right: the only

---

8. B.S.G., MS. 3285, fo. 55, Dom Placide Le Simon to François Boulart, Rome, 23 March 1638, makes this point.
9. The Nanterre seminary was based on a *prieuré* there that was in La Rochefoucauld's grant as Abbot of Ste Geneviève. It began functioning in late 1637: B.S.G., MS. 627, fos. 286–94; MS. 612, fo. 416r, for an account of its inauguration.
10. The following pages are based on the voluminous acts contained in B.S.G., MSS. 622–33, 3241–3, 3250, as well as the numerous accounts of individual reforms in MSS. 611–13. For an account of an individual reform which discusses some of these issues in detail, see my article, 'Ways and Means of Monastic Reform: St Denis de Reims 1630–1633'.

problem was the purely practical one of the extent of support for, or opposition to, change in the house in question. Negotiations for reform could begin at any time – sometimes weeks, sometimes years after La Rochefoucauld's formal acceptance of the petition for reform. Once they began, a *maître des requêtes* from the royal commission was assigned to them, since the commission's jurisdiction covered all 'temporal' matters relating to reform. Representing the crown, the *maîtres* applied pressure on the hesitant or the unwilling, attended important sessions of La Rochefoucauld's council, especially when ordinances for reform had to be issued, and then acted as 'reporters' when the royal commission, sitting as a royal *conseil privé*, published its own decree enabling the cardinal's reform ordinances to take effect. Finally, they often supervised the introduction of reformed communities into abbeys, conducting on-the-spot negotiations on matters like pensions for the *anciens*. Fully sharing the dislike of monastic de-cadence and 'désordres' common to *dévots* and the robe nobility generally, their role in La Rochefoucauld's reforms was essential.[11] Nothing would be more inaccurate than to view them as neutral functionaries protecting royal interests. The most active of them, such as François de Verthamon and Nicolas Lefèvre de Lezeau, vigorously promoted reform, and were among La Rochefoucauld's closest advisers.[12]

Before a reform ordinance could be published, let alone implemented, there was a wide range of issues to be solved by negotiation with the interested parties. Commendators and canons had to be induced to agree on a division of revenues and on responsibility for the upkeep and repair of monastic buildings. Unreformed canons bargained for pensions ranging from around 100 to 500 *livres* annually. While La Rochefoucauld did not object to this, he had to ensure that the remaining revenues would support a reformed community; where this seemed unlikely, reform was often postponed for years. Indeed, it was a further reason for insisting that the *anciens* resign their offices: the revenues from them would revert to the new community, giving it full control of its own internal affairs.[13] *Anciens* who elected to join the

11. Their political careers are better known if only because the provincial intendants were drawn mostly from their ranks, even though not all of them became intendants. Verthamon did, Lezeau did not. See Richard Bonney, *Political Change in France under Richelieu and Mazarin 1624–1661* (Oxford, 1978); Roland Mousnier, *Lettres et Mémoires adressés au chancelier Séguier 1633–1649*, 2 vols. (Paris, 1964). Vol. 1 contains short biographies of some intendants. See also Michel de Certeau, 'Politique et mystique. René de Voyer d'Argenson 1596–1651', *Revue d'ascétique et de mystique* 29 (1963), pp. 45–82.
12. Lefèvre was the biographer of the *dévot* leader, Michel de Marillac, and the manuscript copy of his work in B.S.G., MSS. 2005–6 probably belonged to La Rochefoucauld. His work was never published.
13. B.S.G., MS. 3263, fo. 58, Faure to Baudouin, 24 July 1634, for an admirably clear and concise expression of the congregation's approach to these questions: 'Vous scaves la méthode, premièrement il fault transiger sur le revenu des pensions avec les anciens,

reform would also have to relinquish offices, pensions and outside benefices, and to become novices once again in the reformed observance, a condition which deterred all but a handful of them over the years.

Dealing with commendators was also beset with problems, as most of them claimed certain rights which they were loath to surrender – for example, to nominate to outside benefices, and to receive and profess novices. The congregation absolutely rejected the latter claim as contrary to a basic principle of the reform, but would accept the first if it aided negotiations. Its generally low opinion of commendators tended to complicate relations with those not conforming to the stereotype of the grasping tyrant. Some like Henri de Maupas du Tour, Abbot of St Denis of Reims, and future Bishop of Le Puy and Evreux, were worthy ecclesiastics residing in their abbeys, men whose claims to exercise abbatial rights were all the more difficult to dismiss because they promoted the reform of their abbeys.[14]

These, and other factors, made for protracted bargaining, and ensured that the contract for reform would be a long and detailed document; no party wanted to sign away irrevocably advantages previously held or claimed. Unable to abolish the *commende*, La Rochefoucauld was anxious to protect his reformed communities from its undesirable effects.

The indispensable final step to negotiations was the cardinal's confirmation of the contract and the publication of his reform ordinance, supplemented by a commission to a named delegate – Faure in most cases, but occasionally a bishop – to implement the reform and conduct the formal *prise de possession* of the house in question. Then followed the decree of the royal commission, which also appointed a delegate to handle the final act and terminate unconcluded business locally.

It was by such methods that the Augustinian reform gradually expanded from its original fragile base. By 1637, it included eighteen houses, by 1640, thirty-two. The speed of reform had accelerated during the 1630s, when many long-standing or half-abandoned projects were taken up again and completed. The congregation's autonomous status after 1634 doubtless served to attract new member-houses, and its novitiates had begun producing a growing number of canons available to take over houses seeking reform. The bishops continued to play an important role. For example, three abbeys were reformed in Sens in the late 1630s, after years of entreaties from

---

deuxièmement qu'ilz nous cèdent moyennant ce tous leurs droits et pouvoir, troisièmement qu'ilz consentent qu'à nostre commodité nous prenions possession dudit monastère et introdusions des religieux'. Baudouin was negotiating the reform of St Martin d'Epernay at that time.
14. Bergin, 'Ways and Means of Monastic Reform', pp. 18ff.

Archbishop Bellegarde, a frequent attender at the Ste Geneviève assemblies of bishops.[15] Others, as we shall see presently, were less well disposed, as were many commendators whose opposition, even at the last minute, could prevent reform.[16]

II

A certain number of other developments facilitated the expansion of the reform. Agreement was finally reached with Gallet and Toussaints in 1635, when Gallet's own supporters deserted him, leaving him with little choice but to follow them into the congregation on its terms. La Rochefoucauld promptly re-appointed him prior, although minor differences remained, with the cardinal rebuking him in 1636 for continuing to receive novices and allowing his office to remain technically a benefice.[17] But Toussaints was now firmly within the congregation, and it sent delegates to the 1637 general chapter. Gallet was active as a reformer in the western dioceses, where his role as a delegate of the cardinal and congregation helped to calm mistrustful bishops.[18] Yet the long history of past misunderstandings sufficed to deny him an important role in Génovéfain affairs.

As we saw, the congregation of Val-des-Ecoliers failed to halt or reverse La Rochefoucauld's reform of Ste Cathérine in 1629, which appears to have been the only time the cardinal used the powers given him in his 1628 commission. The renewal of his commission for a further four-year term in 1632 helped to convince Laurent Michel, the general of Val-des-Ecoliers, that reform was inevitable, and that he should himself promote it.[19] However, his efforts in 1633 to enforce the cardinal's ban on novices throughout his congregation met with universal opposition.[20] Two years later, when La Rochefoucauld confirmed his intention to reform the congregation, he offered for

---

15. There are brief accounts of the three reforms in B.S.G., MS. 612, fos. 345–51, 378–80; MS. 613, fos. 3–7.
16. For example, such last-minute intervention, even after La Rochefoucauld had published his reform ordinance, by the commendator halted the reform of St Martin d'Epernay: B.S.G., MS. 612, fos. 187–8.
17. B.S.G., MS. 3263, fo. 81, Faure to François Blanchart, 3 September 1635; MS. 3281, fo. 308, Boulart to Faure, 6 August 1636. See also MS. 612, fos. 176–80, for a Génovéfain account of the union that is less than sympathetic to Gallet, B.S.G., MS. 3250, fo. 307, La Rochefoucauld to Gallet, 19 July 1636.
18. These activities can be followed in Gallet's numerous and informative letters to La Rochefoucauld, Faure and Boulart in B.S.G., MSS. 3266 *et seq.*
19. B.S.G., MS. 612, fos. 325–30. He apparently consulted André Du Val and other doctors of the Sorbonne about the problem, and it was they who resolved his doubts. As general of Val-des-Ecoliers he was, of course, under strong pressure to preserve his congregation's independence.
20. B.S.G., MS. 3250, fo. 204, Michel to La Rochefoucauld, 14 August 1633, where he reports that even those who favoured a reform rejected the ban.

reform his own abbey and mother house of the congregation, Notre Dame du Val, in the diocese of Langres. The acquisition of Notre Dame du Val was clearly important, both strategically and psychologically. The cardinal helped to dispel the reservations of Bishop Zamet of Langres, and an agreement, which safeguarded Michel's rights as abbot, was eventually signed in July 1636. The abbey came under the control of the congrégation de France, to whose novitiates its recruits would in future be sent.[21] But it was not until late 1637 that a Génovéfain community was established there.[22] In subsequent years, smaller member-houses of Val-des-Ecoliers were reformed and, with Michel's assistance, those that were too small to survive independently were grouped together.[23]

If this proved to be the only instance of a successful breakthrough by La Rochefoucauld into an existing non-observant congregation, it was not for lack of interest. In the early 1630s, he expressed his intention of reforming the older congregation of St Ruf, which had a large membership, mostly in the Dauphiné. Word of this elicited an interesting response from one of its leading officials. Conceding its deplorable state, he suggested it would be better to feign willingness to co-operate with the cardinal, in the hope that sufficient grounds for opposition and appeal would arise later. Viewed from the Dauphiné, the cardinal's commission seemed a 'torrent dont il fault éviter l'impétuosité'.[24] This particular alarm proved exaggerated and premature, and it was not until 1638 that a petition to the pope, which formally admitted St Ruf's inability to reform itself, asked him to confide the task to Ste Geneviève or someone else of his choosing.[25] La Rochefoucauld himself was evidently ready to move by then but, as he lacked authority to deal with existing congregations, the royal commission attempted to fill the gap, ordering the local intendant to inquire into, and report, on St Ruf.[26] However, La Rochefoucauld's commission lapsed before the report arrived, and without the protection it provided, the congregation was unwilling to take on St Ruf.

21. Only the confirmation of the agreement by the royal commission has survived: B.S.G., MS. 627, fos. 364–9, 30 October 1637.
22. *Ibid.*, fos. 198–201, La Rochefoucauld's ordinance, 24 August 1637; fos. 412–27, *prise de possession*, 26 November.
23. B.S.G., MS. 628, fos. 92–3, 639–41; MS. 631, fos. 20–3; MS. 632, fos. 22–3.
24. B.S.G., MS. 3278, fo. 318, Berger, *syndic général* of St Ruf, to prior of St Dié, 10 October 1633. Berger was particularly astonished at the facility with which La Rochefoucauld triumphed over all opposition in his recent reform of the abbey of St Denis near Paris.
25. Several petitions and memoranda concerning St Ruf were sent to La Rochefoucauld, probably around 1637–8: B.S.G., MS. 3241, fos. 32, 37–9, 128–30.
26. B.S.G., MS. 3241, fo. 30, commission to intendant Laisné, 27 August 1638; MS. 3297, fo. 270, Boulart to Faure, 28 May 1641, confirming the intendant's enquiry, of which no trace has been found.

The late 1630s also produced a number of attempts at reform that promised to give some substance to the appellation 'congrégation de France'. Not only were some of these significantly different from anything attempted hitherto, but they shed interesting light on the relations between the reform and the crown, this time in provinces where royal authority was less secure.

In 1636, on the initiative of Henri de Sponde, Bishop of Pamiers, La Rochefoucauld delegated Solminihac to conduct the reform of the Abbey of St Volusien near Foix.[27] But Sponde's tough conditions for the preservation of episcopal rights soon produced conflict with Solminihac.[28] The bishop complained bitterly to La Rochefoucauld that his authority was being flouted, and the reform was temporarily abandoned. It was only resumed in 1639 with a direct appeal from the commendator to the cardinal, who replied by incorporating St Volusien into his congregation and by decreeing its reform.[29] Local opponents tried, through an *appel comme d'abus*, to involve the *parlement* of Toulouse, which was thought to be hostile to the reform, but the royal commission intervened, ordering Sponde, Solminihac and the royal intendants in Guyenne to implement La Rochefoucauld's ordinance.[30] Strong measures, it seemed, produced the desired result, yet Sponde blew hot and cold in subsequent years, and the abbot followed his lead. Taking advantage of changed political circumstances after Louis XIII's death, they preferred to see Solminihac's own reform established there.[31]

Even more remarkable was the Génovéfain attempt to reform one of the few cathedral chapters of canons-regular left in France, that of Uzès. The initiative once again came from the bishop, Nicolas Grillet who, dissatisfied with his canons' behaviour, initially offered them the choice between observance and secularisation. They predictably opted for the second, but when he went to Paris to negotiate the details, he became acquainted with the Génovéfain reform, and unilaterally decided to impose it on his cathedral. Charles Faure fell in with his

27. B.S.G., MS. 627, fos. 104–11. Faure argued that Solminihac would not cause trouble as he was by then Bishop of Cahors: MS. 3263, fo. 498, letter to Boulard, 2 July 1636.
28. B.S.G., MS. 3249, fos. 184–5, Sponde to La Rochefoucauld, 11 December 1636. The cardinal had earlier tried to pacify the irate bishop: MS. 3250, fo. 288, letter of 13 October 1636.
29. B.S.G., MS. 3250, fo. 171, petition from the abbot, Etienne Caulet who, as Bishop of Pamiers, later became famous for his opposition to Louis XIV over the *régale*; MS. 628, fos. 340–73, act of incorporation, 2 January 1639.
30. MS. 628, fos. 406–31, decree of 10 May 1639.
31. Sponde's letters to Faure on the subject are in B.S.G., MS. 3250, fos. 432–44. Abbot Caulet was instrumental in obtaining a decree in 1643, which was confirmed the following year, enabling Solminihac to install his own reform at St Volusien: Sol, *Lettres et documents*, pp. 291–2, Caulet to Solminihac, 30 May 1643; *Correspondance de St Vincent de Paul*, ed. Pierre Coste (Paris, 1920–5), ii, p. 464, Solminihac to de Paul, 29 June 1644.

plans, despite warnings from his entourage. In October, 1638, Grillet obtained a reform commission from La Rochefoucauld, and an agreement was signed in December. Arriving in Uzès, Grillet found his canons, the local notables and the *parlement* of Toulouse opposed to him; they had little taste for a reform by strangers who would not be attuned to their customs, ambitions and interests.[32] For its part, the congregation was about to encounter the formidable power of *ancien régime* cathedral chapters and the powerful connections enjoyed by the holders of prized canonical prebends. Isolated, Grillet had to appeal to the provincial intendant for support.[33] In September 1640, the royal commission upheld his policy, and delegated the intendant, des Yveteaux, to supervise the reform.[34] This only intensified the conflict between local interests and those based in Paris, although the former were unable, for the time being, to prevent a reform that was evidently supported by Richelieu, the chancellor, and the intendant. In January 1641, a Génovéfain community was finally installed in Uzès cathedral by des Yveteaux. They received a number of prebends, and in future only those trained by them could become cathedral canons. However, the opposition was so strong that des Yveteaux had to allow the *anciens* to plead their case before the royal commission.[35]

By the time Grillet returned to Paris in 1643 to defend his reform, both Louis XIII and Richelieu were dead. The political and ecclesiastical atmosphere had changed to the extent that some bishops accused him of betraying his chapter to Ste Geneviève, and of irretrievably damaging his own and his successors' authority as bishop.[36] But Faure was determined to hold on in Uzès, and sought a compromise with Grillet which would lessen the opposition while preserving the reform.[37] Perhaps the most revealing item in the ensuing agreement, signed in December 1643, was that future canons should be recruited locally and then trained by the Génovéfains, who were reduced to the role of resident reformers rather than masters of the chapter.[38] The ideal of a fully observant chapter, which would have been unique for France, had been seriously compromised. Yet even these concessions failed to defuse opposition, and the Génové-

32. B.S.G., MS. 613, fos. 49–50.
33. B.S.G., MS. 629, fos. 414–15 [1640].
34. *Ibid.*, fos. 364–7, decree of 11 September.
35. *Ibid.*, fos. 368–408, des Yveteaux's *procès-verbal* of 15 January 1641, which is also the source for opposition demands.
36. B.S.G., MS. 613, fo. 61: '. . .avoir faict un monastère d'une catédrale, et d'avoir aliéné les droits de ses successeurs, et soumis l'évêque d'Uzès à l'abbé de Ste Geneviève; c'étant une chose sans example, et une action qui rendroit sa mémoire odieuse à ses successeurs'.
37. B.S.G., MS. 3250, fo. 361, letter to Bishop Potier of Beauvais, 24 August 1643, asking him to use his influence with the Regent, Anne of Austria, to obtain a favourable ruling from the council.
38. B.S.G., MS. 631, fos. 306–18.

fains were evicted from Uzès during disturbances in 1644, when the *anciens* and their allies defied both Grillet and the intendant. They were to return later that year in the intendant's train, but failed to win ready acceptance in, or secure possession, of Uzès.[39]

Initially, the experiments at Foix and Uzès seemed to herald the expansion of the reform into the Midi. The Archbishop of Narbonne persuaded the congregation to reform the Abbey of Quarante in his diocese, yet that reform, too, appears to have provoked unrest in 1644.[40] The unrest there and at Uzès seems to have shaken Ste Geneviève, and halted any further plans it may have had for the south. Reform never became the 'impetuous torrent' that one of its opponents there had feared so much.

These experiences of expansion highlight the character of royal involvement with the cardinal's reforms in the provinces. The congregation's policy on the recruitment, formation, and random assignment of its members was bound to run counter to local vested interests; it was a parallel to the firmer central control which the crown was trying, in other spheres, to impose on the provinces.[41] In each case, the role of the intendants is noteworthy, and both Richelieu's intendants and La Rochefoucauld's commissioners were drawn from the same corps of *maîtres des requêtes*. It is unnecessary to expatiate here on the unpopularity of this class of royal servant before the Fronde. Indeed, some of the intendants of the 1630s and 1640s were former or actual members of the royal commission, who pursued their efforts on behalf of La Rochefoucauld's reforms while on duty in the provinces. An early commissioner, La Poterie, did so in Provence after the 1630 revolts there, and so did Verthamon in Guyenne in 1634.[42] It was Verthamon who was instrumental in restoring the reform to the Norman priory of St Lo, whence it had been swept away during the celebrated revolts of 1639–40.[43]

39. B.S.G., MS. 632, fos. 140–55, council decree of 6 June 1644, giving details of the troubles; MS. 613, fo. 62, for a Génovéfain account. The letters of Hallay, provost of Nîmes cathedral, to Faure and Boulart, give a fascinating account of the intrigues surrounding this reform after 1643, especially those involving novices and canons drawn from local noble families: MS. 3251, fos. 462–72, 560–8.
40. B.S.G., MS. 630, fos. 310–13, 320–1, 332–47, 368–40, for the official acts. The *parlement* of Toulouse actually came to the rescue of the reform in 1644: MS. 632, fos. 112–13, decree of 27 May.
41. For example, the practice of reserving all appeals arising out of La Rochefoucauld's reforms to the royal commissioners was parallelled by the reservation of appeals against the provincial intendants to the king's council. See Bonney, *Political Change under Richelieu and Mazarin*, especially pp. 24–8.
42. *Lettres et mémoires adressés au chancelier Séguier 1633–1649*, ed. A. D. Lublinskaya, (Moscow, 1966), i, p. 237, La Poterie to Séguier, 21 June 1633. No trace has been found of the letter that he wrote to La Rochefoucauld about problems relating to reform in Provence.
43. *Diaire ou journal du voyage du chancelier Séguier en Normandie après la sédition des Nu-Pieds*, ed. Amable Floquet (Rouen, 1842), pp. 24, 158, 192–3. The author of this journal was

But the reform's alliance with the crown could also prove two-edged in the outlying provinces: not only could changes effected in times of royal strength be reversed in times of weakness, as happened at Uzès and Quarante, but they would be tainted by the very unpopularity of the crown's own policies and agents. Yet La Rochefoucauld never doubted the necessity or propriety of such an alliance, even if it meant that his congregation was slow to expand outwards from its core in the Paris basin.

However, neither the cardinal nor the congregation pinned all their hopes on rapid geographical expansion. They were no less keen, especially after the experiences of 1632, to provide the reform with a strong institutional framework. The extent of their success in doing so can be gauged by the way the 1637 general chapter debated and legislated on its own affairs with little reference to La Rochefoucauld, even if it did ensure that all decisions had his approval. Another sign of the congregation's growing stability and confidence was that this chapter was entirely free of the conflicts that had disrupted that of 1632. It was dominated by the personality and ideas of Faure, whom it duly re-elected coadjutor-abbot and superior-general.[44] Indeed, so indispensable did he seem to its affairs, that the chapter petitioned La Rochefoucauld to request Rome to alter the terms of the 1634 bull, so as to enable generals to be re-elected for an unlimited number of terms.[45]

Many other decisions of the 1637 chapter have an important bearing on the general objectives of reform.[46] The congregation's expansion explains the decision to classify its houses along Jesuit lines, yet another attempt to re-shape the older orders in the image of the new. Given the ancient custom of parents 'presenting' their children to monasteries, there would be schools for the very young, followed by a 'séminaire des enfants' for those between ten and sixteen years. After that came the novitiate, entry to which would be carefully screened, with the transition from one institution to another being designed to test vocations and prevent indiscriminate admissions. Professed members were to be divided between houses of study and retreat, houses with cure of souls attached to them, and those set aside solely

not Séguier at all, but Verthamon, who accompanied him to Normandy to restore order there after the revolts. Further evidence of his activism can be seen from his enquiries into the state of the hospices at Caen, Bayeux and Coutances; he suggested to Faure that the congregation should reform them, and thus expand its presence in the province: B.S.G., MS. 3251, fo. 22, letter of 11 March 1640. For his activities in Guyenne in 1634, see MS. 3279, fo. 77, letter to Faure, 16 November 1634.

44. B.S.G., MS. 627, fos. 348–55, *procès-verbal* of 25 October 1637.

45. *Ibid.*, fos. 494–5, petition to La Rochefoucauld. The papal bull permitted re-election only once.

46. The following account is based on B.S.G., MS. 612, fos. 271–4, 278–81. The original *procès-verbal* of the chapter has not survived.

for prayer and liturgical exercises. La Rochefoucauld and Faure agreed that reform and good learning were inseparable, and the subsequent reputation of the Génovéfains in many fields of scholarship is evidence of the sound foundations that they laid.

Benefices, as we saw, had been a problem for the Génovéfains from the beginning and Faure, as we also saw, had argued in 1623 that only withdrawal from them could eradicate abuses within their communities. The problem remained largely academic for many years, since benefices in newly-reformed abbeys were usually turned over to the *anciens*, in return for their resigning offices and vacating the 'claustral' buildings to accomodate the incoming observant community. But as the *anciens* began to die out, there was growing pressure from bishops for the Génovéfains to take their place, obliging Faure to compromise at the 1637 chapter. In doing so, he insisted on rigorous safeguards for observance, proposing that every new member should vow never to seek or accept a benefice unless with the general's express permission, and to return to his abbey when recalled. When he proposed to add heavy penalties for offenders, he was criticised by Gallet for a lack of compassion. But his reply that laisser-faire practices undermined regular observance convinced the chapter, and even mollified Gallet.[47] Not only did Faure win this particular argument, but his views became an essential part of Génovéfain teaching thereafter.[48]

Finally, the 1637 chapter drafted immensely detailed legislation to define the conduct, duties, and accountability of monastic officials.[49] Its target here was, as ever, the self-perpetuating oligarchies which traditionally governed independent religious houses like those of the canons-regular.

III

Because the traditional superiors of the canons-regular were the bishops, their reform inevitably possessed an episcopal dimension. Even if they approved of reform in principle, bishops' reactions could not but be mixed when abbeys were removed from their jurisdiction, and placed in a congregation which gradually adopted the conven-

47. *Ibid.*, fos. 275–8, 305–7.
48. See the *Instruction du R.P. Charles Faure contenant le desseing de la congrégation sur les Religieux envoyez dans les paroisses, et autres bénéfices pour travailler au salut des âmes, et les précautions qu'elle veut estre gardées, pour empescher les désordres qui peuvent naistre de ces emplois* (n.p., n.d.). This appears to have been composed after the 1637 chapter, and to have been widely used throughout the congregation. It lists, and warns against, the main dangers arising from the services of external benefices.
49. B.S.G., MS. 612, fos. 284–95.

tional attitudes of the orders towards episcopal authority; the argument that their authority over canons-regular was in practice illusory, and obedience to them rarely granted freely, carried little weight with them. Where canons served in benefices, conflicts were almost inevitable, and the anti-regular attitudes of many bishops in this period were bound to affect La Rochefoucauld's reforms. If his efforts at reform served to identify him more closely with the regulars generally, his reputation within the French church greatly benefited the congregation in its relations with the bishops, and he frequently acted as mediator, placating hostile or suspicious bishops. Despite this, the bishops remained extremely sensitive about their rights, even when they were imploring his assistance against recalcitrant abbeys, and their firm opposition could, as we have seen, jeopardise the outcome of any attempted reform. Tensions were unavoidable, not least because the rekindling of the quarrel between the regular and the secular clergy made it more difficult to find workable compromises.

In general, the congregation behaved deferentially towards the bishops, if only because it was too weak and too young to adopt the more robust attitudes of the Jesuits or the Capuchins. Nevertheless, its development during the 1630s into an autonomous congregation with its own *esprit de corps* and structure of authority led it to exhibit some of the traditional reflexes of the orders towards the bishops. By 1633, Faure was firmly instructing priors to refuse episcopal visitations concerning the observance or internal affairs of their houses.[50] For their part, reforming bishops like those of Châlons-sur-Marne and Angers pointedly reminded it of their authority, while in 1636 Bishop Sponde of Pamiers thundered against reform 'à l'espaignolle, ou plustost à la huguenotte', warning that there would be only one bishop in his diocese.[51] In 1634, Bishop Potier of Beauvais, often so close to La Rochefoucauld in ecclesiastical politics, imposed stringent terms for the preservation of his authority over an abbey which the congregation was about to reform, hinting that non-compliance might open the way for takeover by another order.[52]

It is not surprising, therefore, that some bishops at the Assembly of the Clergy in 1635 should have sought a settlement with the Génovéfains. The lead was taken by Bishop Potier, and after months of negotiations, Faure finally agreed in December 1635 to sign an accord for the sake of peace, order, and the good of souls — hardly an

---

50. B.S.G., MS. 3263, fo. 46, letter to Blanchart, 23 September.
51. B.S.G., MS. 3280, fo. 3, Gallet to Faure, 19 January 1635, on the annoyance of the Bishop of Angers, who had to be reassured by La Rochefoucauld; MS 3250, fo. 538, Bishop of Châlons to Faure, n.d.; MS. 3249, fos. 184–5, Sponde to La Rochefoucauld, 11 December 1636. Sponde did not elucidate what he meant by the expressions 'à l'espaignolle' or 'à la huguenotte'.
52. B.S.G., MS. 612, fos. 234–7.

expression of enthusiasm.[53] Pastoral activities had, as one might expect, caused most dispute – as they did in most conflicts between the regulars and the seculars – and here the bishops obtained satisfaction: their permission would be required to preach, confess and administer the sacraments in the congregation's churches, while its members serving in benefices would recognise episcopal authority as the secular clergy did. In the event of scandal, bishops would have a free hand – even over the congregation's own superiors – to punish offenders and, should observance itself decline, they might step in to restore it, as the ultimate guarantors of reform.[54] These and other minor conditions were designed to assert the 'tridentine' claims of the episcopacy, which French bishops generally interpreted in the light of older, Gallican traditions.

The 1635 agreement did not, of course, guarantee perfect harmony thereafter. There were further clashes in the late 1630s, and a separate agreement had to be signed with Potier in 1642.[55] Moreover, those bishops who disliked the reform still remained aloof. There were also several confrontations during the late 1630s, even with well-disposed bishops, on an issue which bedevilled the Counter-Reformation church throughout Europe: whether unreformed religious houses should be turned over to other – mostly new – orders, whose services were felt to be more valuable.[56] Disputes of this kind pitted even reformers against each other; a bishop's priorities for his diocese might clash with those of a congregation like La Rochefoucauld's, especially when the latter, although committed to reforming non-observant houses, was slow in producing results. Throughout the 1630s, the congregation made fierce efforts, not always successfully, to prevent the transfer to other orders of Augustinian houses at Bourges, Amiens and elsewhere, but in doing so made enemies of a number of bishops.[57] More serious for the congregation, however, were disagreements involving royal commissioners like Bishops Séguier and Sanguin, whose support was crucial to it in other respects. In 1638,

53. B.S.G., MS. 3250, fo. 353, Faure to Potier, 13 December 1635. MS. 773, fos. 49–50, refers to discussions still taking place in late November 1635.
54. B.S.G., MS. 612, fos. 227–9, for the text of the agreement. The episcopal signatories were Beauvais, Toulouse, Lisieux, Noyon, Bazas and Chalons.
55. B.S.G., MS. 630, fos. 286–90, 11 March 1642. This agreement covered only Potier's diocese of Beauvais.
56. See L. van Dijck, 'L'Affaire Raguet et le problème du gouvernement central de l'ordre de Prémontré au xviie siècle', *Analecta Praemonstratensiana* 50 (1974), pp. 171–215, especially pp. 196–202. The Jesuits were thought by many to be planning large-scale spoliation of the older orders throughout central Europe.
57. There is extensive correspondence about these cases in Faure's papers, B.S.G., MS. 3623, as well as in MSS. 3278–80. At Amiens, the replacement of the canons-regular by the Celestines was connected to plans for re-building the town's citadel. The dispute thus involved not merely the bishop, but the town council, the governor, the duc de Chaulnes, and ministers in Paris.

Séguier supported the takeover of the Abbey of Juilly by Bérulle's Oratory,[58] while Sanguin saw considerable advantages for his diocese in the Abbey of St Maurice at Senlis becoming a Jesuit college.[59] The Senlis dispute was the more tangled and protracted of the two, since La Rochefoucauld, despite his commission for the canons-regular, instinctively tended to support the Jesuits and Sanguin.[60] It was conflicts like these which convinced the congregation in 1640 that a group of bishops was actively plotting nothing less than its destruction.

IV

It was not the bishops, however, who precipitated the crisis which not only terminated La Rochefoucauld's career as commissioner, but which seemed to threaten much of what he had achieved since 1622. The crisis developed out of a number of unresolved issues which resurfaced in the late 1630s.

Firstly, there was the continuing problem of how to deal with Solminihac. In 1634, La Rochefoucauld gave him a new commission for reform in Guyenne, but remained undecided as to what to do next.[61] Solminihac, supported by the Jesuits and, more suprisingly, by Verthamon, who was intendant in Guyenne in 1634,[62] pressed the cardinal several times over the next few years for his own congregation, only to be thwarted each time by La Rochefoucauld's council.[63] Solminihac became Bishop of Cahors in 1636, with an assurance from Richelieu that this need not prevent him from continuing with his reforms.[64] Such powerful support seemed to presage better fortune,

58. B.S.G., MS. 612, fos. 359v–62v, for a short account. Faure's letters on the takeover are in MS. 3263, fos. 126, 171, 520.
59. B.S.G., MS. 613, fos. 183–96; MS. 3284, fo. 83, Boulart to Faure, 24 January 1638. Numerous letters on this issue throughout MSS. 3284–94.
60. B.S.G., MS. 3294, fo. 281, Boulart to Faure, undated: 'Monseigneur le Cardinal m'a fort parlé de donner St Maurice aux RR. PP. Jésuites, et ce à la solicitation de Msgr. de Senlis...son inclination va à donner contentement à mondit seigneur de Senlis'. The Génovéfains repeatedly appealed to the cardinal to remember that his primary duty was to the order of which he was officially reformer: MS. 3250, fos. 199, 228–9, 289, 321. In the end, Boulart made a formal protest to the Jesuit general, Mutio Vitelleschi, who disowned the efforts to take over St Maurice: MS. 630, fos. 40–3, Vitelleschi to Boulart, 27 February 1641.
61. B.S.G., MS. 3279, fo. 548, Boulart to Faure, 16 November 1634; *ibid.*, fo. 558, same to same, 23 December 1634, giving account of discussions concerning Solminihac in La Rochefoucauld's council.
62. *Ibid.*, fo. 77, Verthamon to Faure, 16 November 1634; MS. 3251, fo. 10, for Faure's guarded, non-committal reply.
63. B.S.G., MS. 612, fos. 199, 205–10, for a Génovéfain account of these discussions which, although biased against Solminihac, is at least based on original sources now lost.
64. Sol, *Lettres et documents*, pp. 136–7, Richelieu to Solminihac, 25 April 1636.

but when he renewed his demands in September 1637, he found, perhaps to his surprise, La Rochefoucauld quite unyielding. Now that Solminihac was a bishop with more pressing responsibilities, he could see no reason for concession and, with the agreement of the general chapter then in session, the incorporation of Solminihac's reform into the congrégation de France was quickly approved.[65]

In fact, Solminihac now decided to bypass La Rochefoucauld altogether.[66] With Richelieu and Père Joseph on his side, he had no difficulty obtaining a letter from Louix XIII to Urban VIII and the French ambassador in April 1638 requesting a separate 'congrégation de Guyenne', of which he would be head.,[67] No immediate result was forthcoming, but the support Solminihac enjoyed in high places was bound to worry La Rochefoucauld. By mid-1638, however, a new and more explosive conflict had blown up elsewhere.

An uneasy peace had reigned between St Victor and Ste Geneviève since 1634, but open conflict only arose in 1637 when the Génovéfains attempted to reform two abbeys in the Paris diocese, Hérivaux and Livry.[68] St Victor appeared to encourage the opposition there to seek the protection of Archbishop Gondi, and suggested that he, as their natural superior, reform the abbeys with canons from St Victor.[69] This patent subterfuge – 'reform' in order to avoid reform – stung La Rochefoucauld, but Gondi, who rebuffed his efforts to explain his intentions, shrank from a final confrontation and, with the royal commission's support, Livry and Hérivaux were reformed in November 1637 and in 1639 respectively.[70]

To La Rochefoucauld and the Génovéfains, St Victor was the real

65. B.S.G., MS. 627, fos. 314–15, ordinance of incorporation; *ibid.*, fos. 362–3, chapter's approval of the ordinance; MS. 612, fos. 298–304, La Rochefoucauld's speech to the chapter justifying his decision. In a surprising reversal of roles, the congregation's leaders agreed a few days later, not to enforce La Rochefoucauld's ordinance against Solminihac: B.S.G., MS. 627, fos. 370–2.
66. Sol, *Lettres et documents*, p. 174, 'Mémoire disant qu'on peut fort bien, à Rome, statuer définitivement sur l'arrêt du cardinal de la Rochefoucault' [1637]. There is no indication, however, of the arguments contained in the memorandum.
67. *Ibid.*, pp. 153–4, letter of 2 April. Similar letters were sent by the king to the ambassador and Cardinal Barberini. Solminihac also enlisted the assistance of the Maurists' envoy in Rome, Dom Placide Le Simon, but as he was simultaneously employed by La Rochefoucauld, he was asked by his superiors to keep his negotiations on Solminihac's behalf secret: B.N., MS. Lat. 12790, fo. 178r.
68. B.S.G., MS. 627, fos. 134–5, commission to Boulart for visitation; MS. 3283, fo. 43, Boulart to Faure, 7 September 1637, reporting on events at Livry.
69. B.S.G., MS. 3250, fo. 536, letter to Boulart, dated 9 September: 'Je scay les excuses qu'on m'a representées, mais plus ou moins en toutes, il y a fort à redire. C'est pourquoy au nom de Dieu et de l'entière charitè, qu'on me laisse en paix'. B.S.G., MS. 627, fos. 308–9, La Rochefoucauld's warning to St Victor not to meddle in the reforms, 22 October; *ibid.*, fos. 309–13, *procès-verbal* of Boulart's visitation of Livry, 23 September.
70. B.S.G., MS. 627, fos. 384–7, Faure's petition to royal commission, October 1637; *ibid.*, fos. 356–61, La Rochefoucauld's ordinance for reform of Livry, 25 October 1637; MS. 628, fos. 615–20, *prise de possession* of Hérivaux, 23 November 1639.

villain in this affair. While the cardinal usually respected the abbey, and would willingly have left it to its own devices, its apparent readiness to act as a bastion against reform in and around Paris, could not be ignored.[71] In June 1638, he finally decreed the incorporation of St Victor into his congregation, and banned the reception and profession of new members there.[72] It was a move that owed more to anger than to cool judgement, and insufficient care was taken to ensure ministerial support for it. St Victor's prior, Jean de Toulouse, quickly put his connections to good use. Richelieu, Séguier and the *premier président* of the *parlement* of Paris all promised him their assistance; when La Rochefoucauld's visitor arrived at St Victor on 23 July, he was promptly turned away.[73] In quick succession, St Victor obtained a decree evoking the whole affair before the king's council, and launched an appeal against La Rochefoucauld to Rome.[74] Disowned by the royal council, and especially by some members of the royal commission, La Rochefoucauld had no choice but to await the papacy's reaction. In retrospect, his action was a tactical disaster, as it drew his reform into controversies and diplomatic manoeuvring which tarnished its reputation and for a time even threatened its survival.

It was perhaps no accident that the cardinal's opponents realised by 1638 that their best hope of success lay with Rome. St Victor had not forgotten its tussle with him there in 1633–4, while Rome had actually quashed his Cistercian ordinances in 1635. Richelieu personally controlled the orders of Cluny, Cîteaux and Premontré in France by 1638, despite Rome's refusal to recognise his administration or attempts at reform – most of which were taken over from La Rochefoucauld. Richelieu's motives were suspect in the curia, which was tiring of reforms which smacked too much of high politics and self-aggrandisement.[75]

None of this augured well for La Rochefoucauld who, as in 1633, was especially angry that the will to limit appeals, which he regarded as the cornerstone of his commission, was no longer in evidence in either Paris or Rome. But even his own advisers were divided on this question. The lawyers distinguished between appeals arising from the 'correction des moeurs' which, they felt, did not have suspensive effect, and from the 'réformation et manutention de la discipline

71. B.S.G., MS. 3238, fo. 410, La Rochefoucauld to prior of St Victor, 5 December 1636; B.N., MS. Fr. 24080, pp. 554–8.
72. B.S.G., MS. 3241, fo. 82, ordinance of 23 June.
73. B.N., MS. Fr. 24080, pp. 600–7; Bonnard, *Histoire de St Victor*, ii, p. 133, quotes from a royal *lettre de cachet* enjoining St Victor to proceed with its own reform, a clear warning to Ste Geneviève to leave well alone.
74. B.S.G., MS. 3243, fos. 134–5, for the decree, 23 July. B.N., MS. Fr. 24080, pp. 615–17, text of the appeal, 26 July. Notice of the appeal was served on La Rochefoucauld on 4 August 1638.
75. See below, pp. 245–6.

régulière', which did. The theologians rejected such a distinction outright, and denied the suspensive effect of any appeal. La Rochefoucauld, who fully agreed with the theologians, demanded a clear statement from Rome which would endorse his move against St Victor.[76] Instructions were sent to Etienne Charlet, French assistant in Rome to the Jesuit general, on the vexed question of referring appeals to minor ecclesiastical judges in France. La Rochefoucauld protested, as before, that it was intolerable to have to answer before a mere *official* for actions performed as a special papal commissioner, and demanded that the judges be at least bishops. Charlet was to explore other possibilities – for example, that the pope establish an episcopal committee of enquiry in France, from whose findings he could make a final judgement of the case.[77] The cardinal then submitted his own remonstrance to Urban VIII in October 1638, reiterating these points, and requesting that his commission be judged at an appropriately high level.[78]

The battle for influence in the curia began when Charlet and Dom Le Simon received their instructions, and began lobbying curial dignitaries and officials. But Urban VIII was content to refer the case to an *ad hoc* congregation, initially headed by the influential secretary of briefs, Marcaurelio Maraldo. This body, which subsequently heard other appeals involving the cardinal's commission, was soon known as the 'congrégation des affaires du cardinal de la Rochefoucault'.[79] Rome was, as usual, in no hurry to proceed, but, initially at least, it was not hostile to him.[80]

St Victor, whose influence extended to Rome as well, was not content merely to defend itself against La Rochefoucauld. It sought to discredit his reforms and prevent the renewal of his commission.[81] Indirectly, St Victor also benefited from Maraldo's strong personal opposition to La Rochefoucauld's reform of the Mathurin order. Another member of the Roman congregation, the datarius, was, if not an open enemy of reform, at least an entrenched defender of curial interests – which was sometimes the same thing. Even Cardinal Francesco Barberini's goodwill towards La Rochefoucauld seems to

76. B.A.V., Barb. lat 8133, fos. 63, 65–6, letter and memorandum from La Rochefoucauld to pope, 13 August 1638; B.S.G., MS. 3285, fo. 303, Boulart to Dom Le Simon, 21 September 1638, for an account of these discussions, and La Rochefoucauld's conclusion.
77. B.S.G., MS. 628, fos. 282–7, instruction to Charlet.
78. *Ibid.*, fos. 262–4.
79. For most of its life, the congregation's president was Cardinal Spada, but his surviving papers in the Vatican archives and the Roman state archives contain no references to it.
80. B.S.G., MS. 3285, fo. 614, Le Simon to Boulart, late September 1638, 'On a donné ordre par deçà que rien ne passe contre l'intention de Son Eminence'.
81. B.N., MS. Fr. 24080, pp. 630–1. The Duke of Atria was an old friend of St Victor, which benefited considerably in 1638 and later from his influence over Urban VIII, and his ability to block requests from La Rochefoucauld and Ste Geneviève.

have been no match for them, and Le Simon wrote in April 1639 that St Victor and the Mathurins were winning the propaganda battle in Rome. Their repeated claims that the cardinal's reforms were so many acts of aggression against them made the curia unwilling to renew his commission.[82]

This setback was all the greater as La Rochefoucauld, unhappy with the one-year commission granted him in 1638, had asked Le Simon to petition for a much longer one which would specifically deny suspensive effect to appeals against his decrees.[83] This request was also sent before the special congregation, while St Victor's vigilant friends prevented any attempt to dispatch a new brief to La Rochefoucauld.[84] The matter was still before the congregation in April 1639, when Le Simon, as we saw, found the curia distinctly unfriendly. From then on, the news from Rome seemed to worsen. The datarius informed Le Simon shortly after this that Solminihac's congregation would be confirmed, but that, too, failed to materialise.[85] Later, in August 1639, Solminihac learned from one of La Rochefoucauld's own councillors that the pope had, in full consistory, actually revoked his commission, declaring that he had often exceeded its terms 'dans ses unions, congrégations et ordonnances'. This report was confirmed by Chancellor Séguier, who added that Solminihac need no longer fear the congrégation de France.[86]

Some of this news was exaggerated. Although there is no independent evidence for the pope's declaration, it is clear that the Roman congregation was ill-disposed towards La Rochefoucauld, 'n'approuvant pas du tout ce qui est faict par delà'.[87] But La Rochefoucauld took the reports seriously, and at a council meeting, during which Faure admitted that the opposition seemed to be winning, the two men agreed on the need for energetic measures of self-defence.[88] A special envoy, Jacques Guérin, was hastily dispatched to Rome. He arrived in November 1639, but then had to wait until April 1640 before receiving proper instructions from Paris.[89] In the meantime, he could only observe the tide turning against the cardinal and the congregation. He reported that, unless Louis XIII

82. B.S.G., MS. 3288, fo. 514, letter to Boulart, 12 April 1639.
83. B.S.G., MS. 3285, fo. 303v, Boulart to Le Simon, 21 September 1638. La Rochefoucauld's own letter to the envoy has been lost.
84. B.N., MS. Fr. 24080, pp. 631, 671–2.
85. Sol, *Lettres et documents*, pp. 194–5, Le Simon to Solminihac, 12 April 1639.
86. *Ibid.*, pp. 197–9, Seraphim de St François, O. Carm., to Solminihac, 20 August 1639.
87. B.S.G., MS. 3290, fo. 127, Le Simon to Boulart, 5 September 1639.
88. Sol, *Lettres et documents*, p. 200, Seraphim de St François to Solminihac, 3 September 1639.
89. Faure seems to have prepared some provisional instructions, limited to the tactics to be employed against St Victor and its allies: B.S.G., MS. 3263, fo. 546, 'mémoire pour Rome, 4 déc. 1639'.

himself wrote to the pope, there was no hope of La Rochefoucauld's commission being renewed, so set was the curia against him.[90] Guérin himself petitioned for its renewal in June 1640, but not even a formal order from Cardinal Barberini could make Maraldo dispatch the commission.[91] La Rochefoucauld's career as a papal commissioner was well and truly finished.

By mid-1640, however, Guérin was far more concerned by reports that certain French bishops had joined the attack on the congregation in Rome. In order to broaden its challenge, St Victor, tactically as astute as ever, seems to have decided to champion episcopal interests, possibly without even consulting the bishops themselves. It had the support of two envoys from the Soissons Abbey of St Jean des Vignes, where efforts at reform had made determined enemies, in particular the Bishop of Soissons.[92] In June 1640, Guérin reported that St Victor was claiming to act on behalf of the French bishops 'qui avoient intérest en ceste cause' – Paris, Chartres, Rouen, Meaux, Soissons and Cahors.[93] Over the following months, inspired perhaps by St Victor, formal statements of opposition to Génovéfain policies did arrive in the curia. Although Guérin had great difficulty discovering either the identity or the complaints of the bishops, he wrote that they were accusing the reform of driving unreformed canons from their abbeys, failing to pay their pensions and reducing them to vagabondage.[94] None of this was to the liking of the curia. More seriously, he concluded they were attempting to undo the reform's congregational structure, and return its individual houses to episcopal control.[95] Indeed, he judged the position to be so critical that he advised Ste Geneviève to drop its quarrel with St Victor, and concentrate on ensuring its own survival. In Paris, Faure took steps to counter St Victor's allegations, and to show that reforms were always conducted in accordance with the cardinal's ordinances. He, too, had difficulty discovering the identity of the bishops in league with St Victor, but

90. B.S.G., MS. 3291, fo. 384, Guérin to La Rochefoucauld, 14 December 1639; MS. 3292, fo. 212, to Boulart, 23 February 1640; *ibid.*, fo. 420, to same, 1 April 1640; MS. 3293, fo. 528, to Boulart, undated: 'Ils ont si mauvaise opinion de ses procédés qu'ils ne peuvent entendre parler'.
91. B.S.G., MS. 3291, fo. 486, Guérin to Boulart, 23 June 1640.
92. B.S.G., MS. 3263, fo. 546, request from Faure to Guérin to oppose vigilantly the envoys from St Jean des Vignes. For the dispute over the abbey, from which the Génovéfains actually withdrew in July 1640, see MS. 628, fos. 312–35. Faure attempted to explain and justify his policy to the Bishop of Soissons: MS. 3250, fo. 402, 6 July 1640.
93. B.S.G., MS. 3293, fo. 129, Guérin to Faure [undated]; MS. 3291, fo. 486, Guérin to Boulart, 23 June 1640. The 'cause' referred to was the congregation's request for permission to re-elect Faure general and to separate the offices of abbot of Ste Geneviève and superior general of the congregation. See below, p. 213.
94. B.S.G., MS. 3291, fo. 489, letter to Faure, 21 July 1640; *ibid.*, fo. 30, to same, 30 August.
95. B.S.G., MS. 3291, fo. 485, letter to Faure, 21 July 1640.

was greatly relieved to learn that neither Séguier of Meaux nor Sanguin of Senlis, both influential royal commissioners who had had recent disagreements with the congregation, were involved.[96] The war of rumours continued, but the alarm itself slowly subsided.[97]

Throughout the critical year of 1640, Guérin stuck to his task in an unfriendly curia, and with what he regarded as inadequate support from La Rochefoucauld. He had also been sent to Rome for purposes of the congregation's own choosing: to sue for the separation of the offices of superior general and coadjutor-abbot of Ste Geneviève, and permission to re-elect a general as often as the congregation's chapter wished. The first request was based on limited faith in royal and papal promises of a return to free abbatial elections after the cardinal's death, and the unnerving prospect that a commendator-abbot of Ste Geneviève would automatically become general of the congregation.[98] The idea of such a separation had been approved by the chapter in 1637. But for some obscure reason, La Rochefoucauld and the congregation differed on both issues, and for a time the former's silence was taken in Rome to mean that he neither knew nor approved of the requests.[99] However, in March 1640, he came round to the Génovéfain view, and wrote to Barberini and Charlet in support of the demands.[100]

Urban VIII also referred these requests to the *ad hoc* congregation.[101] The moment was inopportune from the Génovéfain point of view, as St Victor had no difficulty depicting the demands, especially the second, as examples of Faure's lust for power.[102] Its propaganda, as well as its claim to speak on behalf of the bishops, probably explains why the Roman congregation rejected out of hand the Génovéfain request at its very first hearing.[103]

Defeat was rarely irreversible in the curia which, in the latter phase of Urban VIII's pontificate, seems to have been frequently working at cross-purposes. In July 1640, with the help of Cardinal Bagno, a

96. B.S.G., MS. 3263, fo. 799, Faure to Boulart [undated], outlining the measures to be taken.
97. B.S.G., MS. 3293, fo. 650, Guérin to Faure, 13 September 1640.
98. François Boulart clearly recognised this danger in a letter to Faure: 'Je crains fort que le tiltre d'abbé de Ste Geneviève ne soit un jour cause de la perte et ruine de la réformation de nostre ordre': B.S.G., MS. 3285, fo. 630, 4 September 1638. Richelieu was suspected of coveting Ste Geneviève — had he not already obtained Cluny, Cîteaux and Prémontré? — and who could prevent him from having his way should La Rochefoucauld die before the curia had acceded to the congregation's demands?
99. B.S.G., MS. 3291, fo. 413, Guérin to Boulart, 22 December 1639.
100. B.S.G., MS. 629, fos. 128–9, *avis* of cardinal's council; *ibid.*, fos. 136–7, La Rochefoucauld to Barberini, 8 March 1640; *ibid.*, fos. 134–5, to Charlet, same date.
101. B.S.G., MS. 3293, fos. 514 and 512, Guérin to Boulart, 28 April and 19 May 1640.
102. B.N., MS. Fr. 24080, p. 672.
103. B.S.G., MS. 3293, fo. 129, Guérin to Faure [undated]; MS. 3291, fo. 486, Guérin to Boulart, 23 June 1640.

former nuncio to France, Guérin obtained a brief, postponing for a year the congregation's chapter, due to meet later in 1640, in the hope of securing papal consent in the meantime to the principle of Faure's re-election.[104] This, in turn, was achieved in October 1640, although it required the personal intervention of Urban VIII – by now perhaps better informed or at least anxious to reward La Rochefoucauld for his pro-papal stance during that year's diplomatic crisis – to enable a brief allowing Faure's re-election for up to twelve years to be dispatched to France in November.[105] But the separation of the offices of general and coadjutor-abbot was still unacceptable to the curia, and the renewal of La Rochefoucauld's commission was no longer on the agenda.[106]

Apart from these concessions, the reform's fortunes were slow to recover in Rome. The lapse of La Rochefoucauld's commission was the biggest blow, and he and Ste Geneviève seem to have been at a loss as to how to proceed once it had expired. The main result was that St Victor had its appeal referred to French judges (in accordance with the usual legal practice) and that, once again, despite a fresh appeal from La Rochefoucauld to Urban VIII against what he regarded as humiliating treatment for a cardinal, an *official* was allowed to handle the case. The conflict with St Victor was not settled until 1645, but by then La Rochefoucauld's plans to incorporate it into his congregation had long been forgotten.[107]

During these years, Guérin was also kept busy in preventing the persistent Solminihac from securing the formal approval of his congregation, which had so narrowly eluded him in 1639. The bishop came close again to success in 1643, when the new French ambassador was instructed to plead his cause, only to see his hopes finally dashed later that year by firm instructions to the contrary from the Regent, Anne of Austria.[108] Yet even now, La Rochefoucauld was not satisfied, but was anxious to see his decree confirmed incorporating Solminihac's reform movement into the congrégation de France. After inevitable delays, it was finally ratified in June 1644 but, before it could be implemented, Urban VIII died, leaving the cardinal to begin negotia-

104. B.S.G., MS. 3291, fo. 485, letter to Faure, 21 July 1640; *ibid.*, fo. 349, to Boulart, same date.
105. B.S.G., MS. 3294, fo. 93, Guérin to Faure, 12 October 1640; *ibid.*, fo. 349, to Boulart, 26 October; *ibid.*, fo. 708, to Faure, same date. For the text of the brief: MS. 629, fos. 522–5.
106. B.S.G., MS. 3294, fo. 225, Guérin to Boulart, 23 November 1640.
107. B.N., MS. Fr. 24080, pp. 694, 766, 780; B.S.G., MS. 629, fos. 186–9; Bonnard, *Histoire de St Victor*, ii, pp. 136–7.
108. B.S.G., MS. 3307, fo. 439, Guérin to Boulart, 12 June 1643; *ibid.*, fo. 442, to same, 23 June; MS. 3250, fo. 45, Anne of Austria to Ambassador Fontenay-Mareuil, 25 June 1643; MS. 3307, fo. 192, Guérin to Boulart, 15 July 1643, on the effect of Anne's instructions.

tions all over again.[109] La Rochefoucauld was himself to die before any further progress had been made, and Solminihac's tiny 'congrégation' retained its independence until the French Revolution.

It was fortunate for La Rochefoucauld that the number of appeals against him to Rome dropped after 1640, and that the outburst of episcopal hostility soon abated. Yet the events of 1638–40 made the curia slow to shower him with graces. Guérin was plied with promises, and for several years found himself sent from one curial office to another in his pursuit of the congregation's desire to separate the offices of superior and coadjutor-abbot.[110] Periodic rumours of La Rochefoucauld's death instantly revived fears of the damage that a commendator-cum-general might wreak on the reform. On each occasion, Barberini assured Guérin that Rome would stand by the terms of its 1634 bull, but Guérin was not alone, both inside and outside of the congregation, in setting limited store by such promises.[111]

V

The critical events of 1638–40 inevitably affected the congregation's internal affairs. We have already noted that La Rochefoucauld's role, especially in 1640, was enigmatic. There were differences between him and the congregation over Faure's re-election and the separation of offices, but there were probably others, such as relations with bishops like Sanguin and Séguier, or with the Jesuits and other religious orders over Augustinian houses which they coveted. In any event, the general chapter of 1640 was overshadowed by these problems, and the congregation's delegates were convinced that La Rochefoucauld was under heavy external influence, and found his council impossible to work with.[112] Moreover, the only two successes Guérin could report from Rome during 1640 proved worthless in France. The brief postponing the 1640 general chapter appeared dubious to La

109. B.S.G., MS. 3308, fo. 284, Guérin to Boulart, 31 August 1643; *ibid.*, fo. 303, to same, 18 September; MS. 3309, fo. 7, to same, 7 November; MS. 3311, fo. 483, to same, 29 May 1644; *ibid.*, fo. 581, to Faure, 26 June 1644.
110. See his voluminous correspondence for these years in B.S.G., MSS. 3291–3315.
111. B.S.G., MS. 3298, fos. 209–10, Guérin to Faure, 26 June 1641; MS. 3295, fo. 685, to Boulart, same date. He added that St Victor had been spreading a rumour in curia that La Rochefoucauld was 'aux aboys' and that his abbey had been granted *in commendam* – an indication that Génovéfain fears were not private or unfounded.
112. B.S.G., MS. 629, fos. 516–19, circular letter from Boulart to all Génovéfain houses, 15 November 1640, in which the frustrations of negotiating with the cardinal's council are described. See also MS. 3297, fos. 118v–19r, Boulart to Faure, 24 May 1641: 'Monsieur le Cardinal est dans ses humeurs d'appréhender toutes choses...depuis quelques iours, à un tel point qu'il n'en peut reposer, et le pis que j'y vois est qu'il croit que nous nous moquons de luy et le méprisons'.

Rochefoucauld's councillors, and he took their advice to ignore it.[113] The chapter had to meet as planned, and in late December 1640, it elected François Boulart to succeed the disqualified Faure as coadjutor-abbot and general for three years.[114] However, La Rochefoucauld did support the chapter's determination to keep Faure in a position of leadership: it appointed him 'commissaire général de la réforme', a title which, while relieving him of all administrative burdens, actually placed him above the new general, Boulart,[115] For the next three years, the congregation possessed a hierarchy that contradicted its statutes, but Boulart's willingness to work under Faure ensured that no friction would come of it. The rift with La Rochefoucauld was also healed after 1640, and it was highly symbolic that Faure's delayed re-election as coadjutor and general in 1643 should have taken place at the cardinal's bedside, because he was too ill to attend the chapter.[116] The congregation would probably have continued to re-elect Faure had he not died at the age of fifty in November 1644. He had never entirely won La Rochefoucauld's affection, and occasionally even lost his confidence, but just as often the commissioner acknowledged his good fortune at having a collaborator of Faure's calibre and determination. A hastily-convened chapter elected François Blanchart, already known as a capable administrator, to succeed him in December 1644.[117]

The crisis of 1638 and subsequent years did not absorb all the energies of La Rochefoucauld's congregation, nor did it arrest its development. Of course, the termination of his commission was bound to affect the business of reform, and he was fortunate in having placed the congregation on a firm footing before then, as it enabled its leaders to concentrate on a task which was increasingly beyond an old man in his eighties. In this respect, the figures speak for themselves. Only eighteen houses were represented at the chapter of 1637, but forty-four at that of 1644, while the total membership was probably nearer to fifty.[118] Even now, it remained averse to indiscriminate expansion, and was determined to reform new houses at a pace it could sustain, especially as manpower problems had not disappeared.[119] But there

---

113. B.S.G., MS. 3293, fo. 722, Boulart to Faure [undated]. Faure found it hard to believe that Guérin would go that far: MS. 3263, fo. 790.
114. B.S.G., MS. 629, fos. 492–9, act of 30 October 1640.
115. *Ibid.*, fos. 500–2, 540–1.
116. B.S.G., MS. 631, fo. 192, *procès-verbal* of 1 May 1643.
117. B.S.G., MS. 632, fos. 374–86, 10 December 1644.
118. B.S.G., MS. 3239, voluminous catalogue of information, especially financial, on all the houses of the congregation, prepared for the 1650 general chapter.
119. B.S.G., MS. 3263, fo. 77, Faure to Blanchart, 19 November 1635; 'pour Chaalons je croy qu'il fault s'introduire avant que de plaider, mais je ne scay pas où trouver du monde, car on parle bien tost d'aller à St Quentin, on travaille aussy tost pour Ste Croix, il y a quelque disposition pour St Victor. Je n'ay point de prestres propres.'

was frequently great pressure from allies and patrons, both episcopal and abbatial, to reform individual houses.[120] As in earlier years, Faure had doubts about the wisdom and future of reforms undertaken in such hasty conditions.[121]

It also appears that, after 1639, much of the initiative for the reform of individual houses came from the bishops, their 'natural' superiors. This often took the form of agreements whereby they invited the congregation to reform abbeys under their jurisdiction. At Meaux, for example, Bishop Séguier first conducted his own visitation at Notre-Dame de Chaage, and only then requested the congregation to undertake its reform.[122] Acting as bishop rather than as royal commissioner, he installed the Génovéfains there in December 1642, imposing his own regulations on its *anciens*, and obliging the congregation to respect his episcopal rights. These terms, and the reform contract, were, as in the past, ratified by the royal commission.[123] Although an influential royal commissioner, Séguier had been among the disaffected bishops in 1638–9.[124] If he later accepted that only the congregation was capable of effecting the reforms he desired in his diocese, it may have been because, after 1639, he was, like other bishops, in a position to impose tougher conditions to protect his rights over reformed abbeys. But it is the continuing growth of the reform which provides the clearest evidence that congregation and bishops found each other indispensable.

La Rochefoucauld's methods of reform changed little after 1639. For example, the reform of the Parisian Abbey of Ste Croix La Bretonnerie in 1641 was initiated by the king's nomination of an *ad hoc* commission of bishops and *maîtres des requêtes*. La Rochefoucauld even drafted a reform ordinance after consulting his council, but the question of its validity immediately arose, now that he was no longer papal commissioner. Amidst considerable opposition and political intrigue, a Génovéfain community was duly installed at Ste Croix, which was coveted by several other orders.[125] However, the reform proved short-lived: it collapsed when Richelieu and Séguier were

120. *Ibid.*, fo. 589, Faure to Boulart, 24 May 1641: 'J'ay passé un accord précipité avec M de Noyon tant il a pressé, crié, et agité'.
121. See B.S.G., MS. 3263, fo. 148, letter to Boulart, 8 April 1637.
122. B.S.G., MS. 630, fos. 432–7, text of Séguier's ordinance, 22 November 1640.
123. *Ibid.*, fos. 480–91, contract for reform, and decree of council, 7 and 12 December 1642 respectively; *ibid.*, fos. 511–16, ordinance of 19 December. See MS. 3263, fo. 249, Faure to Blanchart, 8 December: 'Je dois partir le 16 de ce mois pour mener une colonie à Chaage. Monsieur de Meaux a tant pressé pour cela que l'affaire soit résolu de là en 22.'
124. His disaffection apparently arose from his support for the Oratorians' takeover of the abbey of Juilly in his diocese, which the Génovéfains strongly opposed.
125. B.S.G., MS. 630, fos. 90–3, text of royal commission; *ibid.*, fos. 116–49, *procès-verbal* of visitation by Lezeau and Verthamon.

persuaded to oppose it, leaving Boulart with no choice but to withdraw his men.[126]

Throughout the Ste Croix affair, there was acute nervousness about appeals and litigation over a reform whose legal basis was now uncertain. It was suggested that the chancellor assume the role once belonging to the cardinal-commissioner, in an attempt to stem litigation, but this only raised fears that reform might become a purely administrative *affaire d'état*.[127] Clearly, ecclesiastics remained as sensitive as ever about initiatives emanating from seculars, particularly crown officials. In its conception, La Rochefoucauld's commission had been essential in maintaining a balance between the acceptable and the effective, and its termination left a gap that was difficult to fill.

The royal commission continued to function after 1639, but it is virtually impossible to determine how far it was affected by the failure to renew La Rochefoucauld's papal commission. There is no evidence that it tried to fill the ensuing void, and pursue reform purely as an affair of state.[128] The deaths of Louis XIII and Richelieu would have made any such ambitions fanciful, and even had La Rochefoucauld been commissioner after 1643, it is hard to see how the regency government of Anne of Austria could have given him the same support he had enjoyed under Louis XIII.[129]

VI

In 1638, the reform seemed most at risk in Rome; by mid-1643, with Richelieu and Louis XIII dead, the threat shifted to France itself. Open hostility to Richelieu's reforms quickly broke out in Cluny and Cîteaux, where the reform parties lost all influence because of their unpopular alliance with him. More alarming evidence of the change was the Prince of Condé's success in obliging the politically weak Regent, Anne of Austria, to accept the election of his young son, Conti, as abbot-general of Cluny.[130] This turn of events convinced La

126. The affair is well documented in Faure's papers: B.S.G., MS. 3263, fos. 226–8, 587, 595, 609, 677, 684, 685, 699. Boulart tried in vain to persuade Richelieu to change his mind: MS. 3250, fo. 268 [undated, but early July 1641]; he also asked secretary of state Sublet des Noyers to use his influence with Richelieu: *ibid.*, fo. 269; MS. 3251, fo. 105, M. Le Roy to Faure, undated.
127. B.S.G., MS. 613, fos. 62–74v, for a detailed history of the reform.
128. The surviving evidence of its activities consists merely of its decrees in the A.N. V[6] series, which do not suffice to delineate precisely its functions or competence.
129. To appreciate the extent of the change after May 1643, compare the events that occurred in Cluny, Cîteaux and Prémontré after Richelieu's and Louis XIII's deaths: Lekai, *Rise of the Cistercian Strict Observance*, ch. 6; G. Charvin, 'L'Abbaye et l'ordre de Cluny en France de la mort de Richelieu à l'élection de Mazarin 1642–1654', *Revue Mabillon* 33 (1943), pp. 85ff; L. van Dijck, 'L'Affaire Raguet', *Analecta Praemonstratensiana* 50 (1974), pp. 171–215; 51 (1975), pp. 37–71.
130. See sources listed in previous note.

Rochefoucauld that he would have to fight to save his reform and, having consulted his council, he presented Anne with his *Remonstrance à la reine régente*, his last published composition, in which he stressed the labours and successes of twenty years' work.[131] He underlined the role played by Louis XIII at every stage, and urged the regent to preserve and continue this royal commitment. He complained that since 1622, there had been 'bien plus de procès que de restablissement de l'observance', adding that had he foreseen the lack of support from Rome, and the indignity of having to answer appeals against him before a lowly *official*, he would not have accepted the commission at all. His pessimistic conclusion was that the history of his commission should serve as a warning to future cardinals not to risk their reputation and dignity in such a fashion.

For all its pessimism, the *Remonstrance* was both timely and successful.[132] Since Richelieu's death, appeals against reform had flooded into Rome, and Jacques Guérin suspected that the ambassador there was under instructions from ministers hostile to reform.[133] The immediate fruit of La Rochefoucauld's *Remonstrance* was a firm set of instructions to the ambassador in Rome, in which Anne declared she would not permit any reformed congregation – explicitly mentioning Solminihac and Val des Ecoliers – to exist in France other than the congrégation de France.[134] In Rome, Guérin soon felt the beneficial effects of a declaration which reaffirmed La Rochefoucauld's principle of a single reform.

Assured of the regent's personal support, La Rochefoucauld could feel well content. But despite a series of royal patents and a papal bull, he had so far failed to secure a satisfactory guarantee of the congregation's independence after his death. Condé's success at Cluny, by showing how easily identical guarantees could be overturned, seems to have persuaded him, probably in late 1643, to have a successor elected during his lifetime rather than continue the unpromising pursuit of the separation of offices in the curia.[135] Yet even this proved

131. The copy in B.S.G., MS. 631, fos. 342–8 has been used here.
132. It was presented to Anne of Austria by the ubiquitous royal commissioners, Bishops Sanguin and Séguier, and the *maîtres des requêtes*, Lezeau and Verthamon, probably in June 1643. La Rochefoucauld also compiled a large dossier of acts and other papers relating to the reform to be placed before the regent: B.S.G., MS. 631, fos. 320–40.
133. Most suspicions fell on Chavigny, the secretary of state for foreign affairs. See p. 261, n. 56 below.
134. B.S.G., MS. 3250, fo. 45, letter to Fontenay-Mareuil, 21 June 1643. 'Je vous écris celle cy pour vous dire. . . que ma volonté n'est d'admettre ni souffrir en ce royaume autre congrégation de l'ordre de St Augustin que celle des chanoines reguliers iceluy confirmée par lesdits arrêts, et que je ne désire pas que vous poursuivrez aucun autre establissement de congrégarion dudit ordre, comme chose contraire à mon intention et abus d'iceluy.'
135. There is no better illustration of this than the attitude of the provost of Uzès cathedral on hearing of La Rochefoucauld's own death: 'Le sieur prévost ayant appris le décez de Son Eminence de la Rochefoucauld s'est non seulement refroidi de son traité mais encore tasche il de retarder l'accomodement des aultres anciens sous une vaine espérance que les

to be a difficult and hazardous affair, one that underlines the congregation's dependence on its founder until the very eve of his death.

La Rochefoucauld's first attempt to resign Ste Geneviève was apparently frustrated. Some courtiers coveted the abbey itself, and others demanded pensions, threatening to quash his resignation if not given satisfaction.[136] Ste Geneviève was indeed a prize worthy of aristocratic ambition, and La Rochefoucauld's own relatives were loath to see it pass out of family hands. These complications, only vaguely alluded to in the sources, delayed the formal act of resignation until early February 1644.[137] The next stage, that of obtaining royal permission to negotiate in Rome for a return to an elective abbacy, was the most treacherous of all. The diplomatic François Boulart was sent to court to secure the necessary *brevet*, and quickly realised that nothing could be obtained from the regent without the consent of Mazarin, whose eye for a good benefice was already common knowledge. The royal council then declared that the elected abbot should be subject to royal approval, and thus challenged the whole basis of what La Rochefoucauld was planning to do, by leaving the king free to exclude an elected candidate for a nominee of his own. The cardinal had no illusion about the value of elections in such circumstances, and presented a point-by-point rebuttal of the council's case. [138] It proved necessary to mobilise all the cardinal's and the congregation's friends at court – among them Vincent de Paul, Bishops Séguier and Sanguin, and La Rochefoucauld's own niece, the marquise de Sénécey, governess to Louis XIV.[139] De Paul, then high in Anne of Austria's esteem and an influential member of the *conseil de conscience*, worked energetically to produce the desired result,[140] while La

affaires changeront à présent, et que l'on fera de vostre congrégation comme Msgr le prince a faict de celle de Cluny, et qu'il assure avoir prétension à vostre abbaye, ce qui balance les esprits entre l'espoir et la crainte': B.S.G., MS. 3251, fos. 484–5, Hallay, provost of Nîmes, to Boulart, undated.

136. B.S.G., MS. 3310, fos. 561–2, Faure to Boulart, 5 February 1644, where he claims that the regent's *maréchal de logis* had threatened to quash the cardinal's resignation unless assured of a pension. Faure feared such individuals might succeed, 'comme ils ont fait la première fois'.

137. B.S.G., MS. 632, fos. 24–9, act of resignation, 2 February.

138. *Ibid.*, fos. 126–7, 'instruction dressée par le cardinal de la Rochefoucault pour la conservation de l'élection de l'abbaye de Ste Geneviève de Paris, présentée au Roy en 1644'.

139. Boulart's numerous letters from court, in some cases three or four a day, give a full account of these negotiations, and the extraordinary sense of insecurity at Ste Geneviève: B.S.G., MS. 3312, fos. 3, 7, 13, 149, 185, 199; MS. 3311, fos. 624, 626, 633; MS. 3313, fo. 310v. Faure's papers also contain letters and memoranda on this matter: MS. 3263, fos. 710, 713, 720, 736.

140. B.S.G., MS. 3275, fo. 550, Faure to de Paul, 21 June 1644, requesting him to use his influence with Anne of Austria, adding obliquely 'si ce n'est que vous cognoissez quelque cause secrete qui soit pour rendre toute prière et solicitation inutile'. One can only speculate on what he may have had in mind.

Rochefoucauld had to write personally to the enigmatic Mazarin before he would sign the *brevet* in late June.[141] Génovéfain fears were such that there was no relaxation until all the necessary papers had been signed and dispatched to Rome.[142] But, as luck would have it, Urban VIII died shortly after the papers arrived. Fortunately, La Rochefoucauld promptly obtained new letters from the French court, but while Innocent X readily granted his request, it was not until December 1644 that Guérin could finally dispatch the bulls to Paris.[143]

By then, Faure was dead, and had been succeeded by Blanchart. Although La Rochefoucauld knew at the time of Blanchart's election in November 1644 that Innocent X had approved his request, the cardinal nevertheless refused permission to elect Blanchart full abbot of Ste Geneviève, for fear of making procedural mistakes which might be seized upon later.[144] When the bulls arrived, he quickly summoned an extraordinary general chapter for this purpose. It met on 13 February 1645, and immediately elected Blanchart to succeed him as abbot.[145]

The timing of the succession was perfect, for La Rochefoucauld died peacefully the next day. Not surprisingly, contemporaries, early biographers and providentialist historians saw in it the hand of God. From a different perspective, it is plain that the cardinal lived just long enough to keep his reform on a survival course, and clear of the serious dangers that arose in France after the deaths of Richelieu and Louis XIII. Although briefly threatened during the Fronde, it continued to grow steadily following La Rochefoucauld's death. By 1650, its membership had risen to fifty-nine houses, approximately one third of the total number for the kingdom. Ste Geneviève had become an important religious centre, its abbot an influential and respected figure, and La Rochefoucauld's reform a permanent part of the religious map of *ancien régime* France.

---

141. B.S.G., MS. 3263, fo. 708, Faure to Boulart, undated. Only La Rochefoucauld's subsequent letter of thanks to Mazarin has survived: B.S.G., MS. 3250, fo. 329, 28 June. See *Correspondance de St Vincent de Paul*, ii, pp. 463–4, de Paul to Faure, 26 June, announcing the signature of the *brevet*.
142. B.S.G., MS. 632, fos. 174–7, text of *brevet*; *ibid.*, fos. 178–85, letters from Louis XIV to Urban VIII, Cardinal Antonio Barberini, Protector of France, and Ambassador St Chamond.
143. B.S.G., MS. 3314, fo. 450; MS. 3312, fo. 452; MS. 3313, fos. 143–4, 244–7, for Guerin's reports from Rome, October–December 1644.
144. B.S.G., MS. 3312, fo. 425, draft of petition in Boulart's hand for election after Faure's death.
145. B.S.G., MS. 633, fos. 44–6, letter of convocation, 11 January 1645; *ibid.*, fos. 251–70, act of election and *procès-verbal* of the chapter.

9

Cluny and Cîteaux:
Experiences of Failure

I

THERE COULD BE no greater contrast to La Rochefoucauld's reform of
the canons-regular than his stormy encounters with the orders of
Cluny and Cîteaux. Whereas his success with the former was a matter
of immense patience and tenacity, his efforts with the latter two orders
were essentially brief, charged with the dramas of high politics, and
spectacularly unsuccessful. The contrast is likely to be instructive on
several counts and I shall therefore study his dealings with Cluny and
Cîteaux together, with the object of adding a further dimension to the
history of his reform commission.

In view of La Rochefoucauld's failure with Cluny and Cîteaux, it is
ironic that his efforts to reform them are much better known than his
dealings with the other orders. Since the work of the Benedictine Paul
Denis, published over seventy years ago, relatively little has been
added to our knowledge of La Rochefoucauld's reforms in Cluny and
among the Benedictines.[1] But Denis's work was to some extent
marred by his excessive adulation of Richelieu, for in comparison with
his reign as abbot-general of Cluny, La Rochefoucauld's commission
appeared as little more than a curtain-raiser. The more recent work of
Krailsheimer, Lekai and Zakar has shed a searching light on Cistercian
affairs, especially because their accounts are based on authentic
original sources – many of which they published – rather than on
traditional secondary authorities of dubious value.[2] Lekai and Zakar, it

1. *Richelieu et la réforme des monastères bénédictins* (Paris, 1912). The most important additions
   have come from Dom Guy Charvin, especially his edition of Edmond Martène, *Histoire de
   la congrégation de St Maur*, 10 vols. (Ligugé, 1928–56); see also his useful survey,
   'L'Abbaye et l'ordre de Cluny de la fin du xve jusqu'au début du xviie siècle 1485–1630',
   Revue Mabillon, 43 (1953), pp. 85–117; 44 (1954) pp. 6–29, 105–32.
2. A J. Krailsheimer, *Armand-Jean de Rancé, Abbot of La Trappe. His Influence in the Cloister and
   the World* (Oxford, 1974); *idem.*, ed., *The Letters of Armand-Jean de Rancé, Abbot and*

may be noted, are themselves Cistercians, concerned essentially with the rise of their order's Strict Observance. Their perspective on reform is wholly Cistercian, shaped by a tradition which tends to regard outside intereference in the affairs of religious orders as unwarranted, misconceived and destructive. But there is ample justification for a different perspective– that of general church reform. The great merit of their work is that it enables us to take for granted much of the narrative detail and, with the exception of moments where such detail is crucial, to concentrate on the broad issues at stake in La Rochefoucauld's dealings with the two orders.[3]

La Rochefoucauld's failure to reform either Cluny or Cîteaux, which generated so much resistance and controversy, owed much to the highly institutionalised, even centralised, structure of those orders. Their respective heydays had long since passed, but they remained intensely proud of their history and glorious traditions. La Rochefoucauld, however, was to be confronted by more than history and tradition, potent as these might be; their contemporary members and institutions had a more direct bearing on the course of his efforts at reform.

Cluny had been governed since its inception by an abbot-general elected for life. Moreover, the abbey of Cluny and its monks traditionally played a decisive role in the affairs of the order as a whole, as the cardinal's experiences will show.[4] Nothing, therefore, symbolised Cluny's decline more than the fact that it was held *in commendam* without interruption between 1485 and 1622, being from 1528 onwards in the hands of an increasingly incompetent line of Guise abbots-general.[5] In consequence, practical responsibility for the affairs of the order devolved on the abbey's grand prior, but he lacked the authority and status required to bear that burden satisfactorily. Moreover, the affairs of the abbey itself were dominated by a small group of officials and dignitaries known from their place of assembly as the 'senieurs de la Voûte'. They were a proud, self-selecting oligarchy

Reformer of La Trappe, 2 vols. (Kalamazoo, Michigan, 1984); Louis J. Lekai, *The Rise of the Cistercian Strict Observance in Seventeenth-Century France* (hereafter Lekai, *Rise of Strict Observance*); Polycarp Zakar, *Histoire de la stricte observance de l'ordre cistercien depuis ses débuts jusqu'au généralat du cardinal de Richelieu 1606–1635* (hereafter Zakar, *Histoire*). For other works by Lekai, see Bibliography.

3. Two-thirds of Zakar's work is comprised of original sources, many of them from La Rochefoucauld's papers in B.S.G., MS. 3247, and published *in extenso*. He also devoted careful attention to establishing the authenticity and veracity of the manuscript sources, and has clarified many controversial problems relating to them.

4. See David Knowles, *From Pachomius to Ignatius. A Study in the Constitutional History of the Religious Orders* (Oxford, 1966), ch. 2, for a convenient brief survey; Guy de Valous, 'Cluny', in *Dictionnaire d'histoire et de géographie ecclésiastiques*, xiii, cols. 35–174, for a useful historical account.

5. Charvin, 'L'Abbaye et l'ordre de Cluny', pp. 105ff; Bergin, 'Decline and Fall of Guise Ecclesiastical Dynasty', pp. 785, 790; *idem.*, 'The Guises and their Benefices', pp. 46–7.

whose interests led them to clash with grand priors and abbots alike, while their attitudes would be crucial to the outcome of any effort at reform.

Cîteaux, although it began life as a breakaway from Cluny, was a less unified order. Its abbot also claimed to be general of his order, but in practice his authority was either shared with, or contested by the four 'proto-abbots', as they were called, of Clairvaux, La Ferté, Morimond and Pontigny, each of whom exercised direct authority over the houses that constituted what were known as their 'filiations'. This federal structure represented a major limitation on the abbot-general's power, a screen between him and individual Cistercian houses. Clairvaux in particular had traditionally resisted Cîteaux's claims, and was perenially suspected of having separatist tendencies. The ensuing tensions were never far under the surface, and put a strong premium on unity of both policy and purpose among the order's leading abbots.[6] Such unity was increasingly elusive by the seventeenth century, and was more likely to occur when an outsider like La Rochefoucauld intervened in the order's affairs. But the leading Cistercian abbeys were at least more successful than Cluny in escaping the *commende*. This good fortune was not without its negative features, and failed to prevent either wilful government or nepotism by the leading abbots.[7] As La Rochefoucauld would discover to his cost, abbatial elections were crucial events in Cistercian affairs.

Both orders had some experience of reform before 1622, but here, too, the differences between them are instructive. Each had suffered extensive damage to member houses during the wars of religion. Partly because of the *commende*, Cluny was in an especially demoralised state, and failed to generate a reform movement of its own. But it was not immune to changes occurring within the wider Benedictine community, of which it formed part. Older observant congregations like Chezal-Benoît or the Exempts no longer had anything positive to offer – like St Victor among the canons-regular. Reform, when it came, originated in Lorraine in the shape of the congregation of St Vanne which, in 1610, obtained qualified royal permission to expand in France. Eight years later, its French houses assumed the name which would make them famous – the congregation of St Maur. The future Maurists quickly attracted attention within France, even though at first the speed with which they reformed houses was no greater than that La Rochefoucauld was to accomplish among the canons-regular.[8] It was they, as we saw earlier, who were recommend-

6. See Louis J. Lekai, *The White Monks* (Okauchee, Wisconsin, 1953); Knowles, *From Pachomius to Ignatius*, ch. 4.
7. Zakar, *Histoire*, pp. 33–40.
8. They reformed only five houses between 1610 and 1618, with thirty-six monks. Thereafter, the pace of reform accelerated: the congregation had thirty-eight houses by

ed as the agents of a reformed congregation proposed for St Germain-des-Près in 1613, the year in which they also established an initially fragile foothold among the Cluniacs by assuming direction of the Paris College of Cluny.[9]

Within Cluny itself, government lay in the hands of its grand prior from 1612 onwards, Jacques Veny d'Arbouze (abbot-general after 1622), a committed reformer who proved unable to generate much impetus for an internal reform movement. He gradually became convinced that only through some kind of co-operation with St Maur could Cluny reform itself. After initial talks with St Maur and other reformers in Paris in 1618, he decided to aim at creating a purely voluntary observant community within the Abbey of Cluny but, despite the support of the abbot, Cardinal Louis III de Guise, the reform statutes which were approved in May 1621 evoked little enthusiasm in Cluny.[10] D'Arbouze, therefore, continued to look to the Maurists, making successive offers to them in 1621 and 1622, the second of which involved sending a number of Maurists to Cluny to introduce their observance there, in return for which they would receive part of its revenues and certain key offices. But the infant congregation was wary of such a momentous step, and soon concluded – perhaps because of d'Arbouze's own uncertainty and isolation – that the offer was too vague for them to act upon.[11] By the time La Rochefoucauld's commission arrived, there had been some negotiation and legislation, but little practical progress towards reform. Yet the notion of some form of co-operation between Cluny and St Maur had been seriously raised, and was to remain central to all future visions of a reformed Cluny.

Cîteaux, on the other hand, had generated its own reform movement, the famous Strict Observance. Since the Council of Trent, the order had had a series of active abbots, who attempted to promote reform throughout the order, with several proto-abbots making similar efforts within their own filiations. The Abstinent movement, as the Strict Observance was also called, initially developed among the daughter-houses of Clairvaux, under the leadership of Denis Largentier, and was distinguished after 1614 by a total abstinence from meat.[12] But even before then, the reform had raised problems, and it has been

1630 and seventy-eight by 1642: See Terence L. Dosh, 'The Growth of the Congregation of St Maur, 1618–1672' (Ph.D dissertation, University of Minnesota, 1971), pp. 22–3, 87, 110.

9. Martène, *Histoire de St Maur*, i, pp. 19–90, for the most detailed account of the Maurists' early years; Dosh, 'The Growth of St Maur', ch. 1; Denis, *Richelieu*, pp. 3–5. See above, p. 145.
10. Denis, *Richelieu*, doc. no. 5, for the text of the ordinance, dated 19 May 1621.
11. *Ibid.*, pp. 5–13, especially pp. 9–13, where the texts of d'Arbouze's offers and of Maurists' responses are printed in full.
12. Zakar, *Histoire*, ch. 2; Lekai, *Rise of Strict Observance*, ch. 2.

suggested that it was only the election of Nicolas II Boucherat as Abbot of Cîteaux in 1604 which dissuaded Largentier and his followers from forming their own own breakaway organisation.[13] The subsequent course of the reform only served to intensify fears and suspicions of Clairvaux. Largentier gave his blessing as well as positions of importance in his filiation to younger Abstinent leaders like Octave Arnolfini, Etienne Maugier, Jérôme Petit and others. Most of them felt frustrated by the relatively slow progress of the reform – it numbered only about ten houses by 1622 – and were, therefore, predisposed to see La Rochefoucauld's commission as a God-given opportunity to reform the order as a whole.[14]

La Rochefoucauld had had dealings of some significance with both orders well before 1622. In 1612, while in Rome, he received the post of Protector of the Cistercian order and, rather unusually, retained it on returning to France the following year.[15] It did not empower him to interfere at will in the order's concerns, though had he remained in Rome, it would have made him more familiar with Cistercian affairs. However, he was certainly aware of developments within the order: Denis Largentier, knowing his support for reform among the orders, corresponded with him after his return to France.[16] There is some irony in this, since it seems to have been La Rochefoucauld who persuaded Louis XIII to block moves to secure royal and papal confirmation of the election, in 1620, of Denis Largentier's nephew, Claude, as his coadjutor with succession rights, on the grounds of Claude's alleged indifference or hostility to the Strict Observance.[17] If La Rochefoucauld did indeed do so, it was an act which prefigured the stance he would subsequently take when he became reform commissioner.

La Rochefoucauld's pre-1622 involvement with Cluny was more restricted, yet it was directly linked to the problem of its reform. He was, as we saw earlier, instrumental in terminating the *commende* there in 1621–2 by insisting that Cluny revert to elected monk-abbots who alone, he argued, were equipped to promote the reforms that the abbey and order so badly needed.[18] His advocacy enabled d'Arbouze's hasty election as abbot-general in 1621 to win the necessary royal and papal approval the following year. In August 1622, d'Arbouze wrote

13. Lekai, *Rise of Strict Observance*, p. 31. Zakar, *Histoire*, doc. no. 2, for the text of Largentier's letter of 1604 to cardinal Givry, which forms the basis of this argument.
14. Zakar, *Histoire*, especially pp. 52–61.
15. B.S.G., MS. 3247, fo. 11, papal brief of 21 May 1612.
16. *Ibid.*, fos. 26, 28, 30, 38, Largentier's letters to Richelieu, from December 1616 to September 1621.
17. Zakar, *Histoire*, pp. 61–2; Lekai, *Rise of Strict Observance*, pp. 37–8; B.S.G., MS. 3247, fo. 36, Clairvaux community to La Rochefoucauld, 19 February 1621; *ibid.*, fo. 50, 5 February 1623, copy of revocation of royal approval of Claude Largentier's election.
18. See pp. 131–2 above.

to La Rochefoucauld welcoming his commission, which had only just come into force, and offering to co-operate with his plans for Cluny.[19]

II

In the event, it was not until early 1623 that La Rochefoucauld turned his attention to Cluny and Cîteaux. What determined the entire course of his later dealings with them, was the kind of approach he took to their reform. Although his papal commission gave him extensive powers, it did not in itself pre-determine his approach, especially among highly structured orders like Cîteaux and Cluny. Would he take the initiative or would he content himself with a modest, secondary role of assisting reform movements where they already existed? Historians, especially from the orders in question, have generally expressed surprise and incomprehension that he opted to lead from the front, by attempting to engineer large-scale change, both in institutions and observance. With the canons-regular, the specific character of this choice was masked by the amorphousness of the order. This was not the case with Cluny and Cîteaux. It was not tactical considerations which led him to make similar choices for all three orders. The arguments that he deployed in 1619–20 over the reform of the orders reveal clearly his basic conviction that a *general* reform was essential, and that partial ones were too easily overpowered by hostility, indifference, and litigation. It was a conviction that he repeated during his years as commissioner.[20] If this made it likely that, in 1622–3, he would attempt reform on a general scale in Cîteaux and Cluny, it may also have prevented him from appreciating the kinds of conflict it would create.

La Rochefoucauld's council first discussed Cistercian reform in late January 1623, but there had almost certainly been earlier exchanges involving members of the Strict Observance.[21] No Cistercian was present at the first council meeting, but it was the proposals aired there which formed the basis of the 'articles particuliers' for Cîteaux which the cardinal published on 11 March 1623.[22] The fact that his 'articles particuliers' for the canons-regular, and his general ordinances

19. B.S.G., MS. 3240, fo. 81, letter of 30 August.
20. He even sought papal absolution in the early 1630s for not implementing his commission to the letter: B.S.G., MS. 3238, fos. 329–30, letter and memorandum to Etienne Charlet S.J., in Rome, 12 April 1632.
21. B.S.G., MS. 3247, fo. 42, Denis Largentier to La Rochefoucauld, 17 September 1622; *ibid.*, fo. 44, same to same, 17 November 1622; *ibid.*, fos. 48–9, J. Depoutz, prior of l'Isle-Adam, to La Rochefoucauld, 4 February 1623, alluding to earlier talks.
22. The text of the January proposals is in Zakar, *Histoire*, doc. no. 10.

for all the orders were published on the same day, highlights the similarity of his approach to the different orders.

La Rochefoucauld's plans for the Cistercians will be partly familiar from what we have seen of the canons-regular. The most significant of them was his decision to divide the order into reformed congregations, the first of which would be based on Clairvaux and its filiation, in which the Abstinents were already strong. He justified this innovation by a potentially damaging reference to earlier reforms in Spain and Italy, where such congregations had, he argued, been the key to success. With their own elected leaders and officials, the future congregations would be largely removed from effective control by the abbots of Cîteaux or Clairvaux. Even monk-abbots, where they existed, should be elected at regular intervals. This was one of many departures from Cistercian tradition, and reflected the cardinal's dislike of superiors and officials who possessed authority for life. As with the canons-regular, visitations of the abbeys designated as members of the new congregations would follow, during which monks would be divided into two communities – those who accepted his ordinances, and those who did not. Other clauses are equally familiar: certain houses would be designated as novitiates; monastic 'stability' was to be understood in relation to the congregations, not to individual houses; and so on.[23]

These articles were signed – after undocumented but probably limited discussions – by ten Cistercian leaders who, if they did have misgivings, kept them to themselves. But they made it difficult for abbots like Boucherat and Largentier to square their commitment to reform with their obligation to protect the interests of the order. Boucherat conveyed his dilemma to La Rochefoucauld some weeks after their publication, and asked for the cardinal's understanding should circumstances force him to conceal his own personal convictions.[24] He was referring to the order's general chapter, which was then imminent. It met in May 1623 and, although poorly attended, it took a very different view of La Rochefoucauld's statutes. Not only did it denounce them as destructive of the order's unity, it also berated Boucherat for his earlier consent. Clairvaux's separatist reputation made the delegates nervous of the effect of La Rochefoucauld's plans for the order. On the other hand, the chapter, perhaps equally nervous of open confrontation with him, encouraged the immediate implementation of reforms that it held to be consistent with Cistercian traditions and customs.[25] Consequently, Boucherat could write to La

23. *Ibid.*, doc. no. 11.
24. B.S.G., MS. 3247, fo. 60, Etienne Binet S.J., to La Rochefoucauld, 8 May 1623, reporting a conversation with Boucherat.
25. *Statuta capitulorum generalium ordinis Cisterciensis*, ed J.M. Canivez, 8 vols. (Louvain, 1933–41), vii, pp. 342–9.

Rochefoucauld both to defend the propriety of the chapter's decisions, especially its rejection of the proposed congregations, and to express the hope that he would see its work as positive.[26] The cardinal, who had already experienced evasion of his decrees by the orders, may not have been convinced by such arguments but, although he acted quickly to prevent the chapter's statutes from being ratified by Rome, chose to reserve judgement and give Boucherat the benefit of the doubt.[27]

This wait-and-see attitude was reinforced by the reform activities of Boucherat and Largentier immediately after the chapter. Visitations of the major abbeys, including Cîteaux itself, were conducted, and plans laid for the establishment of designated novitiates.[28] More significantly, while stopping short of fostering the Clairvaux-based congregation that La Rochefoucauld had proposed, Boucherat took several steps which further attenuated the chapter's rejection of his ordinances. He not only appointed Etienne Maugier vicar-general of the Strict Observance, but by allowing him to hold chapters of the Observance, he enabled him and his followers to run their own affairs.[29]

The effect of this was to make La Rochefoucauld somewhat redundant as far as Cistercian reform was concerned; had nothing untoward occurred, his subsequent involvement with it might have remained limited and low-key. At any rate, he was in no hurry — perhaps because of his other commitments — to force the pace of Cistercian reform in the eighteen months following the 1623 chapter. It took events of an entirely different order, beginning in late 1624, to precipitate such direct involvement, and to open a very different episode in both the order's history and La Rochefoucauld's commission.

III

By then, however, La Rochefoucauld was deeply immersed in the affairs of Cluny. Formal discussions about its reform began several months later than for Cîteaux, partly because d'Arbouze was engaged in conducting extensive visitations, and partly because he was not installed as Abbot of Cluny until April 1623. Although the general ordinances of March 1623 extended to Cluny, discussion of specific

26. B.S.G., MS. 3247, fo. 69–70, 1 June 1623. Printed in Zakar, *Histoire*, doc. no. 12.
27. B.S.G., MS. 3247, fo. 74, La Rochefoucauld to Christophe Balthazar S.J., in Rome, referring to two earlier letters on Cistercian affairs; *ibid.*, fo. 73, for his letter to Roman agent, Duboucherys.
28. *Ibid.*, fos. 65–7, 71–2. For accounts of the implementation of these measures, Zakar, *Histoire*, pp. 68–70; Lekai, *Rise of Strict Observance*, pp. 44–5.
29. J.D. Lelockzy, ed., *Constitutiones et acta capitulorum strictioris observantiae ordinis Cisterciensis 1624–1687* (Rome, 1967), p. 145, for Boucherat's letter to Maugier, 28 July 1623.

'articles particuliers' did not commence until two months later. But early signs of a lack of enthusiasm within the order for the cardinal's commission had already emerged. In February 1623, the community at Cluny demanded that the forgotten 1621 statutes be implemented, and even agreed to 'suffer', as it put it, the presence at Cluny of a few Maurists in order to learn about their observance.[30] The two delegates whom it then sent to Paris to accompany d'Arbouze in talks with La Rochefoucauld were authorised to accept a Maurist-sponsored reform, but warned not to surrender any of Cluny's privileges.[31] When news spread that Abbot d'Arbouze and Cluny's delegates, Pierre Lucas and Claude Bridet, were in Paris to discuss reform with La Rochefoucauld, St Maur and other religious leaders,[32] an unofficial meeting of Cluniacs protested that the impending changes would destroy Cluny by handing it over to another order, and called for a general chapter which would speak for the the entire order.[33] D'Arbouze argeed to transmit this protest to La Rochefoucauld on 19 June but, possibly because of the recent events of the Cistercian general chapter, the cardinal decided to ignore it and to threaten action against opponents.[34] Within a week, he published his 'articles particuliers' for Cluny.

The articles were drastic and far-reaching, going far beyond anything d'Arbouze had previously conceived. They aimed at a permanent union of St Maur and Cluny in a single congregation. The latter might be called the congregation of Cluny, in deference to its status and history, but its observance would be that of St Maur. La Rochefoucauld's strategy was to reform and control the order through the abbey of Cluny itself. The future congregation's general would be the Abbot of Cluny, elected for five-year terms by those monks who had embraced the reform. As with the other orders La Rochefoucauld was attempting to reform, the *anciens* would be pensioned off, assigned to separate houses, forbidden to receive or profess new members and, consequently, faced with extinction; in that way, the reform would eventually embrace the entire order. Meanwhile, d'Arbouze himself, whose offer to resign had been turned down by La Rochefoucauld, would remain Abbot of Cluny for life, although his coadjutor and eventual successor would be the general of St Maur; real authority over the new congregation would be vested in the general from the outset,

30. A.N., LL 1334, fos. 11–16, *procès-verbal* of 23 February 1623.
31. B.S.G., MS. 3240, fos. 108–10, procuration to Pierre Lucas and Claude Bridet, both of whom had earlier petitioned La Rochefoucauld to unite Cluny with St Maur in the interests of reform: B.S.G., MS. 3240, fo. 243, 13 February 1623.
32. B.S.G., MS. 3240, fo. 243, Lucas and Bridet to La Rochefoucauld, April 1623. These meetings are undocumented, but they are referred to in B.N. MS. Fr. 17669, p. 611.
33. The source for this opposition is the pamphlet entitled *Union entre l'ordre de Cluni et la congrégation de St Maur* (Paris, 1623), pp. 22–6.
34. B.S.G., MS. 3240, fo. 114, *procès-verbal* of 19 July.

with the Abbot of Cluny being confined to governing the unreformed *anciens* and administering the order's non-religious affairs.[35]

That these ordinances were detailed, complex, and even cumbersome suggests that they were a series of compromises worked out by La Rochefoucauld and his advisers, who alone signed them. D'Arbouze, Lucas, Bridet and the Maurists gave a separate undertaking to observe and implement them, and to regard his commission as the proper framework for reform – a precaution which may also have been suggested by recent Cistercian reaction to his efforts at reform.

The next step was to secure acceptance of the articles by Cluny and St Maur. The latter ratified them at its 1623 general chapter, albeit with a certain trepidation, given the size and past of an order as powerful as Cluny, and with the explicit proviso that the union take place on the exact terms laid down by the cardinal.[36]

With Cluny, matters were different – and infinitely more complex. No sooner had the articles been published than La Rochefoucauld commissioned d'Arbouze and others to visit a large number of Cluniac houses in northern and central France, as a result of which the abbot was absent from Cluny for several months.[37] During that interval, the mood in the abbey changed considerably, and opposition to the cardinal's intervention ripened unchecked. Soon after their return from Paris, Lucas and Bridet were accused of exceeding their powers and of agreeing to changes contrary to the order's best interests.[38] A more prosaic squabble over offices between Cluny's leading members further envenomed internal relations, overlapping with, and fuelling the development of, an anti-reform party.[39] Lucas and Bridet continued throughout late 1623 to assure La Rochefoucauld that a majority of Cluny's monks still favoured reform, while their opponents repeatedly challenged them to admit that they had violated their instructions and that, consequently, La Rochefoucauld's ordinances were not binding on Cluny.[40] D'Arbouze returned in September 1623, having encoun-

35. *Ibid.*, fos. 116–17, for the original text with autograph signatures. Printed in Denis, *Richelieu*, doc. no. 22.

36. B.N. MS. Fr. 17669, p. 621.

37. B.S.G., MS. 3240, fos. 126–9, for the visitation commissions, 7 July 1623.

38. *Ibid.*, fo. 149, Lucas and Bridet to La Rochefoucauld, 5 August 1623; B.N. MS. Bourgogne 87, fo. 93, Lucas and Bridet to Mathieu Molé, *procureur général* of the Paris *parlement*, 5 August. For a disavowal of their actions by some of Cluny's members: D.S.G., MS. 3240, fos. 151–3, 5 August 1623, with their rejection of the protest as groundless.

39. This struggle loomed even larger than the question of reform in the second half of 1623, if the volume of surviving documentation relating to it is a reliable guide. The numerous papers on it in B.S.G., MS. 3240 were briefly calendared by Denis, *Richelieu*, pp. 17–18, n. 5.

40. B.S.G., MS. 3240, fo. 170, Bridet to La Rochefoucauld, 3 September 1623; B.N. MS. Bourgogne 87, fo. 99, interrogation of Lucas and Bridet, 16 October; B.S.G., MS. 3240, fo. 194, d'Arbouze to La Rochefoucauld, 29 October.

tered little enthusiasm for the proposed reform during his visitations, but frequent demands for a general chapter.[41] With Cluny itself in turmoil he was soon suggesting to La Rochefoucauld that there might be no alternative but to hold a chapter.[42] The cardinal was against such a concession, and insisted that he would continue with his reforms. This left d'Arbouze with the task of eliciting a decision from his abbey, but he could only persuade thirteen monks to commit themselves to supporting La Rochefoucauld's ordinance in late October 1623.[43] Moreover, it was increasingly evident that d'Arbouze lacked the qualities of leadership that the situation required. His opponents, especially among the leading dignitaries, found it easy to outmanoeuvre him and, by suddenly altering their demands, to keep him on the defensive.[44] In late October 1623, they demanded the implementation of the 1621 statutes, yet by January 1624, they were asking La Rochefoucauld to send Maurists to Cluny for further talks on reform.[45]

Such inaction and deadlock were obviously a serious disappointment to La Rochefoucauld. Moreover, d'Arbouze's pathetic reports on the state of his abbey and pleas for sympathy could not conceal the fact that he was gradually shifting his position, albeit under cover of simply conveying to La Rochefoucauld the views of his monks.[46] If the commissioner was to pursue his designs any further, new talks with Cluny and St Maur were needed. The presence of d'Arbouze and others in Paris in June 1624 provided such an opportunity. When La Rochefoucauld reiterated his determination to continue his efforts, his council advised him to despatch two Maurists to Cluny to establish the abbey's real position, obtain statements of intent on the reform from individual monks, and impose a general ban on receiving or professing novices other than at St Martin-des-Champs in Paris, which La Rochefoucauld intended bringing under Maurist control.[47]

The Maurists were, understandably, perturbed by the turn events

41. B.S.G., MS. 3240, fos. 130–1, 138, 162, 408, 410–13, 417, 421–2, 431; B.N. MS. Bourgogne 87, fos. 102–5, for records of the visitations.
42. B.S.G., MS. 3240, fos. 180, 182, 184, letters to La Rochefoucauld, 9 and 11 October 1623.
43. B.S.G., MS. 3240, fos. 186–7, 199, register of declarations with signatures, 20 and 31 October.
44. *Ibid.*, fos. 172–6, 'Memorial de ce qui s'est passé au fait de la réforme depuis l'arrivée de Monsieur [l'abbé], le jeudy 21 Septembre', written by Lucas and Bridet; *ibid.*, fo. 186, rejection of La Rochefoucauld's articles and threat of *appel comme d'abus* unless the 1621 ordinances were enforced, 20 October; *ibid.*, fo. 188, similar demand, 26 January 1624.
45. Charvin, 'L'Abbaye et l'ordre de Cluny', p. 122, n. 65, for request to negotiate with Maurists. D'Arbouze felt obliged to implement the 1621 statutes on a provisional basis.
46. B.S.G., MS. 3240, fos. 262–3, d'Arbouze to La Rochefoucauld, 6 February 1624; *ibid.*, fos. 277–8, same to same, 7 March; *ibid.*, fo. 279, consultation for La Rochefoucauld on d'Arbouze's letter; *ibid.*, fo. 280, d'Arbouze to La Rochefoucauld, 2 May.
47. *Ibid.*, fos. 335–6, *procès-verbal* of 24 July 1624, which gives details of earlier talks with Cluniacs.

had taken during the past year, and their general chapter would only consent to sending delegates to Cluny on condition that they would not have to re-negotiate any of La Rochefoucauld's original terms for its reform.[48] Their delegates finally arrived at Cluny in early December 1624, to be greeted by effusive expressions of delight and satisfaction.[49] Discussions began in earnest when d'Arbouze returned a few days later, and the euphoria rapidly vanished. Soon a bewildering range of changes and demands was tabled by the 'senieurs de la Voûte', the ordinary monks and, finally, d'Arbouze himself, the cumulative effect of which was to make La Rochefoucauld's planned reforms virtually unrecognisable. The 'senieurs' claimed they wanted union with St Maur and to elect a general from the reform movement; but they also insisted that the ordinary Cluniac observance be preserved, and retain a full role in the future affairs of the order. Some officials presented personal demands which ran counter to La Rochefoucauld's efforts to deprive monastic offices of their semi-proprietary status.[50] The simple monks added their conditions: they would accept the cardinal's reform but insisted on retaining their privileges, on remaining subject to the abbot's authority, and on their 'stability' within Cluny itself.[51] These various demands were compiled and then approved by the abbey. D'Arbouze, still the subject of much animosity, was evidently shaken by this behaviour and, fearing that he might be left empty-handed, decided to formulate his own demands, in which he rejected the need for a coadjutor-abbot: the reform could make do with a simple vicar-general. But above all, he wished to re-claim his unrestricted spiritual and temporal authority as abbot for life.[52]

The final version of these responses − known as the 'Eclaircisse-ments' − was approved on 20 December 1624, and given to the Maurists for transmission to La Rochefoucauld as evidence of Cluny's desires to serve his 'pieux desseins', and of its members' honest efforts 'to satisfy our zeal and charity for the implementation of such a holy undertaking'.[53] But even d'Arbouze, who claimed that Cluny's response did not contradict the tenor of his articles, had to concede that the 'Eclaircissements' contained many things 'which go against

48. Denis, *Richelieu*, pp. 24−5, Maurist chapter to La Rochefoucauld; B.N. MS. Fr. 17669, pp. 738−9, for the chapter's resolutions; Martène, *Histoire de St Maur*, i, pp. 177−81.
49. B.S.G., MS. 3246, fo. 6, Martin Tesnière, general of Maurists to Mareschal, legal adviser to La Rochefoucauld, 9 December; *ibid.*, fo. 4, Henri Girard, *procureur général* of Cluny, to same, 9 December.
50. B.S.G., MS. 3240, fos. 436−7, 441−2; B.N. MS. Fr. 17669, pp. 739−43, 747.
51. B.S.G., MS. 3240, fos. 442−3.
52. *Ibid.*, fos. 437−9; B.M. MS. Fr. 17669, pp. 743−5.
53. B.S.G., MS. 3240, fo. 435, Dom Jean Sesse, grand prior, to La Rochefoucauld, 20 December, 'pour satisfaire au zèle et charité que nous avons à l'establissement d'un si sainct oeuvre'.

the articles issued in Paris...and for which we shall do everything that your lordship shall decree'.[54]

The Maurists, who refused to engage in direct negotiations with Cluny, reported to La Rochefoucauld in early January 1625.[55] By then further additions to the 'Eclaircissements' had reached him, removing whatever illusions either he or the Maurists may have retained on the prospects of his planned reform. Yet for some reason, he took his time before responding to Cluny.[56] When he did so, sometime in mid-1625, his reply was uncharacteristic of a man known for his tenacity: in a private letter to d'Arbouze, he resigned his commission for Cluny, leaving the task of reform to the abbot 'suivant le deub de sa charge'.[57] Shortly afterwards, the Maurists' general chapter followed his lead, finding Cluny's demands so self-contradictory 'que nous n'y avons pu rien répondre'.[58]

Thus ended the most short-lived of all La Rochefoucauld's efforts to reform a major order. We may doubt whether he expected d'Arbouze to succeed where he had failed. The beleaguered, ageing abbot did continue his efforts after 1625, but to no avail.[59] Perhaps the most ironic twist to the Cluny affair came when its first elected monk-abbot in a century and a half, whom La Rochefoucauld had seen as essential for a successful reform, took the first step towards restoring the *commende* there. But it was not to the general of St Maur, with whom relations had virtually ceased, that d'Arbouze turned in his search for a coadjutor with full succession rights, but to a cardinal whose power promised greater results than La Rochefoucauld ever could hope to deliver — Richelieu. The latter accepted with alacrity and, indeed, had to apply firm pressure on the reluctant monks of Cluny in order to secure his 'postulation' as coadjutor.[60] If he did not acquire immediate control of Cluny's affairs, he was in a strong position to veto any important decision about the order. In the event, he did not have to wait long, for d'Arbouze resigned in 1629, leaving Richelieu in undisputed control of Cluny's affairs. By the mid-1630s, he was ready to embark on reform plans which were closely modelled on La Rochefoucauld's — a union of St Maur and Cluny. It is hardly

54. *Ibid.*, fo. 433, letter to La Rochefoucauld, 20 December, 'qui répugnent aux articles accordés à Paris...pour lesquels nous ferons tout ce qu'il plaira à Monseigneur d'ordonner'.
55. Martène, *Histoire de St Maur*, i, p. 181; B.N. MS. Fr. 17669, p. 752.
56. B.N. MS. Bourgogne 87, fo. 124, Tesnière to Henri Girard, 12 January 1625, 'Je ne sçay point la cause de ce silence'.
57. A.N., LL 1334, fo. 34v. This source gives no indication of the date or specific contents of the cardinal's letter.
58. Martène, *Histoire de St Maur*, i, p. 182, for the text of their reply.
59. Denis, *Richelieu*, pp. 30–1.
60. Avenel, *Lettres, Mémoires et instructions diplomatiques de Richelieu*, ii, pp. 369, 460, 501, for his correspondence with d'Arbouze and Cluny over the coadjutorship; the official acts are in Denis, *Richelieu*, docs. no. 49–51(b), especially the 'postulation' of Richelieu as coadjutor, dated 17 April 1627.

surprising, therefore, that at no time after 1627 was there any question, either in France or in Rome, of extending or renewing La Rochefoucauld's commission for the reform of Cluny.

IV

By the time that La Rochefoucauld was ready to turn his back on Cluny in mid-1625, his Cistercian commission was also well on the road to collapse. A new phase had opened in October 1624 with the death of the Abbot of Clairvaux, Denis Largentier, whose leadership had been so central to the growth of the Strict Observance that its future progress seemed to depend on the attitude of his successor. His nephew, Claude, had been elected as coadjutor in 1620 despite Abstinent opposition led by Etienne Maugier, but that election had never been approved by Rome.[61] For his part, Abbot Boucherat of Cîteaux feared that a damaging succession dispute in 1624 would exacerbate relations with Clairvaux, so he immediately recognised Claude Largentier as its legitimate, properly elected abbot, and obtained royal approval of his succession. Maugier and the Abstinents were dismayed by this move, but Boucherat firmly rejected their request for a new election. They turned instead to La Rochefoucauld, who had earlier helped to block papal approval of Claude's original election, and persuaded him that the future of the reform was now at stake. La Rochefoucauld authorised a fresh election, and Maugier was predictably 'elected' Abbot of Clairvaux by those present. The cardinal's intervention on 'abbot' Maugier's behalf led to the royal approval, previously secured by Boucherat for Claude Largentier, being withdrawn, but this success proved to be no more than the beginning of a prolonged and increasingly bitter war of attrition between the two observances, in which La Rochefoucauld lent his full support to the Abstinents.[62] Enlisting the combative support of the *parlement* of Paris at a time when the crown was distracted by foreign and domestic policy problems, Largentier and his followers gradually gained the upper hand,[63] and in February 1626, Louis XIII finally

---

61. Zakar, *Histoire*, pp. 61–2; Lekai, *Rise of Strict Observance*, pp. 37–8. Maugier had pressed Claude Largentier to come out in favour of the Abstinent observance, but he had refused to do so. He was accordingly believed to be opposed to it.
62. B.S.G., MS. 3247, fo. 434; B.N. MS. Fr. 3677, fo. 59v, Ambassador Béthune to Secretary of State Phélypeaux, Rome 4 December 1624; B.N. MS. Fr. 3667, fo. 54v, Louis XIII to Béthune, 3 January 1625, repeating instructions to prevent Largentier's election from being confirmed.
63. Zakar, *Histoire*, pp. 72–4; Lekai, *Rise of Strict Observance*, pp. 46–7. Both Zakar and Lekai assume rather than prove that La Rochefoucauld was simply doing the bidding of the Strict Observance. The texts of the *parlement*'s four decrees against La Rochefoucauld are printed in the appendix to the *Remontrances très-humbles par les religieux de l'ordre de Cîteaux au Roy* (Paris, 1635).

relented and confirmed him as Abbot of Clairvaux. From that moment onwards, the house that had been the best hope for reform was lost forever to the Strict Observance.[64]

Meanwhile, the death in May 1625 of Abbot Boucherat himself threatened to engulf the entire order in conflict, since the matter of his succession had not been settled. La Rochefoucauld, for his part, was less anxious to take a direct part in the ensuing election than to extract from the victorious candidate a promise to implement his articles of 1623, and despatched Charles Boucherat, the young and plausible Abbot of Pontigny, to Cîteaux for that purpose.[65] But Boucherat soon revealed his ambition to succeed his uncle and, although not an adherent of the Strict Observance, it was inevitably assumed that he was the candidate who enjoyed the cardinal's support.[66] The result was another bitterly contested election.[67] Boucherat was initially 'elected' abbot by his supporters at Cîteaux, but a full chapter elected Pierre Nivelle. Disputed elections, which had become increasingly rare in France since the Concordat of Bologna, could only be settled by the crown, and La Rochefoucauld persuaded Louis XIII to set both elections aside, and to fix a new election for November 1625. Nivelle again easily worsted Boucherat.[68] Although Louis XIII approved Nivelle's election, Boucherat refused to acknowledge defeat, and his campaign was successful to the extent that the papacy, uncertain of Nivelle's reputation, refused to confirm him as abbot and, in late December 1625, commissioned La Rochefoucauld to investigate his election.[69] This he duly did, presenting to the king a case against Nivelle which contained many ludicrous and trivial charges which he had no doubt picked up from the Abstinents. It was accompanied by an impassioned appeal for Louis's support for what he had been attempting to do since 1622, and a defence of his decision to found reformed congregations, whose beneficial effects in other countries he underlined. The election of an Abstinent abbot-general, far from encouraging the secession of non-French houses, would preserve the order's unity, fragmentation being far more likely if Cîteaux remained unreformed within France. Finally, since the electors had so manifestly

64. A.N., LL 988, fos. 388–90.
65. B.S.G., MS. 3247, fo. 98, commission dated 23 April 1625. Boucherat did not in fact die until 8 May, and La Rochefoucauld had acted upon a rumour of his death. Such behaviour was common enough for other church offices during this time, as is clear from Richelieu's correspondence: *Les Papiers de Richelieu*, ed. Pierre Grillon (6 vols. to date, Paris, 1975–, in progress).
66. B.S.G., MS. 3247, fos. 100, 102–3, 105–6, for his correspondence with the cardinal.
67. For details on the election(s), see Lekai, 'The Abbatial Election at Cîteaux in 1625', *Church History* 39 (1970), pp. 30–5.
68. A.N., LL 988, fos. 309–17, the 'instrument' of Nivelle's election, which contains a long account of earlier events, and of the king's intervention.
69. Zakar, *Histoire*, p. 77, n. 73, for reference to the papal brief of commission.

abused their privileges, these were now forfeit, and the king might legitimately exercise the right to fill the office and further the cause of reform.[70]

Coming from the pen of a defender of 'ecclesiastical liberties', such a conclusion may evoke surprise, but nothing reveals more clearly the extent to which La Rochefoucauld had espoused the Abstinent cause. His arguments, especially about foreign reformed congregations, also suggest a fear that the king might be swayed by the 'nationalist' charges being made against his ordinances. Yet, perhaps because of the Clairvaux election, the outcome at Cîteaux was no more satisfactory, and the final verdict came even more swiftly. Nivelle's election was confirmed in January 1626, even before that of Largentier, and both were approved by the pope a few months later.[71]

It was events like this, which he did not encounter in any of the other orders, that precipitated the collapse of La Rochefoucauld's first Cistercian commission. He had gambled for high stakes in conventional monastic politics, and lost heavily. The sudden disappearance in such quick succession of Largentier and Boucherat was bound to create problems, and La Rochefoucauld could not remain indifferent to the outcome of the resulting elections. The possession of authority and the pursuit of reform could not be readily separated in an order like Cîteaux. The elections themselves polarised animosities and deflected Cistercian energies into power-struggles in which means and ends quickly drifted apart, particularly in the case of Cîteaux itself. La Rochefoucauld was thereafter compromised by his open support of the Abstinents and their noisy attempts to achieve by a *coup de main* what they had so far failed to achieve through persuasion. Perhaps the surest indication of La Rochefoucauld's mistaken tactics and judgement was the failure of his usually reliable ally, Louis XIII, to support him over either Clairvaux or Cîteaux, and without royal support on major questions his commission became unworkable.

V

In view of the events of 1624–6, the revival of La Rochefoucauld's commission – for three years this time – for the Cistercians in September 1632 must count among the principal surprises of his career as reformer of the old orders. Nothing is known of the background to the pope's decision, apart from his declaration that he

70. B.S.G., MS. 3247, fos. 97–8, 329, 392–5.
71. Lekai, 'Abbatial Election', p. 34. He is almost certainly wrong in claiming that royal approval of Nivelle was given on 13 January 1626, since La Rochefoucauld had probably not conducted his enquiry, let alone submitted it to the king by that date.

was acting in response to a petition from Louis XIII, and that Louis was dissatisfied with the current progress of reform. But who convinced the king of this?[72] Cistercian historians have seen in this move the hand of the Strict Observance, but this can no more be proved than the suggestion that La Rochefoucauld himself persuaded the king to seek a renewal of his commission.[73]

It is clear that Cistercian affairs had gone rather badly since Nivelle's election in 1625. Nivelle's personal support for reform was beyond doubt but, like d'Arbouze in Cluny, he never commanded anything like the respect enjoyed by Boucherat or Denis Largentier, and his leadership was continually contested by the proto-abbots. Although he personally practised abstinence, and confirmed Maugier as vicar-general of the Strict Observance in 1628, he was under strong pressure to curtail the autonomy enjoyed by the Abstinents. The latter had made little progress, controlling no more than fifteen houses in 1630, and would certainly have had grounds for welcoming a new initiative on reform.[74] By 1632 the conflicts of 1624–6 would have faded sufficiently for the king and the pope to contemplate another commission for Cîteaux.

But the renewal of La Rochefoucauld's Cistercian commission was bound to be controversial within the order. The clock could not be put back to 1622, nor previous conflicts ignored. He was now faced with Cistercian leaders who were intensely suspicious of his support of the Strict Observance, and who regarded his previous reform ordinances as destructive. The unknown factor was how the cardinal, now in his mid-seventies and as suspicious of the order's leaders as they were of him, would use his new powers as commissioner.

If La Rochefoucauld had sought a new brief in order to put Cîteaux to the test, he took an unconscionably long time to make his first move. This was probably due to other commitments and distractions, such as the St Victor affair and his efforts to reform the great Benedictine Abbey of St Denis near Paris.[75] It was not until August 1633 that he summoned a large number of Cistercian leaders to talks at Ste Geneviève, but these had to be postponed twice until early November.[76] Even then, Nivelle declined to attend, alleging that his

---

72. B.S.G., MS. 3247, fos. 3–7, for the text of the brief [printed in Zakar, *Histoire*, doc. no. 19]; *ibid.*, fos. 7v–9, for the royal letters-patent, 17 December 1632.
73. Zakar, *Histoire*, pp. 85–6; Lekai, *Rise of Strict Observance*, p. 52.
74. Lekai, *Rise of Strict Observance*, pp. 49–51; Zakar, *Histoire*, pp. 78–84.
75. This reform, which even Richelieu regarded as unlikely to succeed, made a considerable impact on contemporaries, and underscored the continuing co-operation between La Rochefoucauld and the Maurists. La Rochefoucauld saw it as the best way to begin exercising the reform commission for the Benedictines that he also received in 1632; MS. 3240, fos. 554–5. The voluminous, official acts of the reform are in A.N. L 833. Further accounts and papers in B.S.G., MS. 3240, fos. 522–37.
76. B.S.G., MS. 3247, fos. 131–6, 138, for the invitations to talks issued at different dates. They were delivered by notary, lest the recipients attempt to claim they had not been properly informed.

poverty prevented him from travelling to Paris until the spring of 1634.[77] One did not need to be as suspicious as La Rochefoucauld to regard this response as hostility to his plans, yet as if to underline his determination, the cardinal pressed ahead with his consultations on 8 November. Less than half of those summoned actually attended, and among those who did the Abstinents were in a comfortable majority. While this was significant in that it set a pattern for the rest of the cardinal's term as commissioner, the November discussions were important above all in that they laid the foundations for his subsequent decisions.

The timidity with which the Common Observance admitted the need for certain changes and improvements contrasted sharply with the readiness of the Strict Observance to take control of the entire order. In a well-supported attack, Maugier asserted that the best means of reforming the order would be to entrust to the Abstinents the spiritual and temporal administration of its leading abbeys, although he conceded that this would require the co-operation of the proto-abbots. But no decisions were taken at the November meetings, except to send Maugier to Cîteaux to brief Nivelle and persuade him to participate in the discussions.[78] The abbot's response was again evasive – he would only travel to Paris if La Rochefoucauld genuinely required his presence and promised to uphold his authority as general.[79]

Meanwhile, the cardinal had begun receiving written proposals for reform. Charles Boucherat, speaking for the Common Observance, argued that each proto-abbot should undertake to reform his own filiation, in accordance with Cistercian and Gallican traditions. Abstinence he dismissed as divisive and unimportant in comparison with the effects on monastic observance of the *commende*, which he urged La Rochefoucauld, for whom he appears to have envisaged no other role, to tackle.[80] In early 1634, the Strict Observance elaborated on their earlier suggestions, the full scope of which was gradually unfolding. Their takeover of the order would begin with Cîteaux and Clairvaux, and thereafter reform would develop along lines familiar from other orders subject to La Rochefoucauld's commission: the two abbeys, and later their filiations, would be peopled with Abstinents,

77. *Ibid.*, fos. 144–5, letter of 6 October. Printed in Zakar, *Histoire*, doc. no. 20. Nivelle's lack of co-operation and delaying tactics were evident from his insistence on seeing the cardinal's brief, and from his failure to inform his fellow-abbots. La Rochefoucauld's suspicion of him must have increased when, on 1 November, he summoned a general chapter to meet in May 1634.

78. *Ibid.*, fos. 146–50, *procès-verbal* of 8 November; *ibid.*, fo. 151, *procès-verbal* of 15 November; *ibid.*, fo. 154, for résumé of speech made by Charles Boucherat at assembly.

79. *Ibid.*, fo. 160, letter to La Rochefoucauld, 20 December 1633.

80. *Ibid.*, fos. 157–8, dated 19 November. Printed in Zakar, *Histoire*, doc. no. 22. The effects of the *commende*, which La Rochefoucauld was powerless to interfere with, was a common theme of Boucherat's interventions in the Cistercians' encounters with the cardinal.

their unreformed *anciens* transferred elsewhere, deprived of the right to participate in the order's affairs, to receive or profess novices, and so on. The audacity of this plan was clear to its authors for, although they still expressed the hope of gaining the proto-abbots' co-operation, they stressed the need to win the prior support of Louis XIII, of Richelieu, of Séguier (keeper of the seals), of Séguier's brother (Bishop of Auxerre and a royal commissioner), and even of the Prince of Condé who, as governor of Burgundy, would be useful in countering the anticipated hostility of the *parlement* of Dijon.[81]

In subsequent years, even after La Rochefoucauld had ceased to be commissioner, the Abstinents remained faithful to the basic elements of this strategy. But what they regarded as zeal for God's house, appeared to their opponents as the delusions of reckless power-hungry conspirators. In early 1634, however, everything still depended on La Rochefoucauld and his close advisers. While he had not made up his mind which steps to take, his commission had reached half-term, and Nivelle and the other Cistercian leaders seemed to be intent on evasion and time-wasting. He therefore launched further consultations in mid-February 1634, but as no member of the Common Observance attended, the discussions inevitably served to further the aims of the Abstinents. Maugier reported on his fruitless mission to Nivelle, but the dominant figure in the assemblies was Eustache de St Paul, a leading member of another reformed Cistercian congregation, the Feuillants, and an influential adviser to La Rochefoucauld on religious reform. If, he argued, the measures previously tabled were the proper way to achieve reform, the cardinal should appoint his own vicar-general for the reformed observance, place the strategic College of St Bernard in Paris and the Roman office of *procureur général* in Abstinent hands, delegate commissioners to supervise the transfer of Cîteaux and the exchange of monks between monasteries and, above all, erect special novitiates.

These recommendations were accepted by La Rochefoucauld's advisers, but no decisions were taken, as La Rochefoucauld still hoped to obtain the co-operation of Nivelle and his fellow abbots.[82] Their continuing unwillingness to come to Paris prompted him to use, for the only time during his commission, royal *lettres de cachet* to oblige them to do so, and to postpone the general chapter Nivelle had summoned for May 1634.[83]

The final and decisive confrontation began on 2 May, with La Rochefoucauld declaring to the assembled Cistercian abbots that the

81. *Ibid.*, fos. 163—8.
82. *Ibid.*, fos. 168—75, *procès-verbal* of meetings of 16 and 18 February 1634.
83. No copy of the *lettres* has come to light, but the abbots' replies on receiving them are in B.S.G., MS. 3247, fos. 197—203.

task of reform was theirs, 'nous contentant en cela de mestre seulement nostre nom de commissaire apostolique pour l'honneur de Sa Saincteté'. They admitted the need for certain reforms, but urged La Rochefoucauld to visit houses first and only issue decrees later, imploring him not to believe hearsay evidence about the state of the order – an obvious reference to the Abstinents' tactics. Apparently, he took none of this amiss, and even adjourned the meetings for a few days when the abbots requested further time for reflection.[84] By 5 May, however, Nivelle and his colleagues had changed their tactics, and proposed that La Rochefoucauld's *general* ordinances of 1623 for all the orders, but not his 'articles particuliers' for Cîteaux, should be the basis of reform, because 'à présent il n'estoit poinct besoin d'en faire d'aultres'.[85] But La Rochefoucauld was infuriated by what he saw as Nivelle's efforts to restrict even these ordinances, and angrily accused him and his supporters of bad faith and a lack of genuine religious spirit. The exchanges quickly degenerated into invective, and Nivelle led his fellow-abbots in a dramatic walk-out.[86]

In the event, this was not to be the final break between the two sides, but if a break had come closer, this was partly because La Rochefoucauld was also under great pressure from the Strict Observance to deliver the order into their hands. He was increasingly influenced by a future leader of the Strict Observance, the young Abbot of Prières, Jean Jouaud. He had been urging La Rochefoucauld to give the Strict Observance full independence from the order's superiors, and to visit and transfer to the Abstinents the College of St Bernard, which Jouaud claimed was corrupt and riddled with abuses; as the principal Cistercian house of study, it could easily be transformed into a seminary for the entire order.[87] Within days of the confrontation of 5 May, La Rochefoucauld swooped on the college for a visitation. But while the records of his inspection prove that Jouaud's charges were unfounded, the cardinal accepted the hostile evidence supplied by members of the Strict Observance there, and promptly invited the royal commissioners to Ste Geneviève to take the appropriate decisions.[88] This move shook Nivelle and the proto-abbots, and prompted them to make a further effort to conciliate La Rochefoucauld by offering to receive Abstinents in a number of major abbeys, to impose total abstinence for half of the year, to establish full

---

84. *Ibid.*, fos. 209–12, *procès-verbal* of 2 May.
85. *Ibid.*, fos. 217–22, for the text of Nivelle's proposals.
86. *Ibid.*, fos. 212–14, *procès-verbal* of 5 May.
87. *Ibid.*, fos. 406, 418–19, for Jouaud's papers. Printed in Zakar, *Histoire*, docs. no. 24–5.
88. *Ibid.*, fos. 229–41, *procès-verbal* of visitation. Printed in L.J. Lekai, 'The Parisian College of St Bernard in 1634–1635', *Analecta Cisterciensia* 28 (1972), pp. 194–204. The visitation record was also signed by several royal commissioners – Bishops Sanguin and Séguier, Lezeau, Verthamon – and by Maugier and Jérôme Petit, Cistercian abbot of l'Etoile.

novitiates, to relegate unworthy monks to other abbeys, and to confirm whoever the cardinal might appoint as vicar-general in France and *procureur général* in Rome. But they also defended the order and the reputation of the College of St Bernard, and again urged La Rochefoucauld to tackle the problem of the *commende*. Their gesture came too late: La Rochefoucauld was no longer capable of believing in their promises, and he informed Nivelle that he would press ahead with his own plans.[89]

The Cistercian leaders took this threat seriously, and quickly made a secret appeal against La Rochefoucauld to Louis XIII, using a mixture of religious and political arguments to persuade him to defend one of the glories of his kingdom. They also requested permission to convene their general chapter, and expressed a willingness to discuss reforms with royal councillors not compromised by involvement with La Rochefoucauld, whose plans they rejected outright.[90] Equally alert to political realities, they sought the personal protection of the 'génie tutelaire de l'estat' – Richelieu.[91]

The Cistercians also appealed to Rome where, in view of his earlier experiences, especially with St Victor, La Rochefoucauld was himself taking steps to protect his interests.[92] At the same time, no doubt anticipating trouble, he hastily assembled his reform ordinances and attempted to use the Séguier brothers to secure their approval and implementation.[93] What happened next is not fully clear. Ubaldini wrote from Rome on 15 July informing him that the Cistercian appeal had been lodged there, and that it had royal support, but the Cistercians had probably served formal notice of their appeal on him before the letter arrived.[94] La Rochefoucauld realised that he had a struggle on his hands and, in order to regain the initiative, he took a step that was unprecedented in the history of his reforms – that of publishing his as yet unapproved ordinances.[95] The *Projet de Sentence*, as it was called, was prefaced by a letter to the king in defence of his actions as reformer of Cîteaux, and couched in terms familiar from his other appeals. The *Projet* itself encapsulated most of the ideas that had been aired in his council since November 1633: the order would be handed over to a minority, beginning with the abbey of Cîteaux but

89. B.S.G., MS. 3247, fos. 250–2, for the Cistercian proposals. Printed in Zakar, *Histoire*, doc. no. 27.
90. Zakar, *Histoire*, doc. no. 28, for appeal, undated but probably June 1634.
91. *Ibid.*, doc. no. 29, undated letter.
92. He relied on the ex-nuncio and vice-protector of the Cistercian order in curia, Cardinal Ubaldini. La Rochefoucauld's letter to him has been lost, but it can be inferred from Ubaldini's reply of 15 July 1634: B.S.G., MS. 3247, fo. 256. Printed in Zakar, *Histoire*, doc. no. 33.
93. B.S.G., MS. 3247, fo. 464, 14 July 1634. Printed in Zakar, *Histoire*, doc. no. 32.
94. B.S.G., MS. 3247, fo. 264–5. Printed in Zakar, *Histoire*, doc. no. 34.
95. For a discussion of the problems surrounding the composition, dating and publication of this document, see Zakar, *Histoire*, pp. 126–31.

gradually spreading to others as well; the leading abbots would be left in place but, flanked by Abstinent assistants – a tactic La Rochefoucauld later attempted with the Mathurin general – they would become virtually powerless.[96]

La Rochefoucauld's controversial tactic of publishing the *Projet* sparked off a bitter pamphlet war which lasted several decades, turning the gap separating the two Cistercian observances into a chasm.[97] These events elicited a perceptive and almost despairing comment from the Abstinent Abbot Arnolfini of Châtillon:

> I am afraid that the Cardinal does not fully understand the power of our order, or the weakness of the houses that wish to band together...the good cardinal's advanced age, the times we are living in, Rome's lack of concern for reform, our dependence on a privy council which changes in accordance with the way in which favours are dispensed, the *parlement* here in Burgundy, the powerful friends that our abbots possess in the royal council – all this keeps me in a state of uncertainty.[98]

In the event, La Rochefoucauld failed to win approval for his *Projet* from Louis XIII and his ministers, a failure which undoubtedly stems from Richelieu's willingness to accept the Cistercian appeal for protection.[99] Although Richelieu kept his true intentions to himself, his attitude ensured that the initiative rapidly slipped away from the commissioner. Abbot Arnolfini's prediction of a tangle of politically-induced intrigue proved correct and, in the following year, events turned, as might be expected, entirely to the advantage of Richelieu, whose tactics were straightforwardly opportunist. Slowly at first, he and his advisers began to take a discreet interest in Cistercian affairs. Talks began in earnest in November 1634, leading to an important conference at Royaumont in March 1635 at which Richelieu's confident, the Capuchin Père Joseph, proposed a set of measures that were quite generous to the Strict Observance. Despite this and some ap-

96. Zakar, *Histoire*, doc. no. 31. The cardinal's prefatory text, known as the *Motifs de la Sentence*, is in B.S.G., MS. 3247, fos. 274–81. Zakar, *Histoire*, p. 95, n. 51, sees the hand of abbot Jouaud in it.

97. See Lekai, 'A Bibliography of Seventeenth-Century Pamphlets and Other Printed Material relating to the Cistercian Strict Observance', *Analecta Cisterciensia* 19 (1963), pp. 105–44.

98. '(Je) crains que Monsieur le Cardinal ne comprend pas bien la puissance de nostre Ordre et la foiblesse des maisons qui se veulent unir...L'aage du bon seigneur, et le temps auquel nous sommes, le peu de sentiment qu'on a à Rome de reforme, dépendre du privé conseil qui varie à mesure que les faveurs roulent, ce parlement de Bourgogne, le amis de nos Messieurs qui entrent au conseil...me font tenire en suspends.' Zakar, *Histoire*, doc. no. 35, letter to his nephew and coadjutor, Joseph Arnolfini, 10 August 1634. The corruption of this text is due to the fact that the letter was intercepted and published by the Common Observance; the original has been lost.

99. Despite a personal appeal from La Rochefoucauld in August 1634: Zakar, *Histoire*, doc. no. 36.

proving statements about La Rochefoucauld's reforms, Richelieu succeeded in retaining the goodwill of the Cistercian abbots.[100] La Rochefoucauld was still commissioner, and his pro-Abstinent stance continued to worry them.[101] By remaining personally aloof and working through Père Joseph and other advisers, Richelieu allowed the abbots to see him as their saviour. Above all, in acceding to their demand for the general chapter that La Rochefoucauld had denied them, he both increased their gratitude and further tightened his grip on the order's affairs.[102]

La Rochefoucauld, predictably, disliked these developments, and his council was severely critical of the Royaumont proposals.[103] But although his legendary determination remained as strong as ever, his room for manoeuvre was now drastically limited. In early July 1635, he approached Richelieu through Père Joseph in a last effort to get his reform ordinances approved before his commission lapsed in early September.[104] The reply was surprisingly positive: the cardinal himself supported his aims, and sent two members of his entourage to confer with him on how best to implement them. The unsuspecting commissioner requested a rapid transfer of the principal abbeys to the Strict Observance while he still had the authority to do so.[105] While awaiting Richelieu's reply, La Rochefoucauld took a decision that he would repeat for the Mathurins in 1638. He may have had doubts about Richelieu's intentions, but the latter proved as good as his word – or almost.[106] On 2 September, with only a week to spare, Louis XIII approved the cardinal's ordinances, but limited their application to the College of St Bernard.[107] If this artful piece of brinkmanship disappointed La Rochefoucauld, he did not show it, for within a few days of his commission's lapsing, he visited St Bernard and handed it over to the Strict Observance.[108]

100. Zakar, *Histoire*, doc. no. 40, Royaumont articles of 25 March 1634. See *ibid.*, pp. 100–5; Lekai, *Rise of Strict Observance*, pp. 63–5.
101. For instances of his pro-Abstinent actions, see the texts in Zakar, *Histoire*, docs. no. 38–9, and the Cistercian abbots' renewed appeal to Richelieu for his protection in December 1634; *ibid.*, doc. no. 39.
102. *Ibid.*, doc. no. 43, Louis XIII to Nivelle, 6 May 1635, permitting the convocation of the chapter for 1 October 1635; *ibid.*, doc. no. 44, Nivelle's summons of chapter, 1 June 1635.
103. B.S.G., MS. 3247, fos. 323–6. Printed in Zakar, *Histoire*, doc. no. 41.
104. B.S.G., MS. 3247, fo. 330. letter of 6 July, accompanied by an explanatory memorandum: *ibid.*, fos. 332–3. Printed in Zakar, *Histoire*, docs. no. 45–6.
105. B.S.G., MS. 3247, fos. 338–9. Printed in Zakar, *Histoire*, doc. no. 49.
106. This, and the realisation that the Abstinents were numerically small, may explain why he issued a provisional decree on 20 August 1635 preserving the autonomy of the Strict Observance should the planned general reform fail to materialise: B.S.G., MS. 3247, fos. 366–9. Printed in Zakar, *Histoire*, doc. no. 51.
107. B.S.G., MS. 3247, fo. 370. Printed in Zakar, *Histoire*, doc. no. 53.
108. B.S.G., MS. 3247, fos. 346–50, 354–8. The first document is printed in Lekai, 'The Parisian College of St Bernard in 1634–1635', pp. 205–8.

This proved to be his last act in a drama that would reach its climax only after he had left the stage. It had the effect, as Richelieu doubtless intended it should, of making the beleaguered Cistercian leaders even more dependent upon him. Once La Rochefoucauld's commission had expired on 9 September, Richelieu had an entirely free hand to pursue his own policies. By the time the general chapter met a few weeks later, its original purpose of enabling the Cistercians to regain control of their own affairs and to distance the order from La Rochefoucauld, had become irrelevant; it had been replaced by one that had been slowly evolving in previous months – the resignation of Pierre Nivelle in order to pave the way for the election of Richelieu as abbot-general of Cîteaux.[109]

La Rochefoucauld gave no sign of resenting Richelieu's opportunism in exploiting his commission for personal ends. Indeed, when the younger cardinal later revealed his own plans for the reform of Cîteaux, which proved – as at Cluny – to be remarkably similar to La Rochefoucauld's, the latter expressed his wholeheated support. It was probably from Rome that La Rochefoucauld's greatest disappointment was to come, one that almost certainly fuelled the despondency of his last years at papal policies over reform. In September 1635, he set about convincing the curia that the Cistercian appeal against him should be judged promptly in Rome, and not sent before a minor French ecclesiastical judge.[110] What the papacy denied him in the case of St Victor, Solminihac and, later, the Mathurins, it provided in that of the Cistercians, though he can hardly have anticipated either its speed or decisiveness. In mid-November 1635, the congregation of bishops and regulars roundly condemned the transfer of St Bernard to the Abstinents.[111] Three weeks later, which was exceptionally rapid by Roman standards, the pope condemned all ordinances contrary to the statutes and privileges of Cîteaux.[112] La Rochefoucauld was not mentioned by name, but there was no doubt about the implication of the decision. La Rochefoucauld had never been so comprehensively disowned by the papacy as a reformer of the orders.

The papacy's haste, which contrasts so sharply with its dilatoriness in respect of other appeals against La Rochefoucauld, was probably conditioned more by political than by religious factors, and chief

---

109. This dependence is perfectly clear from the hyperbolic letter addressed to Richelieu by the general chapter delegates: *Statuta capitulorum generalium*, vii, pp. 388–90, 1 October 1635.
110. B.S.G., MS. 3247, fos. 382–3, (September) 1635. Printed in Zakar, *Histoire*, doc. no. 56.
111. Zakar, *Histoire*, doc. no. 60, 16 November 1635.
112. *Ibid.*, doc. no. 65, brief of 5 December 1635. Perhaps the greatest irony of events in 1635 is that Richelieu prevented the publication in France of the brief condemning La Rochefoucauld's ordinances, because, given its broad scope, it might have hindered his own projects for the order.

among these was Richelieu's success in adding control of Cîteaux and, in 1636, of Prémontré, to that of Cluny. La Rochefoucauld had unwittingly proved to be a stalking horse for Richelieu in both Cluny and Cîteaux, if much less directly in the case of Cluny. Success in acquiring Cluny probably bred in Richelieu the ambition to add Cîteaux, and the confrontation between La Rochefoucauld and the Common Observance provided the opportunity he so skilfully exploited.

Nevertheless, Richelieu's efforts to reform Cluny and Cîteaux were to be equally unhappy failures, albeit masked while he lived by his combined powers as abbot-general and chief minister, which were infinitely greater than those La Rochefoucauld possessed as papal commissioner. Within a short time of his death in 1642, his reforms had collapsed, and there was no one either powerful or determined enough to resume the challenge thereafter.

Did La Rochefoucauld's reforms fail because his entire approach was misconceived? Cistercian historians would have little hestitation in agreeing. What he proposed for both Cîteaux and Cluny only differed slightly from what he partly achieved among the canons-regular, but the presence among the former of powerful interests and traditions, as Abbot Arnolfini intimated, made it particularly difficult to get such measures accepted, let alone implemented. Nor did La Rochefoucauld sufficiently realise that in such orders, the more general the kind of reform being planned, the greater his need of a broad measure of support from within them. It is not clear, especially from Richelieu's failures, what anyone could have achieved in Cluny, and La Rochefoucauld did not take long to see the hopelessness of the whole entreprise. On the other hand, it was precisely because Cîteaux offered some hope of success that he persevered in his quest for results. If he did not create the order's internal divisions, his involvement in the election battles and his other confrontations with its leaders, denied him the authority to implement reforms which enjoyed a wide measure of support.

In more general terms, the experience of Cîteaux and Cluny shows how far La Rochefoucauld had become convinced that an enduring reformed observance could only survive within a congregational system with elective superiors and officials similar to the kind practised by the newer orders. But Cîteaux and Cluny posed particular problems that were more intractable than elsewhere. In Italy and Spain, reformed congregations received support and protection, partly because greater independence from the hegemony of French superiors was, for various reasons – some of them political – both popular and desirable. In France itself no such support could be counted upon. The Cistercians, and later the general of the Mathurins, both played this card against La Rochefoucauld to considerable effect. His advocacy of observant congregations along Spanish and Italian lines was far too guileless, blinding him to the fact that other forces were at work, and that they worked against him. He might well have royal support for his objectives, but with Cîteaux at least, he did not retain it for his methods.

10

La Réforme Introuvable: The Mathurins

I

IN MARCH 1635, the reformist group within the Mathurin order sent one of their number, Aléxis Berger, on a mission to Rome. Nothing is known of his activities there apart from their outcome – the despatch to La Rochefoucauld in October 1635 of a six-year commission for the reform of the Mathurins in France that was virtually identical to those issued to him since 1622.[1] Given the cardinal's long involvement with the orders, such a commission appears as the logical, almost inevitable conclusion to Berger's mission. Yet its genesis and subsequent history provide many significant points of contrast with his other commissions.

Several questions arise almost immediately. The most obvious is why the Mathurin *réformés* sought a commission at all, and then not until 1635? Why did the papacy, which in October 1635 was about to condemn La Rochefoucauld's Cistercian ordinances, grant him a new commission without a formal petition from the crown, as had hitherto been the rule? Furthermore, what was the validity in France of a commission issued in reply to an unofficial petition, and how would La Rochefoucauld attempt to implement it? Only some of these questions can be answered satisfactorily for lack of evidence, but a brief sketch of the order's internal history up to 1635 may provide a basis for understanding the events of that and subsequent years.

The Mathurins, also known in France as the *Trinitaires*, were a distinct branch of the canons-regular who had been founded in the twelfth century for the purpose of redeeming Christian captives from Islam.[2] Membership of the order is difficult to estimate, but a survey

---

1. B.S.G., MS. 3244, fo. 32, original text of the commission.
2. Paul Deslandres, *L'Ordre des Trinitaires pour le rachat des captifs*, 2 vols. (Toulouse-Paris, 1903), La Rochefoucauld's reform is briefly dealt with in vol. i. But Deslandres's narrative and interpretation of the cardinal's action is sketchy and often inaccurate – e.g. he claims that La Rochefoucauld died in 1641. Vol. ii is a collection of documents, some of which are relevant to this chapter, and will be cited by the number given them by Deslandres.

conducted by La Rochefoucauld in 1638 accounted for sixty-six French houses.[3] Although Spanish and Italian houses were both more numerous and more observant, the order's general was traditionally French, since only the four 'provinces' of northern France had the right to elect him. This monopoly was, not surprisingly, a source of internal division, with the French regarding it as a 'Gallican' privilege, and the non-French houses, especially those of Spain, pressing for greater autonomy for themselves. The split widened in the post-Tridentine period, when foreign houses were experiencing reform, and those of France civil war. Reform itself, when it got under way in France, exacerbated existing tensions, since reform groups there tended to seek closer ties with reformed houses abroad, thus placing them in the invidious position – one exploited by their opponents – of being suspected of complicity with separatists abroad.[4]

The first stirrings of Mathurin reform in France were confirmed in 1601 when Clement VIII made provision for superiors and visitors for the reformed houses, while safeguarding the general's own authority. François Petit, who was general at the time, responded positively to the pope's decision, and contributed to the growth of the reform. But this promising chapter ended abruptly in 1612, when Petit died and was succeeded by his nephew, Louis Petit. He treated the *réformés* as subversives, conspirators, and even criminals, and regarded the reform as a threat to his authority. He aimed not only to prevent its future growth, but also to undo Clement VIII's concessions and reduce the *réformés* to complete subordination. He pursued this policy unremittingly for over thirty years, and in doing so reduced the order to a collection of mutually antipathetic groups. He played off the desire of both crown and the papacy to promote internal reform against the former's instinct to underwrite Gallican privileges, and the latter's anxiety to protect legitimate, constituted authority.[5] But from the mid-1610s onwards his tactics began to annoy the curia, and in particular the order's protector, Cardinal Bandini, who consistently supported the *réformés* against Petit.[6] Indeed, it was Bandini who drew

3. B.S.G., MS. 3244, fos. 225–8, 'dénombrement, revenu annuel et taxes deues à la redemption des captifs...de ce royaume'.
4. Deslandres, ii, doc. no. 164, 28 March 1615, *réformés* seek union with the 'discalced' branch of the order, based in Rome.
5. For Petit's appeals to the crown, see B.N., MS. Fr. 18007, fo. 450v, Ambassador Brèves to Marie de Medici, 8 December 1612; B.N., MS. Nouvelles acquisitions françaises 460, fo. 284, Puysieux to marquis de Tresnel, ambassador in Rome, 17 June 1615; MS. Fr. 16050, fos. 314–15, Puysieux to Archibishop Marquemont, 20 May 1618; MS. Fr. 17364, p. 217, Louis XIII to Ambassador Coeuvres, undated [but *c.* September 1619].
6. Bandini's stance is well documented in his correspondence with the nuncios, Ubaldini and Bentivoglio: B.N., MS. Ital. 1268, fos. 384–5, Ubaldini to Bandini, 30 June 1614; MS. Ital. 1269, fos. 41–2, same to same, 6 September 1616. Bandini's extensive correspondence with Bentivoglio on Mathurin affairs between 1616 and 1619 is in Ferrara, Archivio di Stato, *fondo* Bentivoglio 18/40, fos. 133–4, 154–5, 157–60, 162–4. Rome's complaints against Petit are listed in Steffani, *Nunziatura di Bentivoglio*, ii, pp. 414–16.

La Rochefoucauld into the order's affairs during the later 1610s, by using him as an unofficial patron of the *réformés*.[7]

This pattern of internal dissension set in the 1610s continued into the 1630s. The *réformés* virtually achieved the status of an observant congregation in 1619, when Paul V confirmed his predecessor's concessions, and allowed them to elect vicars-general of their own for the provinces where they were strong, Provence and 'France', and also gave them the right to accept new houses anxious to join them.[8] Practical responsibility for implementing this decision was given to La Rochefoucauld, who presided over the *réformés'* first general chapter in March 1621.[9] But with few powers and faced with Petit's resolute hostility, La Rochefoucauld seems to have done little more than mediate in the internal disputes that continued during the 1620s.[10]

In many respects, the Mathurins' problems illustrate perfectly La Rochefoucauld's criticisms in 1619–20 of reform 'secondo il modo canonico'. Yet it is surprising that the order was not included in his 1622 commission. Gregory XV appears to have wished to see it return to its primitive rule, but confined himself in August 1622 to commissioning La Rochefoucauld to reform Cerfroid and Fontainebleau, two of its leading houses.[11] This approach might have generated a strategically-placed reform movement, but Gregory died soon after dispatching the brief, and it was not renewed by Urban VIII. Thereafter, it appears that the *réformés* were increasingly left to face Petit alone, and that by 1635, he had regained much lost ground, interfering almost at will in the *réformés'* affairs and thereby negating the effects of the papal grants of 1601 and 1619.[12] His success bred increasing resentment, and over the years the *réformés* seem to have become at least as much an anti-Petit party as an observant movement.[13] It is reasonable to suppose that it was Petit's growing

7. B.S.G., MS. 3248, fo. 225, Bandini to La Rochefoucauld, 26 July 1618. Other references to La Rochefoucauld's activities are contained in the sources listed in the previous note.

8. Its terms are given by B.N., MS. Dupuy 493, fos. 286–90.

9. B.S.G., MS. 3244, fo. 33, Bandini to La Rochefoucauld, 22 May 1622. La Rochefoucauld's letter, giving an account of his activities, to which Bandini refers, has not been found.

10. B.S.G., MS. 3244, fos. 51–6; B.N., MS. Fr. 3676, fo. 12, Louis XIII to Ambassador Béthune, 5 September 1624, requesting the pope to revoke recent concessions made to Petit; A.D., Seine-et-Oise 53 H 1, *avis* on Mathurin affairs signed by La Rochefoucauld and others, January 1627; B.N., MS. Dupuy 493, fos. 286–90, decree of king's council based on the *avis*, 19 March 1627.

11. Deslandres, ii, doc. no. 170, brief of 4 August 1622, for return to the primitive rule; *ibid.*, doc. no. 172, brief to La Rochefoucauld, 8 February 1623.

12. Abundant evidence in A.D. Seine-et-Oise 53 H 5, fos. 1–4, acts of chapters of *réformés* held at Montmorency, 1634–6; A.N. V⁶ 105, decree of *conseil privé*, 19 June 1635; B.S.G., MS. 3244, fos. 51–6, text of Petit's *appel comme d'abus* against La Rochefoucauld's reform commission in 1637, containing several references to earlier conflicts.

13. These disputes were frequently aired in public. See, for example, the pamphlet entitled

power which induced them to turn again to Rome in 1635, and to seek a reform commission for La Rochefoucauld. It was a move that was bound to open a new chapter in the order's internal conflicts.

II

Events moved very slowly after the grant of the commission in October 1635. Issued without royal support, the 1635 brief was of dubious validity, and was open to attack as having been obtained under false pretences. La Rochefoucauld rightly chose to virtually ignore it until it had received royal endorsement by letters-patent. Sovereign impartiality was essential in such matters, especially when faced by an opponent as experienced in exploiting procedural mistakes and other 'vices de forme' as Louis Petit. When royal confirmation of the papal commission seemed finally in sight, in April 1637, Petit appealed *comme d'abus* to the *parlement* of Paris, even citing La Rochefoucauld personally as a defendant in the case.[14] This roused the cardinal from his neutrality, but also provoked the intervention of the royal commission, where his allies were dominant. Having examined Petit's appeal, they cleared the way in early September 1637 for the issue of letters-patent to activate La Rochefoucauld's commission.[15] But years of experience and the warnings of his advisers made La Rochefoucauld unwilling to make any move until late December 1637, when the royal council had formally evoked Petit's appeal from the *parlement*.[16]

With the legal obstacles to his commission finally lifted, over two years after it had been issued, La Rochefoucauld was understandably anxious to press ahead. Most of what he attempted to do for the Mathurins was put together during six busy months between late December 1637 and June 1638. The sources for this period are abundant, and enable us to examine at uncommonly close range the

---

Défense pour le Révérendissime Père Général de tout l'ordre de la Sainte Trinté et Rédemption des captifs. . .contre la coniuration de frère Simon Chambellan et ses adhérens, sous le nom de Réformez dudit ordre (Paris, 1636) [B.N. Ld⁴³ 8].

14. B.S.G., MS. 3244, fos. 51–6, for the text of the appeal which the *parlement* upheld. Petit described La Rochefoucauld as 'non seulement suspect, mais aussi partie formelle' in the case. For La Rochefoucauld's own appeal to the royal commissioners against the *parlement*'s action: *ibid.*, fos. 7–8. Evidently Petit had succeeded in delaying the grant of the letters-patent in 1636, if we can judge by a letter from him to Chancellor Séguier, 6 October 1636: B.N., MS. Nouvelles acquisitions françaises 6210, fos. 53–4.

15. B.S.G., MS. 3244, fo. 169, decree of 7 September 1637; *ibid.*, fo. 31, for the letters-patent, also 7 September. The royal commission for the Mathurin reform included familiar figures like Lezeau, Verthamon and Bishops Sanguin and Séguier.

16. B.S.G., MS. 3244, fo. 49, decree of 4 December 1637. When formal notice of this was served on Petit on 12 December, he continued to protest against the cardinal's commission. *ibid.*, fo. 38.

genesis of his reforms, as well as the twists and turns in his dealings with the order and its different factions.[17]

La Rochefoucauld began his career as commissioner with a plenary meeting of his council on 20 December 1637, during which he alluded to the delays since 1635, the poor state of the order and the plight of the Christian captives in Muslim hands it seemed incapable of redeeming. He also expressed a desire to work in conjunction with the order in his efforts at reform. Petit both defended his own attempts at reform and promised to do whatever La Rochefoucauld judged necessary, while Simon Chambellan, visitor of the *réformé* province of 'France', also spoke in conciliatory fashion, recommending an enquiry into the state of the order. In reply, La Rochefoucauld asked him to submit his own views on the defects in its observance.[18]

Chambellan's report on the order, which was submitted within a few days, noted many inadequacies of observance, but emphasised the failure to use revenues designated for the redemption of captives, the order's *raison d'être*; money had indeed been raised, but Petit had never accounted for it. Invited to comment on these allegations, Petit blamed lack of funds and of co-operation from the *réformés* for this; he had, he insisted, held regular chapters at Cerfroid, at which he had given accounts of his stewardship. If there were relaxations in observance, these were the result of perfectly normal papal dispensations; allegations could surely be tested by a full visitation of the Paris house.[19]

La Rochefoucauld evidently hoped that Chambellan's report and Petit's response would form the basis of his council's discussions on 27 December, but he was soon reminded that as reform commissioner he had also inherited the bitter personal and factional feuds which continued to divide the order.[20] Despite his efforts to persuade Petit and the *réformés* to drop their quarrels, no sooner had the Chambellan and Petit submissions been read out, than the general declared the cardinal's commission to have been improperly obtained, demanding that the culprits be handed over to him. Their 'reformed' observance, he alleged, was spurious, and no more than a conspiracy to reject his own legitimate authority. Chambellan dismissed these charges as 'inventions' and pressed La Rochefoucauld to persevere with his aim of

---

17. The care with which these records were kept may well spring from La Rochefoucauld's fear of making procedural mistakes that Petit might pounce on. He had been given precise advice on this point at the beginning of his commission: B.S.G., MS. 3244, fos. 328–9.
18. B.S.G., MS. 3246, fos. 192–5, *procès-verbal* of 20 December 1637.
19. B.S.G., MS. 3244, fos. 65–7, memorandum of 24 December; *ibid.*, fos. 179–83, Petit's reply.
20. B.S.G., MS. 3244, fos. 57, 59–62, 71–2, 312–15, papers relating to one of these disputes.

a general reform. The cardinal's response was to delegate Charles Faure and Etienne Binet to examine the more detailed memoranda on the order that he now called for; in the meantime he strictly forbade both Petit and Chambellan to receive or profess novices without his express permission.[21] By the time his council next met, a few days later, memoranda, many of them highly critical of Petit, had evidently begun to pour in to Ste Geneviève, and La Rochefoucauld, in his anxiety to press on with matters of substance, had to warn the general to refrain from attacking opponents.[22] When the deliberations were finished, the cardinal commissioned Faure and Binet to visit the Paris house, which Petit himself governed.[23]

Faure completed his visitation before the next council meeting, at which La Rochefoucauld concluded that there was a 'deffaut essentiel d'observance regulière' in Petit's community, and declared that further visitations were necessary. This assignment also fell to Faure, who was to enquire into lapses of observance and ascertain which individuals were capable of promoting reform.[24] That La Rochefoucauld's list of houses for visitation included some belonging to the *réformés* may reflect a desire to be seen to be even-handed, but it is more likely that he was already having doubts about the nature of the existing reform.

The vastly experienced Faure was ideally suited for the difficult task of visitation. His reports, which reveal his thoroughness, unveiled the intense confusion which reigned within the order. Both sides, but especially the *réformés*, seemed to move their members around so much that their communities lacked real stability and, more seriously, regular observance. Few of those he questioned seemed to believe that the reform was superior to the old observance. Neither at Cerfroid or Montmorency, both leading houses, was a genuine reform felt to exist. Most of the simple members of the order appear to have been content to draw pensions and live off their families. Almost inevitably, the visitation provided yet another occasion for the venting of personal animosities against the leaders of the different factions, some *réformés* even inveighing against their own leaders, Chambellan in particular. In accordance with La Rochefoucauld's established practice elsewhere, Faure ended each visitation by banning the independent reception and profession of novices.[25]

Faure's visitation may have covered only the Paris-centred province of 'France', but it gave La Rochefoucauld and his council a solid basis

21. B.S.G., MS. 3246, fos. 195r–7v, *procès-verbal* of 27 December 1637.
22. *Ibid.*, fos. 197v–8v, *procès-verbal* of 30 December; MS. 3244, fo. 324, charges against Petit; *ibid.*, fos. 171–4, charges against Chambellan.
23. B.S.G., MS. 3244, fos. 73–4, commission to Faure and Binet, 30 December.
24. B.S.G., MS. 3246, fos. 198v–9r, *procès-verbal* of 7 January 1638; MS. 3244, fo. 75, commission to Faure, same date.
25. B.S.G., MS. 3244, fos. 80–105, records of Faure's visitation.

for their deliberations; his reports were also used for cross-examinations of both Petit and Chambellan, the first privately, the second in full council.[26] The council met no less than three times in the week following Faure's return to Paris in early February. The first session launched a debate on the shape of a future reform. Petit, whom La Rochefoucauld had again admonished to refrain from invective, admitted that the Mathurins 'ne vivoient en Capucins', but warned the cardinal that he would destroy the order if he tried to use the *réformés* as the basis of his reform. His only positive suggestion was that a central novitiate be established at Cerfroid, but then added, characteristically, that it should come under his personal jurisdiction. While Faure's reports probably increased La Rochefoucauld's suspicion that the *réformés* were less observant than they claimed to be, he had no desire to entrust the future of the reform to the vindictive general. No decision was taken about Chambellan's future either, despite his unconvincing self-defence under close questioning.[27] A few days later, La Rochefoucauld announced to an enlarged council meeting that their next task would be to discuss articles that he was having prepared for the restoration of the Mathurin observance.[28]

The consultations which began on 18 February reveal the full extent of the conundrum facing the commissioner. His council agreed that a new start was necessary; given the shortcomings of the existing reform and the lack of capable individuals within the order, external help would have to be sought. If the inadequacies of the *réformés* were a disappointment, the task of reforming Petit's followers raised the crucial question of what to do with the general himself. Here opinions within the council were divided: some members felt that nothing should be done without Petit's formal consent; others, while admitting the advantages of such constitutional propriety, argued that nothing would be achieved unless intense pressure was brought to bear on him. In the end, it was agreed that Petit should be flanked by assistants, without whose consent he could do nothing as general. More significant still was the decision, which evinced a serious lack of confidence in the *réformés*, to choose these assistants from *outside* the Mathurin order. There were also divergent views on how and where to begin the actual process of reform, but it was finally resolved to send non-Mathurin reformers to Petit's Paris house in the hope of nursing an observant community into existence there. Acknowledging that the existing reform was unsatisfactory and the order's divisions serious, La Rochefoucauld commissioned a group of his councillors to catalogue

26. B.S.G., MS. 3246, fos. 199v–200v, *procès-verbal* of 30 January; *ibid.*, fos. 200v–1r, *procès-verbal* of 3 February.
27. *Ibid.*, fos. 201r–3v, *procès-verbal* of 6 February.
28. *Ibid.*, fos. 203v–4r, *procès-verbal* of 10 February.

the Mathurins' failings and lack of observance.[29] At the same time, he announced a more momentous decision – to hold a general chapter in May 1638, with a view to ascertaining the state of the order in France as a whole, and to assess the calibre and attitudes of its members.[30]

That decision, far from imposing a moratorium on discussion, actually intensified the activities of La Rochefoucauld and his advisers. During late February and March 1638, they met regularly to work on a general *règlement* for submission to the chapter. Producing a coherent statement of the order's privileges and constitutions, obtaining exact information on houses and their revenues and, particularly, investigating the practice of raising money for the freeing of captives, was a slow and difficult business, in which there were, as the participants themselves admitted, no ready-made solutions.[31] But a twelve-point *règlement* was prepared for La Rochefoucauld, and it contained some controversial suggestions. The most novel of these was the proposal to give the general six assistants who, as outsiders with other duties, would exercise their office in pairs and in rotation. Under such a scheme, the general could take no decision without their consent. The reform itself would be launched at Cerfroid and Paris. Complex and unusual provisions for the recruitment of a new generation of Mathurins were also tabled. Whenever postulants presented themselves at Mathurin houses, the local superiors would be obliged to seek the cardinal's permission to admit them. The application would be channelled through the rector of the local Jesuit college, who would submit a report to La Rochefoucauld on the suitability of the candidates involved. Other questions were also raised, among them that of centralised novitiates.[32] All these proposals suggest a loss of confidence, unparalleled elsewhere in the cardinal's dealings with the orders, in Mathurin leaders and institutions, not only for the task of reform but even for that of ordinary day-to-day government.[33]

The equally onerous task of preparing a digest of the Mathurin's constitutions was also taken on by the cardinal's council before the chapter. While no Mathurin appears to have been regularly involved in this, there was a certain amount of consultation with Petit and other Mathurin leaders, if only because of the uncertainty as to which

29. There are three separate accounts of these crucial exchanges B.S.G., MS. 3244, fos. 42–4, MS. 3246, fos. 138 and 204v–5r. The last of these is the formal record of the meeting of 18 February.
30. B.S.G., MS. 3246, fo. 137, printed copy of the summons to attend.
31. B.S.G., MS. 3263, fo. 524, Charles Faure to Boulart, 15 March 1638: 'l'affaire des Mathurins sera plus aysé à consulter qu'à déterminer'.
32. B.S.G., MS. 3246, fos. 139–41, undated consultative document.
33. The *réformés* themselves sensed the drift of the discussions, and petitioned the cardinal to visit at least some of their houses. This, they claimed, would convince him that their reform was a satisfactory basis for his own planned reforms: B.S.G., MS. 3244, fo. 142, undated request.

constitutions were being observed by the order in 1638.[34] La Rochefoucauld continued to find himself arbitrating the bitter internal feuds of the Mathurins during the period leading up to the chapter.[35]

III

After months of hard work, La Rochefoucauld and his advisers could only wait for the general chapter. Not surprisingly, his proposals for the government of the order convinced Petit and his followers, like the Cistercian abbots before them, that the cardinal was in league with their enemies. Nevertheless, La Rochefoucauld's reduced faith in the *réformés*, and his growing reliance on his own council to manage the order's affairs, even to the extent of revising its constitution, is proof that he was not the prisoner of a faction, as Petit and his followers claimed. It now remained to be seen how the order would react to the unprecedented pressure under which it found itself.

The principal feature of the general chapter, which La Rochefoucauld personally opened on 3 May 1638, was that it was primarily a sounding-board for his own proposals. Previous experiences with Cluny and Cîteaux had convinced him that general chapters were potentially dangerous as platforms for opposition to reform. In the Mathurin case, nothing was left to chance. Being too ill to preside the chapter in person, his place was taken by Bishop Sponde of Pamiers. The exchanges at the chapter seem to have been mostly of a formal kind. Once Sponde had the terms of La Rochefoucauld's commission and his draft *règlement* read out, certain remonstrances were presented by a number of leading superiors.[36] These, along with detailed reports on individual houses, were then debated by the cardinal's council, after which Sponde informed the chapter that the cardinal had agreed to modify parts of the *règlement*. The delegates then continued their discussions, and it was not long before the inevitable antipathies surfaced. Petit, who had evidently not renounced his ambition to return to the status quo ante 1635, submitted several petitions against his opponents, and strongly opposed the idea that future generals should be elected exclusively from among the reformed Mathurins.[37]

At this juncture there was little left to do but dismiss the chapter,

34. B.S.G., MS. 3246, fos. 205v–6v, fo. 208; MS. 3244, fo. 44, record of these discussions. See also MS. 3284, fo. 375, Boulart to Faure, 14 March 1638: 'on continue à s'assembler pour les affaires des Mathurins chez les révérends pères feuillans pour revoir la règle'. Both Boulart and Faure, who was briefly absent from Paris, were actively involved in these discussions.
35. B.S.G., MS. 3246, fo. 208r–9r, *procès-verbal* of 14 April, referring to previous meetings.
36. *Ibid.*, fos. 148–9, *procès-verbal* of 3 May.
37. *Ibid.*, fos. 150–2, *procès-verbal* of 5 May.

which in La Rochefoucauld's view had served its limited purpose, especially that of informing him of the state of the order. The reports brought by the delegates provided clear evidence that neither Petit nor the *réformés* were honouring their obligation to spend the stipulated one-third of their revenues on the redemption of captives.[38] Sponde thus disbanded the chapter after only four days, promising that the cardinal's *règlement* would soon be published, repeating the ban on novices, and asking superiors to furnish La Rochefoucauld with a detailed list of their novices and postulants.[39]

The events of this brief chapter demonstrated the paralysis that beset the order. Both sides looked to the commissioner for support, and referred to him for decisions on even minor administrative matters.[40] Petit was evidently discredited, and his authority over the order had all but vanished. The *réformés* were incapable of trusting him, while his limited co-operation with the cardinal probably compromised him in the eyes of his own supporters. In such circumstances, it seems safe to assume that La Rochefoucauld entertained substantial doubts about the prospects of a genuine reform of the whole order. No other explanation seems possible for the unusual statement that he issued only a few days before his reform ordinance for the entire order was published. While reaffirming his objective of a full-scale reform, he declared that should his reforms prove impossible to enforce for any reason, he wished the *réformés* to retain their separate status and privileges within the order, and that provisions in his forthcoming ordinance for their suspension or abolition should not take effect.[41] It seems likely that the *réformés* themselves canvassed such a declaration, but they would hardly have obtained it had not La Rochefoucauld realised how limited were the means at his disposal for a general reform. For all his reservations about them, he acknowledged that any future reform would have to rely heavily on them.

The long-awaited general ordinance followed on 1 June 1638, and was divided into a *Sentence de réforme* and a *Règlement perpetuel*. Its unusually broad scope reflects La Rochefoucauld's continuing dilemma over Mathurin reform. The *Sentence* was designed for the purpose of achieving actual reform, and was intended to lapse once that happy state had been reached. The *Règlement perpetuel*, together with a set of constitutions which La Rochefoucauld promised to publish in due course, would then come into force. If reform required extraordinary

38. The memoranda on individual houses are in B.S.G., MS. 3244, fos. 191–311.
39. B.S.G., MS. 3246, fos. 152–3, *procès-verbal* of 7 May.
40. Numerous petitions from the different factions to La Rochefoucauld in B.S.G., MSS. 3244 and 3246. They include requests for permission to transfer members from one house to another, and to hold elections.
41. Deslandres, ii, doc. no. 184, 26 May 1638.

measures, they could be justified by the order's wilful neglect of its *raison d'être*, the ransoming of Christian captives.

The terms of the *Sentence* were adapted, with some minor modifications, from the proposals considered by La Rochefoucauld's council since December 1637. Petit was to be given two, not six assistants; an eight-man council, which the royal commissioners might attend, would meet weekly to oversee Mathurin affairs. Should the general die, La Rochefoucauld would personally supervise the election of a successor, who would have to have been a member of the reform for at least four years. For the rest, he left existing procedures to stand, while expressing determination to see proper forms respected. Reform at Paris and Cerfroid would be initiated by outsiders, Jesuits and Feuillants, and prospective members of the order would have to be examined by the commissioner's delegates.[42]

By contrast, the *Règlement perpetuel* was a lengthy document which spelled out in unusual detail the kind of Mathurin observance La Rochefoucauld wished to see develop. That it was so detailed is further evidence of his lack of confidence in the Mathurins of his day. Among other things, he prescribed a return to their primitive, communal observance, attempted to regulate the proper administration of conventual revenues, and established rules to ensure the kind of responsible internal government without which reformed observance was impossible. He also decreed that, as with the canons-regular, 'stability' should be understood in relation not to individual houses but to the order as a whole. Novitiates would be established in Paris and Cerfroid for northern France, and in Arles and Marseille for the Midi.[43]

By 1638, La Rochefoucauld had more experience than most reformers of the limits of good intentions and fine ordinances. Yet even now the latter seemed important to him as a means of staking out the future and of establishing a claim on the conscience of an order. As we have seen, it had taken months of hard work even to get this far by mid-1638. But he was no less anxious to take practical steps towards reform, and had not waited for the chapter or the general ordinance before doing so. In early March 1638, he had sent pairs of Jesuits, Feuillants, Génovéfains and Carmelites to Cerfroid, Paris and other houses to supervise the practice of the Spiritual Exercises by their younger members.[44] In late July, he finally dispatched two Jesuits to Cerfroid and two Feuillants to Paris to begin reform in these two leading houses.[45] He took rather longer to appoint Petit's two

42. B.S.G., MS. 3244, fos. 10–16.
43. *Ibid.*, fos. 16v–22.
44. *Ibid.*, fos. 44, council meeting of 2 March.
45. *Ibid.*, fos. 128, 130, commissions dated 31 July.

assistants, perhaps because none of his councillors coveted such an unenviable post. When he finally announced his decision in December 1638, the nominations went to Charles Faure and the Feuillant Eustache de St Paul, two of those who had been most active in Mathurin affairs.[46] As was his habit, La Rochefoucauld also sought royal approval of his ordinances, and this was granted by the royal commissioners on 23 November 1638, and ratified by letters-patent published shortly afterwards.[47] The commissioners also responded to his demands that the Mathurins honour their obligations towards Christian captives, and laid down the sums that each of their houses should contribute towards redemptions.[48] Finally, he dispatched his ordinances to Urban VIII for ratification; conscious of the debatable course he had taken, he argued that the Mathurins' neglect of their duty to Christian captives had forced him to take drastic measures.[49]

IV

What La Rochefoucauld cannot have known when approaching Urban VIII was that, in August 1638, Petit had formally appealed to Rome against the cardinal's decrees. La Rochefoucauld may well have learned of it over the following months, but Petit only served notice of it to him in December 1638.[50] The timing of the general's appeal, however, coincided roughly with that of St Victor (26 July), but there is no evidence that he concerted his action with the abbey's leaders. Be that as it may, Petit's case was certainly strengthened in Rome by that coincidence. La Rochefoucauld regarded the appeal as a frivolous, purely negative tactic, and insisted that it should not prevent his *Sentence* from being implemented, a view that he repeated in his instructions to the Maurist envoy in Rome, Dom Le Simon, in March 1639.[51] Yet the pope's decision to refer the appeal to the *ad hoc*

46. B.S.G., MS. 3246, fo. 164, minutes of the commission. Reluctance to accept such responsibility is hinted at by François Boulart in a letter to Faure: 'Monseigneur. . . insiste tousiours à vous donner la subdélégation pour les Mathurins avec le père Eustache. Si une fois vous estes embarassé en cette commission, cela vous arrestera de veoir nos maisons': B.S.G., MS. 3286, fo. 99, 10 September 1638.

47. B.S.G., MS. 3244, fos. 136–8, decree of 23 November; *ibid.*, fo. 135, letters-patent. Louis Petit also had notice of this approval served on him: *ibid.*, fo. 138v.

48. A.D., Seine-et-Oise 53 H 1, copy of the 'état des revenus' on which the decree of 23 November was based.

49. B..A.V., Barb. lat. 7952, fo. 34, La Rochefoucauld to Cardinal Francesco Barberini. The end of this letter, which contained the date, is missing.

50. B.S.G., MS. 3244, fo. 243, appeal dated 18 August. Petit refused to reveal the grounds of his appeal at this time, reserving the right to do so before judges-delegate at a later stage.

51. B.N., MS. Fr. 15787, fos. 69–70, 29 December 1638. B.S.G., MS. 3286, fo. 514, Le Simon to Boulart, 12 April 1639, summarising the contents of the cardinal's (lost) letter. A draft of his instructions is in MS. 3246, fo. 165, 12 March 1639.

'congrégation des affaires du cardinal de la Rochefoucauld', where the influential Maraldo openly championed Petit's cause, did not augur well. Petit's allegations, when they became known, were sweeping. He prudently refrained from questioning the validity of the 1635 brief — such criticism would not have been welcome in the curia, which had, after all, issued the brief — but asserted that La Rochefoucauld had clearly exceeded its terms, altering 'lo stato' of his order by his constitutional changes; his ordinances were replete with 'molte cose parte contrarie e parte disordinate'. Worst of all, by consulting seculars, establishing a council consisting of other regulars and seculars, and appealing to the royal council for support, he had seriously infringed ecclesiastical liberties — something Rome had surely never intended. Such arguments show Petit's tactical skill, and were an adroit flattery of superior curial wisdom and prudence. They proved so effective that after the *ad hoc* congregation's first meeting, Barberini wrote to La Rochefoucauld in July 1639 to suspend his reforms until the case had been judged, and to send all the relevant papers to the congregation.[52]

This was a severe blow. During 1639–40, the Mathurin and St Victor affairs severely dented La Rochefoucauld's reputation in a curia which, in the last years of Urban VIII, seems to have been more incapable than ever of reaching decisions and sticking to them. La Rochefoucauld did not remain passive in the face of Petit's claims, and was all the more offended by Rome's response because he had not sought the Mathurin commission in the first place.[53] The importance that he attached to the Mathurin case is abundantly clear from the continual pressure he attempted to put on the curia throughout 1639–41 via the papal nuncio, who had been entrusted with investigating the issue in France.[54] It brought him to within an ace of success in August 1641 when the congregation and the pope himself finally approved his *Sentence*, only for confirmation of the decision to be halted by a timely letter which Petit had secured from Louis XIII

52. B.A.V., Barb. lat. 8150, fos. 32–3, Barberini to nuncio Bolognetti, 12 July 1639. This letter lists Petit's charges under a number of headings, and added that he had defended them 'con molta efficacia'.
53. B.A.V., Barb. lat. 8217, fo. 82, undated minute of letter from nuncio Grimaldi, where this point is strongly put.
54. B.S.G., MS. 3290, fo. 127, Dom Le Simon to Boulart, 6 September 1639; B.A.V., Barb. lat 8188, fo. 153, Ranuccio Scotti, papal nuncio, to Barberini, 30 December 1639; B.S.G., MS. 3244, fo. 337, 'pièces à recouvrer pour faire veoir à M. le nonce'; *ibid.*, fos.161–8, a defence of the reform, also probably for submission to the nuncio; B.A.V., Barb. lat. 8201, fos. 64v–5r, Scotti to Barberini, 20 April 1640; *Correspondance de Scotti*, ed., Pierre Blet, pp. 296, 399, for further letters. La Rochefoucauld's persistence is also evident from the correspondence of another of Barberini's confidents, Valerio di Sant'Anna: B.A.V., Barb. lat. 8257, fo. 83, Valerio to Barberini, 20 April 1640. See Valerio's letter to La Rochefoucauld in B.S.G., MS. 3246, fo. 178, 21 March 1641.

defending his authority as general, and the 'probité' and 'bonne vie' of his subjects.[55] With the support of Chavigny, the secretary of state for foreign affairs (who had probably obtained the royal letter in the first place), the French ambassador in Rome, and Maraldo, Petit was able throughout the early 1640s to prevent La Rochefoucauld's *Sentence* from being approved.[56] The curia's own state of confusion was also an advantage to him. At one point, in early 1644, Maraldo and Cardinal Spada, ex-papal nuncio and president of the *ad hoc* congregation, drafted totally different decisions on the *Sentence*, the first damning it outright, the second upholding it. But neither was ever confirmed.[57] Whatever hopes La Rochefoucauld might have had of living to see his *Sentence* confirmed were dashed when Innocent X decided, soon after his election, to leave the affair in the hands of Spada's congregation.[58]

The only noteworthy outcome of these years of tedious, fruitless negotiation in Rome was that Petit's appeal was actually referred to French judges-delegate in 1643. The case was handled by Claude Martin, *official* of St Germain-des-Prés, who had also heard the St Victor appeal. It was no secret that he was favourable to the appellants in both cases, and no surprise that in December 1643 he declared that La Rochefoucauld's Mathurin *Sentence* should be suppressed as seriously infringing the constitutions of the order.[59] But, as La Rochefoucauld himself never tired of arguing, decisions by a minor judge on major questions settled nothing, and negotiations continued uninterrupted in Rome. La Rochefoucauld received posthumous vindication in November 1645, when the royal council quashed Martin's judgement and bravely ordered the full implementation of the cardinal's *Sentence*,

55. A.S.V., Nunz. Fr. 394, fo. 214, Louis XIII to pope, 1 August 1641. The Génovéfain envoy in Rome, Jacques Guérin, regularly reported on Mathurin affairs to La Rochefoucauld and Ste Geneviève: B.S.G., MS. 3298, fos. 522–3, letter to Faure, 10 August 1641, where La Rochefoucauld's cause seemed vindicated. For an account of events in Rome around this time, compiled from missing La Rochefoucauld papers, see the memorandum in B.S.G., MS. 3244, fo. 335.
56. B.S.G., MS. 3298, fo. 437, Guérin to Boulart, 20 October 1641; MS. 3246, fo. 186, undated minutes of letter from La Rochefoucauld to a Roman correspondent; MS. 3304, fos. 391, 395, 406–7, 427–8, letters from Guérin to Boulart, December 1641 to March 1642, documenting the ambassador's position. Ironically, the latter admitted to Guérin that Petit's case was unjustified, but he had formal instructions to uphold it! Chavigny's earlier support for Petit is evident from his instructions for the new French ambassador in Rome, Fontenay-Mareuil, asking him to drop the policy of opposing La Rochefoucauld: B.N., MS. Fr. 16066, fo. 243v, 30 March 1642. The change is recorded by Guérin: B.S.G., MS. 3304, fos. 408–9, letter to Boulart, 15 June 1642.
57. B.S.G., MS. 3311, fo. 122, Guérin to Boulart, 25 March 1644; *ibid.*, fo. 489, to same, 23 May. He described the terms of Maraldo's proposed brief as 'mesme honteux à Mons. nostre Cardinal', while Spada proposed to include the entire text of the cardinal's 1638 *Sentence* in his brief as a means of confirming it.
58. B.S.G., MS. 3313, fo. 246, Guérin to Boulart, 4 December 1644. To Guérin's even greater dismay, Innocent also retained Maraldo as secretary of Latin briefs.
59. Deslandres, i, pp. 253–4.

but such a vindication was wholly symbolic: it neither promoted reform nor terminated the Mathurins' long-standing divisions.[60]

V

La Rochefoucauld's hopes of supervising a general reform of the Mathurins had, of course, disappeared long before his death in February 1645. Yet, he refused to throw in the towel on hearing of Petit's appeal in late 1638. His commission was due to run until 1641, and Rome failed to answer his demands for clarification as to whether Petit's appeal affected the validity of only certain decisions or whether it placed the entire commission in cold storage. This was crucial to him because, while St Victor's appeal affected only a few houses of canons-regular, Petit's concerned the entire Mathurin order. In the event, Rome's negative attitude obliged him to accept that any new attempts on his part to deal with the whole order might provoke further appeals, either to the council, or to the *parlement* of Paris, or to the curia.

Until Rome could reach a decision, there was little he could do but devote his attention to the *réformés*. In this respect, his decision in May 1638 to preserve their autonomy proved to be an advantage, as it enabled them to dissociate themselves from Petit's appeal, and to continue to regard the cardinal as their protector, even after his commission had expired in 1641. By appointing first Alexis Berger, and then Chambellan, 'promoteur et scindic pour l'execution du bref', he had also signalled his intention of employing their leading members in the business of reform shortly after the publication of his *Sentence* in June 1638.[61] Their exact duties are unknown, but the post was evidently no sinecure and required them to reside in Paris, in order to be at the commissioner's disposal and to liaise with his council.[62] The cardinal was also determined to impose order on the *réformés'* own affairs and to eliminate internal rivalry,[63] and to that end, he controlled elections carefully, quashing some and, and on occasion, appointing men of his own choice. When their provincial chapters met, it was La Rochefoucauld who vetted their deliberations and elections.[64] These chapters also provide evidence that the *réformés*

60. A.D., Seine-et-Oise 53 H 1, decree of 28 November.
61. Berger so describes himself in December 1638: B.S.G., MS. 3246, fo. 162.
62. B.S.G., MS. 3244, fo. 190, 12 June 1639, commission to Charles Dangneaux to succeed Chambellan, recently elected 'minister' of the Montmorency house.
63. *Ibid.*, fos. 146–53, for several instances of this.
64. E.g. B.S.G., MS. 3246, fo. 162, petition from Berger, and La Rochefoucauld's decision on filling offices; *ibid.*, fos. 174–5; MS. 3292, fo. 455, Boulart to Faure, 25 April 1640, referring to an assembly held by the cardinal to examine decisions and confirm elections by recent chapters.

became keener than they had been to implement reform, and particularly to adhere to the provisions of the *Sentence*.[65] It is impossible to judge the short-term consequences of this development, but the fact that a number of *réformés* were active about this time as missionaries around Meaux, Bellegarde and La Rochelle suggests that improvements had taken place in their ranks.[66]

Yet despite La Rochefoucauld's continuing patronage, the number of reformed houses remained few. Petit stood firmly in the way of expansion, refusing to allow houses subject to him to pass to the *réformés*. Indeed, there is only one recorded instance of success against Petit, when La Rochefoucauld and Bishop Séguier of Meaux combined to force through the reform of the important Mathurin house at Meaux in 1639.[67] It survived subsequent upheavals as well as the travails of the cardinal's commission in Rome.

For their part, the *réformés* continued to hope for a general reform. They sent an envoy to Rome in early 1642 to seek permission for La Rochefoucauld to convene their first general chapter.[68] The negotiations there proved successful, and the chapter which met in May that year at Lambesc in Provence solemnly accepted the cardinal's *Sentence* as binding on them all. By then, however, such a move possessed little more than symbolic value.[69] Like the Cistercians and the Cluniacs, the Mathurins were still quarrelling over La Rochefoucauld's ordinances well into the reign of Louis XIV, long after any hope of a general reform had vanished.[70]

In retrospect, there is every reason to doubt whether La Rochefoucauld, even if he had enjoyed a free hand after July 1638, could ever have produced widespread reform in the Mathurin order, bearing in mind its internal condition and lack of positive leadership. No doubt prospects would have been far better had Petit resembled his predecessor as general but, by the mid-1630s, it was too late to expect him to abandon the policies of a lifetime. At best, La Rochefoucauld might have 'captured' a few leading houses for the reform, enforced his ban on taking novices except in general novitiates and, in time, helped to produce a new generation of observant Mathurins. But, as we saw

---

65. This is clear from the decisions of the provincial chapter held at Cerfroid in January 1639: A.D., Seine-et-Oise 53 H 5, fos. 18–20v, and from the visitation ordinances at Montmorency, 29 April 1639: *ibid.*, unfoliated.
66. See Bernard Jacqueline, 'Missions en France', in *Sacrae Congregationis de Propaganda Fide memoria rerum*, ed. Josef Metzler (Rome, 1972), i, p. 121.
67. B.S.G., MS. 3244, fo. 330, undated petition for reform from members of house at Meaux; MS. 3246, fo. 170, commission to Bishop Séguier, 26 August 1639; Deslandres, i, p. 253.
68. B.S.G., MS. 3304, fos. 414–15, Guérin to Boulart, 5 April 1642.
69. *Ibid.*, fos. 397–8, Guérin to Boulart, 27 April 1642. The acts of the chapter are in A.D., Seine-et-Oise 53 H 5, fos. 22 *et seq.*
70. Deslandres, i, pp. 255–6. For Petit's own efforts to make peace around 1645, see *ibid.*, ii, doc. no. 194.

in the case of the canons-regular, even these were objectives that were not easy to attain. Both the lateness and the short lifespan of his commission precluded a significant breakthrough outside the realm of ordinances and legislation.

Conclusion:
Leadership and Reform

PERHAPS THE MOST universal assumption made about the Catholic church, both past and present, is that it is characterised by a strongly hierarchical structure which governs the manner in which it operates. So general is this view that the church is often referred to in common parlance as simply 'the hierarchy'. This is hardly the place to examine the appropriateness of such an assumption, but it may serve as a starting point for some concluding reflections on the French church of the Counter-Reformation.

The term hierarchy usually serves as shorthand to indicate the location of authority and the exercise of leadership in the church. But a curious feature of the French church of the sixteenth and seventeenth centuries is that, while it genuinely respected rank and status, it had surprisingly few institutional sources of unity and authority and, therefore, of leadership. From one angle, it can be seen as a federation of over a hundred episcopal republics; over the centuries, Gallican traditions had the effect of turning dioceses into as many republics, whose bishops resented external interference, whether from Rome or from ecclesiastical superiors nearer home. In particular, the archbishops who headed France's fourteen ecclesiastical 'provinces' seem to have exercised relatively few powers over their suffragans; the provincial councils which the Council of Trent had so strongly recommended as instruments of ecclesiastical cohesion and reform, but which might also have tightened hierarchical bonds, met more rarely in France than anywhere else in Catholic Europe. To the extent that archbishops did exercise leadership over the episcopate, they did so more through their personal ability than they did through institutional prerogative, and that leadership could just as well have been exercised by bishops of less exalted rank or title.[1] In some ways, the same could be said of the cardinals, whose elevated status could indeed enhance a position of leadership, but could not create one where none existed, as is only too evident from the careers of several of La Rochefoucauld's fellow-cardinals. In retrospect, the papacy's fear, voiced in 1593 at the time of Henry IV's conversion, and in 1639–40 during Richelieu's conflicts with Urban VIII, that the French crown, supported by part of the episcopate, wished to establish a national church under the leadership of a French-born patriarch, appears devoid of real substance. Such a prospect contained very few attractions for the majority of French bishops, who would almost certainly have found themselves corseted by a more immediate, functioning hierarchy of authority and leadership dominated by the crown.

Indeed, one important consequence of the religious wars, and especially of the League, was to make the French upper clergy much less docile and compliant towards the crown than they had previously been, or would later become under Louis XIV. For that reason they were capable, during the early decades of the Counter-Reformation, of producing leaders from within their own ranks who were not 'king's men' in the conventional sense or who, like a Bérulle or a Vincent de Paul, had not followed a conventional episcopal career at all. It is difficult to imagine La Rochefoucauld, with his notorious anti-Gallican and pro-Jesuit sympathies, emerging as a major figure in the French church in the age of Louis XIV, when access to, and especially promotion within, the ranks of the episcopate were much more carefully screened than in previous generations.

Of course, throughout the period of the Counter-Reformation the crown possessed the right to appoint bishops, but that in itself did not suffice to produce a highly unified church hierarchy. For its own purposes, the crown obviously relied on chosen bishops to provide leadership, but the 'political' bishop to which this gave rise did not necessarily command a wide range of loyalties within the episcopate. The Wars of Religion also temporarily discredited the political prelate, either because of his partisanship, or because, at a time when the crown began making real financial demands on the clergy, churchmen who were perceived as being too close to the crown became suspect to their colleagues, and could exercise little influence over them. When La Rochefoucauld joined the episcopal bench, a long period of domination by the Guise cardinals and their allies was drawing to a close; their record made Henri IV less than anxious to continue the

---

1. The growth of the regular assemblies of the clergy after 1560 may have done something to offset this development, as many of the procedures of the assemblies – from the election of deputies to voting procedures during debates – were based on provincial structures. See Lucien Serbat, *Les Assemblées du clergé de France*, part 3.

tradition, and it was not resumed until the rise of Richelieu. Yet for all their immense power, neither Richelieu nor Mazarin exercised exclusive or effective leadership within the French church, and on several major occasions the church managed to distance itself from them and their policies.[2]

But the French clergy's aversion to leadership from a single source had other roots, too. They were divided by a whole range of issues, which either appeared for the first time or took on a new importance during the seventeenth century. The Council of Trent and the Counter-Reformation generally obliged the various Catholic churches throughout Europe to reconsider their attitudes to Rome and to papal authority to a degree that had been hitherto unnecessary. In France, for example, the experience of the League and the prolonged debate about whether the decrees of Trent should be formally accepted, demonstrate the strength of feeling generated by papal claims, and shattered for some time the 'Gallican' tranquility that had long prevailed in the church there. While the church and its leaders continued to have a mind of their own on crucial questions in the age of Louis XIV, it is clear that they were far more divided in their loyalties to pope and king in the half century or so following the League.[3] Likewise, the controversy between the seculars and the regulars, although centuries-old, again raged fiercely in the seventeenth century, not because of any hankering for controversy, but because Counter-Reformation developments re-opened the closely intertwined questions of episcopal authority and pastoral reform. The Jansenist affair would then follow from the early 1640s onwards, encapsulating and complicating earlier forms of conflict, and weakening and dividing the French church still further.

Thus, in addition to the institutional sensitivities of the kind already alluded to, the French church was itself divided on a range of issues – doctrinal, political and pastoral – which made it virtually impossible for any figure within the church to exercise a form of leadership which was not subject to dissent from one quarter or another. Leadership tended to flow in channels which not only failed to merge, but which might subdivide further in the course of subsequent re-alignments. The well-known clashes between Richelieu and the *dévots* over the Huguenots and foreign policy around 1630, and over 'l'amour pénitent' around 1637–40, provide the best-known illustrations of this process.[4] It is not surprising that La Rochefoucauld,

2. See Pierre Blet, *Le Clergé de France et la monarchie*, i, pp. 335ff, 478ff; ii, pp. 3ff, 120ff, 396ff.
3. Blet, *Les Assemblées du clergé et Louis XIV de 1670 à 1693* (Rome, 1972), for an important revision of earlier views on the age of Louis XIV.
4. Orcibal, *St Cyran et son temps*, chs. 10–11, which remains the most sensitive account of these developments.

although he was widely admired for his life-long commitment to reform, should have been hopelessly separated from many of his colleagues by his Ultramontane, pro-Jesuit convictions.

By the same token, this continuing process of fracturing has much to do with the French church's slowness in generating a united movement for reform capable of commanding a broad measure of support. Any progress towards reform was, of course, considerably slowed by the task of physically reconstructing dioceses heavily damaged during the Wars of Religion, especially but not exclusively in the west and the south. This handicap increased the existing time-lag between France and those areas of Catholic Europe which did not have to face such problems, and accounts for much of the pessimism expressed in the reports of both visitors and nuncios about the state of the French church until well into the 1620s and 1630s. When reform did begin to gather some impetus, it was frequently criss-crossed by internal divisions and differences of emphasis – over episco-pal authority, the place of the regulars in pastoral activities, the frequenting of the sacraments, the reform of popular religious practice, and so on.

The crisis of the religious wars not only altered the relationship between the crown and episcopate, but it was decisive in other ways for a younger generation of ecclesiastics. Those who, like La Rochefoucauld, threw themselves wholly into the League, retained thereafter a firm commitment to the defence and reform of the church which contributed greatly to their influence in the decades that followed the end of the Wars of Religion. The latter left them with a monumental task that reduced all but the most determined of them to despondency. Like La Rochefoucauld himself, few could boast of lasting successes in restoring their authority, disciplining their clergy, or eliminating what they viewed as superstition and irreligion. On the other hand, the ideals that they set for bishops and clergy alike, as exemplified by La Rochefoucauld's *Estat ecclésiastique*, were taken up and amplified by later generations, and became the most original con-tribution of the French church to the European Counter-Reformation. They more than any of its other features ensured that the French Counter-Reformation would aim at more than simply 'restoring' the church to some earlier, purer state.

Perhaps the most important consequence of this concern with perfecting the clergy was a failure to give full attention to the distinctive demands and religious life of the laity. Of course, as La Rochefoucauld himself stressed in his writings and decrees as a bishop, clerical reform was intended to be a means to an end, namely general religious reform. The impossibility of a full-scale study of his diocesan administration and reforms prevents us from seeing just how far this conviction might have been translated into practice. At any rate, as the French Counter-Reformation gathered momentum, the means often seemed to become ends in themselves, and to lead in the longer term towards a clericalisation of Catholicism. Certainly, the failure to develop a genuine spirituality for the laity corresponding to that developed for the clergy had such an effect.

This failure conceals an important feature of the early French Counter-Reformation – the intensity of lay involvement in promoting religious reform and innovation. It is increasingly apparent that, while the church reacted to the initial challenges of the Protestant Reformation in a rather negative and conventional way, the experience of the Catholic League did more than either the decrees of Trent or the example of Borromeo to generate a conviction of the need for positive reforms.[5] In this, the educated laity of the towns were often to the forefront, making their contempt for unworthy clergy perfectly clear in the process. When the smoke of war cleared, and reform could get underway, lay activism was essential to it. The League might have lost heavily in the political field, but its defeat did not necessarily spell ruin for the social or religious ambitions of its protagonists.[6] Without the continuing but often critical support of these lay *dévots*, who remained suspicious of a clergy, both upper and lower, which was in many ways inadequately prepared for its responsibilities, the seventeenth-century church would have achieved far fewer of its objectives.[7] If this dimension of the early Counter-Reformation is not obtrusive in La Rochefoucauld's work and career, it is not entirely absent either. Without the support of a lay *dévot* like Marillac, the idea of a commission for the reform of the orders might not have mustered and retained the support it enjoyed at court around 1620. Even more significant is the extent to which throughout his years as commissioner, La Rochefoucauld relied for advice and assistance on royal officials and magistrates whose support for his reforms owed more to their own

---

5. On the inadequacies of the church hierarchy for much of the sixteenth century, see Frederic J. Baumgartner, *Continuity and Change in the French Episcopate 1547–1610* (Durham, N.C., 1986). The change in church attitudes is tentatively suggested for Rouen by Philip Benedict, 'The Catholic Response to Protestantism: Church Activity and Popular Piety in Rouen 1560–1600', in James Obelkevich, ed., *Religion and the People 800–1700* (Chapel Hill, N.C. 1979), pp. 168–90.

6. Their 'social' and professional survival, not to mention subsequent advancement, is a central theme of the recent work of Robert Descimon. See in particular his *Qui étaient les seize? Mythes et réalités de la ligue parisienne (1585–1594)* (Paris, 1983).

7. The attitudes of the *dévots* who filled the ranks of the Company of the Holy Sacrament between 1630 and 1660 are particularly striking in this regard. They kept their distance from all but the most favourably disposed bishops, regarding many of them and the lower clergy as failing to discharge their duties adequately; the Company was only too willing to fill the breach. The best accounts are in Raoul Allier, *La Cabale des Dévots* (Paris, 1902), and Emmanuel Chill, 'The Company of the Holy Sacrament' (Ph.D dissertation, University of Columbia, 1960). For a spirited account of the religious life of Paris in the early seventeenth century, see Orest Ranum, *Paris in the Age of Absolutism* (Paris, 1968), ch. 3, 'A Generation of Saints'.

personal commitment than to any formal duty to implement royal policies. Indeed, one of the accusations made against him in 1639 by the general of the Mathurins was that the cardinal had permitted laymen to deliberate on questions of reform to an unprecedented extent.[8]

As practised by La Rochefoucauld in his successive capacities as bishop, grand almoner, and commissioner for the orders, reform was conducted 'par voie d'autorité'. If it was to produce results, it needed to balance the 'rigueur de la contrainte' with the the 'douceur de l'exemple'.[9] Episcopal authority might be among the oldest and most legitimate forms of authority in the church, but where the right balance was not struck, efforts at diocesan reform were readily seen by opponents, particularly among the entrenched clergy, as exercises in episcopal absolutism; as such they met with as much resistance as did absolutism in its other, better-known guises. A drift towards episcopal absolutism, enjoying the increasingly open support of the crown, is apparent by the later seventeenth century, by which time one can detect in episcopal action a growing dissociation of authority, leadership, and reform. But in the age of Henry IV and Louis XIII, the crown remained too weak in the provinces to pursue anything like the systematic efforts of Louis XIV to confirm and reinforce episcopal authority. Efforts at reform were thus blunted by the autonomy not merely of local religious traditions and ecclesiastical institutions, but also by that of royal officialdom itself.

A further characteristic of the early French Counter-Reformation is the range and diversity of interests of virtually every one of its leading figures. If many of them have subsequently become identified with specific aspects of its history – de Sales with spiritual writing and counsel, Bérulle with the Oratory, St Cyran with Port-Royal and Jansenism, Vincent de Paul with charitable activities – this is the end result of a process of simplification which fails to do justice to the true scope of their activities. The extent of their concern for church affairs and reform in the broadest sense remains one of the impressive things about them, and one is constantly surprised to encounter the same figures involved in church affairs far removed from their alleged centres of interest. La Rochefoucauld's own career can be taken as an example of this versatility. As we have seen, he composed substantial works on the authority of the church and the reform of the clergy, even if these lack the literary elegance of de Sales, the profundity of Bérulle, or the erudition of Saint-Cyran. Yet perhaps the most illuminating, because the most unexpected, instance of this range of interests is his

---

8. B.A.V., Barberini latini 8150, fo. 33, 12 July 1639.
9. These terms were used in the 1621 reform ordinance for Cluny composed by Jacques Vény d'Arbouze: Denis, *Richelieu et la réforme des monastères bénédictins*, p. 393.

career as grand almoner, during which he attempted to promote reform in areas with which he had previously had little opportunity to deal – the court, the hospices and charitable institutions, and the episcopate itself.

The campaign for the reform of the orders must rank among the most important instances of this diversity. The idea of conducting a nation-wide reform of the great monastic orders was also typical of the ambition of the early French Counter-Reformation to encompass all spheres of religious life. This, too, went considerably beyond efforts at restoration, for not only did it often entail altering the constitution and structure of the orders but, even more ambitiously, grafting onto them some of the practices and observance of the more recent orders. Any attempt to do this was certain to encounter resistance, given the fierce attachment of individual orders to their traditions, and suspicion of others claiming to practise a more 'perfect' observance than their own. Contemporaries fully realised the peculiar difficulties besetting such a reform, and not a few despaired of success. It is not especially surprising that, although the cause of reform gained the support of the king and his entourage in 1619, La Rochefoucauld was the only senior ecclesiastic prepared to pursue the argument with the papacy and, in the end, to shoulder the burden of attempting to reform the orders.

As the negotiations of 1619–22 show, a no less significant feature of his commission is the extent to which the reformers of his generation were ready to associate the papacy with their ambitions and projects. This had not always been so, and for most of the sixteenth century, the common points of reference for most French reformers were the great royal ordinances of Orléans, Blois and Moulins. The change that subsequently took place can be charted through the clergy's efforts to see the decrees of Trent applied in France as elsewhere in Catholic Europe, but it was by no means limited to such a pious aspiration.

It was certainly La Rochefoucauld's intention to strengthen this trend towards closer ties with Rome, yet his commission was to have unforeseen consequences for the relationship of the French church and the papacy. Firstly, the fact that his reforms were instrumental in enabling Richelieu to take over Cluny and Cîteaux revived the belief, the short-lived nature of Richelieu's policies notwithstanding, that the problems of the orders could be dealt with by the direct application of political power by royal ministers. Secondly, the role of the royal commission made it plain that La Rochefoucauld's reforms depended for their effectiveness more on the crown than they did on the papacy. The fact that the commission could continue to function in the early 1640s, when La Rochefoucauld was no longer papal commissioner, shows how much it had become detached from its roots in the original papal decision of 1622; its work and decisions over a twenty-year period almost certainly encouraged the view that the crown itself possessed the machinery needed to pursue policies of its own in respect of the religious orders.

On the other hand, the papacy's role in the history of La Rochefoucauld's commission after its initial grant in 1622 was not particularly distinguished. It seems probable that, although he was prepared to renew La Rochefoucauld's successive commissions when petitioned to do so by Louis XIII, Urban VIII would have preferred to imitate Paul V rather than Gregory XV and to reject any call for exceptional measures in France, where he had once been papal nuncio. But as his pontificate wore on, there were more and more French churchmen who believed, even before the curia upheld the different appeals against La Rochefoucauld during the 1630s, that papal advocacy of reform had dwindled to a point where it could not be relied upon to support any significant initiatives. The notion that the Counter-Reformation was led and sustained by a dynamic, reformed papacy is not borne out by the history of La Rochefoucauld's commission.

The limited successes – or outright failures, in some cases – of La Rochefoucauld's reform commission also taught his contemporaries the limitations of good intentions in such an important sphere of church reform. La Rochefoucauld stated in his remonstrance of 1643 to Anne to Austria, that the history of his commission should constitute a warning to future cardinals. He need not have worried – there were to be no successors, nor is there any sign that anyone was anxious to imitate him. A generation later, in the 1660s, it was Colbert, and not one of La Rochefoucauld's fellow-cardinals, who planned a general reform of the French orders without any reference to the papacy and, even more significantly, in accordance with criteria of social 'utility' and the 'good of the state' which a previous generation would not have recognised.[10] By the age of Louis XIV ideas for the reform of the orders were markedly different from those of La Rochefoucauld's years.

This particular development may stand as a symbol of what had happened to the French Counter-Reformation in general. Its early, creative phase had seriously run out of steam, a process which the church's own divisions did not serve to arrest. The crown had strengthened its grip on the church as on the kingdom; if it lent its support to bishops and church authorities, it did so on its own terms, and with one eye firmly on the political advantages of such a policy. Above all, the crown was in a position to determine the kind of church leaders and reforms it wished to promote.

10. Vladimir N. Malov, 'Le Projet colbertiste de la réforme monastique', in *Un Nouveau Colbert*, ed. R. Mousnier (Paris, 1985), pp. 167–76.

APPENDICES
Biographical Index

ARNOUX, Jean: born at Riom 1575; enters Jesuits in 1592; well-known preacher; confessor to Louis XIII 1617; disgraced December 1621; died 1636.

BAUDOUIN, Robert: born 1590; canon of St Vincent de Senlis in 1606; prior of St Vincent, 1618; prior of St Jean de Chartres 1625; *procureur général* of congrégation de France; died February 1639.

BERULLE, Pierre de: born 1575; son of Claude, *conseiller* at *parlement* of Paris, and Louise Séguier; founded Oratory, 1611; influential adviser to Marie de Medici, leading figure in *parti des dévots*; cardinal 1627; died October 1629.

BINET, Etienne: born at Dijon, 1569; entered Jesuits 1590; rector of Rouen and Paris colleges; provincial superior in 'France', Champagne and Lyon; composed numerous works of spirituality and devotion; died July 1639.

BLANCHART, François: born at Amiens 1606; canon of St Acheul of Amiens in 1624; ordained in 1630; sub-prior of Ste Cathérine of Paris; prior of St Denis de Reims 1633; abbot and general of congrégation de France 1644–50; 1656–62, 1659–62, 1667–75; died February 1675.

BOUCHERAT, Nicolas: born 1562; doctor in theology; prior of Cîteaux; abbot of Vaucelles in 1592; coadjutor-abbot of Cîteaux before becoming abbot-general in 1604; died May 1625.

BOULART, François: born at Senlis 1605; canon of St Vincent in 1621; secretary to La Rochefoucauld; prior of Ste Geneviève in 1633; coadjutor-abbot and superior-general 1640–3; abbot and general 1653 and 1665; died January 1667.

CHARLET, Etienne: origins obscure; rector of College of La Flèche to 1615; provincial of Jesuit province of 'France', 1616–19; Assistant for France to Jesuit superior-general, Rome 1627–46; died Paris 1652.

D'ARBOUZE, Jacques Vény: son of Michel, *premier maître d'hotel* of François duc d'Anjou, and Péronnelle de Marillac; grand prior of Cluny; vicar-general of cardinal of Guise for order of Cluny, 1615; abbot-general 1622; resigned 1629.

DU PERRON, Jacques Davy, cardinal: born near St Lô, 1556; raised as Huguenot; became Catholic, 1576; rallied to Henri IV, 1590; received see of Evreux, 1591, confirmed by pope, 1595; cardinal 1604; archbishop of Sens and grand almoner of France, 1606; died September 1618.

ETAMPES de Valençay, Léonor d': born at Valançay, 1588; son of Jean and Sarah d'Applaincourt; succeeds cousin Nicolas Hurault as bishop of Chartres 1620; archbishop of Reims, 1642; died April 1651.

FAURE, Charles: born near Paris 1594; entered St Vincent de Senlis 1613; canon in 1615; ordained priest 1619; sub-prior of St Vincent 1623; vicar-general of reformed canons-regular, 1628, 1633; coadjutor-abbot of Ste Geneviève and superior-general of congrégation de France 1634–40, 1643–4; died November 1644.

GALLET, Philippe: born in Angers diocese, 1567; canon of Toussaints of Angers in 1593; ordained priest *c*. 1600; doctor in theology, adviser to successive bishops of Angers; prior of Toussaints, 1620; entered congrégation de France 1635; died July 1654.

GUERIN, Jacques: born 1598; canon of Toussaints of Angers in 1614; entered congrégation de France 1635; *procureur général* in Rome 1639; died May 1681.

LARGENTIER, Claude: born at Troyes, 1584; nephew of Denis Largentier; entered Clairvaux *c*. 1599; bachelor in theology; prior of Rosières; vicar of uncle, 1616; abbot of Clairvaux 1624; died September 1653.

LARGENTIER, Denis: born 1557 at Troyes; entered Clairvaux *c*. 1573; doctor in theology; *procureur-général* of order in Rome 1592; abbot of Clairvaux 1596; died October 1624.

LEZEAU, Nicolas Lefèvre de: born 1581; *conseiller* at *grand conseil* 1603; *maitre des requêtes*, 1618; commissioner for the orders, 1622; councillor of state, 1657; *doyen* of council; died 1680.

MAUGIER, Etienne: born at Châteaudun, 1573; professed as Cistercian 1589; bachelor of theology, 1594; abbot of La Charmoye in 1608; vicar-general for reformed observance within Clairvaux filiation; leader of Strict Observance of Cistercian order; died August 1637.

NIVELLE, Pierre: born at Troyes, *c*. 1583; entered Cistercians *c*. 1606; doctor in theology 1608; provisor of College of St Bernard in Paris until 1621; abbot of St Sulpice (Burgundy) 1621; abbot of Cîteaux, 1625; resigned in favour of Richelieu, 1635; bishop of Luçon 1636; died 1660.

PHELYPEAUX, Jean: born at Angers 1577; entered Jesuits 1594; professor at college of La Flèche; secretary to La Rochefoucauld in 1620s; died August 1645.

POTIER, Augustin: son of Nicolas Potier de Blancmesnil, and Isabeau Baillet; succeeds brother René as bishop of Beauvais, 1616; *grand aumonier* to Anne of Austria, 1624; hostile to regulars during 1630s; briefly rival to Mazarin and candidate for cardinalate, 1643; died June 1650.

RETZ, Henri de Gondi, cardinal de: born in 1572; son of Albert de Gondi and Claude Catherine de Clermont; succeeds cardinal Pierre de Gondi bishop of Paris, 1596; first cardinal de Retz and president of king's council, 1618; died August 1622; succeeded by brother, Jean-François, first archbishop of Paris, 1622–54.

RICHER, Edmond: born 1559; syndic of Faculty of Theology, 1608; published *Libellus de ecclesiastica et politica potestate*, 1611; condemned in 1612; retracts Gallican opinions, 1629; died 1631.

ST PAUL, Eustache de: born Eustache Asseline, in Paris, 1573; doctor of Sorbonne 1604; entered congregation of Feuillants 1605; held numerous offices in congregation; composed widely-used philosophical and theological works; died December 1640.

SANGUIN, Nicolas: born in Paris 1580; son of Jacques, *conseiller* at *parlement* of Paris, and of Marie du Mesnil; *conseiller-clerc* at *parlement*; *conseiller* to Marie de Medici (1621); bishop of Senlis 1622; royal commissioner for orders, 1622; resigned see to nephew, Denis Sanguin, 1652; died 1653.

SEGUIER, Dominique born in St Denis, 1593; son of Jean, *conseiller* at *parlement* of Paris, and of Marie Tudert; younger brother of Pierre, keeper of seals and chancellor of France; *premier aumonier* to Louis XIII in 1631; bishop of Auxerre 1631, of Meaux 1637; commissioner for reform of orders, 1631; died 1659.

SEGUERAN, Gaspar de: born at Aix-en-Provence, 1569; entered Jesuits in 1584; missionary and preacher; confessor to Louis XIII, 1621–5; died 1644.

SOLMINIHAC, Alain de: born in November 1593; abbot *in commendam* of Chancelade, 1614; professed as canon-regular, 1616; priest in 1618; bishop of Cahors, 1636; died December 1659.

SPONDE, Henri de: born at Mauléon, 1568; brought up as a Huguenot; became Catholic in 1595; priest in 1606; spent several years in Rome, wrote sequel to Baronius's ecclesiastical history; bishop of Pamiers 1626; resigned 1641; died May 1643.

SUFFREN, Jean: born 1565; entered Jesuits at Avignon, 1579; college professor at Lyon; preacher in Rouen and Paris; confessor to Marie de Medici, 1615, and to Louis XIII, 1625; exile with Marie de Medici, 1631; died 1641.

VERTHAMON, François de: son of François and Marie de Versoris; *conseiller* at *parlement* of Paris, 1618; *maître des requêtes* 1623; commissioner for the orders, 1628; intendant in Guyenne 1630–8; councillor of state, 1643; died October 1666.

Glossary

abstinence	feature of religious or monastic observance, usually referring to practice of not eating meat
anciens	unreformed members of religious order
annates	tax on benefices, equivalent to one year's revenue, payable to Apostolic Chamber in Rome
appel comme d'abus	appeal to a secular court against an alleged abuse of ecclesiastical power
aliénation	sale of church property which is in theory inalienable
brief	form of papal letter granting petitions or communicating wishes or instructions, characterised by simplicity of form
brevet	public act of nomination to an office (hence *brevet de nomination*)
bull	most solemn form of papal letter, used for matters of general or public interest, often in relation to benefices
canons	clergy living in community and attached to service of a collegiate church
chapter	college of clerics (regular or secular) possessing legal personality
commende	practice of giving a monastic or other 'regular' (s.v.) benefice *in commendam* to secular cleric or laymen not technically competent to hold it
confidence	practice whereby one person holds a benefice in trust for another in defiance of canon law, usually involving transfer of revenues to that person
congregation	group of houses belonging to same religious order bound together by common observance and superiors; in Rome, the 'departments' entrusted with government of the church

grand conseil	one of the 'sovereign' courts of Paris, specialising in ecclesiastical affairs
datary/datarius	tribunal through which pope exercises his jurisdiction 'of grace and favour', in reply to petitions and appeals; its head is the datarius
expectatives	favours (usually benefices) granted in anticipation of their becoming available at some unspecified date
filiation	group of daughter-houses of major Cistercian abbeys – Cîteaux, Clairvaux, La Ferté, Pontigny and Morimond – and subject to authority of their abbots
maître des requêtes	senior royal officials serving at the king's council and frequently used on special judicial or administrative missions
novitiate/novice	period and/or place of probation (usually one year) for individuals seeking to become members of a religious order
official	head of the bishop's tribunal known as the *officialité*
priory/prior	religious house usually subject to an abbey, whose superior is known as prior
procès-verbal	Formal record or certificate of a meeting, visitation etc
procureur-général	official entrusted by religious orders with handling of their affairs, especially legal, usually in the papal curia
profession	act whereby a novice (s.v.) takes three vows of religion (poverty, chastity and obedience) and is admitted to membership of a religious order
provisor	superior of certain religious houses; principal dignitary of the Sorbonne
réformés	reformed group or party within religious orders
regular	clergy belonging to religious orders; (adj.) pertaining to religious orders generally
rescript	type of papal letter issued in reply to appeal or petition
stability	permanence inhering in membership of religious order, either in respect of way of life, or of monastery to which one 'belongs' by virtue of profession
synod	assembly of clergy under control of bishop
visitation	formal procedure permitting church authorities to inspect observance of church law by institutions and individuals, clerical or lay

Political and Ministerial Changes 1617–24

1617: April: assassination of Concini; replaced as favourite by Charles d'Albert de Luynes; Nicolas de Neufville de Villeroy and Pierre Brûlart de Puysieux secretaries of state; Pierre Jeannin *surintendant des finances*; Nicolas Brûlart de Sillery chancellor; Guillaume du Vair keeper of seals; December: death of Villeroy; Puysieux in charge of foreign affairs

1618: September: Cardinal de Retz president of king's council

1619: September: resignation of Jeannin; Gaspar de Schomberg *surintendant*

1621: March: Luynes constable of France; August: death of Du Vair; Luynes keeper of seals; December: death of Luynes; Merry de Vic keeper of seals

1622: August: death of Cardinal de Retz; September: La Rochefoucauld enters council; death of de Vic; Lefèvre de Caumartin keeper of seals (d. January 1623)

1623: January: Schomberg disgraced; La Vieuville *surintendant*

1624: January/February: disgrace of Brûlarts; Aligre keeper of Seals; Beauclerc secretary of state for war; April: Richelieu enters council; August: arrest of La Vieuville; Richelieu becomes Chief Minister; Marillac and Bochart *directeurs des finances*; October: Death of Sillery; Aligre chancellor

The Old Orders in Seventeenth-Century France

o = order; c = congregation

BENEDICTINES
Independent houses
Cluny (o)
Exempts (c)
St Maur (c)

CISTERCIANS
Common Observance
Strict Observance
Feuillants (c)

CANONS-REGULAR
Independent houses
Génovéfains (c)
Chancelade (c)
St Victor (c)
Val des Ecoliers (c)
Saint-Sauver (c)
St Ruf (c)
St Antoine de Viennois (o)
Mathurins (o)
Prémontré (o)

OTHERS
Carthusians
Grandmontains
La Merci
Servites

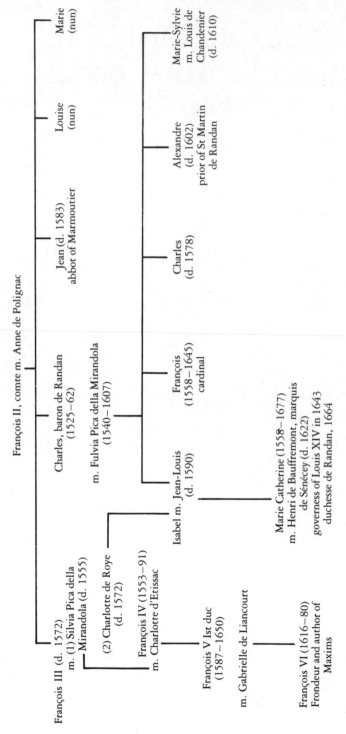

Genealogy of the La Rochefoucauld Family

Map 1.   Diocese of Clermont (*Dictionnaire d'histoire et de géographie ecclésiastiques*).

Map 2.   Some Houses of Religious Orders in Seventeenth-Century France.

Houses in italics were held *in commendum* by La Rochefoucauld.

CR   Canons-Regular
B   Benedictine
M   Mathurin
Cx   Cîteaux
C   Cluny

Sources and Bibliography

1. MANUSCRIPT SOURCES

Paris

Archives Nationales (A.N.)

G 8* 643F, 1221, 1282; L 833; LL 988, 1333−4, 1457; M 241; S 1445; V^6 105, 113, X^{1}a 1767; X^{2}b 195; Z^{1}O 239−40

Archives des Affaires Etrangères (A.A.E.)

Mémoires et Documents (Mems et docs) France 802, 804
Correspondance politique, Rome 18

Bibliothèque de l'Arsénal
MS. 2028

Bibliothèque de l'Institut de France

MS. Godefroy 15, 492

Bibliothèque Nationale (B.N.)

a. MS. Bourgogne 87
b. MS. Français (MS. Fr.) 3483−4, 3487, 3542, 3633, 3652−3, 3676−8, 15518, 15699, 15787, 16050−2, 16066, 16508, 17363−4, 17669, 17835, 18001−19; 18453, 24080
c. MS. Nouvelles Acquisitions Françaises (N.a.f.) 460−1, 6210, 24159−61
d. MS. 500 Colbert 89, 159
e. MS. Dupuy 35, 379, 438, 493, 557, 812
f. MS. Latin 9758, 12790
g. MS. Italien 38, 64−5, 1264−9, 1773, 1778
h. MS. Clairambault 1126

Bibliothèque Sainte Geneviève (B.S.G.)

MS 366, 607, 611−13, 621−33, 712, 720, 741, 745, 2131, 3238−51, 3263, 3266−3314

Archives Départementales (A.D.)

Seine-et Oise (Versailles) 53 H 1, 53 H 5

Puy-de-Dôme (Clermont) 1 G 153, 979, 1626

Senlis

Bibliothèque Muncipale, MS. Afforty vol. vi

Ferrara

Archivio di Stato
Fondo Bentivoglio 18/11, 18/12, 18/13, 18/14, 18/38, 18/40

Rome

Archivum Romanum Societatis Jesu (A.R.S.I.)

Francia 37–8; Francia, Epistolae Generalium 2; Gallia 35, 61; Tolosa 20

Corsini Library

MS. 713

Archivio Segreto Vaticano (A.S.V.)

a.   Fondo Borghese I, 636c; III, 46c
b.   Fondo Consistoriale: Acta Miscellanea 36; Acta Vicecancellarii 15; Processus Consistoriales 17
c.   Nunziatura di Francia (Nunz. Fr.) 42, 57–8, 60–5, 72, 74, 74a, 76, 295a, 299, 301–2, 394, 401, 416
d.   Miscellanea Armarium XLIV, 37
e.   Segretaria dei Brevi 658

Biblioteca Apostolica Vaticana (B.A.V.)

MS. Barberini lat (Barb. lat.) 7952, 8054–6, 8058, 8133, 8150, 8188, 8201, 8217, 8257

London

British Library (B.L.)
a.   Additional MS. (Addit. MS.) 8721, 8724, 8730
b.   Egerton MS. 1673

2.   PRINTED SOURCES

Acta Nuntiaturae Gallicae: iii, *Correspondance du nonce Girolamo Ragazzoni 1583–1586*, ed. Pierre Blet, Rome 1962; v, *Correspondance du nonce Ranuccio Scotti 1639–41*, ed. Pierre Blet, Rome 1965.

Advis pour la réforme et nourriture des religieux à qui Sa Majesté voudroit donner les abbayes de leur ordre, n.p., n.d.

Anatipophile Bénédictin aux pieds du Roy et de la Royne pour la réformation de l'ordre de St Benoist en ce Royaume, par un père du noviciat de l'observance regulière, Paris 1615.

Articles faits par l'ordonnance de Monseigneur le cardinal de La Rochefoucauld, grand aumosnier de France, pour le restablissement de l'observance régulière ès monastères qui en ont besoin ès ordres de Sainct Augustin, S Benoist, Clugny et Cisteaux, Paris 1623.

Articles proposez à la noblesse du pais d'Auvergne par Monsieur le comte de Randan, avec un discours sur la réplique de ladite noblesse et villes du contraire party par M. l'évesque de Clermont, Paris 1590.

Avis à Messieurs des Estats pour l'Ordre de St Benoist en France, Paris 1614.

Aubery, Antoine, *Mémoires pour l'histoire du cardinal-duc de Richelieu*, Paris 1660.

Bérulle, Pierre de, *Correspondance*, ed. Jean Dagens, 3 vols., Paris 1937–9.

Chartonnet, A.F., *La Vie du révérend père Charles Faure, abbé de Sainte Geneviève où l'on voit l'histoire des chanoines réguliers de la congrégation de France*, Paris 1698.

Collectio iudiciorum de novis erroribus, ed. Charles Duplessis d'Argentré, 2 vols., Paris 1728.

Collection de procès-verbaux des assemblées générales du clergé de France depuis l'année 1560 jusqu'à présent, ed. A Duranthon, 9 vols., Paris 1767–8.

Constitutiones et acta capitulorum strictioris observantiae ordinis Cisterciensis 1624–1687, ed. J.D. Lelockzy, Rome 1967.

Correspondance de Mayenne, ed. E. Henry and C. Loriquet, 2 vols., Reims 1860–2.

Correspondance du nonce Giovanni Francesco di Bagno 1621–27, ed. Bernard de Meester, 2 vols., Brussels 1938.

Courtier, Jean (trans.) *Procopii sophistae christianae variorum in Esaiam prophetam commentariorum epitome*, Paris 1580.

——, *Historia ecclesiasticae scriptores graeci*, Paris 1571.

Défense pour le réverendissime père général de tout l'ordre de la Sainte Trinité et rédemption des captifs et les révérends pères ministres des provinces dudit ordre, contre la coniuration de frère Simon Chambellan et ses adhérents, sous le nom de réformés audit ordre, Paris 1636.

Desbois, Jean, *Biographie du cardinal de La Rochefoucauld, par Jean Desbois son secrétaire*, ed. Gabriel de La Rochefoucauld, Paris 1923.

Diaire ou journal du voyage du chancelier Séguier en Normandie après la sédition des Nu-Pieds (1639–40), et documents rélatifs à ce voyage et à la sédition, ed. Amable Floquet, Rouen 1842.

Documents inédits pour servir à l'histoire du christianisme en orient, ed. A. Rabbath, vol. i., Paris n.d.

Duchesne, André, *Généalogie de l'ancienne et illustre maison de La Rochefoucauld*, Paris 1622.

Examen d'une apologie pour les chanoines-réguliers de l'ordre de Saint Augustin, Paris 1624.

Héroard, Jean, *Journal sur l'enfance et la jeunesse de Louis XIII*, ed. E. Solié et E. de Barthélemy, 2 vols., Paris 1868.

Inventaire sommaire des archives communales antérieures à 1790. Ville de Clermont-Ferrand: Fonds Montferrand, 2 vols., Clermont-Ferrand 1902.

Inventaire sommaire des archives de la ville de Riom, Riom 1892.

Inventaire sommaire des archives de l'hôpital de Tournus, Mâcon 1887.

Jaitner, Klaus, ed., *Die Hauptinstruktionen Clemens VIII für die Nuntien und Legaten an die Europäischen Fürstenhofen 1592–1605*, 2 vols., Tübingen 1984.

Jaulnay, Charles, *Histoire ou annales contenant plusieurs remarques particulières des choses plus mémorables arrivées depuis plus de 1500 ans sous l'épiscopat de chacun evesque de Senlis au nombre de quatre-vingt huit*, Paris 1648.

Juenin, Pierre, *Nouvelle histoire de l'abbaie royale et collégiale de St Philibert et de la ville de Tournus*, Dijon 1733.

La Rochefoucauld, François de, *De l'Authorité de l'église en ce qui concerne la foy et la religion*, Lyon 1597.

——, *De l'estat ecclésiastique*, Lyon 1597.

——, *Statuts renouvelez par le R.P. François de la Rochefoucauld evesque de Clairmont*, Clermont 1599.

——, *Institutio baptizandi aliaque sacramenta qua simplex sacerdos conferre potest administrandi, juxta ritum ecclesiae cathedralis Claramontanensis atque S. Flori, avec l'instruction aux curez et vicaires pour faire le prosne*, Clermont 1608.

——, *Avertissements pour les révérends curez de Senlis dressés par l'authorité de Monseigneur le cardinal de La Rochefoucauld*, 2nd ed., Paris 1638.

——, *Statuts synodaux du diocèse de Senlis 1620*, in *Actes ecclésiastiques de la province de Reims*, ed. Thomas-J. Gousset, vol. iii., Reims 1843.

——, *Raisons pour le désaveu fait par les évesques de ce roiaume d'un livret publié avec ce tiltre Jugement des cardinaux archevesques évesques et autres qui se sont trouvés en l'assemblée générale du clergé de ce roiaume sur quelques libelles diffamatoires*, Paris 1626.

L'Estoile, Pierre de, *Journal pour le règne de Henri IV*, ed. L.R. Lefèvre, vol. i., Paris 1948.

Lettres du cardinal d'Ossat, ed. Amelot de la Houssaye, 5 vols., Amsterdam 1714.

Lettres et mémoires adressés au chancelier Séguier 1633–1649, ed. Roland Mousnier, 2 vols., Paris 1964.

Lettres et mémoires adressés au chancelier Séguier 1633–1649, ed. A. D. Lublinskaya, 2 vols., Moscow 1966–80.

Lettres inédites du roi Henri IV à Monsieur de Sillery ambassadeur à Rome du 1 avril au 27 juin 1600, ed. E. Halphen. Paris 1866

Lettres missives de Henri IV, ed. X. Berger de Xivrey and J. Guadet, 9 vols., Paris 1843–76.

Molé, Mathieu, *Mémoires*, ed. A Champollion-Figeac, 4 vols., Paris 1855–7.

Martène, Edmond, *Histoire de la congrégation de St Maur*, ed. G. Charvin, 10 vols., Ligugé-Paris 1928–56.

Mignet, Abbé Etienne, *Histoire de la réception du concile de Trente dans les differens états catholiques*, 2 vols., Amsterdam 1756.

Montchal, Charles de, *Mémoires contenant des particularitez de la vie et du ministère du cardinal de Richelieu*, 2 vols., Rotterdam 1728.

Morinière, Michel-Martin de la, *Les Vertus du vray prélat représentées en la vie de Monseigneur l'Eminentissime Cardinal de La Rochefoucauld*, Paris 1646.

Négociation commencée au mois de mars de l'année 1619 avec la reine Marie de Medicis par M. le comte de Béthune, et continuée conjointement avec M. le cardinal de La Rochefoucauld, Paris 1673.

Négociations diplomatiques de la France avec la Toscane, ed. Abel Desjardins, 5 vols., Paris 1859–75.

Négociations, lettres et pièces diverses relatives au règne de François II, ed. Louis Paris, Paris 1841.

Nunziatura di Francia di Guido di Bentivoglio, ed. Luigi di Steffani, 4 vols., Florence 1863–70.

Palma-Cayet, Pierre-Victor, *Chronologie novenaire*, ed. J.A.C. Buchon, Paris 1836.

Paul, Vincent de, *Correspondance, documents et entretiens*, ed. Pierre Coste, 14 vols., Paris 1922–5.

La Prise et réduction de plusieurs villes et chasteaux du pay d'Auvergne à l'union des catholiques, par Monsieur le comte de Randan gouverneur dudict pays, Paris 1589.

Rapin, René, *Mémoires sur l'église et la société, la cour, la ville et le jansénisme*, ed. L. Aubineau, 3 vols., Paris 1865.

Recueil des actes titres et mémoires concernant les affaires du clergé de France, 14 vols., Paris 1768–71.

Remerciements des Bénédictins au Roy Très Chrestien Louis XIII de France et de Navarre sur la proposition faicte par S.M. en l'Assemblée de Rouen de remettre les Abbayes en régularité.

Remonstrance au très chrestien roy de France et de Navarre Henry IIII sur la réformation necessaire et ja ordonnée estre faicte en l'ordre de St Benoist, Paris 1606.

Remonstrances très-humbles par les religieux de l'ordre de Cisteaux au Roy, Paris, 1635.

Response des abbez et religieux de l'estroitte observance de l'ordre de Cisteaux à l'apologie du révérend abbé de Foucarmont, Paris, 1635.

Resolution des trois estats du bas pais d'Auvergne, avec la prise de la ville d'Issoire, par Monsieur le compte de Randan, Paris, 1589.

Retz, Cardinal de, *Oeuvres*, ed. Marie-Thérèse Hipp and Michel Pernot, Paris 1984.

Richelieu, Armand-Jean du Plessis, cardinal de, *Lettres, instructions diplomatiques et papiers d'état*, ed. D.L.M. Avenel, 8 vols., Paris 1853–77.

——, *Les Papiers de Richelieu: politique intérieure, correspondance et papiers d'état*, 6 vols. to date, Paris 1975–85.

——, *Mémoires*, ed. Société de l'Histoire de France, 10 vols., Paris 1908–31.

Richer, Edmond, *Histoire du syndicat d'Edmond Richer*, Avignon 1753.

Rouvier, Pierre, *De Vita et rebus gestis Francisci cardinalis de la Rochefoucauld libri tres*, Paris 1645.

Saint-Julien de Baleurre, Pierre de, *Recueil de l'antiquité et choses plus mémorables de l'abbaye et ville de Tournus*, Paris 1581.

Sentence pour la réforme des chanoines réguliers de St Augustin en ce royaume, portant règlement pour la réformation dudit ordre, et l'union de tous les monastères d'iceluy congrégation de France, Paris 1636.

Solminihac, Alain de, *Lettres et documents*, ed. E. Sol, Cahors 1930.

Sponde, Henri de, *Annalium ecclesiasticorum Em. Cardinalis C Baronii continuatio*, 3 vols., Pavia 1675–82.

Statuta capitulorum generalium ordinis Cisterciensis, ed. J.M. Canivez, 8 vols., Louvain 1933–41.

Sully, Maximilien de Béthune, duc de, *Les Oeconomies royales*, ed. Bernard Barbiche and David Buisseret, vol. i., Paris 1970.

Union entre l'ordre de Cluni premier chef entre les chefs d'ordre en France, et la congrégation de St Maur, où se voit comme l'ordre de Cluni se remet en l'ancienne et estroitte observance de la règle de St Benoist, Paris 1623.

Vernyes, Jean de, *Mémoires 1589–93*, Clermont-Ferrand 1838.

3. SECONDARY WORKS

Adam, Antoine, *Du Mysticisme à la révolte*, Paris 1968.

Alberigo, Giuseppe, 'Carlo Borromeo come modello di vescovo nella chiesa post-tridentina' *Rivista Storica Italiana* 79 (1967), pp. 1031–52.

——, 'Carlo del mito, Carlo della storia' in *Il Grande Borromeo tra storia e fede*, (Milan 1984), pp. 127–219.

Allier, Raoul, *La Cabale des dévots*, Paris 1902.

Arneth, Michael, *Das Ringen um Geist und Form der Priesterbildung im Säkularklerus des 17 Jahrhunderts*, Würzburg 1970.

Babelon, Jean-Pierre, *Henri IV*, Paris 1982.

Barbiche, Bernard, 'L'Influence française à la cour pontificale sous Henri IV', *Mélanges d'histoire et d'archéologie de l'ecole française de Rome*, 77 (1965), pp. 277–99.

Barrau-Dihigo, L., ed., 'Voyage de Barthélemy Joly en Espagne, 1603–4', *Revue hispanique* 20 (1909), pp. 459–70.

Baumgartner, Frederic J., 'The Catholic Opposition to the Edict of Nantes 1598–1599', *Bibliothèque d'humanisme et renaissance* 40 (1978), pp. 525–37.

——, 'Crisis in the French Episcopacy: The Bishops and the Succession of Henri IV' *Archiv für Reformationsgeschichte* 70 (1979), pp. 276–301.

——, 'Henry II's Italian Bishops: A Study of the Use and Abuse of the Concordat of Bologna', *Sixteenth Century Journal*, 11 (1980), pp. 49–58.

——, *Change and Continuity in the French Episcopate: The Bishops and the Wars of Religion*, Durham, North Carolina 1986.

Benedict, Philip, 'The Catholic Response to Protestantism. Church Activity and Popular Piety in Rouen 1560–1600', in James Obelkevich ed. *Religion and the People 800–1700* (Chapel Hill, North Carolina, 1979), pp. 168–90.

Bergin, Joseph, 'The Crown, the Papacy and the Reform of the Old Orders in Early Seventeenth-Century France' *Journal of Ecclesiastical History* 33 (1982), pp. 234–55.

——, 'The Decline and Fall of the House of Guise as an Ecclesiastical Dynasty', *Historical Journal* 34 (1982), pp. 781–803.

——, 'The Guises and their Benefices 1588–1641', *English Historical Review* 99 (1984), pp. 34–58.

——, *Cardinal Richelieu. Power and the Pursuit of Wealth*, London-New Haven, 1985.

——, 'Ways and Means of Monastic Reform in Seventeenth-Century France: the Case of St Denis de Reims 1630–33' *Catholic Historical Review* 72 (1986), pp. 14–32.

Berlière, U., 'La Congrégation bénédictine des exempts de France', *Revue Bénédictine* 14 (1897), pp. 398–414.

—— and Kaiser, J.B., 'Le Cardinal de Givry et les Bénédictins', *Revue Bénédictine* 42 (1930), pp. 244–62; 343–71.

Blet, Pierre, 'Jésuites et libertés gallicanes en 1611', *Archivium Historium Societatis Jesu* 24 (1955), pp. 165–88.

——, 'L'Article du tiers aux états-généraux de 1614', *Revue d'histoire moderne et contemporaine* 2 (1955), pp. 81–106.

——, *Le Clergé de France et la monarchie 1615–1666*, 2 vols., Rome-Paris, 1959.

——, 'Le Concordat de Bologne et la réforme tridentine', *Gregorianum* 45 (1964), pp. 241–79.

——, *Les Assemblées du clergé et Louis XIV de 1670 à 1693*, Rome, 1972.

——, 'Le Nonce en France au xviie siècle. Ambassadeur et délegué apostolique', *Revue d'histoire diplomatique*, 88 (1974), pp. 223–53.

——, *Histoire de la représentation diplomatique du Saint Siège*, Rome, 1982.

Bonnard, Fourier, *Histoire de l'abbaye royale et de l'ordre des chanoines réguliers de St Victor de Paris*, 2 vols., Paris, n.d.

Bonney, Richard, *Political Change in France under Richelieu and Mazarin 1624–1661*, Oxford, 1978.

——, *The King's Debts. Finance and Politics in France 1589–1661*, Oxford, 1981.

Bonnot, Isabelle, *Hérétique ou saint? Henry Arnauld, évêque janséniste d'Angers au xvii siècle*, Paris 1984.

Bosatra, Bruno Maria, 'Ancora sul "vescovo ideale" della riforma cattolica. I lineamenti del pastore tridentino-borromaico', *Scuola cattolica* 112 (1984), pp. 517–79.

Bossy, *Christianity in the West 1400–1700*, Oxford 1985.

Boucher, Jacqueline, *La Cour de Henri III*, Rennes 1986.

Broutin, Paul, *La Réforme pastorale en France au xviie siècle*, 2 vols., Tournai-Paris 1956.

——— and Jedin, H., *L'Evêque dans la tradition pastorale au xvie siècle*, Bruges 1953.

Calendini, Paul, 'Henri IV et les Jésuites de 1602 à 1604', *Annales Fléchoises* 12 (1911), pp. 69–92.

Canivez, J.M., 'Cîteaux', in *Dictionnaire d'histoire et de géographie ecclésiastiques*, vol. xii, cols. 851–997.

Certeau, Michel de, 'Politique et mystique. René de Voyer d'Argenson 1596–1651', *Revue d'ascétique et de mystique* 29 (1963), pp. 45–82.

Chartier, R., Compère, M.-M., Julia, D., *L'Education en France du xvie au xviiie siècle*, Paris 1976.

Charvin, G., 'L'Abbaye et l'ordre de Cluny de la fin du xve au début du xviie siècle 1485–1630', *Revue Mabillon* 43 (1953), pp. 85–117; 44 (1954), pp. 6–29, 105–30.

———, 'L'Abbaye et l'ordre de Cluny en France de la mort de Richelieu à l'élection de Mazarin 1642–1654', *Revue Mabillon*, 33 (1943), pp. 85–114.

Chatellier, Louis, 'Société et bénéfices ecclésiastiques. Le cas alsacien 1670–1730', *Revue historique* 244 (1970), pp. 75–98.

Chaunu, Pierre, *Le Temps des réformes*, Paris 1975.

Chesnay, Charles Berthelot du, *Les Missions de Saint Jean Eudes*, Paris 1967.

Chesneau, Charles de, *Le Père Yves de Paris et son temps*, 2 vols., Meaux 1946–8.

Chevallier, Pierre, *Louis XIII roi cornélien*, Paris 1979.

Chill, Emmanuel, 'The Company of the Holy Sacrament', Ph.D dissertation: Columbia University 1960.

Choné, J., 'La Spiritualité sacerdotale', *XVIIe Siècle* nos. 62–3 (1964), pp. 112–32.

Church, William F., *Richelieu and Reason of State*, Princeton, N.J. 1972.

Cognet, Louis, *La Réforme de Port Royal*, Paris 1950.

———, 'The Leadership Position of France' in *History of the Church*, ed. Hubert Jedin, vol. vi (London 1981), pp. 3–106.

———, 'Charles Faure', *Dictionnaire d'histoire et de géographie ecclésiastiques*, vol. xvi, cols. 714–19.

Coste, Pierre, *Monsieur Vincent. Le grand saint du grand siècle*, 3 vols., Paris 1932.

Cottret, Monique, 'Edmond Richer: le politique et le sacré', in *L'Etat baroque*, ed. Henri Méchoulan (Paris 1985), pp. 159–77.

Couzard, Rémy, *Une Ambassade à Rome sous Henri IV*, Paris 1901.

Crouzet, Denis, 'Recherches sur la crise de l'aristocratie en France au xvie siècle: les dettes de la maison de Nevers', *Histoire economie et société* 1 (1982), pp. 7–50.

Dagens, Jean, *Bérulle et les origines de la restauration catholique*, Paris 1952.

———, *Bibliographie chronologique de la littérature de la spiritualité et de ses sources 1500–1601*, Paris 1952.

Dainville, François de, *Les Jésuites et l'éducation de la société moderne*, Paris 1940.

———, *L'Education des Jésuites*, Paris 1978.

Darricau, Raymond, 'La Postcrità spirituale di San Carlo Borromeo in Francia nei secoli xvii–xix', *Scuola cattolica* 112 (1984), pp. 733–64.

Davis, Natalie Z., 'From "Popular Religion" to Religious Cultures', in Steven Ozment, ed. *Reformation Europe: A Guide to Research* (St Louis, Missouri 1982), pp. 321–41.

Degert, Antoine, *Histoire des séminaires français des origines jusqu'à la révolution*, 2 vols., Paris 1912.

———, 'St Charles Borromée et le clergé français', *Bulletin de littérature ecclésiastique* 4 ser., 4 (1912), pp. 145–59, 193–213.

Delattre, P, *Les Etablissements des jésuites en France depuis quatre siècles*, 5 vols., Enghien (Belgium) 1940–57.

Delumeau, Jean, *Le Catholicisme entre Luther et Voltaire*, Paris 1971. English translation: *Catholicism between Luther and Voltaire*, London 1977.

——, *Le Peché et le peur. La culpabilisation en occident xiiiᵉ–xviiiᵉ siècles*, Paris 1983.

Demante, Gabriel, 'Histoire de la publication des livres de Pierre Dupuy sur les libertés de l'église gallicane', *Bibliothèque de l'ecole des chartes* 5 (1843–4), pp. 585–600.

Denis, Paul, *Richelieu et la réforme des monastères bénédictins*, Paris 1912.

Descimon, Robert, *Qui étaient les seize? Mythes et réalités de la ligue parisienne 1585–94*, Paris 1983.

Deslandres, Paul, *L'Ordre des Trinitaires pour le rachat des captifs*, 2 vols., Toulouse-Paris, 1903.

Dhotel, Jean-Calude, *Les Origines du catechisme moderne*, Paris 1967.

Dijck, L.C. van, 'L'Affaire Raguet et le problème du gouvernement central de l'ordre de Prémontré au xviiᵉ siècle', *Analecta praemonstratensiana* 50 (1974), pp. 171–215; 51 (1975), pp. 37–71.

Dodin, André, 'François de La Rochefoucauld' *Dictionnaire de Spiritualité*, vol. ix, cols. 304–5.

Dosh, Terence L., 'The Growth of the Congregation of St Maur 1618–1672', Ph.D. dissertation: University of Minnesota 1971.

Doucet, Roger, *Les Institutions de la France au xviᵉ siècle*, 2 vols., Paris 1948.

Drouin, A., 'L'Expulsion des Jésuites sous Henri IV et leur rappel', *Revue d'histoire moderne*, 3 (1901–2), pp. 5–28, 593–609.

Duby, Georges, ed., *Histoire de la France urbaine*, vol. iii., Paris 1981.

Duccini, Hélène, 'La Vision de l'état dans la litérature pamphlétaire au moment des états généraux de 1614', in *L'Etat baroque*, ed. Henri Méchoulan, Paris 1985, pp. 147–58.

Dupont-Ferrier, Gustave, *Du Collège de Clermont au lycée Louis-le-Grand*, 3 vols., Paris 1921–5.

Dupront, Alphonse, 'Vie et créations religieuses dans la France moderne', in *La France et les français*, ed. Michel François, Paris 1972.

Dupuy, Michel, *Bérulle et le sacerdoce*, Paris 1969.

——, 'Hiérarchie', *Dictionnaire de Spiritualité*, vol. vii, cols. 441–51.

Elliott, J.H., *Richelieu and Olivares*, Cambridge 1984.

Evennett, H. Outram, *The Spirit of the Counter-Reformation*, Cambridge 1968.

Febvre, Lucien, 'Aspects méconnus d'un renouveau religieux en France entre 1590 et 1620', *Annales: economies, sociétés, civilisations* (1958), pp. 639–50.

Féret, Pierre, 'Le Cardinal de La Rochefoucauld réformateur' *Revue des questions historiques*, 23 (1878), pp. 115–75.

——, *L'Abbaye de Ste Geneviève et la congrégation de France*, 2 vols., Paris 1883.

Fouqueray, Henri, *Histoire de la compagnie de Jésus en France des origines à la suppression*, 5 vols., Paris 1910–25.

Greengrass, Mark, *France in the Age of Henry IV. The Struggle for Stability*, London 1984.

Guitton, Georges, *Le Père de La Chaize confesseur de Louis XIV*, 2 vols., Paris 1959.

Halkin, Leon-E., 'La Formation du clergé catholique après le concile de Trente', in

Miscellanea Historiae Ecclesiastica, ed. Derek Baker, vol. iii (Louvain 1970), pp. 109–25.

Hallman, Barbara Mc Cluny, *Italian Cardinals, Reform and the Church As Property 1492–1563*, Los Angeles 1985.

Hamscher, Albert N., 'Les Réformes judiciaires des grands jours d'Auvergne', *Cahiers d'histoire* 21 (1976), pp. 425–42.

Harding, Robert R., *Anatomy of a Power Elite. The Provincial Governors of Early Modern France*, New Haven 1978.

Hayden, J. Michael, 'Continuity in the France of Henry IV and Louis XIII: French Foreign Policy 1598–1615', *Journal of Modern History* 45 (1973), pp. 1–23.

——, *France and the Estates General of 1614*, Cambridge 1974.

Hoffman, Philip T., *Church and Community in the Diocese of Lyon, 1500–1789*, New Haven 1984.

Houssaye, Michel, *Vie du cardinal de Bérulle*, 3 vols., Paris 1872–5.

Huppert, George, *The Public Schools of Renaissance France*, Chicago 1984.

Imbart de la Tour, Pierre, *Les Origines de la réforme*, 4 vols., Melun 1909–35 [new ed. of vol. ii: Melun 1946].

Imberdis, A., *Les Guerres religieuses en Auvergne*, 2 vols., Moulins 1840.

Imbert, Jean, 'Les Préscriptions hospitalières du concile de Trente et leur diffusion en France', *Revue d'histoire de l'église de France* 42 (1956), pp. 5–28.

Jacqueline, Bernard, 'Missions en France' in Josef Metzler, ed., *Sacrae Congregationis de Propaganda Fide memoria rerum*, vol. i., (Rome 1972), pp. 111–48.

Jaitner, 'De Officio Primario Summi Pontificis. Eine Denkschrift Kardinal Bellarmins für Papst Klemens VIII', in Erwin Gatz, ed. *Römische Kurie, kirchliche Finanzen, Vatikanische Archiv. Studien zu Ehren von Hermann Hoberg*, vol. ii. (Vatican City, 1979), pp. 377–403.

Janssen, P.W., *Les Origines de la réforme des Carmes en France au xviie siècle*, The Hague 1963.

Jedin, Hubert, 'Zur Vorgeschichte der Regularenreform, Trid. Sess. XXV' *Römische Quartalschrift* 44 (1936), pp. 231–81.

——, *Geschichte des Konzils von Trient*, 4 vols., Freiburg-im-Breisgau 1949–75.

——, *Kirche des Glaubens, Kirche der Geschichte. Gesammelte Aufsätze*, 2 vols., Freiburg-im-Breisgau 1966.

——, *Riforma cattolica o controriforma?* Brescia 1967.

——, ed. *Handbuch der Kirchengeschichte*, vols. iii–iv, Freiburg-im-Breisgau 1967–70. [English translation, vols. v–vi, London 1980–1].

——, 'Le Concile de Trente a-t-il formé l'image-modèle du prêtre?', in *Sacerdoce et célibat. Etudes doctrinales et historiques*, ed. Joseph Coppens, Louvain 1970, pp. 11–31.

Julia, Dominique, 'La Réforme post-tridentine en France d'après les procès-verbaux de visites pastorales: ordres et résistances', in *La Società religiosa nell'eta moderna*, Naples 1973, pp. 311–433.

——, 'Les Bénédictins et l'enseignement aux xviie et xviiie siècles', in *Sous la règle de Saint Benoît. Structures monastiques et sociétés en France du moyen âge à l'époque moderne*, Geneva 1982.

Knecht, R.J., 'The Concordat of 1516: A Reassessment', *University of Birmingham Historical Journal* 9 (1963), pp. 16–32.

Knowles, David, *From Pachomius to Ignatius. A Study in the Constitutional History of the Religious Orders*, Oxford 1966

Krailsheimer, Alban J., *Armand-Jean de Rancé, Abbot of La Trappe, His Influence in the Cloister and the World*, Oxford 1974.

——, ed., *The Letters of Armand-Jean de Rancé, Abbot and Reformer of La Trappe*, 2 vols., Kalamazoo, Michigan, 1984.

Lacroix, L., *Richelieu à Luçon. Sa jeunesse, son épiscopat*, Paris 1890.

Laemmer, H., *Melematum Romanorum Mantissa*, Ratisbon 1875.

La Rochefoucauld, Gabriel de, *Un Homme d'église et d'état au commencement du xviie siècle: le cardinal de La Rochefoucauld*, Paris 1926.

Le Bachelet, X.M., 'Robert Bellarmin et les Célestins en France', *Revue des questions historiques*, 104 (1926), pp. 257–94.

Lebigre, Arlette, *Les Grands jours d'Auvergne: désordres et répressions au xviie siècle*, Paris 1976.

——, *La Révolution des curés. Paris 1585–1594*, Paris 1980.

Lebras, Gabriel, *Etudes de sociologie religieuse*, 2 vols., Paris 1955–6.

——, 'Mariage', *Dictionnaire de Théologie Catholique*, vol. ix, cols. 2123–317.

Lebrun, François, ed., *Histoire des catholiques en France*, Toulouse 1980.

Leclerc, Francine, 'Les Etats provinciaux de la ligue en Basse Auvergne de 1589 à 1594', *Bulletin philologique et historique du comité des travaux historiques* (1963), pp. 914–30.

——, 'Le Temps des troubles', in *Histoire de l'Auvergne*, ed. Aimé-Georges Manry (Toulouse 1974), pp. 253–86.

——, 'Le Temps des troubles' in *Le Diocèse de Clermont*, ed. Abel Poitrineau (Paris 1979), pp. 91–126.

Lekai, Louis J., *The White Monks*, Okauchee, Wisconsin 1953.

——, 'Cardinal de La Rochefoucauld and the Cistercian Reform', *American Benedictine Review*, 6 (1955–6), pp. 429–49.

——, 'Moral and Material Status of the French Cistercian Abbeys in the Seventeenth Century, *Analecta Cisterciensia* 19 (1963), pp. 199–266.

——, 'A Bibliography of Seventeenth-Century Pamphlets and Other Materials related to the Cistercian Strict Observance', *Analecta Cisterciensia*, 19 (1963), pp. 105–44.

——, *The Rise of the Cistercian Strict Observance in Seventeenth Century France*, Washington D.C. 1968.

——, 'The Abbatial Election at Cîteaux, 1625', *Church History* 39 (1970), pp. 30–5.

——, 'The Parisian College of St Bernard in 1634–35', *Analecta Cisterciensia*, 28 (1972), pp. 184–208.

Lemarchand, Guy, 'Les Monastères de la Haute-Normandie au xviii^c siècle' *Annales historiques de la révolution française*, 37 (1965), pp. 1–28.

Lemoine, Robert, *L'Epoque moderne. Les religieux. [Histoire du droit et des institutions de l'église en occident*, vol. xv, t. ii]. Paris n.d.

Léonard, Emile-G., *History of Protestantism*, vol. ii, London 1967.

Lovett, A. W., *Early Habsburg Spain 1517–1598*, Oxford 1986.

Lutz, Georg, *Kardinal Giovanni Francesco Guidi di Bagno. Politik und Religion im Zeitalter Richelieus und Urbans VIII*, Tübingen 1971.

Magendie, M., *La Politesse mondaine et les théories de l'honnêteté en France au xviie siècle, de 1600 à 1660*, 2 vols., Paris n.d.

Malov, Vladimir, 'Le Projet colbertiste de la réforme monastique', in *Un Nouveau Colbert*, ed. Roland Mousnier (Paris 1985), pp. 167–76.

Mandrou, Robert, *Magistrats et sorciers en France au xviie siècle*, Paris 1968.

Martin, Georges, *Histoire et généalogie de la maison de La Rochefoucauld*, n.p. 1975.

Martimort, Aimé-Georges, *Le Gallicanisme de Bossuet*, Paris 1953.

——, *Le Gallicanisme*, Paris 1973.

Martin, Victor, *Le Gallicanisme et la réforme catholique. Essai historique sur l'introduction des décrets du concile de Trente en France*, Paris 1919.

——, *Les Négociations du nonce Silingardi, évêque de Modène, relatives à la publication du concile de Trente en France, 1599–1601*, Paris 1919.

——, *Le Gallicanisme politique et le clergé de France*, Paris 1929.

Marvick, Elizabeth Wirth, *The Young Richelieu: A Psychoanalytical Study of Leadership*, Chicago 1983.

Massaut, Jean-Pierre, *Josse Clichtove, l'humanisme et la réforme du clergé*, 2 vols., Paris 1968.

Michaux, G., 'Les Professions dans la congrégation de Saint-Vanne et Saint-Hydulphe', *Annales de l'Est* 27 (1975), pp. 63–78.

Michel, A., *Les Décrets du concile de Trente*, Paris 1938.

Mollat, Guillaume, 'L'Aumônier du roi de France du xiiie au xve siècle', *Comptes-rendus des séances de l'Académie des Inscriptions et Belles-Lettres* (1939), pp. 514–25.

Mousnier, Roland, *La Plume, la faucille et le marteau*, Paris 1970.

——, *The Assassination of Henry IV*, London 1973.

——, *Paris capitale au temps de Richelieu et de Mazarin*, Paris 1978.

Neveu, Bruno, 'L'Erudition ecclésiastique du xviie siècle et la nostalgie de l'antiquité chrétienne', in Keith Robbins, ed. *Religion and Humanism* (Oxford 1985), pp. 195–225.

——, 'Archéolatrie et modernité dans le savoir ecclésiastique au xviie siècle', *XVIIe Siècle* 33 (1981), pp. 169–84.

O'Connell, Marvin R., *The Counter Reformation 1560–1610*, New York 1974.

Orcibal, Jean, *Jean Duvergier de Hauranne, abbé de St Cyran, et son temps*, 2 vols., Paris 1948.

——, *St Cyran et le jansénisme*, Paris 1961.

Orlea, Manfred, *La Noblesse aux états-généraux de 1576 et 1588*, Paris 1980.

Oro, José Garcia, *La Reforma de los religiosos españoles en tiempo de los reyes católicos*, Valladolid 1969.

Oroux, Abbé, *Histoire ecclésiastique de la cour de France*, 2 vols., Paris 1773.

Pantin, W.A., *The English Church in the Fourteenth Century*. Cambridge 1955.

Pastor, Ludwig von, *History of the Popes*, London 1923–53.

Péronnet, Michel, *Les Evêques de l'ancienne France*, 2 vols., Lille 1976.

Perrens, François-Tommy, *L'Eglise et l'état en France sous Henri IV*, 2 vols., Paris 1872.

Petit, Jeanne, *L'Assemblée des notables de 1626–27*, Paris 1936.

Peyrous, Bernard, 'La Réforme institutionnelle de l'archidiocèse de Bordeaux au temps du cardinal de Sourdis (1599–1628), *Revue d'histoire ecclésiastique* 76 (1981), pp. 5–47.

Philippson, Martin, *Heinrich IV und Philip III*, 3 vols., Berlin 1870–6.

Pillorget, René, 'Réforme monastique et conflits de rupture dans quelques localités de la France méridionale au xviie siècle', *Revue historique* 252 (1975), pp. 77–106.

——, *La Tige et le rameau. Familles anglaise et française, xvie–xviiie siècles*, Paris 1979.

Plongeron, Bernard, *La Vie quotidienne du clergé français au xviiie siècle*, Paris 1974.

Pocquet du Haut-Jussé, Barthélemy, 'Les Evêques de la Bretagne dans la renaissance religieuse du xviie siècle', *Annales de Bretagne*, 54 (1947), pp. 1–30.

Portal, Michel, 'Le Grand aumonier de France jusqu'à la fin du xviie siècle', *Revue de l'assistance publique* 29 (1954), pp. 291–306.

Powis, J.K., 'The Nature of Gallicanism in Late Sixteenth Century France' *Historical Journal* 26 (1983), pp. 515–30.

Prat, J.M., *Recherches historiques et critiques sur la compagnie de Jésus en France du temps du Père Coton*, 5 vols., Lyon 1876–8.

Préclin, Edmond, 'Edmond Richer 1559–1631. Sa vie, son oeuvre, le richerisme', *Revue d'histoire moderne*, 5 (1930), pp. 241–69, 321–36.

Prodi, Paolo, *Il Cardinale Gabriele Paleotti*, 2 vols., Rome 1959–66.

——, 'San Carlo Borromeo e il cardinale Paleotti: due vescovi della riforma cattolica', *Critica storica* 3 (1964), pp. 135–51.

——, *Il Sovrano pontefice. Un animo e due corpe. La monarchia papale nella prima età moderna*, Bologne 1982.

Puyol, Edmond, *Edmond Richer. Etude historique et critique sur la rénovation du gallicanisme au commencement du xviie siècle*, 2 vols., Paris 1876.

Quéniart, Jean, *Les Hommes, l'église et dieu dans la France du xviiie siècle*, Paris 1978.

Ranum, Orest, *Paris in the Age of Absolutism*, New York 1968.

Rapp, Francis, *L'Eglise et la vie religieuse en occident à la fin du moyen âge*, Paris 1971.

Ravitch, Norman, *Sword and Mitre. Government and Episcopate in France and England in the Age of Aristocracy*, The Hauge 1966.

Reinhard, Wolfgang, 'Reformpapsttum zwischen Renaissance und Barock', in Remigius Bäumer ed., *Reformatio Ecclesiae. Beiträge zu kirchlichen Reformbestrebungen von der Alten Kirche bis zur Neuzeit* (Paderborn 1980), pp. 779–96.

——, 'Kardinaleinkünfte und Kirchenreform', *Römische Quartalschrift* 77 (1982), pp. 157–94.

Ranaudet, Augustin, *Humanisme et préréforme à Paris pendant les premières guerres d'Italie 1495–1517*, Paris 1916.

Richard, Pierre, *Pierre d'Epinac. La papauté et la ligue française*, Paris 1902.

Richet, Denis and Chartier, Roger, *Répresentation et vouloir politiques. Autour des états généraux de 1614*, Paris 1982.

Roberg, Burkhard, 'Päpstliche Politik am Rhein. Die römische Kurie und der Jülich-Klevische Erbfolgestreit' *Rheinische Vierteljahrsblätter* 41 (1977), pp. 63–87.

Romier, Lucien, *Les Origines politiques des guerres de religion*, 2 vols., Paris 1913.

Salmon, J.H.M., *Society in Crisis. France in the Sixteenth Century*, London 1975.

Sauzet, Robert, *Les Visites pastorales dans le diocèse de Chartres pendant la première moitié du xviie siècle*, Rome 1975.

——, *Contre-Réforme et réforme catholique en Bas-Languedoc. Le Diocèse de Nîmes au xviie siècle*, Louvain 1979.

Serbat, Lucien, *Les Assemblées du clergé de France, Origines, organisation, développement 1560–1615*, Paris 1906.

Skinner, Quentin, *The Foundations of Modern Political Thought*, 2 vols., Cambridge 1978.

Sol, E., *Le Vénérable Alain de Solminihac, abbé de Chancelade et évêque de Cahors*, Cahors 1928.

Solé, Jacques, *Le Débat entre protestants et catholiques français de 1598 à 1685*, 4 vols., Lille 1985.

Soman, Alfred, *De Thou and the Index*, Geneva 1972.

Sommervogel, C., *Bibliographie des auteurs de la compagnie de Jésus*, 12 vols., Brussels 1890–1932.

Tackett, Timothy, *Priest and Parish in Eighteenth-Century France. A Social and Political Study of the Curés in a Diocese of Dauphiné 1750–1789*, Princeton, N.J., 1977.

Tapié, Victor-Lucien, *La Politique extérieure de la France et les débuts de la guerre de trente ans*, Paris 1934.

Taveneaux, René, *Le Catholicisme dans la France classique 1610–1715*, 2 vols., Paris 1980.

Urbain, Charles, *Nicolas Coëffetau, dominicain, évêque de Marseille, un des fondateurs de la prose française 1574–1623*, Paris, 1893.

Valous, Guy de, 'Cluny', *Dictionnaire d'histoire et de géographie ecclésiastiques*. vol. xiii, cols. 35–174.

Venard, Marc, 'Le XVIe siècle', *Dictionnaire d'histoire et de géographie ecclésiastiques*, vol. xviii, cols. 51–78.

——, 'Pour une sociologie du clergé au xvie siècle: recherches sur le recrutement sacerdotal dans la province d'Avignon', *Annales: économies, sociétés, civilisations* (1968), pp. 987–1016.

Vissac, Marc de, *Chronique de la ligue en Basse-Auvergne*, Riom 1888.

Voitel-Grenon, Geneviève, *La Chambre de la générale réformation des hôpitaux et maladeries de France 1612–72* (Unpublished thesis, Ecole des Chartes 1972).

Welter, Louise, 'Les Aliénations des biens ecclésiastiques en Auvergne au xvie siècle', *Bulletin historique et scientifique de l'Auvergne* 66 (1946), pp. 115–48.

——, 'Les Communautés de prêtres dans le diocèse de Clermont du xiiie au xviiie siècle' *Revue d'histoire de l'église de France*, 35 (1949), pp. 7–32.

——, 'Le Chapitre cathédral de Clermont' *Revue d'histoire de l'église de France* 41 (1955), pp. 5–42.

——, *Le Réforme ecclésiastique au diocèse de Clermont au xviie siècle*, Paris 1956.

Wright, A. D., *The Counter Reformation*. London 1982.

——, 'The Religious Life in the Spain of Philip II and Philip III', in W.J. Sheils ed., *Monks, Hermits and the Ascetic Tradition* (Oxford 1985), pp. 251–74.

Zakar, Polycarp, *Histoire de la stricte observance de l'ordre cistercien depuis ses débuts jusqu'au généralat du cardinal de Richelieu*, Rome 1966.

Zeller, Berthold, *Richelieu et les ministres de Louis XIII, de 1621 à 1624*, Paris 1880.

——, *Louis XIII, Marie de Medici, Richelieu ministre*, Paris 1899.

Index